Human Communication
ELEMENTS AND CONTEXTS

PHILIP EMMERT
WILLIAM C. DONAGHY

University of Wyoming

ADDISON-WESLEY PUBLISHING COMPANY
Reading, Massachusetts
Menlo Park, California
London • Amsterdam
Don Mills, Ontario • Sydney

This book is in the
ADDISON-WESLEY SERIES IN COMMUNICATION

Library of Congress Cataloging in Publication Data

Emmert, Philip, 1940-
    Human communication.

    Bibliography: p.
    Includes index.
    1. Communication. I. Donaghy, William C., joint author. II. Title.
P90.E47   001.51   80-17595
ISBN 0-201-03597-9

Copyright © 1981 by Addison-Wesley Publishing Company, Inc. Philippines copyright 1981 by Addison-Wesley Publishing Company, Inc.

All rights reserved. No part of this publication may be reproduced, stored in a retrieval system, or transmitted, in any form or by any means, electronic, mechanical, photocopying, recording, or otherwise, without the prior written permission of the publisher. Printed in the United States of America. Published simultaneously in Canada.

ISBN 0-201-03597-9
ABCDEFGHIJ-DO-8987654321

PREFACE

The means by which humans communicate with one another has been of interest to both students and teachers since the beginning of recorded history, yet the importance of human communication study in the total realm of education has fluctuated drastically. The content and direction of the field have often been defined by whatever happens to be currently in vogue with its most prominent teachers and practitioners. To some extent, this is still the case today. However, on the whole, the centrality of communication study to the entire education process is once again becoming widely recognized throughout the world at a time when teachers and students of human communication are beginning to reach some consensus as to the central content and most profitable directions for the field. It was our hope when we began this book to bring together this central content in a clear and unified perspective that could be easily understood by a beginning student. We believe we have succeeded to a great extent in fulfilling that purpose, yet we fully realize that we still have a long way to go. We hope to have a chance in future editions to come closer to realizing our goal. We see this book as a project that we hope will grow and evolve over time with the help of teachers, practitioners, and students of human communication.

Recent texts in human communication that have followed a behavioral-empirical orientation have seemed to neglect strengths in speech communication's past. We believe that students better understand today's theories and research if they understand our past. Although our approach throughout this book is not historical-critical, the material presented in the first chapter should, we hope, provide a historical perspective for the student about the study of human communication, which will enrich the student's understanding of the material presented throughout the rest of the book.

Central to our goal of presenting a clear and unified presentation of the major content of human communication is the concept of system theory. The successful use of this approach for similar goals in many other disciplines and, to some extent, in earlier publications concerned with human communication, has convinced us of its value to our discipline. We find the basic elements of the systems approach to be the least complicated and most useful of all approaches for an understanding of human communication. Further, we find the systems approach to be entirely consistent with the traditional and widely accepted "process" view of communication, as well as with the newer but equally important "transactional" view. We see the systems approach simply as a more complete theory, which is a natural outgrowth of these as well as several other approaches. It has allowed us to carry a single viewpoint throughout the text and

Preface

to tie together its various parts. This continuity and unification of communication concepts is what we and our students have found missing in many of the earlier human communication books. The fragmentation of principles tends to confuse students and makes the learning of those principles more difficult.

The concepts of systems theory have enabled us to include discussions of materials that were once always a part of speech communication texts but that, for reasons not clear, are often neglected today. For instance, the systems view of human communication in this book almost required us to include a chapter focused on the physiology, development, and improvement of communication sending and receiving mechanisms. This chapter integrates material related to verbal communication, nonverbal communication, motivation, perception, and reasoning rather than leaving them as isolated topics.

In trying to unify the basic principles of human communication and explain them in such a way that students will understand them, we have made some interesting discoveries. We constantly found ourselves being forced in new directions within chapters. We quickly found that we could not write chapters out of sequence. We discovered that we needed to constantly edit each other's work and to make changes. Many topics we originally intended to include in one chapter are now found in a different chapter because they fit so much better. Often these changes went against the common practices of other human communication texts. A good example of this deviation from the norm is to be found in the section on communication contexts. Similar chapters in other books often appear to be tacked on to the main body of the text and unique from one another. The systems model provided a basis for distinguishing among these different contexts, as well as a basis for considering them to be conceptually related phenomena. The chapters on communication contexts build upon the systems perspective presented in earlier chapters as they extend the principles to each context.

Because of this approach, we did not discuss some topics as they are traditionally covered. For example, concepts such as evidence and reasoning, which are usually found discussed with public communication, are placed much earlier in this text because they relate to all of the contexts and are merely referred to in the chapter on the public communication context. Our main criteria in making these changes, as well as in making omissions and substitutions within the book, have always been the following.

1. Are we reflecting the central content of our field, which a beginning student needs to know?
2. Is the material unified and does it flow smoothly with the other material that precedes and follows it?
3. Are we explaining it clearly enough and in enough depth so that it can be understood by the average freshman- and/or sophomore-level student?

We have written this book to be used in the first, mostly "content-oriented" course in human communication. This book is in no way "skills-oriented." We have intentionally left out any suggested exercises, study problems, and so forth. Anything of that sort can be supplied by the instructor, if desired. We would not pretend to guess what types of exercises work best for different teachers and students or if exercises are even suitable for such a course.

We would like to acknowledge the contributions of many teachers and scholars within the field of human communication from whom we have learned so much and whose ideas we have incorporated in this book. Your names appear in our list of references, and we would like to thank you all. Many thanks also go to our families, colleagues, and students who helped us in many ways, not the least of which was being patient with us when our attention was split between them and this project. Finally, we would like to acknowledge the potential help of each one of you who will read this text, which can further develop and mature in the future with your feedback. You may contact us by writing to the Department of Communication, University of Wyoming, Box 3341, University Station, Laramie, Wyoming 82071. We will be looking forward to hearing from you.

December, 1980 PE/WCD
Laramie, Wyoming

CONTENTS

PART 1 INTRODUCTION TO HUMAN COMMUNICATION

1

Chapter 1 The Study of Human Communication

3

- 4 Communication is all around us
- 7 Communication as a survival tool
- 9 Historical evidence of communication
- 20 Overview
- 24 Summary

Chapter 2 Human Communication Perspectives

- 29 Perspectives on human communication
  - Using models 29
  - The stimulus-response perspective 30
  - The motivational perspective 31
  - The transactional perspective 32
  - The systems perspective 33

- 33 Characteristics of communication systems
  - Interdependence 33
  - Holism 34
  - Goal-seeking 34
  - Inputs and outputs 35
  - Transformation 36
  - Entropy 36
  - Regulations 37
  - Hierarchy 38
  - Differentiation 39
  - Equifinality 39

- 40 Communication systems
  - Communicators 40
  - Interfacing and intrafacing 41
  - Relationships 42
  - Feedback 42
  - Environment 42
  - Interference 43

- 43 Definitions of communication
  - Two points of view 44
  - Definitions based on the intent to influence 45
  - Definitions based on perceived meaning 46
  - Which is correct? 46

- 47 Types of communication systems
  - Interpersonal communication systems 48
  - Organizational communication systems 48
  - Public communication systems 48
  - Mass communication systems 48

- 49 Summary

PART II INTRAPERSONAL PROCESSING ELEMENTS 51

Chapter 3 Motivation 53

55 The intraface of motivational components
56 The drive-reduction need component
   Maslow's need classification system 56
60 The consistency need component
61 The interpersonal need component
   Communication responses to inclusion needs 63
   Communication responses to control needs 64
   Communication responses to affection needs 65
67 The value component
   The function of the value component 69
71 Environmental effects on motivation
73 Summary

Chapter 4 Perception 75

78 The process of perception
   Basic principles 79
85 Person perception
   Perceiving communicator intent 85
   Forming impressions 87

- 96 Message perception
  - Selectivity 96
  - Social judgment involvement 98
- 103 Summary

Chapter 5
Reasoning
105

- 106 Why people reason
  - Dissonance theory 106
  - Other consistency theories 108
- 109 How people reason
  - Classifications of evidence 110
  - Types of evidence 110
- 113 Forms of reasoning
  - Deductive reasoning 114
  - Inductive reasoning 116
  - Inferential reasoning 117
- 119 Fallacies of reasoning
  - Fallacies in invalid arguments 120
  - Fallacies in valid arguments 124
- 127 Barriers to effective reasoning
- 128 Summary

PART III
COMMUNICATION INPUTS AND OUTPUTS
131

Chapter 6
Verbal Communication
133

134 The power of language
    Time-binding power 134
    Abstraction power 135

137 What is language?
    Linguistic competence 138
    Communicative competence 138
    Cognitive competence 138

139 The vocabulary component
    Our word pool 139

149 The grammar component
    Sentence structure 149
    Word appropriateness 150

152 Language and thought

153 Problems in language
    Multiple meaning 153
    Emotional words 154
    Language intensity 155
    Meanings change 155
    Stereotypes 156
    Cultural differences 158

160 Improving language effectiveness
    Moderation 160
    Use feedback 160
    Audience analysis 161
    Observe all output systems 161

162 Summary

Chapter 7

Nonverbal Communication

165

166 Verbal versus nonverbal communication
167 Characteristics of nonverbal communication
169 Nonverbal communication and interaction
    Vocalics 170
    Facial expression 170
    Eye behavior 171
    Head and hand movements 172
    Body posture and orientation 173
    Proxemics 174
    Interrelationship of verbal and nonverbal interaction channels 175

179 Nonverbal communication and interpersonal attitudes
    Facial expression 180
    Eye behavior 180
    Body posture and orientation 181
    Touch 182
    Personal artifacts 184
    Proxemics 184

185 Communicating emotion nonverbally
    Facial expression 186
    Eye behavior 186
    Hand and leg movements 187
    Vocalics 188
    Posture 188
    Personal artifacts 188

189 Nonverbal communication and personality
    Physical appearance 189
    Personal and public artifacts 190
    Vocalics 191

192 Summary

Chapter 8
Sending and Receiving Mechanisms

195

196 The physiology of human communication
    The speech chain 198
    Other receptor organs 200
    The brain 202

203 The development of human communication
    The child's equipment 204

210 Communication sensitivity
    Developing verbal communication sensitivity 211
    Developing nonverbal communication sensitivity 214

217 Summary

PART IV
COMMUNICATION CONTEXTS
221

Chapter 9
Context Components
223

- 225 Structure
  - Physical structure 225
  - Relationship structure 227
- 230 Function
  - Individual functions 230
  - System functions 231
- 233 Evolution
- 236 Summary

Chapter 10
Dyadic Communication
239

- 240 Classifying dyadic systems
  - Dyadic structure 240
  - Dyadic function 240
  - Dyadic evolution 241
- 242 Dyadic structure
  - Status and power 244
  - Status and role 244
  - Status conflict 244
  - Transactional analysis 245
- 247 Dyadic function
  - The consummatory dyad 248
  - The instrumental dyad 252

- 257 Dyadic evolution
    - Stage one: initiating 257
    - Stage two: experimenting 257
    - Stage three: intensifying 258
    - Stage four: integrating 258
    - Stage five: bonding 259
    - Stage six: differentiating 260
    - Stage seven: circumscribing 260
    - Stage eight: stagnating 261
    - Stage nine: avoiding 261
    - Stage ten: terminating 261
- 262 Dyadic conflict
    - Conflict types 263
    - Conflict intensity 263
    - Value of interpersonal conflict 263
    - Value of content conflict 264
    - Conflict management 264
- 266 Integrating dyadic structure, function, and evolution
- 269 Summary

Chapter 11
Small Group Communication

273

- 274 Public discussions
- 275 The triad
- 276 Classifying small groups
- 276 Small group structure
    - Small group networks 277
    - Small group leadership 280
- 281 Small group function
    - Consummatory small groups 281
    - Cohesiveness 284
    - Instrumental small groups 288
- 292 Small group evolution
    - Orientation phase 292
    - Conflict phase 294
    - Emergence phase 295
    - Reinforcement phase 296
- 297 Summary

Chapter 12 Organizational Communication   301

- 302 What is organizational communication?
  - Communication and organizations 303
- 304 Organizational communication structure
  - Formal communication structure 304
  - Informal communication structure 308
  - Communication subsystems 311
- 311 Organizational communication function
  - Instrumental organizational communication 311
  - Consummatory organizational communication 313
- 316 Organizational communication evolution
- 319 Summary

Chapter 13 Public Communication   321

- 322 The importance of public communication systems
  - Public communication in society 322
  - Public communication and you 324
- 324 Public communication structure
  - The public speaker 326
  - The audience 327
- 330 Public communication function
- 332 Public communication evolution
  - Initiation 332
  - Operation 333
  - Termination 333
  - The speech 333
- 338 Presenting the speech
  - Practice 340
  - Feedback 340
- 341 Summary

Chapter 14 Mass Communication

345

- 346 Mass communication structure
  - Structural elements 346
  - Relationships among the elements 350
  - Relationship models 351
- 359 Mass communication functions
  - The economic function 360
  - The entertainment function 361
  - The educational function 361
  - The socializing function 363
  - The tranquilizing function 363
  - The persuasive function 364
- 365 Mass communication evolution
  - The print media 366
  - The electronic media 372
- 378 Summary

381 Bibliography

389 Index

I

INTRODUCTION TO HUMAN COMMUNICATION

1

The Study of Human Communication

Human communication is important because we are constantly bombarded by it. From the time we awaken in the morning until we go to sleep at night, we send and receive messages. Without such messages, we could not survive in our modern society. Humans have learned to depend on communication for survival since the age of the caveman. They have constantly tried to learn more about communication. These early attempts to study communication provide a background for understanding contemporary communication principles. Contemporary communication study involves both the methods by which people receive, process, and send messages and the contexts in which communication normally takes place.

Communication is like breathing; we usually do it without thinking about how we do it. If you were going to be a singer, a voice teacher would teach you how to breathe correctly. With some voice students, the teacher would make very little change in their breathing because they had been doing it well all along; with others, major changes would have to be undertaken. Learning to be a good communicator is very similar. For some of you, the principles you will learn in this text will suggest very minor changes in your normal communication behavior; for others, major overhauls may be needed. Like breathing, these changes will involve not only learning new patterns of behavior but also unlearning old habitual patterns. The latter task is what makes communication so difficult for some people. In most of the courses you are taking, you have only the one task of learning new material, not that of unlearning the old.

At this point the question becomes, "Well, is it worth it to learn the new patterns? I don't seem to be getting along too badly." That is a question you must answer for yourself. There is nothing in this book that can force you to change.

COMMUNICATION IS ALL AROUND US

Most of us spend much more of our time in communicating than we realize. For most of us, the amount of time devoted to communicating breaks down statistically to something like the following: 42%-48%, listening; 32%-35%, talking; 10%-15%, reading; and 7%-11%, writing. Now let us consider our daily activities and the part communication plays in them.

The average individual normally follows about the same routine every day. First comes the awakening period. This time span usually involves a battle with the alarm clock, then a cup of coffee, a shower, and related preparations, followed perhaps by a little breakfast and a glance at the newspaper or television. These procedures prepare us for the main activities of the day. If we live with other people, these early activities are coordinated so that although everyone is not in the bathroom at the same time, they are all at the table together or out the door on time. In some of our homes, at least, verbal communication during this period is kept to a minimum of grunts and groans and occasional choppy sentences. We have found, through years of experience, that this is not the best time to express complaints, carry on weighty discussions, plan difficult tasks, and so on. We have discovered that such communication in the morning can often lead to disagreements and hostilities that will last throughout the whole day and will prevent us from getting anything accomplished. In this case, then, silence has real communicative value. However, this understanding within our own families was not reached without mistakes being made. Communication mistakes and misunderstandings as simple as these can lead to separations, divorces, and permanent scars.

The second set of routine activities of the day for almost everyone begins somewhere between eight and ten in the morning. Many of us try to get over the morning activities slowly. We may sit down to have a cup of coffee with those people we will be coming in contact with for the rest of the day. Students may meet at the Union, faculty members may meet in someone's office, business people may meet in a lunchroom or "over the water cooler," homemakers may

The social climate for the rest of the day is often helped by a cup of coffee and small talk among coworkers.
PHOTO BY CAROLE DUGAN

meet in someone's kitchen, and so on. The exchange of "small talk" during these meetings can have significance throughout the day. It not only gets us over the waking period but also sets a tone or climate for the rest of the work period. Absenteeism, work loss, and turnover can often result from the kinds of communication that take place during these early social periods. If you don't believe this is true, just ask someone who is not invited to these gatherings.

Once the work period formally begins, all kinds of communication take place. For students, these include lectures, discussions, conversations, tests, reports, term papers, textbooks, library research, club meetings, bull sessions, and many other similar activities. For business people, these include memos, letters, business meetings, telephone conversations, sales pitches, orders, interviews, planning, reporting, overseeing, and negotiating. All of these communicative endeavors can be positive or negative. They can accomplish their purpose or they can lead to significant problems. Handling these communication activities that occur during the work period is at least as important as handling the other activities that go on during this period. Communication activities often have a direct effect on the success of the activities to which they are related. For example, there is a direct relationship between how much you learn in college and in your past training about how to receive and record transmitted information, and how and when you should ask questions that will clarify matters that are not understood. It is very hard to think of a single area of activity in which communicative ability is not directly related to the overall success in that

The Study of Human Communication

activity. The worlds of work and communication are tightly linked. Even those people who do their work alone, like accountants, foresters, and draftsmen, must ultimately report the results of their efforts to someone as well as acquire information through communication in order to do their work.

The evening period can be a time of relaxation. Weekends also fall into this routine for many of us. We turn our attention to other matters around which our lives revolve. We partake in sports, either actively or passively. We maintain our homes and rooms. We indulge in hobbies. We watch TV. We read. We take walks. We talk to one another in a less pressurized, less stressful, and more leisurely manner. These are the periods when our communication failures can catch us unprepared. We let down our guard during these evening and weekend periods. Because our communicative failures do not seem to have the same consequences, we tend to become sloppy. However, when we stop to consider with whom we are interacting during these periods, it becomes apparent that our communicative relationships during this time can have more devastating consequences than those during the working period. It is with our friends and relatives that we have many of our most meaningful interactions. We can always change jobs, but it is much harder to change friends. For many of us, our work is important, but it only has meaning when put in the context of all of the other activities we deem important in our lives.

We have taken this much time in trying to demonstrate why communication is important to you directly because it is often difficult to really estimate the value of communication when your head is being filled each day with all of the technical information that other university courses offer. It is an easy matter to let the more practical classes like communication slide with little or no concentrated effort. Once you begin to think about the information you have learned in college, however, you will realize that you normally have time to check back on those technical aspects of your training before you have to commit yourself, and you can also usually go back and make corrections when technical mistakes occur. But communication problems have a way of occurring that cannot be changed without a great deal of effort. You cannot check back with this text in the middle of a conversation, formal presentation, or meeting.

Communication affects you in your everyday life not only directly but also indirectly because of its importance in such nonpersonal areas as advertising and politics. All of us are indirectly influenced by these areas, which are related to communication. Communication occurs all over the world at all hours of the day and night. We are frequently unaware of it, but it has the potential to affect our lives directly. Examples of such communication encounters might be an advertising executive discussing a campaign that will air on your television screen and will convince you to try a new product; a group of congressmen debating new tax reforms that will affect people in your tax bracket; a business executive planning new openings in the company, one of which you will eventually fill; or you yourself planning a summer vacation during which you will meet someone and begin a lifelong relationship.

Communication is a vitally important part of our society. It is almost impossible to imagine society without communication. It is through advertising, for example, that people are made aware of new services and new products. The production of these services and products accounts for the employment of

Indirect communication constantly surrounds us.
PHOTO BY CAROLE DUGAN

much of our population. Without communication, the services and products would not be used, and the people would not be employed. Without communication, we would be unable to elect capable officials to represent us in our local, state, and federal government agencies. This could mean no police force, no water supply, no streets, no parks, and no laws to guide the behavior of society. All of us would be, more or less, islands unto ourselves. Our society might well regress to the age of the caveman or further. No matter how much some of us long for the "good old days," none of us really want to go back that far. Many of the problems that face our society and make us feel that life was better in the "good old days" are due in great part to ineffective communication. Today, more than ever, we need people who are aware of communication strengths and weaknesses in order to reclaim for our society the more satisfying level of the "good old days."

COMMUNICATION AS A SURVIVAL TOOL

Although there are many theories regarding human communication, the position with which we are in most agreement is that *people communicate in order to survive* (Ardrey, 1970). The way communication facilitates survival is by influencing other people's behavior so that they will do things that help satisfy our needs. A young child asks a parent for a drink of water to satisfy the body's need for liquid. This request is an example of communication being used to satisfy a physical need.

Less obvious is the case of a young man saying "I love you" to his girlfriend. At first, this might seem to be a simple expressive statement. If you consider it for a while, however, it should be clear that at the very least the young man expects a response like "I love you, too," a hug, an affectionate squeeze of the hand, or maximally, sexual behavior. The original statement may be intended to persuade the young woman that her boyfriend has feelings that make sexual behavior appropriate, thus satisfying physical needs. Or the statement may be intended to persuade her to say she loves him, too, and thus to satisfy his social needs (because this response reinforces their relationship).

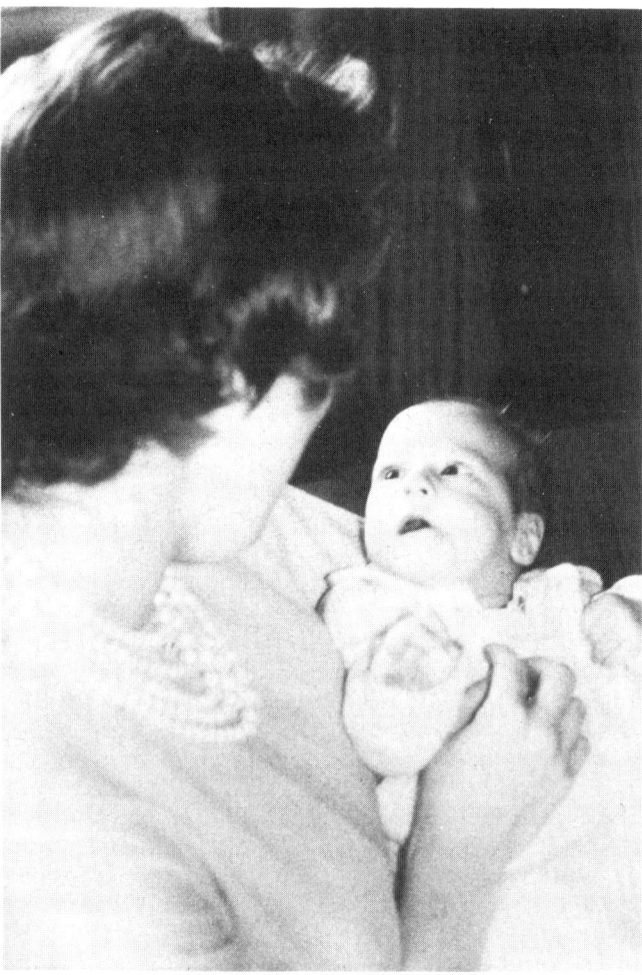

Cuddling fulfills the stroking need of both the mother and the child.
PHOTO BY CAROLE DUGAN

All of us need this kind of stroking. Babies will actually shrivel and die without physical stroking. Adults can get by with verbal stroking, although they, too, desire physical stroking and respond favorably to it. It is not uncommon for people to "fish for compliments." An employee may say, "I don't think I did this job very well" to his boss. He may say this in order to hear his boss respond, "You did it very well, better than I could have done." Although the employee's social needs might be satisfied to some extent by the comment, we suspect the real satisfaction would be that of ego, or esteem satisfaction. Thus, communication can also be used to satisfy our ego needs or the need to think well of ourselves.

By using communication to satisfy our physical, social, and ego needs, we are more likely to survive. Keep in mind that physical survival alone is not enough. If we don't have enough social acceptance or if we think too poorly of ourselves, we may also actually become mentally ill and unable to cope with our environment. Communication is a tool we use to cope with our environment. When we cannot satisfy our own needs directly, we employ communication to influence other people in ways that will satisfy those needs and that will thus permit our survival within our environment. This is certainly not a recent development. Communication has always been a survival tool.

HISTORICAL EVIDENCE OF COMMUNICATION

Perhaps we can best understand the value of communication as a survival tool by looking at it from a historical perspective. Homo sapiens, as we more or less know the species now, has existed on earth for around a half million years. The earliest discovered genus of humans seems to be the "ape man" (Pithecanthropus). Another very early human genus is the "China man" (Senanthropus). There is strong evidence that both the ape man and the China man were able to communicate simple ideas. Analysis of their otherwise underdeveloped brain cavities shows that they were well developed in the areas associated with speech. We assume that this area of the brain was highly developed because of its potential as a survival mechanism, since these early people seem to have had little time for anything other than trying to survive.

There is also evidence of communication survival by the Neanderthals, who lived during the early Paleolithic era. These people were able to kill and eat very thick-skinned animals such as the hippopotamus, rhinoceros, and elephant. In order to accomplish such a task, they would have had to form some type of cooperative union under some form of leadership. The formation of such a cooperative effort and the development and exercise of leadership would necessarily involve at least some primitive form of communication. The famous cave drawings of horses, deer, bison, reindeer, fish, and humans also provide early evidence of a desire to communicate.

It was not until the Neolithic age that humans settled down. Rather than hunting, they had discovered farming and the raising of animals as a means of supplying food. At this point, our ancestors began to live in villages. Around 3000 B.C., the first crude forms of writing appeared. During this period, the intellectual life of the community was centered around the oral legends that grew up in each village. These legends were as important in motivating the survival behaviors of those who heard them as our own attitudes and values are in motivating ours.

The end of the Neolithic period came when new and more complex civilizations developed. The Sumerians, who settled in Babylonia, comprised

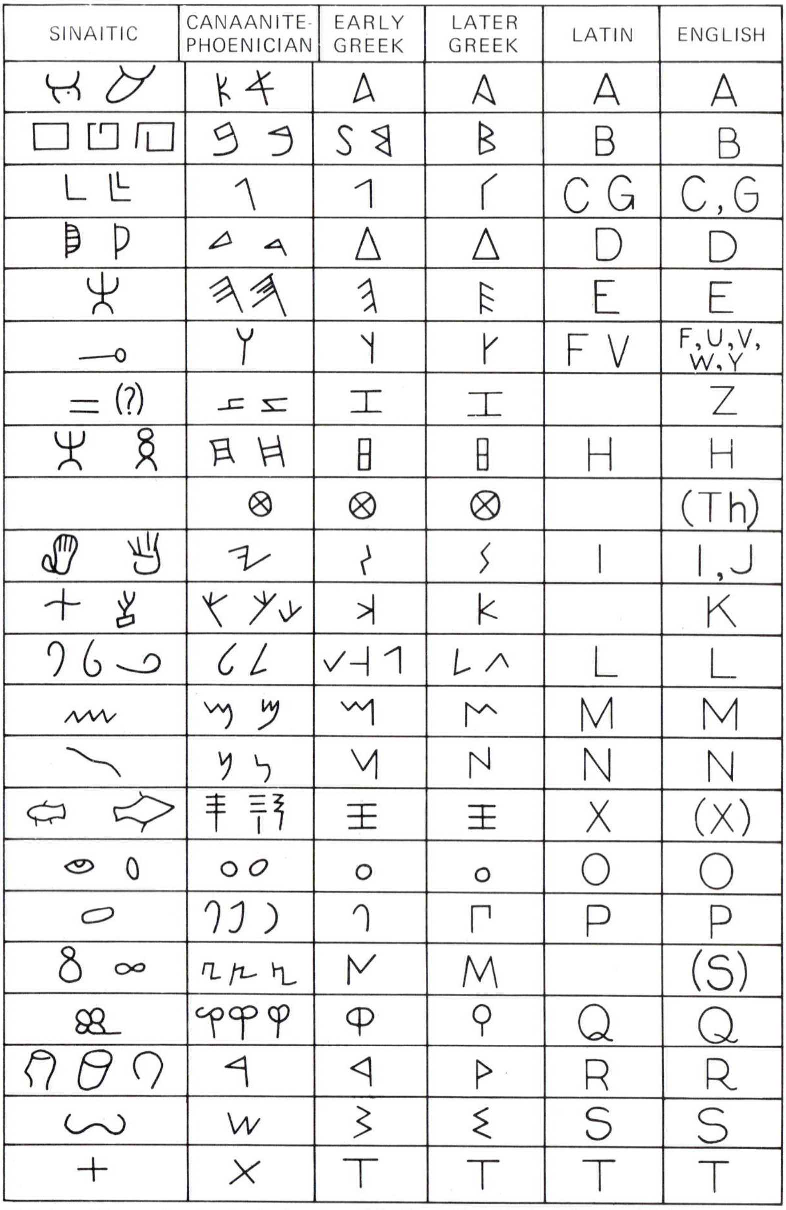

The Study of Human Communication

SINAITIC	CANAANITE-PHOENICIAN	EARLY GREEK	LATER GREEK	LATIN	ENGLISH
⊬ ⋎	𐤊 𐤀	A	A	A	A
▢ ▢ ▢	𐤁 𐤁	S ᗷ	B	B	B
L L	𐤂	𐌂	Γ	C G	C, G
⍙ ⍙	△ △	Δ	Δ	D	D
⍦	⋛ ⋛	⋛	E	E	E
⊶	Y	Y	Υ	F V	F, U, V, W, Y
= (?)	⊏ ⊏	I	I		Z
⍦ ⍦	ᖴ ᕼ	⊟	⊟	H	H
	⊗	⊗	⊗		(Th)
✋ ✋	Z	⌒	⌒	I	I, J
+ ⚮	⋏ ⋎⋎	⋋	k		K
⋎ 𝟨 ⌒	𐌂𐌋	⋎ ⊣ ⊐	L ⋏	L	L
⋀⋀⋀	𝑚 𝑚	𝑚	𝑚	M	M
⌒	𝑚 𝑚	Μ	N	N	N
⋐ ⋑	⋤ ⋦	⋤	⋤	X	(X)
⌾ ◯	○ ○	○	○	O	O
⌒	𐤐 𐤐	⌒	Γ	P	P
𝟠 ∞	𐤑 𐤑 𐤑	Μ	M		(S)
𐌒	𐤒 𐤒 𐤒	Φ	ϙ	Q	Q
𐤀 𐤀 𐤀	⊲	⊲	P	R	R
⋍	W	𐌔	⧢	S	S
+	×	T	T	T	T

Alphabets: Diagram showing the development of the Phoenician, Greek, and Latin alphabets.

Fig. 1.1 Early forms of writing.

From *Ancient Times*, 2nd ed. by James Henry Breasted. © copyright 1935 by James Henry Breasted. Used by permission of the publisher, Ginn and Company (Xerox Corporation).

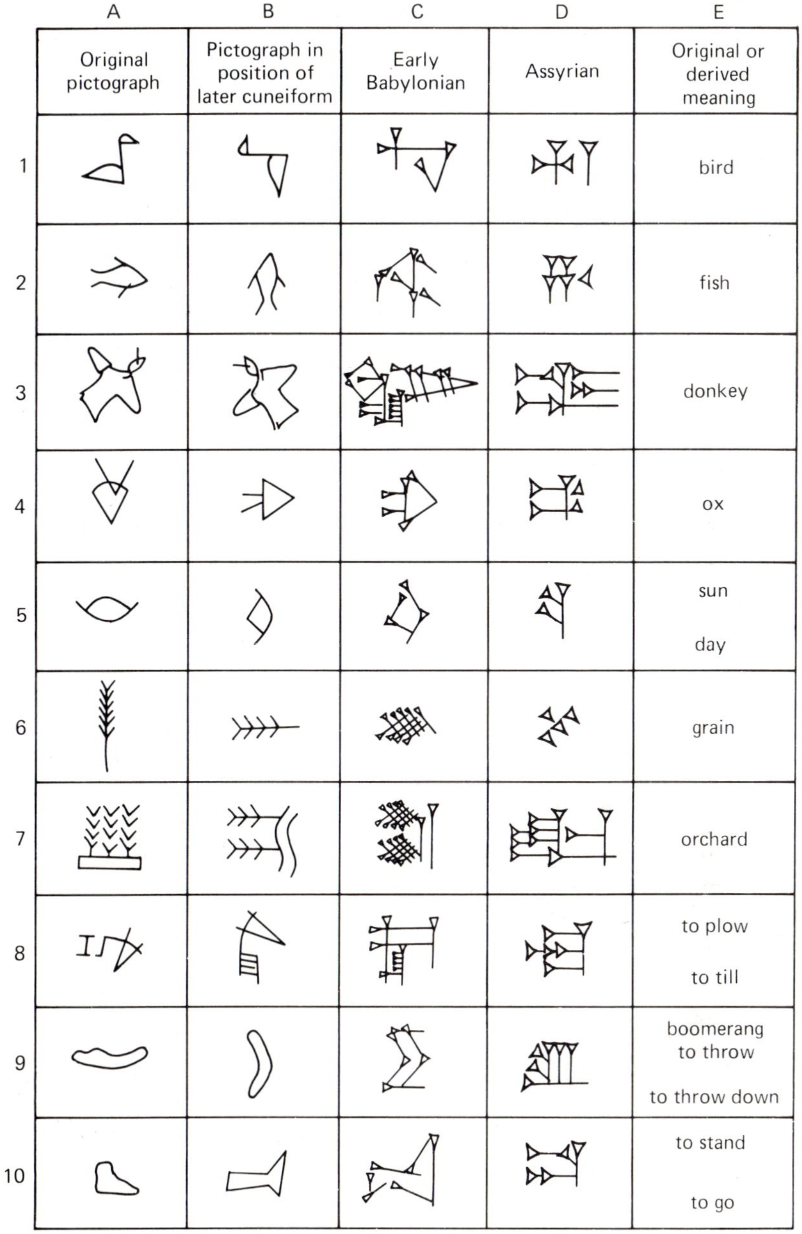

Historical Evidence of Communication

	A Original pictograph	B Pictograph in position of later cuneiform	C Early Babylonian	D Assyrian	E Original or derived meaning
1					bird
2					fish
3					donkey
4					ox
5					sun day
6					grain
7					orchard
8					to plow to till
9					boomerang to throw to throw down
10					to stand to go

Babylonian characters: This diagram shows pictorially the origins of ten cuneiform signs.

the first really distinct group of this era. They developed the first written characters and a cheap, practical writing material—clay tablets. The first writings were pictures called "cuneiforms," but later they took on conventional forms. Some of the marks retained their iconistic nature, that is, they were derived directly from the earlier picture, while others stood only for the sound of a word. Several such marks could be written to make a longer word for which a picture could not be drawn. This form of writing lasted until a couple of centuries before Christ. In the Sumerian law courts, presided over by priests and agents of the king, oral communication was used to argue a case. In the development of both writing and oral communication in the law courts, we can again see the importance of communication as a survival tool. Writing was developed because the business people needed a means of keeping records and conducting business, while oral communication in the law courts provided a means of defending oneself.

The Egyptian culture developed about the same period as the Sumerians. Egyptian writing retained its pictorial qualities longer than Sumerian writing. Even after the scribes developed a shorthand form of writing (hieratic), they retained the formal sacred form (hieroglyphic). They wrote on "papyrus" made from the stalks of the papyrus plant. Because of the cheapness of the paper, the Egyptians tended to write down things the Sumerians retained only in oral form. We can discover how important the oral form of communication was in Egypt from the "oldest book in the world," *The Instruction of Ptah-Hotep and the Instruction of Ke'Gomni*. The book is filled with the speeches of the period and the importance of communication for future kings.

There were many other cultures that developed prior to the "Golden Age" of Greece. Only two have any direct relation to the history of communication—the Phoenician and the Hebrew. The Phoenicians' contribution to civilization was the alphabet. We are deeply indebted to them for that one contribution. They first tried to write in hieroglyphics and cuneiform but discovered they could do it with fewer letters. The change was slow in developing, but by 1000 B.C., the classic Phoenician alphabet of twenty-two letters was complete. Both the idea of alphabetic writing and the forms we give the various letters today are of Phoenician origin.

The Hebrews are important not because of the size of their population, which was very small, but because of their religious ideas and literature, which inspired much interest and thought about the principles of communication down through the ages. The Hebrew belief in Yahweh and in one great community of worship has had a profound influence on civilization and on communication study and practice.

The Greeks began their history with the Trojan War. The story of the war was told by Homer in the *Iliad*, but this book is also an important part of the history of communication. It makes reference to types of speakers and it is filled with speeches. To Homer, some communicators were reputed to speak without thought and to be disorderly and redundant, while others were said to weave a web of words. In some ways, things have not changed much since that time. Homer also suggested that the ability to communicate effectively was a natural gift, which some people had and others did not have.

The Greek culture prospered because of its trade and industry. Trade was promoted in part by the invention of the Greek alphabet based on that of the Phoenicians. As in earlier times, writing was first used by business people, then by rulers, and later by teachers to record ideas. In Athens, public communication grew in importance because of the public-forum mode of government in which all citizens could speak in favor of, or in opposition to, each issue. It was because of these public communication contexts such as forums and law courts that the art of communicating became so important.

It was during this Greek period that the first systematic study of communication or rhetoric, as it was then called, began. Corax formulated a series of basic communication principles to help the average citizen argue for his rights in the courts. He proposed dividing a speech into its basic parts: proem (introduction), narration (main idea), argument (proof), and peroration (conclusion). This same basic division can still be seen in many of our public communication textbooks today. Corax felt, in opposition to Homer, that one's ability to communicate was not a natural gift but a skill that could be mastered by anyone with proper training. He believed communication to be a democratic tool that should be learned by everyone and not just by a favored few. He also felt, as we do, that a knowledge of communication was essential to survival in a democratic society.

The most substantial beginnings of the study of communication came from the fifth to the third centuries B.C. in Athens. Early teachers, called "sophists," taught students to emphasize communication style sometimes to the neglect of content. This sort of embellishment is not an uncommon problem with some messages we receive 25 centuries later. The sophists had no formal university or school. Each one lectured on any subject that interested him. Some of you may have heard the term "sophist," or its derivative, "sophistry," which refers to reasoning that seems plausible but is actually deceptive. During the Greek period, however, the term did not carry such connotations. It merely referred to those teachers who set up private schools, charged a fee, and taught "new" ideas in literature, science, philosophy, and especially oratory. During that period, communication was considered one of the most important disciplines a person could learn.

The most successful of the sophists was Isocrates. He was the most influential of the Greek rhetoricians during his time. Isocrates was a highly intelligent, moral, and gifted teacher. He believed that the successful communicator should be a well-rounded person who understood human nature and had good moral habits. An understanding of the self and self-control were central to his teachings. That focus is paralleled by the approach you will find in this book. Because the sophists became so rich, many less gifted and less ethical persons were drawn into the teaching profession, and the term "sophist" began to take on a negative meaning.

During this same time period, Protagoras was teaching his pupils that one should carefully examine both sides of any question or issue before communicating. Once one was in full command of all of the arguments and reasoning on both sides of an issue, then one should prepare speeches of affirmation or negation. For this reason, Protagoras is called the "father of debate." For him the content or "what one says" was at least as important as how something is said, if not more so.

The Study of Human Communication

All of the foregoing discussion sets the stage for two of the most important early teachers of communication: Plato and Aristotle. Plato was perhaps rhetoric's greatest critic and Aristotle its greatest benefactor. Plato attacked oratory because he thought it did not seek truth but instead rested on flattery and appearances. He believed that rhetoric had an unhealthy influence on the youth of Athens. According to Plato, one could best seek truth through the use of the question-and-answer approach to learning (Socratic method) rather than through public speaking. Obviously, his attacks were primarily aimed at the sophists who, he felt, put style above content.

Plato's student, Aristotle, reacted to the sophists in much the same way as Plato. But instead of condemning all rhetoric for the excesses of a few, Aristotle sought to raise rhetoric to a higher level. He divided his rhetoric text into three sections dealing with the speaker, the audience, and the message, in much the same manner as modern communication models. The key to Aristotle's lasting impact on communication was his careful analysis of its elements and his understanding of the basic nature of communication.

Aristotle realized, better than those who preceded him and perhaps as well as many of those who followed him, that it is not truth or reality that guides human affairs but what people *think* is the truth. He understood that communication is based on attitudes and beliefs, not on demonstrable universal truth or reality. He realized that people do not perceive reality clearly, but that they filter and distort it to meet their own needs. This same approach underlies our view of communication as well as every contemporary communication text. Aristotle said that communication is based on probability and thus defined rhetoric as "all of the *available* means of persuasion." He believed that the effort we put into our communication is as important, if not more important, than the success of the communication attempt, or the results. Probably the most insightful part of Aristotle's analysis of the elements of communication was his examination of the modes of proof. He believed that all people are persuaded by an appeal to reason (*logos*), an appeal to emotion (*pathos*), or an appeal to ethics (*ethos*). No matter how hard we try, communication teachers cannot seem to come up with any better listing of the basic communication appeals. Whereas Plato dreamed up answers to important questions, Artistotle set his pupils to work collecting information. Plato was a philosopher, whereas Aristotle was a scientist.

Before we leave the Ancient Greek period, we must discuss the five canons of rhetoric. They have had a profound influence on all of communication. At first, they were thought to be written by Aristotle, but we have since discovered that they were in existence long before his time. They are important because they form the basis of so much contemporary communication study. The five canons of rhetoric are inventio, dispositio, elocutio, memoria, and pronuntiatio. They describe the essential processes necessary to the production of a message. *Inventio*, or invention, refers to the thought, reasoning, and background that goes into a message. *Dispositio* refers to the arrangement of the ideas in a particular order. *Elocutio* is the style of the message, including word and phrase choice. *Memoria*, or memory, is the lost or least important canon. People seldom memorize a message any longer. Finally, *pronuntiatio* refers to the delivery, including the nonverbal cues that accompany the message.

Historical Evidence of Communication

Raphael's *The School of Athens* (fresco in the Vatican) depicts Plato (left) and Aristotle (right) surrounded by students.

During the Greek Age, just as in modern times, everyone wanted peace but no one knew how to achieve it. However, in an amazingly short period after the rise of Rome as a major power, the world was civilized under her control and people enjoyed peace as never before or since in history. The most famous of the Latin rhetoricians was Cicero, Rome's most important man of letters. Like Isocrates, Cicero believed that the true communicator should have a wide range of knowledge. Under Cicero's teaching, rhetoric more or less became the study of the liberal arts. Cicero preached democracy at a time when most politicians were dictators. He focused heavily on the five canons of rhetoric. Much of his teaching was done by example, since he himself was an outstanding speaker, with Caesar only second best. Cicero felt a speech had six parts: introduction, narration, division, proof, refutation, and conclusion. He also discussed the nonverbal gestural behaviors that should accompany one's verbal message.

Some years after Cicero died, another rhetorician came to the forefront in Rome. He was Quintilian, a man who took the best of Cicero and Aristotle and combined them. He emphasized not only the broad education necessary for a communicator but also the importance of good moral training. He defined the perfect communicator as "a good man skilled in speaking." Both Cicero and Quintilian had a significant influence on the teaching of communication in the early English and American school systems.

The Middle Ages were characterized by religious fervor. The Christian clergy comprised the intellectual class, and they discouraged all thought except that which interested them. This situation continued until about the thirteenth century. Education consisted primarily of the seven "liberal" arts. They were made up of the "trivium"—grammar, rhetoric, and logic, and the "quadrivium"—arithmetic, geometry, astronomy, and music. During this period, parchment began to be used for writing. The Middle Ages saw a definite change in the study of communication. The emphasis on style and imitation of the sophists again became prominent. This focus on religious communication and style continued for almost 900 years.

The true Renaissance did not begin until the sixteenth (or late fifteenth) century, but in the fourteenth century the general population began to renew its interest in the surrounding world. Students and teachers started being interested in more than the "seven liberal arts." This was certainly a new age of intellectual thought, but it was not yet "modern" in the sense we know the term today. A great deal of credit for this awakening can be traced to the discovery of paper as a means of communication. The Chinese first invented paper, and it was in general use by the fifteenth century. Of comparable importance was the invention of printing. "Block printing" through the use of carved blocks of wood was used in China as early as the second century. It came to Europe in the fifteenth century. The only major change from the Chinese process was the use of movable type, letters that could be rearranged and used over and over again. Johann Gutenberg produced his famous Bible in 1455 by using a movable-type press. Printing would not have expanded very rapidly if it had not coincided with the emergence of a reading public capable of buying books and of speculators willing to invest in book publishing. By 1500, more than 40,000 books and pamphlets had been printed.

With the advent of printing and the large number of books during this period, you might expect that there would have been much progress in the understanding of communication. Such was not the case. Unlike art, architecture, sculpture, music, engineering, science, and other disciplines that took great strides forward during the Renaissance, the humanists' enthusiasm for the Greek and Latin periods caused them to turn backward instead of forward. Little, if any, progress in the understanding of oral communication can be found during this period. A hundred years ago, historians praised this period as a magnificent "rebirth" of civilization after the "Dark Ages," but they have since discovered that the Middle Ages were not so dark as we once imagined and that the people of the Renaissance were not so very different from their predecessors.

The sixteenth century brought a total collapse of medieval thought. Many people feared the change at first, but this was the actual beginning of the new age of science. It was during this period that both Aristotle and the Scriptures were dethroned as the final word in intellectual circles. Persons of learning turned from deductive to inductive methods of thought. This was the age of astronomy's Nicholas Copernicus, physics' Galileo Galilei, and, above all, Sir Isaac Newton. This was the age of discovery: Columbus discovered America and the world discovered the scientific method.

The most famous figure in the development of the scientific method was Francis Bacon. Whereas others had attacked Aristotle's deductive method and suffered for their ideas, Francis Bacon succeeded. He replaced deductive logic with the idea of experimentation and observation (inductive logic). He proposed that general laws can grow only out of research. Bacon's writings on communication reflect this same approach. He believed that the discovery, selection, and arrangement of ideas were as important as phrasing and delivery. He defined rhetoric as the application of "reason to imagination for the better moving of the will." According to Bacon, communicative symbols need meet only one rule—that they provide the vehicle by which the "variety of actions" can be conveyed from one person to another. He further stated that no one method of orderly, systematic communication of ideas can fit every purpose and every situation. He made the listener the key to the communication process, not the speaker. He believed that language in part determines how people understand, respond, and survive in the world. He viewed language, thought, and behavior as inseparable. We could go on and on talking about the similarities between Francis Bacon's thoughts and the contemporary approach to communication study. Suffice it to say that we believe Francis Bacon to be the father of modern communication study.

It was during the 1500s that the first rhetoric texts were published in English. Some of these were merely translations and syntheses of the Greek and Roman writings, while others began to develop some new ideas. Most of these writers saw little difference between the arts of oral and written communication. The connection of the term rhetoric to written communication has recently been renewed in modern English departments. In the Renaissance, it was a recognition on the part of teachers of the debt literature owes to its much older cousin—oral communication.

A major contributor to our understanding of communication during the sixteenth and seventeenth centuries was a poet—John Milton. His importance does not, however, derive from his poetry but from his classic plea for the freedom of spoken and written communication. When Parliament passed an act establishing censorship he proposed that when freedom of speech and the press is denied, civilization itself soon declines. He saw, perhaps more clearly than anyone before or after him, how important communication is for survival, not only for individuals but also for society as a whole.

Rhetorical training did not end during the sixteenth and seventeenth centuries in spite of the attacks it received. American rhetoric in the early eighteenth century was strongly influenced by the British models as well as by early colonial pulpit rhetoric. Oratory and disputation were central and important aspects of college education during this period. At Harvard University, for example, weekly practice in oratory and disputation was supervised by the president who earlier in the day had given a lecture on rhetoric. The first truly American rhetoric text was written by John Witherspoon (a signer of the Declaration of Independence) in 1810. It consisted of his lectures on rhetoric, given while he was president of Princeton University. His text took the colonial oratory of the clergyman and transformed it into the American rhetoric of the statesman. One of Witherspoon's many students was James Madison. In a similar vein, Benjamin Franklin, in 1744, called for courses that emphasized speaking and reading skills. He believed these to be essential for religious, legal, commercial, and political endeavors.

By 1785, an outgrowth of the stylistic rhetorics had taken hold—the elocutionary movement. The movement focused on the rhetorical canon of delivery. The elocutionists were well aware of the power of oral presentation in public persuasion. Not surprisingly, this was the same period that saw a marked increase in interest in the theatre. A restless, dynamic, and industrious American population wanted self-improvement and entertainment, and the elocutionary movement offered both. Reading groups, lyceums, and chautauquas grew up almost overnight. The public lecture was in constant demand and teachers of elocution began to open professional elocutionary schools. Some examples of such schools were the Vocal and Polyglot Gymnasium, the National School of Elocution and Oratory, Columbia School of Expression, the School of Practical Rhetoric and Oratory, and the Leland Powers School of the Spoken Word. These schools taught a combination of rhetoric, stage practices, and science. Most took a strong psychological approach to their discipline. This interest in psychology and science is what makes the elocutionary movement important to modern communication. The elocutionists made scientific studies of the voice that were the forerunners of speech correction. They combined scientific observation and recording and invented symbols to understand the communication process. Perhaps their most significant contribution came in the area of nonverbal communication where they made careful studies of facial expression, gestures, and body orientation. The elocutionists firmly believed an art should rest upon science.

By the 1850s, the elocutionary movement received harsh, stiff criticism because its performance orientation was not meeting the needs of lawyers, ministers, and business people. Although the first national communication organization founded in 1892 was called the National Association of Elocutionists, the choice of name provoked some very heated debate. The name was changed to the National Speech Arts Association in 1906, but even that organization lasted only eight years. As the elocutionary movement died, these teachers joined the rhetoricians either in college and university departments of rhetoric or elocution or in departments of English. The relationships between speech and English, never very strong, started breaking up by 1913.

The term "speech" was not found in department titles until about 1920. The national organization at that time (established in 1914) was called the National Association of Academic Teachers of Public Speaking. It later became the National Speech Arts Association, then the National Association of Teachers of Speech, then the Speech Association of America, and it is currently called the Speech Communication Association. By the 1930s, most colleges had established separate departments of speech. Using the concept of the symbolic processes and the spoken message as its area of interest, the discipline of speech permitted itself freedom to move into all areas related to human discourse.

Early speech departments usually included courses in public speaking, debate, oratory, rhetoric, drama, interpretation, elocution, voice, and gesture. By the 1930s, parliamentary law and phonetics had been added. By the 1940s, argumentation, business speech, speech correction, extemporaneous speaking, and radio were coming into their own as well. Members of the profession had basically agreed upon the goal of a sound education in speech by then, including both the skills and techniques of speech as well as knowledge of the principles on which the skills are based. But they differed radically on how this goal could best be obtained.

Pages from Professor C.P. Bronson's 1845 book entitled, *ELOCUTION; or, MENTAL AND VOCAL PHILOSOPHY: Involving the Principles of READING AND SPEAKING; and Designed FOR THE DEVELOPMENT AND CULTIVATION of BOTH BODY AND MIND, in Accordance with the NATURE, USES, AND DESTINY OF MAN: Illustrated by Two or Three Hundred Choice Anecdotes; Three Thousand Oratorical and Poetical Readings; Five Thousand Proverbs, Maxims and Laconics, and Several Hundred Elegant Engravings.*

The Study of Human Communication

With autonomy for the field of speech came many developments. As we have seen, the curricular offering greatly increased. Graduate study developed. The first Ph.D. in speech was granted in 1922. Specializations within speech began to develop. The area of speech pathology and speech therapy found an affinity with the natural and medical sciences. Drama and interpretation discovered a kinship with the humanities, fine arts, and literature. Broadcasting found a community of interest with journalism and the other mass media. In time, the specialists in each of these areas formed their own professional organizations, and many left the speech association.

The "communication" approach has its roots not only in speech and rhetoric but also in such areas as public opinion, marketing and sales, the nonverbal expression of emotions in human beings, reflective thinking, industrial sociology, sociometrics, group leadership, psychotherapy, general semantics, and many others. We conclude our historical treatment of the study of communication at this point because we discuss the principles developed during the modern era throughout the rest of this text. However, we should point out that the communication approach as we present it in this text is a blending of the best of the older rhetorical and humanistic speech approaches to human discourse with the newer, more scientifically and psychologically oriented approaches of modern behavioral science. With this blending, communication scholars have never lost sight of the basic goal of speech education since earliest times: the use of communication knowledge to help people survive. Dr. David Berlo, one of the founders of the modern approach, points this out.

> A basic assumption of the communication discipline is that an understanding of the process, the determinants, and the effects of communication improve a man's basic ability to handle the communication problems that he faces on his job, regardless of the kind of work in which he is engaged. (Berlo, 1960, p. 7)

OVERVIEW

As in the past, contemporary communication specialists continue to focus on two aspects of the human communication process. The first aspect is continued investigation of the *elements of communication*, that is, the discovery and understanding of how communication works regardless of whether it takes place in a large auditorium with an audience, within a family, on the job, or in any other environment. The second aspect is how the basic principles change depending upon the *context*, or environment. In this book we will consider both the elements and the contexts of human communication.

In Chapter 2, you will find our definition of communication. We do not claim to have the "correct" definition. Our definition is really a compromise between two different points of view which seem to pervade the study of communication. We do not see such definitional disagreements as unhealthy. On the contrary, we believe such disagreement and debate lead to better understanding and progress in any field of study. Chapter 2 also presents several communication perspectives and models. We believe the *systems* theory perspective provides the most complete and easily understood approach to communication. Systems theory is defined and explained, and a simple model is provided for student reference throughout the book.

We hope, as you read Chapter 2, that you constantly will be challenging the various perspectives and models presented, including our own. You should attempt to develop your own point of view regarding communication. We believe that a student should not merely read and accept every idea that is presented in a book. Your approach should be one of constantly challenging and mentally testing the ideas presented. We sincerely hope you will approach this book in that manner. You will get more out of the book if you do.

Parts II and III of the text grow directly out of our model of communication. The model suggests that each communicator is capable of receiving inputs from the environment, processing those inputs, and responding to them in the form of both verbal and nonverbal communicative outputs. The input, processing, and output mechanisms are highly interrelated. Even though we handle them in six chapters, you must constantly be aware of this interrelationship.

Part II deals with the intrapersonal processing elements. We have broken the processing function into the elements of motivation (Chapter 3), perception (Chapter 4), and reasoning (Chapter 5). A concern for what motivates people has been a part of scientific and philosophical thought for centuries. We believe, along with many in the past, that an understanding of motivation can grow only out of an understanding of the "self." How a person sees his or her "self" will determine, in great part, that person's needs and values. These needs and values provide the motivation to both input and output communicative stimuli. People must have a motive to communicate.

Perception is intimately related to motivation in a number of ways. We form our "self" through the process of perception. As a child, our "self" is initially formed through our perceptions of the environment around us. As we grow older, our "self," our needs, our motivations, our reasoning, and our communication change, based on further perceptions of our environment. Our perceptions are random and undifferentiated, but as we grow older we begin to discriminate among the possible stimuli available to us. We begin to filter our perceptions. This filtering is a product of reasoning and motivation. We tend to protect our "self" by filtering out or distorting certain perceptual stimuli. In this way, communication can be seen as a transaction in which people act upon the things perceived. Both physical and person perception are involved in this process. Many times we will choose to accept or reject our physical or direct perceptions, based on our perceptions of the people involved. Our communication, then, is determined not only by our own motivations and reasoning but also by our perception of the motivations and reasoning of those around us.

So far we have discussed our motivations and perceptions as having a rather emotional basis. In fact, however, they are based on both emotion and logic. In the chapter on reasoning we will consider the logical aspect of communication processing. All of us want to be logically consistent in our motivations and perceptions so we look carefully for the reasoning underlying our perceptions and motivations. Reasoning includes the evidence and lines of argument found in the inputs we receive and in our own outputs. For most of us, our "self" image demands that we be a rational human being capable of balancing emotion with logic. Reasoning has been a central focus of communication study since the classical Greek and Roman periods.

The processing elements of motivation, perception, and reasoning discussed in Part II of this book are not only interrelated with one another but are also intimately connected to communication inputs and outputs discussed in Part III. The aspects of communication inputs and outputs we discuss in Part III are verbal communication (Chapter 6), nonverbal communication (Chapter 7), and sending and receiving mechanisms (Chapter 8).

In order to communicate ideas (based upon motives, perceptions, and reasoning) and to receive the communicated messages of others, we need to understand the means by which communication takes place. These means include both linguistic (verbal) and nonlinguistic (nonverbal) behaviors. Verbal communication is made up of symbols that have referents and, therefore, meaning. In order to understand how verbal communication works, you must understand the relationships between symbols, referents, and meaning. We have chosen to demonstrate this relationship by discussing how a child learns to communicate in the first place. Not only are the acquired symbols used to output the results of the processing elements but they also directly affect the processing elements themselves. In other words, our symbols in large part determine what we are capable of perceiving, how we reason, and, ultimately, why we are motivated in particular ways. Language, then, can have both positive and negative effects on our "self" and on our communicative relationships with others.

Nonverbal communication rests on the same basic principles as verbal communication and is a complementary means of information input and output. Nonverbal cues include such things as our tone of voice, gestures, posture, clothing, facial expression, and use of space. Nonverbal cues are useful in areas where language effectiveness is limited and vice versa. We use nonverbal communication to help regulate our verbal interactions. We also use it to communicate attitudes, emotions, and personality. Language is not very good in these areas. Most of what we know about the people with whom we are communicating and the environment in which the communication takes place comes to us nonverbally. The ideas that are communicated are usually handled through verbal communication. We process both kinds of information, and they are both vitally important.

In order for efficient communication inputting and outputting to take place, you must also be familiar with the mechanism you use for these purposes. We send information not only with our mouth but also with our face, eyes, body, and so on. We receive information through our five senses. Without an understanding of our mechanisms of sending and receiving communication, we are incapable of diagnosing our communication problems. Our perception, motivation, and reasoning processes are all dependent on these mechanisms. In Chapter 8 the mechanisms are not only explained but suggestions are also given for their improvement.

Parts I, II, and III of this text discuss the elements necessary to understand human communication systems. By then, you will be ready to examine how these elements actually operate in the various communication systems or contexts. Obviously, context has a powerful effect on the communication that takes place. The importance of this effect is demonstrated in Part IV.

Overview

The systems discussed in Part IV are the dyadic, small group, organizational, public, and mass communication contexts. Each of these contexts involves a somewhat different set of problems and potentialities that you must understand before you can successfully participate in any one of them.

There are, however, a number of similarities among the various contexts. These common contextual components are presented in Chapter 9. The remaining chapters deal with the various contexts. The dyad, or two-person communication context (chapter 10), represents the most common interaction context. It is at this basic level of interaction that you will become aware of the importance of such factors as the different consummatory and instrumental dyads, the status of the individual participants, the stages of dyad development, and the environment in which communication takes place. This is not to say that these factors are important only in the dyad; they are also important in the other contexts discussed. It is with the dyad, however, that we can most easily examine them.

Small group communication (Chapter 11) adds the element of size or multiple participants to the dyadic principles discussed in the previous chapter. Size of the interaction group might, on the surface, seem to be a relatively minor matter, but in reality it accounts for many added problems and potentialities. For example, with size come leadership, group pressure, increased numbers of interaction channels, and a host of alternative methods of problem-solving and decision-making. The types of small groups that will be discussed in this chapter are the family, sports teams, discussion groups, and club meetings.

Beginning with Chapter 12, the focus of the text shifts to very large communication contexts. The first of these large group contexts is the organization (Chapter 12). We deal with the organizational communication context first because it, like dyads and small groups, involves extensive interpersonal communication. Messages are also not as carefully planned as in public and mass communication. The sheer complexity of organizational communication often bewilders students. The types of organizations with which we will be concerned include businesses, schools, and governmental organizations. Such organizations have very specific kinds of communication problems. Many of these problems stem from the fact that organizations have a strict hierarchy or status structure. Organizations also exist to serve a purpose, and the success or failure of the organization's communication is directly related to the organization's ability to accomplish its purposes. An organization that fails in either its internal or external communication soon goes out of existence.

Public communication (Chapter 13) involves a different type of large group communication. Public communication refers to situations where one or a few people are trying to communicate to a group of listeners face-to-face. A presidential speech, a lawyer before a jury, and a panel discussion on UFOs are examples of public communication. Few people are ever called upon to make such a presentation, but all of us are constant receivers of such communication. In order to be an effective receiver of public communication, you must be able to understand its elements, including the viewpoint of the speaker. Problems of public communication include such matters as message organization, use of evidence, audience analysis, delivery, and critical analysis by receivers.

Many of the principles of public communication apply equally to mass or media communication (Chapter 14). The media consist of radio, television, film, newspapers, books, and magazines. The influence of the media on our lives is tremendous. The influence of the media and the aspects of communication that are important in understanding them are in some ways very different from those of public communication. The purposes are often different, the channel is different, the sources and receivers are often different, and the environment in which they are received is different. When the mass media are combined with face-to-face channels, they become a very powerful tool for diffusing information.

As technology is deemphasized as the means by which we judge the quality of our lives, our attention becomes focused on such areas as communication. This is already happening in business and industry where managers are shifting away from technology as a means of increasing profit to the less tangible aspects of the company such as human relations and communication. Job openings that used to go to engineers are now going to social science and humanities graduates. It is a strong belief of the authors that we are just on the brink of a communication revolution in our society and that those students who have prepared themselves for such a revolution will be increasing in demand in the future.

SUMMARY

This chapter has focused on the study of human communication. We first discussed why communication study has become so important to all of us. We are constantly either communicating ourselves or are receiving communication. Probably the main reason why communication study is so important, however, is because it is one of our most significant survival tools. We traced the survival value of communication back to its very earliest beginnings with the caveman, through the Sumerians, Egyptians, and other historic cultures. We then focused on the systematic study of communication, beginning with the Greeks and Romans and ending with the beginning of the contemporary period. We did not go into the contemporary period because that is presented in future chapters. The last section provided an overview of what you will study in this book, including the intrapersonal processing elements, communication inputs and outputs, and finally, the contexts of communication.

KEY TERMS AND CONCEPTS

ARISTOTLE
BACON, FRANCIS
CICERO
COLONIAL RHETORIC
COMMUNICATION CONTEXTS
COMMUNICATION ELEMENTS
DEVELOPMENT OF ACADEMIC DEPARTMENTS
DEVELOPMENT OF PRINTING
DEVELOPMENT OF WRITING
DYADIC COMMUNICATION
ELOCUTIONARY MOVEMENT

"ENGLISH" VS "SPEECH"
FIVE CANONS OF RHETORIC
GREEK RHETORIC
IMPORTANCE OF COMMUNICATION
INPUTS
MASS COMMUNICATION
MEDIEVAL RHETORIC
MOTIVATION
NONVERBAL COMMUNICATION
ORGANIZATIONAL COMMUNICATION
OUTPUTS

PERCEPTION
PLATO
PREHISTORIC EVIDENCE OF COMMUNICATION
PROCESSING ELEMENTS
PUBLIC COMMUNICATION
"PUBLIC SPEAKING" VS "SPEECH"
QUINTILIAN
REASONING
RENAISSANCE RHETORIC
RHETORIC
ROMAN RHETORIC
SMALL GROUP COMMUNICATION
SOPHISTS
"SPEECH" VS "COMMUNICATION"
SURVIVAL VALUE OF COMMUNICATION
VERBAL COMMUNICATION

SUGGESTED READINGS

BERLO, DAVID K., *The Process of Communication: An Introduction to Theory and Practice.* New York: Holt, Rinehart and Winston, Inc., 1960. This book is commonly recognized as the beginning of the interdisciplinary, behavioral approach to human communication. Although the field has long since gone far beyond the principles suggested in this text, the basic concepts of process, empathy, social systems, meaning, and inference are still important to an understanding of human communication. Many of the insights presented in this book have never been fully investigated.

HARPER, NANCY, *Human Communication Theory: the History of a Paradigm.* Rochelle Park, N.J.: Hayden Book Company, Inc., 1979. This book examines the major historical communication trends in the classical, medieval, Renaissance, and modern periods. The areas of categorization, conceptualization, symbolization, organization, and operationalization, from the Greek-Roman paradigm, are examined for each period. A text of this type has been badly needed in the communication field for a long time, and this book not only fills the bill but is also extremely well done.

WALLACE, KARL R., ed., *History of Speech Education in America: Background Studies.* New York: Appleton-Century-Crofts, Inc., 1954. This is a classic collection of readings on the history of human communication. Discussions of the English background of rhetoric and rhetorical theory and practice in colonial America, the rhetorical and elocutionary colleges, the development of departments of speech and speech organizations, and a great deal more are included in this book. Although it is somewhat dated, it is still "must" reading for anyone interested in the historical background of the communication field.

2

Human Communication Perspectives

The attempts to explain human communication continue to be varied. Why and how people communicate are questions we all need to answer. This chapter discusses human communication as a complete, survival-oriented system. The most important components in every human communication context are the people involved. In addition, the ways people can relate through communication, as well as the ways people deal with their environment are considered. The view presented in this chapter serves as the base upon which the rest of the book is constructed.

In recent years, human communication has been studied by people in academic disciplines as widely disparate as electrical engineering, psychology, speech communication, journalism, education, political science, and biology, to mention just a few. Although this is a legitimate field of study for all of these areas, you should not for a moment consider that people in these disciplines are studying the same thing. The process of communication as it occurs in various contexts, whether educational, political, or within electronic or biological systems, can vary considerably. However, the perspectives provided by these various approaches can be both valid and complementary.

The first question we must ask is why people communicate at all. There are as many answers to that question as there are people who have tried to answer it. Whenever we have asked this question in our communication classes, the answers we have received have included such responses as the following:

"**We communicate to share information.**"
"**We communicate in order to persuade people.**"
"**We communicate in order to understand one another.**"
"**We communicate to give direction.**"
"**We communicate in order to express emotions.**"
"**We communicate in order to find ourselves.**"

Each of these statements is probably true in some respects. When we do any of the things just listed, we are communicating. However, to better understand why we communicate, it is useful to consider a more basic question: Why do people ever engage in any sort of behavior? The answer to this question is more difficult to come by than the answer to the earlier question. However, in order to answer our first question, it is necessary to consider the second.

As you read in Chapter 1, people have been attempting to determine the causes of human behaviors for centuries. One of the first statements ever uttered must have been, "Why did you do that?" How many times have you been asked this question? Probably often. Frequently, we have trouble answering that question about our own behavior, much less anyone else's behavior. The body of evidence already presented suggests that human beings behave the way they do in order to survive, even though they are not always conscious of the survival motivation. This statement is somewhat simplified and does not distinguish humans as being very different from other living things. Cattle, grazing in a field, munch on grass to survive physically (at least for a time). They ingest enough food to provide the fuel needed to maintain their biological systems. But people do more than that.

We do not mean to imply that human beings are the only communicating animals. For instance, you may be aware of the current research suggesting considerable communication abilities of apes and porpoises. (However, many scholars do not accept the validity of this research.) Because our concern is with human communication, we will not examine communication as a survival tool in other animal species, although it is a topic of considerable interest. Suffice it to say that people have become dependent on effective communication for their survival.

Without communication, we could not pass knowledge from one generation to another, and our species could not evolve, grow, and increase its ability to survive within its environment. There are those who would suggest that possibly we are destroying our environment. This may be true, since communication, like any other tool, can be used constructively or destructively. However, we may also use communication to become more aware of our environment so as to reduce our destruction of it, increase our concern for it, and thus, save it. Whatever finally happens, communication will play a significant role in the way we exist within our environment.

In the second half of this chapter, as we begin to present our perspective of the communication process, we will make more clear the ways people use communication. At this point, we would like to turn our attention to some major perspectives on communication.

PERSPECTIVES ON HUMAN COMMUNICATION

We will now examine several perspectives on the communication process. We will do this by considering representative communication models that have evolved over the years.

Using Models

Most of you at one time have played with scale model cars, doll houses, and other toys. Each of these is a model that represents some reality so that the person using the model can experience the phenomenon without having to go to the real thing. For instance, it is very common in designing airplanes for aeronautical engineers to construct a model of the plane they are designing and test it in a small wind tunnel. In this way, they can detect flaws in the design before they have committed the time, effort, and resources to construct the real plane. Likewise, the communication models we will consider have been developed so that we might have a way of studying the communication process that is less resource- and time-consuming than looking at real communication events all the time. These models are usually verbal, diagrammatic, or three-dimensional in form. Models are important in communication teaching and research. They frequently enable us to pinpoint variables in the communication process that we might wish to study.

We will discuss several communication models in order to make the communication process more understandable to you. We will not concentrate on any given variable within the communication process, but rather we will try to look at the process as a whole. By looking at these models, we can also demonstrate the ways in which our views of communication have developed over time. We will discuss four different perspectives that have been or currently are in existence: *the stimulus-response perspective, the motivational perspective, the transactional perspective, and the general systems perspective.* Each of these perspectives has value and provides insight into the process of human communication.

The Stimulus-Response Perspective

This approach to communication rests on an underlying assumption that is in keeping with the stimulus-response model used by psychologists. This perspective assumes that when an organism (i.e., a person) receives a stimulus (i.e., a noise, a touch, an odor, or light), it responds in some way.

The first people who systematically studied the communication process were the ancient Greeks. We have already discussed the primary communication theorists during the "Golden Age" of Greece. As we said, the greatest of them all was Aristotle. His model was actually a fairly simple one. The three variables in Aristotle's model were: the speaker, the audience, and the message. He used words to describe the communication process and thus his was a *verbal model*. From this beginning with Aristotle, other rhetoricians developed further verbal models.

An outgrowth of the rhetorical approach of Aristotle and others was a public speaking approach to communication in which the concern was with the person giving a public speech before an audience. These students of the communication process expanded their view of the process to include other variables such as language, gestures, delivery, and attitudes of the audience. These approaches have also been reviewed in Chapter 1.

The twentieth-century version of this approach is what we are calling stimulus-response models. One of the most famous of these models, which is concerned with mass communication, is that developed by Harold Lasswell (1948). This verbal model asks: "Who? Says what? In which channel? To whom? With what effect?" Having five variables, this verbal model is more complex than earlier ones. It is a model that represents the act of someone saying something to someone else with an intent to influence.

In addition to making a basic assumption about the stimulus-response behavior of people, it is important that we point out that these models have one other characteristic in common. They are all essentially *one-way models*. These models suggest that communication flows from one person to another and stops there. A basic problem with these models is the assumption that communication is one-way, or *linear*. It places the burden for the success or failure of any communication outcome on the person who initiates the message, because this is the person "doing communication to someone" and thus controlling whatever happens. Stimulus-response models view the other person as simply responding to messages.

Although these models have the value of helping us identify the various components of the communication process and of calling our attention to them, this one-way approach to communication is misleading. Too much evidence suggests that the person who receives the message has almost as much effect (if not as much) on the person sending the message as the person sending the message has on the receiver. In fact, it is frequently hard to tell who is "sending" and who is "receiving" in any given communication situation. About the only situation we can imagine that would actually be one-way is when one person could speak and be seen by another without the other being able to speak or be seen by the first person. This is not a common human occurrence, with possible exceptions in the mass media or of a person using a loudspeaker, and even in these cases there is delayed feedback.

Perspectives on Human Communication

The Motivational Perspective

The motivational sequence of Ehninger, Monroe, and Gronbeck (1978) illustrates the motivational perspective on speech construction. This verbal model focuses on the processes of human thinking. It suggests that the thought

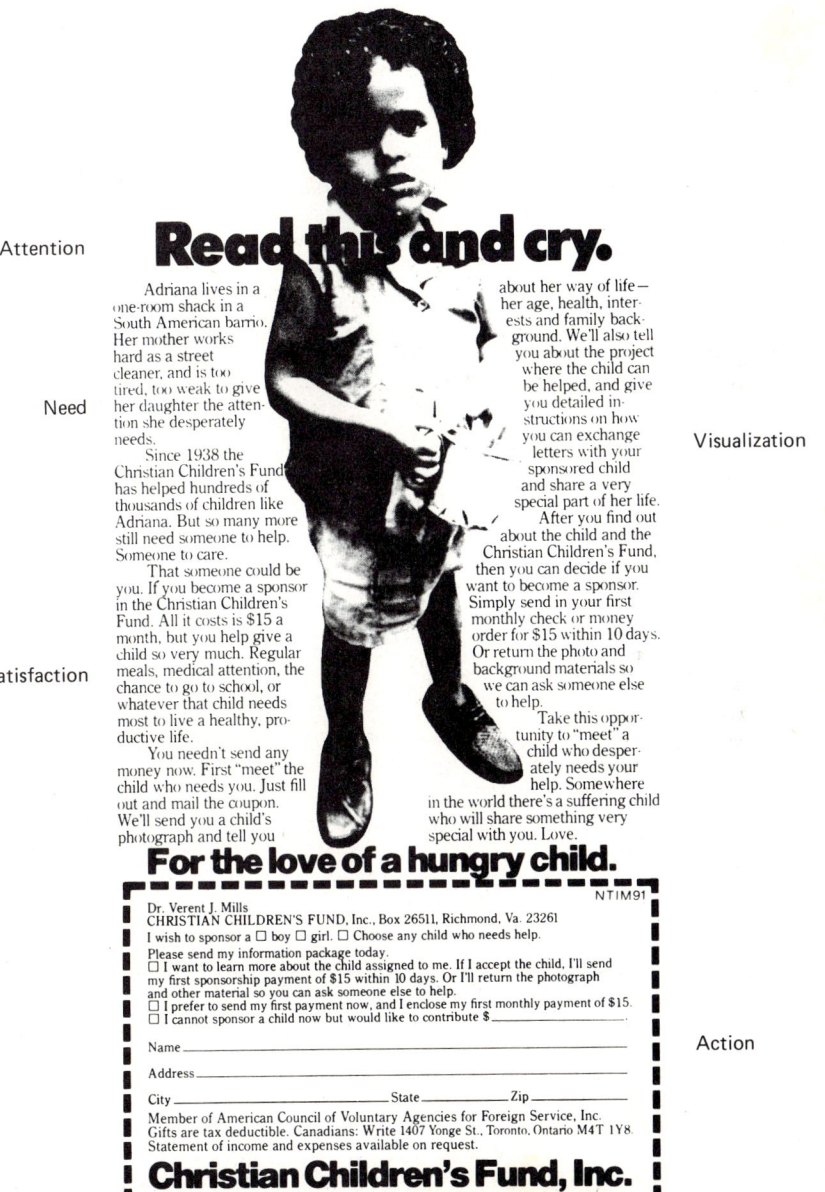

Fig. 2.1 Advertisement with motivational sequence steps noted.

processes in listeners who respond to various sorts of messages are uniform enough to provide a basis for a standard guide to speech organization. This standard guide is called "the motivated sequence" and consists of five steps.

1. The attention step: The receiver's attention is caught.
2. The need step: The listener is made to feel a definite need regarding the topic presented in the message.
3. The satisfaction step: The listener is shown a way in which the need can be satisfied. The way to satisfy this need is to adopt or accept whatever is advocated by the speaker.
4. The visualization step: The benefits to the listener for accepting the recommendations of the speaker are visualized for the listener. The listener is shown in a graphic form what acceptance of the recommended course of action will do for him or her.
5. The action step: The speaker gives the listener a specific course of action that can be followed in order to achieve the satisfaction suggested in the message.

Although this is not strictly a model of the entire communication process, it is a view of the way in which messages relate to listeners. Other models that follow similar patterns can be found in advertising, public relations, and journalism.

The Transactional Perspective

The transactional approach to communication assumes that people engage in transactions with their environment, including the people in it. This perspective contrasts with the stimulus-response approach, in which people react to their environment and to the people in it. A transactional view of communication is concerned with relationships and suggests that you cannot describe the persons in a communication system separately; they can be considered only in terms of the way they relate to each other. Further, the transactional perspective suggests that it is misleading to examine the sender, message, or receiver independently and apart from the events that preceded the communication event. This perspective assumes that the environment shapes the motivations, perceptions, and reasoning of the interactants and thus the communication process.

The transactional perspective assumes that all messages contain information about communicators as well as topics. The transactional point of view shifts our focus from the individual to relationships. This perspective on communication, at the very least, focuses on a dyad (or larger units), since with anything less there would be no relationships to observe.

This approach is very holistic. The concern is with the communication system as a whole. Previously discussed models have tended to focus on individual components in isolation. This approach has much in common with the next approach discussed, the systems approach. In fact, it probably would be fair to say that the transactional approach is one type of systems theory.

The Systems Perspective

The systems approach to viewing communication is organismic. Rather than trying to divide the act of communication into separate parts and treating each of them in isolation, systems theorists attempt to study the whole process as a single entity in which interaction is occurring. This is similar to the approach already discussed, called the transactional perspective. It is a *way of thinking* about natural phenomena. Something as complex as communication within a large factory is viewed as a single organism or system with components and interrelationships within it. Rather than looking at "speakers," "messages," and "listeners" separately, we attempt to consider them jointly as a system. We try to view everything at once rather than focus on one component at a time. We can speak of "marriage communication systems," "political communication systems," "two-person communication systems," "mass communication systems," etc. To be sure, we will discuss different components of these systems in separate chapters of this book because it is impossible to write and read about it all at once. However, you should always try to think of communication systems as whole and complete entities.

A second important point made in the systems perspective is that we should be content with an *adequate* knowledge of communication systems rather than be overly concerned with obtaining an *accurate* knowledge of it. No one has a completely accurate understanding of human communication in all of its subtleties and nuances. Because of this, we try for, at best, an understanding adequate enough to permit us to *predict* and to *effectively engage* in communication behavior.

CHARACTERISTICS OF COMMUNICATION SYSTEMS

In his discussion of general systems thinking, A. Litterer (1969) listed ten characteristics that are important in a consideration of communication systems.

Interdependence

This concept is an extension of the organismic point of view. Rather than discussing communication acts in terms of who causes what to happen to whom, it is more useful to think in terms of everyone involved in the communication process as interrelated with and mutually affecting one another. When two friends talk with each other, they are mutually affecting each other. It is not something that one is doing to the other, but rather a case in which they are "doing with" each other. It is the composition that is important, not the parts.

When Charles begins to explain to his professor why he does not have a paper prepared on the due date, the professor may influence Charles as much as Charles influences her. If, while Charles is talking, the professor frowns, or begins to irritably tap her pencil on the desk, Charles may begin to "soften the snow job." If the professor nods in agreement and smiles while Charles is talking, he may continue his preplanned message. In other words, how Charles talks is affected by the professor at the same time the professor is affected by Charles' message. The room, chair arrangement, and time of day are also relevant elements in this situation. There are no elements that are unrelated to any others.

All elements have some effect on all other elements and in turn are affected by all other elements. This means that if we change a component such as the verbal language within the communication process, we also will change the nonverbal language, meaning, attitudes, etc. Likewise, person A will behave differently with person B from the way he or she behaves with person C. Whether the component is a person, a language, an attitude, or anything else, a change in any single component of a communication system will change everything else in the system. In our earlier example, Charles' language was affected by the professor's nonverbal behavior of frowning or smiling. A stone thrown into a pond causes ripples throughout the water. One marble removed from a bowl of marbles causes all the rest to shift positions.

Holism

For hundreds of years our approach to the communication process was analytical. We attempted to break the process down into its individual parts and treat them separately. Sometimes this resulted in our becoming so focused on one part, such as the message or the use of words within a message, that we forgot about the ways in which this element interacted with all other elements.

The Gestalt approach to perception views people as perceiving things as wholes rather than in parts. In communication, also, we should not look at the speaker alone, nor the message. The whole communication process should be viewed as a single entity or composition. It is such that it cannot be divided without changing it. The minute we take out the message to look at it, we have affected everything else. It is a little bit like trying to view a human body part by part. If we remove the heart to study it, we alter the entire system. The human body also is a system, and we cannot remove one part without affecting everything else. Likewise, when we look at the words in typed form from a romantic conversation, they seem lifeless without the accompanying nonverbal behaviors of eye contact, touching, lowered voices, and the like.

Goal-Seeking

Many people forget that all of us are goal-seeking creatures. We have already discussed our survival-oriented behavior. We engage in behaviors that will satisfy our physical, social, esteem, and consistency needs in order to survive. Animals in the wild seek out food and shelter in order to survive. Talk between a clerk in a store and a teenager looking for a record is also goal-seeking. The teenager has the goal of acquiring a record (possibly to satisfy social or ego needs), the clerk has the goal of making money (possibly to satisfy physical needs), and the two of them together have the goal of a successful transaction between them.

A husband and wife in a conversation together constitute a dyadic system, a two-person system. This dyadic system can be considered to have a goal—

Characteristics of Communication Systems

maintenance of the relationship—although each individual may have personal goals as well. All communication systems are goal-seeking systems.

Inputs and Outputs

All systems receive inputs and produce outputs. In human communication, inputs are stimuli received from outside the system. We are constantly receiving stimuli such as heat, light, food, and verbal and nonverbal messages. All of these can be considered inputs. Likewise, we produce outputs. In communication systems, the outputs usually include verbal and nonverbal messages, such as spoken words, gestures, and facial expressions.

The goals of the salesperson and customer do not have to be the same to satisfy the needs of both.
PHOTO BY CAROLE DUGAN

Different systems have varying amounts of inputs from and outputs to the environment. Those systems with maximum amounts of inputs and outputs are called *open systems*, while those with minimum amounts are called *closed systems*. Actually, there are probably no *totally* closed or open systems. In the real world it is more reasonable to think in terms of "opening" and "closing" systems, since few, if any, systems ever have complete or total absence of interaction with their environments. An opening system is one that is attempting to have more inputs and outputs, while a closing system is one that is attempting to restrict inputs and outputs. Each system tries to reach a level of interaction with its environment that is optimally conducive to its survival.

Transformation

Every system transforms inputs into outputs. A large system such as a factory receives raw materials and transforms them into outputs called products. In communication, transformation is the processing we do within our minds. Once we have received inputs in the form of messages or other stimuli, we convert the inputs into symbols so we can think about them. We generate and create ideas and then convert them into symbols such as words, or outputs.

It is not enough for a person to observe combustion. That observation must be interpreted as fire and thought about in order to assess the probability of danger. Once the visual stimuli are received and processed, the person may then produce the output of a scream of "Fire!" The process of transformation thus is circular, involving reception, processing, and transmission of stimuli.

Entropy

The concept of entropy denotes the tendency toward maximum disorganization. For instance, maximum entropy in our solar system would mean completely random movement of all planets, stars, and other parts. There would be no more organization in the system.

Perhaps the following analogy will help you understand the concept of entropy. You are all familiar with a treadmill. That is the kind of moving path that people exercise on in a gym. The faster you walk, the faster the path moves under you. If you stop walking, the path moves you backward. Entropy operates in the same way. In order to stay even, you must move forward or entropy will cause you to lose ground. Another example with which you are all familiar is inflation. You need to make more money to maintain the same standard of living. Entropy is the tendency for all systems to become disorganized, fall behind, and lose ground. It is a tendency that is in opposition to survival.

Within a person, total entropy could simply be interpreted as death. People are opening systems because they interact with their environment. Although some mentally ill persons may be closing systems when they refuse to interact with anyone in their environment, it is difficult to imagine most people ever reaching a point at which they have absolutely no interaction with any other person. Because human communication involves people, it should be clear that human communication systems are opening systems. Within a communication system involving two or more people, entropy would be a complete disorganization among the people or the absence of any relationships.

Since the major goal of the human system is survival, it follows that people behave in ways to combat entropy. Likewise, since people use communication to survive, it follows that communication can be considered to be "antientropic." For instance, when we begin a new job we communicate in order to learn the rules and norms of the job system we have entered. We do this so that we can be a part of our new system. If we don't learn the "right" way of doing things, we will either be asked to leave the system or we will stay in the system until we have destroyed it. Effective communication creates order and organization and combats entropy.

Characteristics of Communication Systems

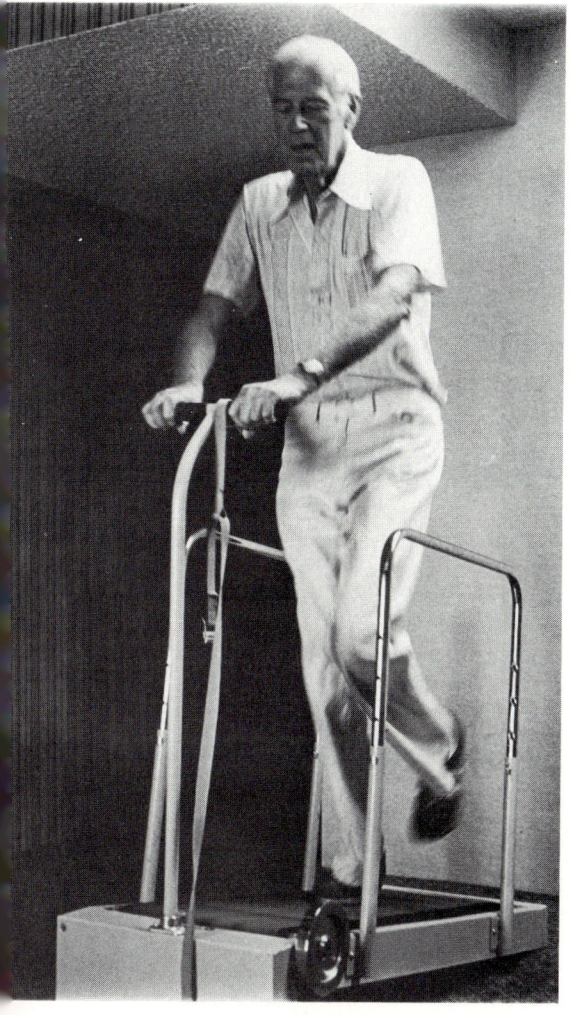

A runner on a treadmill must constantly expend effort in order to avoid entropy.
PHOTO BY CAROLE DUGAN

Regulations

If a system is goal-seeking and if all of the components within a system are interrelated, then there must be regulations governing component relations that enable the system to progress toward its goals. This means we must have planning and control within any system. In a communication system, this regulatory behavior is called *feedback*.

Feedback in human communication systems is the response of a receiver to a message produced by the person who began the communication process. Once the process is started, all communicators are responding to each other, so it might be possible to suggest that all messages (except for the first message) are feedback for someone. It is important to understand that feedback from one communicator to another is regulatory behavior engaged in by one communicator, which controls the behavior of another. Since regulation and control are basic to the survival of any system, we would suggest that a communication system cannot survive without feedback. In other words, feedback is not simply a nice thing to include in a discussion of communication. It may well be the essence of a communication system. It is a main factor that differentiates the transactional and systems perspectives from the stimulus-response and motivational perspectives.

When Carole begins to speak to Bill, the feedback she receives is in the form of Bill's facial expressions, head nods, bodily posture, and comments he makes in response to her statements. If Bill's verbal and nonverbal responses are positive, Carole continues to talk in the same manner. However, if Bill's responses are negative, Carole may alter her message or the way she presents her message. Thus, she will be regulated by the verbal and nonverbal feedback she receives from Bill.

It is also useful to remember that we are "governed" by a number of different "rules" for interaction. If our mate says "I love you," the "rules" for interaction require a response of "I love you, too." It has been "against the rules" to use obscenities in the company of both males and females together, as it also is on some formal occasions. These "rules" are unstated yet widely accepted norms within a culture. They serve to regulate human communication behavior in ways that permit progression of our communication systems toward their goals. If you think for a while, we are sure you can think of some "rules" you have encountered and their regulatory function.

Hierarchy

Hierarchies are systems within subsystems. Systems theorists refer to hierarchy as the "nesting" of systems within other systems. An analogy would be a set of measuring cups that cooks use. Each smaller size (1 cup, 1/2 cup, 1/4 cup, etc.) "nests" inside the next size up.

In a small-group communication system, the people within the system are components and/or subsystems. (See Fig. 2.2.) Within the larger system of the small group there can be smaller subsystems. For instance, two people within a group of five may be friends and may carry on conversations off to the side while the group is functioning. Thus, their dyad becomes a dyadic communication subsystem. Of course, within that subsystem there are at least the two components, consisting of each individual carrying on his or her own intrapersonal thought processes. Likewise, we could even subdivide the individuals into their various biological and mental components.

Later, as we talk about types of human communication systems, we will classify the type of communication that is occurring from the point of view of how many levels of hierarchy there are within the communication system. For instance, a communication system involving only two people (a dyadic communication system) has fewer subsystems and components within it than does a mass communication system such as a television network.

Characteristics of Communication Systems

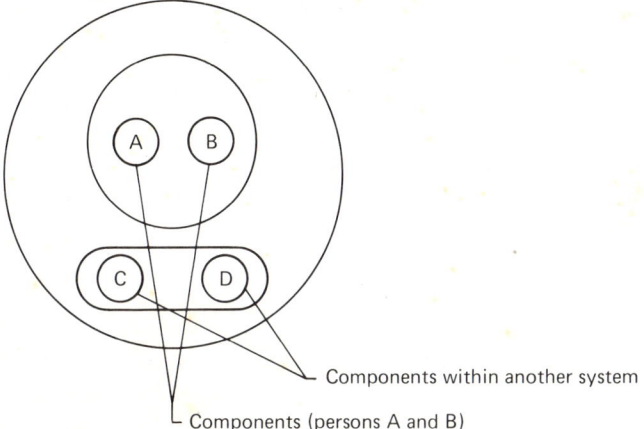

Fig. 2.2 Small group system.

Differentiation

Within any communication system, the various components perform specialized functions. For instance, within the small group, one component, individual A, may perform the function of gathering information for the group. Individual B may perform the function of planning the analysis of the information. Individual C may serve as a leader of the group. Each subsystem, or component, of a system will perform functions that are specialized yet oriented toward satisfying the needs of the larger system. Greater differentiation requires more regulation in order to combat entropy. That is why very large systems require more formal rules than small systems.

Equifinality

Equifinality refers to the ability of a system to reach a goal by several different routes, and even from different starting points. For instance, two small groups may wish to solve the problem of pollution. They may start from different points in their analysis. One may start with an analysis of the problem of emissions from automobiles. The other may start by considering the smog problem in a large city. Both may reach the goal of solving the pollution problem, even though each has started from different points. They will take different routes to the solution of the problem. An opening communication system has the ability to solve problems by different strategies with similar (or "equal final") outcomes.

These ten characteristics are not intended to be complete. They also overlap, to some extent. However, by considering them all together, we gain a fair understanding of the kind of thinking employed by general systems theorists about human communication. It is this approach to the analysis of human communication phenomena you will grasp more fully as you read this book.

Human Communication Perspectives

COMMUNICATION SYSTEMS

The basic elements within any communication system are fairly simple. Our model is of a very basic interpersonal communication system: the dyad. The concepts we will discuss are, however, applicable to more complex communication systems.

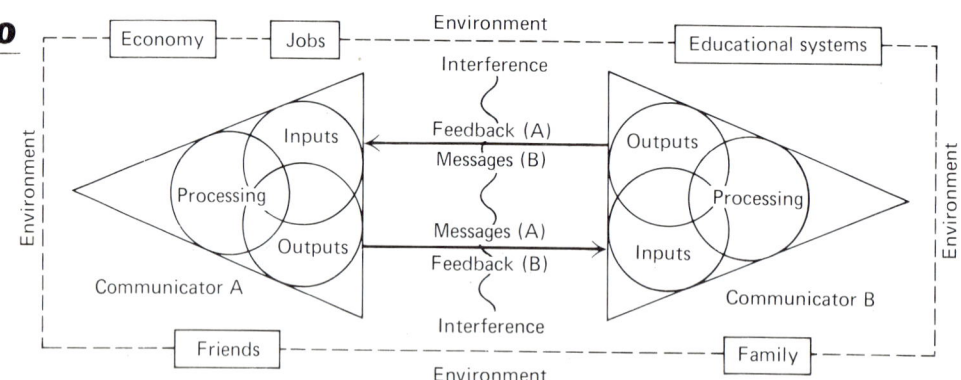

Fig. 2.3 Emmert-Donaghy model of a dyadic communication system.

Communicators

Within every communication system there are people called *communicators*. The system theorist usually refers to them as the "components" of a system. Another way to think of them is to consider them subsystems within the communication system. Each communicator is, of course, composed of further subsystems. These include input, output, and processing subsystems. The input subsystem permits the communicator to receive messages and stimuli from outside. The input subsystem involves the reception of light, temperature, touch, sound, and odors via our eyes, skin, ears, nose, and taste buds. There is more involved here than just physical reception, however. We also interpret these input stimuli through a process called "perception."

The processing subsystem of a communicator includes all thought processes. As we process, we generate, organize, and reflect on ideas in response to the stimuli received. This entire process is determined not only by the stimuli just received, but it is affected also by all stimuli ever received, such as past experiences, education, health, genetic inheritance, and all other factors in our environment. Intrapersonal processing subsystems will be considered more completely in the chapters on motivation, perception, and reasoning.

The output subsystem includes the messages and other behaviors produced by the communicator. These include nonverbal messages, verbal messages, and other physical behaviors. All of these become inputs for other people and can have both intentional and unintentional effects on them. Output subsystems will be discussed further in the chapters on verbal and nonverbal communication.

Figure 2.3 shows how these subsystems mutually interact with each other. Those messages we receive as inputs affect our thinking processes and in turn both affect and are affected by the things we say to others. Since each communicator is a system, all subsystems within a communicator constantly interact with one another.

Interfacing and Intrafacing

There are two basic ways in which systems or components of systems can interact with or relate to one another. The first is called an *interface*. An interface allows information to flow between two or more independent parts of the system or between two or more independent systems. Figure 2.4 illustrates how an interface is usually diagrammed. This is a common relationship between systems and elements of systems. Human communication is a type of interface.

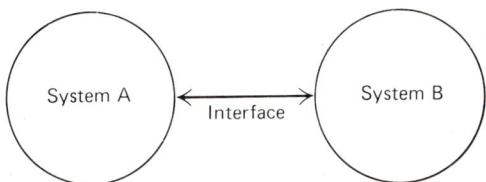

Fig. 2.4 An interface relationship.

However, there are times when two or more systems or components of systems are so intertwined and dependent upon one another that the term interface does not accurately represent their interdependence. Perhaps a good example of such an interdependent relationship between two systems would be Siamese twins who share such important body components in common that they cannot be separated without the death of at least one of them. We call this interdependent relationship an *intraface*. An intraface occurs much more frequently within components of a system than between systems themselves. Figure 2.5 illustrates how an intraface will be diagrammed in this text. You will notice that in our model of communication systems we have already illustrated intrafacing between the components of inputs, outputs, and processing. This is an example of a three-way intraface. In this text, we discuss each of these elements separately, but we want you to understand that they are inseparable and interdependent. An intraface relationship between components or subsystems has often been termed "intrapersonal communication." The intraface

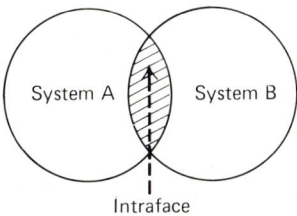

Fig. 2.5 An intraface relationship.

relationships among the various human subsystems are important enough to our understanding of human communication so that we have devoted several chapters to this topic in Part II, Intrapersonal Processing Elements.

Relationships

Communicators within a communication system are constantly interfaced with each other. As one communicator speaks, the other responds, in turn affecting the first communicator, as their respective roles permit. The roles of friend, parent, or boss, for example, define the ways in which these subsystems within a communication system relate to each other and thus affect the way the communicators will interact. Therefore, one of our concerns in analyzing a communication system should be: What are the relationships of one person to another? The concept of role is important in describing what is happening in any communication interaction, and thus it will be alluded to throughout this book.

Feedback

As mentioned earlier, all components within a communication system regulate all other components to some degree. The outputs of communicator A in Fig. 2.3 can be considered as messages by communicator A and as feedback by communicator B if the outputs of A are in response to the outputs of B. If the outputs of communicator A become feedback within the communication system for communicator B, then communicator B will adjust to this feedback in order to achieve his or her goal(s) within the communication system. Feedback thus serves a *regulatory function* within the communication system.

In keeping with the regulatory characteristic of systems discussed earlier, it should be clear that communication is essential to the maintenance of many kinds of systems. It is necessary because feedback is accomplished through communication and regulation is accomplished through feedback. Remember that without regulation, disorganization, or entropy, would occur, thus ending the system. Over time, both communicators produce nothing but feedback for one another.

Environment

The communication system just described occurs within an environment. The environment is everything external to the communication system that can affect the system in one way or another. For instance, as indicated in Fig. 2.3, other systems such as family, friends, schools, the economy, and government exist within the system's environment.

Each of the systems within the environment interfaces with the communication system to a different degree. For instance, a communicator's family probably interfaces more with a communicator than the economy, although that statement could be debatable from situation to situation. Because they are opening, communication systems interface with their environment. Therefore, it is important to remember that we can never analyze a communication event only from the point of view of the people who seem obviously involved. Since

Definitions of Communication

the environment does interact with the system, we must frequently consider environmental effects in order to explain the interaction that occurs within any human communication system.

Interference

Figure 2.3 also indicates the presence of interference. Anything present within the system or within the environment that can alter or distort inputs and outputs is interference. If two people are talking in a room full of noisy machinery, the noise may be interference, since it would distort the spoken messages (inputs and outputs) between the people. Other types of interference *within* the person can affect the communication system. Emotions such as fear, love, anxiety, etc. can affect the way inputs and outputs are perceived and processed. Although emotional states occur within the communicator, they distort inputs and outputs as much as or more than interference that occurs within the system but outside the communicator.

Interference can take many forms.

DEFINITIONS OF COMMUNICATION

There are two schools of thought regarding the definition of communication. Although communication specialists may argue over different definitions, remember that none of them is absolutely right and none of them is absolutely wrong. Both approaches have merits as well as shortcomings. When we present our definition, the same could be said of it as well.

Human Communication Perspectives

We find it useful to think of each of these definitions as providing a different viewpoint from which to consider human communication. It is a little bit like standing at different points in a room and trying to describe a table in the middle of the room. If you stand at the end of the table that is the "long end," then the description of the table will follow one pattern. If, on the other hand, you lie down on the floor underneath the table and describe it, the description will be very different. Neither of the descriptions is wrong. In each case, you are simply looking at the same physical phenomenon from a different point of view. Likewise, various definitions of communication simply reflect differing points of view or perspectives, not different amounts of "truth."

Two Points of View

What are the two points of view? The first assumes that for something to be communication the person producing the message or engaging in the behavior in question must have intended to influence someone's behavior through a symbolic message. In other words, this school of thought focuses on whether or not there is an intent to influence.

The second point of view does not assume the presence of intent to influence. Rather, this school of thought assumes that it is impossible for someone to not communicate and that everything we do or say and every event or physical occurrence around us is communication, if someone perceives meaning in it. This means that if it is possible for someone who perceives a behavior or event to assign meaning to it, communication has occurred.

To make a little clearer what these two approaches imply consider the following example. Picture two people in a room seated in two chairs next to each other. Person A has a cold and sneezes, using tissue to handle the problem. Person B observes the sneeze and the tissue and moves his chair further away from person A. If we subscribe to the point of view that intent to influence must be present for communication to have occurred, then we do not consider that either the sneeze or the use of the tissue communicates anything to person B. In fact, people subscribing to this school of thought would suggest that no communication has taken place because person A was not attempting to communicate with or influence person B. This point of view suggests that the sneeze and the use of the tissue existed as simple stimuli within person B's environment, which person B could observe and respond to—or not. This perspective would suggest that no *message* was present, but rather simply a stimulus to which someone responded.

People adopting the other point of view would interpret this occurrence quite differently. They would maintain that the sneeze and the use of the tissue by person A communicated the existence of a cold to person B because person B attached meaning to what he or she saw. The message in this particular case would be the sneeze itself and/or the use of the tissue paper. These behaviors become messages because the receivers are able to interpret and assign meaning to them.

We hope it is obvious to you that in either case, the same event has occurred. No matter how you define communication, person A sneezes and person B moves further away from person A. The question is whether you want to explain this event in terms of communication or in terms of stimuli and

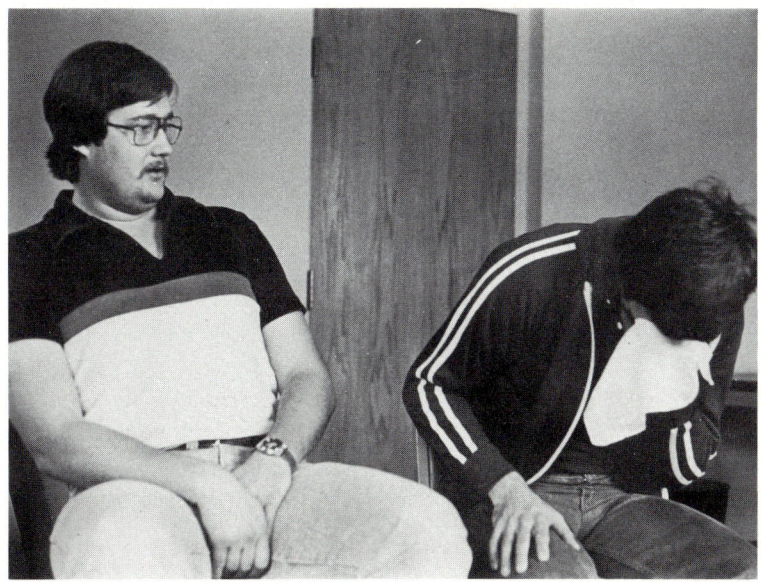

Is communication taking place in this situation?
PHOTO BY CAROLE DUGAN

responses to stimuli. There will be a time or two as you read through this book when it will become evident that there is more than one way of looking at any phenomenon. Use these different perspectives to develop your own point of view about the communication process. Remember, the important thing is not which perspective you take, but whether you understand human communication and are able to improve your own communicative skills as a result of your understanding.

To give you an idea of the form that definitions can take from each of the two schools discussed, we would like to present a few for you to consider. Think about each of these definitions in light of the preceding discussion and begin to formulate your own perspective.

Definitions Based on the Intent to Influence

Communication . . . is . . . all the procedures by which one mind may affect another. This, of course, involves not only written and oral speech, but also music, the pictorial arts, the theater, the ballet, and in fact, all human behavior. (Shannon and Weaver, 1963)

. . . the primary goal of most communication is to influence the behavior of the receiver in some way. (Arnold and Hirsch, 1977)

. . . what is normally thought of as perfect or effective communication implies the control and manipulation of a receiver of messages by the sender. (Ruben, 1972)

Many people adopt definitions such as those just listed without realizing that intent to influence is implied in the definitions. When we discuss communication as a mechanism of control or influence affecting another human being, it would be inconsistent to consider it as something occurring unintentionally. We don't unintentionally seek to control, affect, or influence.

Critics of this perspective frequently point out that if we adopt this point of view, we lose the ability to explain those verbal and nonverbal behaviors in which people engage that are apparently subconscious attempts to communicate feelings or fears. Those who try to justify the intentional approach suggest that intent can be either conscious or subconscious.

Most of us never really know the exact reason we are doing everything all of the time. There are times, of course, when we can explain to someone the reasons we have done something. But frequently, if we are interrupted in the process of engaging in a behavior or making a comment by the question "Why are you doing this?", we discover that it is very difficult to explain exactly why we are doing what we are doing.

Definitions Based on Perceived Meaning

All behavior—oral, verbal, written verbal, tonal, postural, contextual, tactile—is communicative. Moreover, the behavior does not have to be intentional for communication to occur. The term "communication" is broad enough to include unintentionally sent stimuli which receive responses. (Brooks, 1974)

. . . communication occurs whenever an individual assigns significance or meaning to an internal or external stimulus. (Thayer, 1961)

In these definitions, the common element is that communication occurs whether someone engages in an intentional act or not. Simply for another person to perceive meaning in a stimulus makes a behavior communication. The color of a room or the temperature outside can be communication if someone attaches meaning to it. This approach to defining communication suggests that we must pay attention to everything in our environment because all of it can be meaningful for us.

Which is Correct?

We suspect that those persons who adopt the intentional approach would agree that many elements not intentionally produced by people in a communication situation can have meaning for someone seeing, hearing, smelling, or feeling them. Those who espouse the intentional approach would also probably agree that because it is possible to interpret these unintentional stimuli meaningfully, the stimuli can have a significant effect on the communication process. Likewise, we think persons who take the second point of view would agree that if we consider communication to be survival-oriented, it is reasonable to assume that we do not produce messages unintentionally and accidentally. Behavior that is oriented toward survival is a goal-seeking type of behavior. The goal, of course, is survival. It seems reasonable, also, that implicit in the notion of goal-seeking is intention, either conscious or subconscious.

Although we can defend either point of view, we feel that this discussion is important mainly so that you can realize the different ways we can view the process of communication. We would also like to emphasize that neither of these approaches is necessarily correct and that both contain some truth. Ultimately, you should try to determine a view of your own that seems most reasonable and develop your own definition.

Our definition of communication is derived from the preceding discussion of systems theory. We define human communication as a process in which two or more persons attempt to consciously or unconsciously influence each other through the use of symbol systems in order to satisfy their respective needs. Given the systems perspective, we must assume that this process occurs within an environment and that all communicators within the system are interrelated and interdependent. By considering human communication a process, it should be obvious that in order to study it most validly, we should study it as a whole rather than as isolated parts. The ideal book on communication would consist of one very large chapter. This is not a convenient way to study, however, so we will consider components of the process in separate chapters. As you read, please keep in mind the wholeness of the process with all the interrelationships.

Our definition requires two or more persons because any fewer than two would consist of what we consider to be intrapersonal processing elements, as indicated earlier in our discussion of intrafacing. Although this definition refers to an attempt to influence, we make no requirement regarding the success or failure of the attempt. The objective is to change another person's behavior, whether to get that person to respond, to give us money, or to behave in ways that make us feel more loved.

We employ common symbol systems such as the English language, facial expressions, or mathematical symbols. These symbol systems will be discussed more completely in later chapters.

Just as all systems are goal-oriented, so, too, are human communication systems. People are oriented toward survival as a goal. In order to survive, needs must be met, most often by manipulation of others through human communication. These needs will be discussed, along with other intrapersonal processing elements. We do not believe that people are always consciously aware of the needs motivating their communication behaviors. Motivation is not always obvious, but it is present at all times.

TYPES OF COMMUNICATION SYSTEMS

Earlier we mentioned that systems are hierarchical in nature. This means that there are different types of communication systems, or contexts, depending on their complexity. These types range from the very simple to the extremely complex. The traditional classification of communication contexts is consistent with the hierarchical approach to communication systems. The very simple systems often nest within the more complex systems.

Interpersonal Communication Systems

At the basic level of interpersonal communication systems is the dyadic context. A dyad consists of two people, or two major subsystems. As interpersonal communication becomes more complex and more subsystems are added, we find the small group context. The upper level of complexity for interpersonal communication is limited only by the ability of all individuals, or subsystems, to interact with each other face-to-face and to have the opportunity to mutually affect each other. You can see that the concepts of mutual causality and interdependence assume importance in that we can define interpersonal communication as reaching an upper limit when all subsystems within the system can no longer interact equally and have a mutual effect on each other. At that point, the small group is no longer a small group, and we find ourselves considering a different type of communication system. The upper limit on the small group is usually around 15 or 20 people. At this point, the group must impose artificial regulations on itself, such as parliamentary procedure.

Organizational Communication Systems

Moving from interpersonal communication, we discover a much more complex system termed the organizational communication context. Examples include a university, a factory, or a government. These systems include a *large* collection of subsystems, all organized with a common goal. The subsystems can become incredibly complex, as in the federal government, or they can be as simple as those in a small business or fraternity. Nevertheless, the subsystems all exist as separate entities, yet interrelate with each other in such a way as to further the survival and other goals of the organization.

Public Communication Systems

This type of system involves communication usually from one person to a large group of people. Although everyone affects everyone else to some degree in every communication system, in a public communication context such as a speech from a politician to people standing behind a platform of a campaign train, the speaker does most of the speaking. The speaker has the primary effect on the people who are listening in that system. Public communication systems involve a different type of feedback for the speaker—a less obvious, very subtle kind of feedback that requires considerable sensitivity in order to detect. This feedback is frequently nonverbal, such as facial expressions or bodily postures assumed by listeners during a speech.

Mass Communication Systems

The mass communication context exists when there is even less opportunity for people to interact freely with one another and to mutually affect one another. Although there is feedback in mass communication (i.e., letters, phone calls, etc.), the distinguishing characteristic of a mass comunication system is that all feedback is delayed. In such a system, the originator of the mass message can not possibly receive immediate feedback from all the people who receive the message. Therefore, someone like Dan Rather must depend on the delayed feedback of television ratings, letters, and phone calls that occur after the message has been presented. The same thing is true for authors of books who have to write all of their message and have it published before they receive the feedback sometime later.

SUMMARY

In this chapter we have discussed the purpose of communication. We have considered the various ways of looking at the communication process, with survival as its goal. We have provided our definition of human communication, which grows out of the two most prevalent points of view held by communication specialists. There have been many communication perspectives developed over the years for studying communication, and we have suggested that the use of general systems theory as a perspective for discussing the communication process is extremely useful. Using the general systems approach, we have also discussed the five contexts of communication systems that are covered in this book.

KEY TERMS AND CONCEPTS

CLOSED SYSTEMS
COMMUNICATION MODELS
COMMUNICATORS
DEFINITIONS BASED ON INTENT TO INFLUENCE
DEFINITIONS BASED ON PERCEIVED MEANING
DIFFERENTIATION
EHNINGER, DOUGLAS
ENTROPY
ENVIRONMENT
EQUIFINALITY
FEEDBACK
GENERAL SYSTEMS PERSPECTIVE
GOAL SEEKING
GRONBECK, BRUCE
HIERARCHY
HOLISM
INPUTS
INTERDEPENDENCE
INTERFACING
INTERFERENCE
INTERPERSONAL COMMUNICATION SYSTEMS
INTRAFACING
LASSWELL, HAROLD
LINEAR MODELS
MASS COMMUNICATION SYSTEMS
MONROE, ALAN
MOTIVATED SEQUENCE
MOTIVATIONAL PERSPECTIVE
ONE-WAY MODELS
OPEN SYSTEMS
ORGANIZATIONAL COMMUNICATION SYSTEMS
OUTPUTS
PROCESSING SUBSYSTEMS
PUBLIC COMMUNICATION SYSTEMS
REGULATIONS
RELATIONSHIPS
STIMULUS-RESPONSE PERSPECTIVE
TRANSACTIONAL PERSPECTIVE
TRANSFORMATION
VERBAL MODELS

SUGGESTED READINGS

BUCKLEY, WALTER, ed., *Modern Systems Research for the Behavioral Scientist*. Chicago: Aldine Publishing Company, 1968. This book of readings contains some of the classic statements on systems theory. Although the readings are advanced, the applications of systems theory in diverse disciplines provide considerable insight into this theoretical perspective for the serious reader.

Fisher, B. Aubrey, *Perspectives on Human Communication*. New York: Macmillan Publishing Co., Inc., 1978. Fisher presents both a historical view and a philosophical analysis of theoretical approaches to the study of communication. This book is of value both for understanding the different theoretical viewpoints in the field of communication and for understanding theory analysis and construction.

Ruben, Brent D., and John Y. Kim, eds., *General Systems Theory and Human Communication*. Rochelle Park, N.J.: Hayden Book Company, 1975. This book presents readings in three areas: general systems theory, communication and levels of human organization, and human communication in systems perspectives. Although all the readings are of value, those in the third section should be of particular interest to the student of human communication. Much in this third section not only expands on what we have presented in this chapter but also provides excellent supplementary material for later chapters in our book.

II
INTRAPERSONAL PROCESSING ELEMENTS

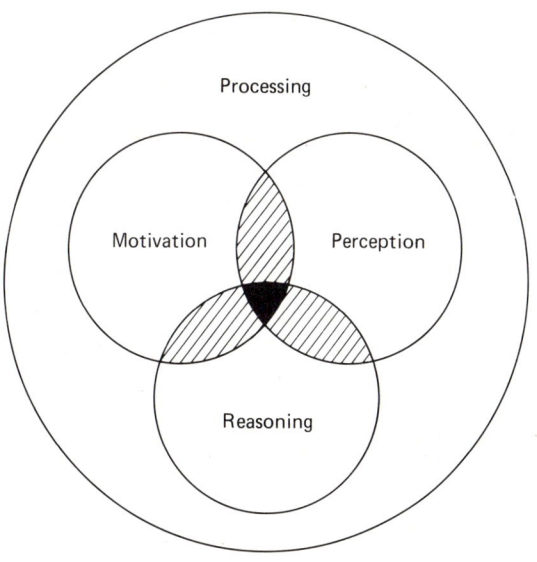

3
Motivation

In order to use messages to affect others' behavior, it is important to understand why people do the things they do. Unfortunately, there is no single cause to which we can trace people's behaviors. In order to understand a given behavior, we must consider the interaction of various motivational components such as interpersonal needs, conditioned needs, consistency needs, and values. In addition, these different components influence our behavior in response to the environment in which we exist. We cannot explain or predict a person's behavior apart from the environment in combination with the other components.

In the systems approach to communication, we must remember that the three intrapersonal processes of motivation, perception, and reasoning intraface with each other. In the figure that opens Part II, the shaded and striped areas represent the ways in which the three subsystems mutually influence and intraface with each other (striped areas). Sometimes all three subsystems intraface with and influence each other (shaded area). All three intrapersonal processes are responsible in one way or another for the filtering that takes place in the human communication system.

Motivation

Why does a person sit on a small platform on top of a flagpole for days on end? Why does a couple try to see how long they can kiss each other? Or, for that matter, why do dozens of people try to go up in small structures attached to hot-air balloons and attempt to ride the wind across the Atlantic Ocean, at considerable risk to their lives? These are some of the more unusual things people do, and it's not so unusual to wonder why people do them. We also can ask similar questions about behaviors that seem a lot more "normal" to us.

The crew of the Double Eagle II was motivated by needs and values different from millions of other Americans.

UNITED PRESS INTERNATIONAL PHOTO

Why do people go to work every day? Why do people get married? Why do we sit and talk about what we saw on a television show the previous night? These are fairly common behaviors among people, and yet the question of why we engage in them is probably as difficult to answer, if not more so, than the question of why people do the more unusual things.

It is important for us to try to answer questions of this sort, however, if we are to understand communication and be able to increase our effectiveness as communicators. In the previous chapters, communication has been related to the satisfaction of needs. In order to satisfy our needs through communication, we employ messages to get someone else to do something for us. In order to use a message to change someone else's behavior, it is very important for us to understand why the people we're trying to influence do what they do. What we have been talking about is motivation.

Simply defined, motivation is whatever causes people to do and not to do things. However, motivation is a very complex topic—one that will probably seem more complex as we progress in our discussion. An awareness of the different factors that affect people's behavior should greatly improve your understanding of communication.

In many discussions of motivation, it is common to focus on intrapersonal needs and to suggest that people are motivated to do the things they do in response to the needs they feel. Indeed, we have earlier referred to people's need systems. However, it is our feeling that a complete understanding of motivation requires that we concern ourselves with more than simply intrapersonal needs. It is to your advantage to consider various influences on behavior so that you may be better able to construct and receive messages effectively.

THE INTRAFACE OF MOTIVATIONAL COMPONENTS

As we pointed out earlier, a systems view of communication implies that we cannot look at one isolated component in the human communication system without keeping in mind other components and subsystems with which each component may interrelate. Nothing could be more illustrative of the importance of the interdependence of the subsystems than the topic of motivation. A given observable behavior within a communication system is the result of several different components intrafacing to motivate the behavior we have observed.

People are motivated by at least four different factors, each a component within the whole motivational subsystem. These four components include drive-reduction needs, consistency needs, interpersonal needs, and values, each intrafacing with the system's other intrapersonal subsystems of perception and reasoning as well as the environment. Any given behavior we can observe a human being performing is the result, at the very least, of all of these components and subsystems intrafacing with each other.

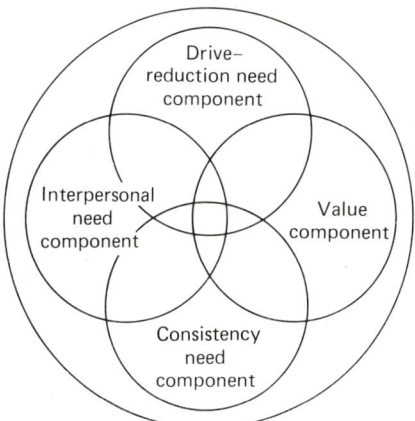

Fig. 3.1 Motivational processing subsystem.

In the past, it has been popular to talk about behavior being motivated by a specific need or a specific value. People have also talked about behavior being motivated by the context, or environment, in which one finds oneself. Finally, people have talked about a person being motivated by interactions with others. The reason why none of these suppositions ever appeared to be a satisfactory explanation of motivation is that no single one was sufficient. Since all these components are in an intraface relationship, it is not a simple matter to come up with an adequate explanation of the motivation behind behavior. In order to discuss a given behavior or the response of a person to a message, we must look at all of these components before we have anything approaching a complete understanding of the person's motivational subsystem.

We must cover each of these motivational components separately because of the constraints imposed on us by the book format. However, we hope you will keep in mind the systems view of human behavior as you read each of these discussions. In that way, you will be able to assess the interdependence of these components and you will be able to develop a view of motivation that is a genuine system view, integrating the three intrapersonal components and the environment into a holistic explanation of motivation.

THE DRIVE-REDUCTION NEED COMPONENT

One of the most often used approaches to motivation has focused on drive-reduction needs. Proponents of this approach suggest that internal needs, or drives, exist within the individual and provide an intrapersonal force, causing the individual to engage in a behavior that is intended to reduce the felt needs, or drives. Probably the example most frequently cited in textbooks is that of hunger. We internally experience feelings of hunger that cause us to eat, and this action in turn reduces the sensation of hunger or the drive or need we originally experienced.

Maslow's Need Classification System

Although there are numerous discussions of needs, the most widely recognized drive-reduction theory has been that proposed by Abraham Maslow (1943, 1954). Maslow's need classification system consists of five parts. He suggested that we have five different need levels: physiological, safety, social, esteem, and self-actualization needs. Maslow believed that these needs are arranged in a hierarchical fashion, with physiological needs as the most basic at the bottom of the hierarchy, up through safety, social, and esteem needs to self-actualization needs at the top level.

Physiological needs can be considered primary physical needs. A person lacking food, sleep, and/or water has what Maslow called physiological needs. These are the needs we must have satisfied before we can be concerned with any others. One way to think of physiological needs is to consider them as day-to-day, or *short-term maintenance needs*. These are the needs we must meet in order to physically survive on a day-to-day basis.

Safety needs are another type of physical need, but they can be considered *long-term maintenance needs*. Safety needs cause a person to be concerned with his or her long-term physical well-being. Safety needs cause us to put money aside for retirement so that we can be assured that sometime in the distant future we will be able to satisfy our immediate, day-to-day, physiological needs. Likewise, safety needs cause workers in a manufacturing plant to be concerned with safety on the job.

Hard hats and orange vests are a result of safety needs.
PHOTO BY CAROLE DUGAN

Social needs have been given many different labels by scholars. They have been called interpersonal needs, belongingness needs, and even love needs. Social needs are those needs we have to relate to other people and to have relationships that are positive and satisfactory. Human beings have been called social animals, and this level of needs refers to our desire to have interaction with other members of our species. It has been suggested that people do not survive well alone. We can often observe people talking about things they have no interest in at all simply so that they can be with another person. They are willing to interact with another individual for almost any reason, as long as they can have human contact. Maslow's social needs closely parallel what we will call the interpersonal need component later in this chapter.

Esteem needs are what some people call "ego needs." These revolve around the need to think well of ourselves. According to Maslow, all people have a basic need to think that they are competent, worthwhile human beings. It isn't unusual for us to see someone engage in a communication behavior such as bragging. This is an example of a person with very high esteem needs who is attempting to communicate in a way that will satisfy these needs. Esteem needs can be satisfied in at least two ways. First, we may be held in high esteem by other people, and second, we may hold ourselves in high esteem. Thus, we can have those needs satisfied by others as well as by ourselves.

Maslow called the final level of needs *self-actualization*. Once we have achieved a high level of self-esteem and think well of ourselves, we apparently need to go beyond that level. Self-actualization refers to the need to reach maximum self-fulfillment or the maximum potential we think we possess. We suggest that this need level is very much intertwined with the previous level of esteem needs. What we believe our potential to be seems highly dependent on the esteem in which we hold ourselves. Self-actualization and esteem needs are so interrelated that it is difficult to tell where one begins and the other ends. The self-actualization need causes a golfer to go out on the course and to try repeatedly to improve his or her score. The self-actualization need drives musicians to constantly try to improve on their last performance. The need to self-actualize is a feeling that we are somehow capable of just a little bit more, so we must achieve that little bit more in order to be satisfied. According to Maslow and many other authorities, people rarely reach the self-actualization level. Most often we are so concerned with satisfying our other needs (and we so rarely get them all satisfied) that it is an unusual case when any of us reaches self-actualization.

Although there have been varying degrees of empirical support for Maslow's classification system, one of the more important research findings is that his hierarchy is probably more flexible than he originally indicated. For some people, the top level of needs may be self-actualization, whereas for other people the top level of needs may be social. This variation is very likely the result of conditioning during early developmental years. For example, someone who grew up in a home in which both parents were gone all the time and in which there may have been no brothers, sisters, aunts, uncles, or grandparents would have spent considerable time alone during childhood. This person could easily have a very heightened set of social needs. As an adult, such a person might constantly seek the company of other people and might look for interaction wherever possible to make up for the lost social satisfaction of the childhood years.

In addition to problems with the rigidity or flexibility of the hierarchy, there is also some question as to whether there are actually five separate needs that exist. Aldefer (1972) has modified Maslow's categories into three, which he refers to as existence needs, relatedness needs, and growth needs. This classification system is, to a certain degree, parallel to Maslow's category system. Although empirical data do seem to fit Aldefer's classification system a little more closely than that of Maslow, there has been very little research to test Aldefer's system specifically.

Another condensation of Maslow's hierarchy is that of Brooks and Emmert (1980). Brooks and Emmert suggest the existence of physical, social, and ego needs. They further believe that this three-part classification system is useful to persons concerned with interpersonal communication. Again, as with Alderfer, this classification system has not received the empirical testing of Maslow's, but research originally designed to test Maslow's theory does tend to support the three-part classification system more than it does the five-part classification system.

The evidence concerning Maslow's theory also calls into question the idea of one need being predominant over another need. Because a person has not yet satisfied his or her basic physiological needs, we cannot necessarily assume that this person does not experience or respond to any social needs. Rather, we would suggest that whatever needs we have exist simultaneously to different degrees. As you are reading this book, there are very likely needs related to esteem as well as social needs that you want to satisfy. You want to earn good grades as well as make friends while you are in school. At the same time, you may also be experiencing some sort of basic long-term physical needs; you are thinking that if you do well in school you're going to be able to get a good job, make money, and have a secure life.

You may be experiencing all sorts of needs at once, and yet there may be one set of needs that is predominant over the others. For instance, although you may be concerned about long-term survival, it wouldn't surprise us if the primary motivator for learning the material in this book and doing well in your communication class (as well as your other classes) has more to do with self-esteem. You don't want to fail. You don't want to think that you are incompetent. Although we could say that all of these needs are existing simultaneously and that you are motivated by more than one need at a given time, it may also be, as suggested by Maslow, that one need will predominate.

There are numerous other need theories that we could discuss, but by focusing on Maslow's system we hope that you understand how drive-reduction needs have been classified. Although there is no one single truth, we could summarize this discussion of the drive-reduction component by suggesting that we do experience some kind of intrapersonal drive mechanism that is a motivating force for many of our behaviors. If we had complete knowledge about human beings, we could classify these drive forces or needs more exactly. Given current knowledge, however, our best guess is that there are at least three needs: physical, social (or interpersonal), and self-esteem. This classification system is as valid and practical as we can hope to achieve at the present time.

As we communicate, we must be aware that in order to get someone to do something we must show the person that what we are requesting will help that person satisfy his or her own needs. For instance, an employer might try to show his or her employees that they should do good work because of the pride they can feel in a job well done. This message would be directed toward the employees' self-esteem needs. Likewise, messages can be directed toward social and physical needs.

We should also realize that people's backgrounds (childhood experiences, illnesses, individuals they have known, critical incidents, etc.) play a significant role in shaping their needs. The needs of primary importance to a person are significantly affected by the environmental experiences during that person's lifetime. However, we very likely inherit some "genetic starting point" for our drive-reduction-need component. Most behavioral scientists think there is an inherited need component with which we begin. However, we would urge that you not attach too much importance to the needs we have at birth because there is too much evidence suggesting that what we are is, to a great extent, a result of what we have experienced.

For communicators to understand the people with whom they are com-

Motivation

municating, it is imperative to find out as much as possible about their backgrounds in order to better assess their need components. As communicators, we can never assume that another person's need component is at all similar to our own. Differences in wealth, race, gender, health, and many other factors too numerous to mention will cause us all to have different experiences in our lives, thus reinforcing and developing different need priorities. From this discussion of needs you should have learned that first, all people's needs are not the same, and second, communicators must adapt to many different needs. We must get to know the people with whom we are communicating so it will be possible for us to understand and adapt to their drive-reduction component.

THE CONSISTENCY NEED COMPONENT

A second type of need we will mention is not usually discussed in reference to need components by people such as Maslow. It is our feeling, however, that there is an abundance of evidence that supports the existence of what is called the *need for consistency*. The consistency component is a need to have our behaviors, beliefs, perceptions, and attitudes consistent with each other.

If you believe in "honesty," you must behave honestly in order to satisfy your consistency need. This may seem like a fairly obvious statement. However, there are many people today who say vehemently that they believe everyone should be a law-abiding citizen, and yet these very same people do not think twice about driving their automobile faster than the 55 mph speed limit. We may step on a couple of toes when we use this example, but it is one with which we all have had contact. When we drive our cars faster than 55 mph, we are breaking a law. When we are not being law-abiding citizens, the problem is what to do in order to satisfy our own need for consistency.

We have several ways of restoring consistency. First, we can distort our perception of reality. For example, many people actually believe they aren't breaking the speed limit. They distort what they see on the speedometer of their cars so that even if they are traveling 70 mph, they "see" 55 mph.

Probably the most frequent response to inconsistency in our behavior is rationalization. We generate a reason that "justifies" those aspects of our behavior that are contrary to our beliefs or values. For instance, if you drive faster than 55 mph but say that you believe in being a law-abiding citizen, you may actually convince yourself that it is a "bad law" and therefore moral to disobey. Thus, you have really changed from being a law-abiding citizen to being a law-abiding citizen only when you agree with the law. Nevertheless, you have restored consistency for yourself. Another way to resolve inconsistencies is simply to change the original attitude or belief. For instance, the person who speeds may finally decide that it is not so important to be a law-abiding citizen.

This need for consistency is a concept that overlaps with reasoning, so it will be discussed in detail in chapter 5. People do experience this need to be consistent in their lives. For the communicator, this fact can be important. For instance, if you want to change people's behavior, you may want to point out in

Do you rationalize if you break the law?
PHOTO BY CAROLE DUGAN

a message that their behavior is inconsistent with an attitude, belief, or value they have. In this way, you have used the need for consistency as a motivator for change. If you wish to change people's speeding behavior, you may have to demonstrate, for example, that they are setting a bad example for their children by breaking the law. This message would call to their attention that the behavior of speeding is inconsistent with a) their belief in being law-abiding citizens and b) with their desire to set a good example for their children. Obviously, this doesn't always work. You could end up only in making them angry for having pointed out an inconsistency they did not want to face in the first place. Such an outcome could happen because another way to restore consistency is to discredit the originator of any message that points out inconsistency.

Many messages we encounter throughout our lives are designed to point up inconsistencies. Probably the most obvious examples are the antismoking commercials on television and radio. Most of these commercials are designed to point out that smoking cigarettes is inconsistent with other values we hold. For instance, it is inconsistent with the values of maintaining good health, taking care of our family, and keeping up an attractive appearance. We should be concerned with the need for consistency if we are interested in effective communication, because we can make use of it when constructing messages to cause people to change their perceptions, attitudes, beliefs, and behaviors.

THE INTERPERSONAL NEED COMPONENT

In 1958, William C. Schutz presented a model of interpersonal needs and their relation to interpersonal behavior. Several times we have mentioned the need for social relationships, or social needs. Schutz (1958, 1966) suggested that people not only have a need to be with people, but they also have needs regarding what should occur in the social relationship. He called these interpersonal needs. The building blocks of the interpersonal need component are inclusion, control, and affection. Each of these need areas represents a different dimension or different type of interpersonal, or social, need that concerns our relationship with others.

Inclusion refers to our desire to establish and maintain satisfactory relationships with people in our interaction with them. We all feel a need to have positive, fulfilling relationships with other people. We want to be associated with other people, and we want others to desire our company. This concept can be thought of in terms of our needing other people to initiate interactions with us and to take an interest in us (as well as our being able to take an interest in other people).

Control refers to the aspect of who influences whom in the relationships we maintain with people. We all want relationships with other people in which we maintain neither too much nor too little control over the other person and in which the other person maintains neither too much nor too little control over us. There appears to be a need both to have some influence over other people and to be influenced to a certain extent by them.

Our need to control others and to be controlled is probably related to our self-esteem, the amount of competence we feel we have, and our perceptions of other people's competence. If we have a personal feeling of competence and if we accord that same kind of respect to others, we probably will exhibit a need for and a need to control that is moderate. Brooks and Emmert (1980) define interpersonal communication ideally as a situation in which there is mutual influence between two or more individuals in a face-to-face situation. In essence, that point of view reflects this moderate point in terms of control between two people. The point of view taken by Schutz is similar to what we have already discussed in terms of human communication systems, in which all subsystems are interdependent and mutually intraface with one another.

Affection refers to our desire to establish and maintain satisfactory degrees of love with other people. The ideal with respect to affection is an average between the extremely affectionate person who must initiate an intensely close relationship with other people and the very distant person who never initiates close relationships with other people at all. The need for affection is very much related to the need to feel that we are lovable and that other people perceive us that way. Affection may in some respects be related to the earlier discussed need for self-esteem. We said that sometimes the interaction among these need levels makes it difficult to tell which level we are really talking about at any given time. The intertwining of the needs for affection and self-esteem is a good example. Although self-esteem is referred to as something separate from social needs, it must be apparent that to perceive ourselves as lovable it is also necessary for us to have some degree of positive self-esteem. Thus, we would suggest that our need for affection may in some ways be related to our perceived self-esteem, as discussed earlier.

Of significance to those concerned with human communication is the effect of interpersonal needs on human communication behavior. It is not enough to indicate that people possess these needs. What is of interest to us in terms of communication is the *response* of people to their interpersonal need component. Schutz has suggested that there are at least four different kinds of responses to these interpersonal needs. These responses can be defined in terms of interpersonal communication behavior:

> (1) deficient—indicating that the individual is not trying directly to satisfy the need, (2) excessive—indicating that the individual is constantly trying to satisfy the need, (3) ideal—indicating satisfaction of the need, and (4) pathological. (Schutz, p. 25)

In order to make the communicative response to the needs more clear, we will discuss the first three communication response patterns to each of the three interpersonal needs. Although there are also pathological responses to these needs, they are more appropriately discussed in an abnormal psychology book.

We most feel the need for inclusion when we are left out.
PHOTO BY CAROLE DUGAN

Communication Responses to Inclusion Needs

A *deficient response* to the need for inclusion results in what Schutz has called the *undersocial person*. No doubt you have seen this kind of individual quite often in your life. This sort of person tends to be introverted, quiet, and withdrawn. An undersocial person frequently appears to avoid other people and to reject invitations to join in activities with them. The undersocial person appears to represent a closing system that desires only very limited inputs and outputs.

This deficient response to inclusion needs is often a defense mechanism in which, at the conscious level, individuals insist that they want to maintain distance between themselves and others and want to be loners. They may even

Motivation

make statements to the effect that they really "don't need people." However, as is the case with many defense mechanisms, these people's real feelings (which probably exist at the subconscious level) are the reverse of their stated feelings. They have a high need for inclusion; they need to interact with others and to have others pay attention to them.

Underlying the defense mechanism is a decision by undersocial individuals that no one wants to pay attention to them. They will not risk being ignored, so they assume the posture of not wanting to be involved. Again, if we relate this interpersonal need to one of the needs earlier discussed, we would say that these individuals frequently feel that they are worthless. They frequently suffer from low self-esteem. Undersocial individuals have high esteem needs, but they engage in communication behaviors that, tragically enough, become a self-fulfilling prophecy: They evoke behaviors in others that confirm their negative self-images and that further convince them of their worthlessness. Thus their interpersonal need for inclusion becomes even greater.

The *excessive response* to the need for inclusion results in the *oversocial person*. This is the "good-time Charlie," or "good-time Charlotte," as the case may be—the extrovert who many of us know so well. This is the person who always seeks out friends, who waves across the cafeteria at the student union or shouts across the street to a person he or she knows vaguely—simply in order to have them pay attention. These people are very similar to undersocial individuals in that they are convinced that nobody wants to pay attention to them, but their response is to go all out and make people pay attention to them as much as they can. These people cannot stand to be alone, and they are always dropping in on groups in the dormitories to talk, even though they are not invited. They call friends up on the phone, hurry across campus to meet someone, and very rarely even walk from class alone. This "I try harder" communication behavior frequently turns off other people, resulting in a confirmation of the individual's negative self-image.

The *ideal response* to the interpersonal need for inclusion is exemplified by the *social individual*. These individuals very likely had a happy childhood in which they were adequately included in activities by many people. They are comfortable with others and also comfortable when no one else is around. This kind of person is comfortable taking a minor role and communicating to a very small degree in a group activity, and is also comfortable being a dominant force within a group. Social individuals never have to "prove anything," because basically these people feel they are worthwhile and valuable. They have found an adequate and satisfactory balance between their inputs and outputs.

Communication Responses to Control Needs

A person with a *deficient response* to the need for control is called *the abdicrat*. Although these individuals have a high need to control and to be controlled, their communicative response to this need is so deficient that they become submissive and completely abdicate all power and responsibility in their interpersonal relationships. In small group discussions, for example, these people move toward subordinate positions where they do not have to take charge or make decisions. Abdicrats want other people to take charge of, or regulate, their lives, although subconsciously they have the need to control as well as to be controlled. These people are very good followers and loyal lieutenants, but they are not living their lives as they wish. They carry with them feelings of considerable anxiety, hostility, and lack of trust toward others around them. These people will frequently resist cooperating with others as a way of handling these feelings.

A person with an *excessive response* to the need for control is called *the autocrat*. This is an overbearing person, whose communication behavior is such that he or she attempts to dominate everyone and to always occupy a position at the top of any power hierarchy. The autocrat is the competitor who is always out to grab power. Interestingly enough, autocrats are afraid that other people will try to control and dominate them. This fear probably results from a defense mechanism called "projection," in which one's own motives and thoughts are projected onto other people rather than accepted as part of oneself.

The autocrat is very similar to the abdicrat in the sense that neither individual really feels that he or she is capable of being in a position of power. Whereas the abdicrat simply gives up and becomes submissive, the autocrat decides to overcompensate for these inadequacies and "show everyone that I am capable of making decisions." Autocrats are very unlikely to trust others who make decisions for them. Likewise, autocrats feel that other people don't trust them. Again, autocrats project many of their own feelings onto other people. Because they don't trust others, they feel others don't trust them.

The person with an *ideal response* to the need for control is called *the democrat*. The term refers to an individual who has successfully resolved his or her relations with others in the control area. Democrats are comfortable both in giving and in not giving orders. System differentiation is no problem for such a person. This person can follow well and lead well, depending on the situation. The communication behavior of democrats is usually appropriate to the situation because they feel capable, they have no defense mechanisms to speak of, and they are not trying to "prove anything" to anybody. These people are also more likely to be trusting toward others and less likely to suspect others of not trusting them.

Communication Responses to Affection Needs

The *deficient response* to the need for affection is personified by the *underpersonal individual*. This is a person who avoids close relationships with other people, tends to maintain superficial and distant relationships, and is most comfortable in situations in which other people do the same thing. These individuals always communicate so as to maintain an emotional distance in relationships, and they are afraid, at the subconscious level, that no one loves them or that they are unlovable. As a defense mechanism, they try to avoid developing any emotional involvement in which that perceived lack of lovability might be brought into conscious awareness.

It is very likely that at one time or another, underpersonal individuals have had their attempts to obtain affection thwarted or have felt rejected.

Motivation

Therefore, they try to keep everyone at a "safe" distance in order to prevent that rejection from ever occurring again. The many people who have "failed at love" provide good examples of this phenomenon. Because their experience has been so painful, they resolve that they will never love again so they can avoid the pain. At the root of these people's feelings is the conviction that they are basically unlovable. As Schutz (1966, p. 31) indicated: "As opposed to the inclusion anxiety that the self is of no value, worthless, and empty, and the control anxiety that the self is stupid and irresponsible, the affection anxiety is that the self is nasty and bad."

The *excessive response* to the need for affection is exemplified by the *overpersonal person*. It is difficult to be around these people, because they wish to be so extremely close to others that they almost suffocate them. Overpersonal individuals have also experienced the pain of rejection, but their response is to try harder and do everything in their power to make sure they get affection the next time. They do their utmost to gain approval. They are extremely personal and intimate in their communication behavior, and they often say things that can make people uncomfortable.

Overpersonal communicators can become excessively possessive in their relationships. They may become so possessive that they do not want their friends to have any other friends but them. We see this situation frequently in the kind of dating relationship in which a female does not want her boyfriend to have any other friends but her. Also, it is not uncommon to see a husband who is jealous of any friendships his wife may develop outside of her relationship to him. As with underpersonal communicators, overpersonal communicators are very concerned about whether or not they are lovable, and they therefore have considerable hostility and anxiety regarding their lovableness—the result of their constant anticipation of rejection.

The *ideal response* to the need for affection is exemplified by the *personal individual*. Personal individuals have had a fairly satisfying childhood in which they received an adequate amount of affection and were not excessively rejected. They are comfortable with close personal relationships as well as emotionally distant relationships with other people. Emotional distance in a relationship is not threatening to them because they don't have fears about their own lovability. These people can even tolerate being disliked by others—the extreme of emotional distance. Because they do not fear that they cannot be loved, personal individuals can assume that being disliked is a situational matter that does not reflect on them personally. The personal individual is not a very anxious person, and because of this fairly well-adjusted state he or she can genuinely give affection.

From this discussion of the three interpersonal needs developed by Schutz and the possible communication behavior related to each, you can see that our interpersonal need component can have a significant effect on the way we communicate with other people. We should also realize that much communication behavior that seems obnoxious or even pathetic may be quite revealing of a person's interpersonal needs.

We do not suggest that you use Schutz's approach to psychoanalyze your friends. Rather, you should keep this information in the back of your mind in order to adjust your own messages to better satisfy the interpersonal needs of the people with whom you communicate. As you become more aware of and more sensitive to the interpersonal needs of others, it will be possible for you to help satisfy those needs in your own messages and thus to become a more effective communicator. Likewise, if you are like us, you may discover some revealing and helpful insights into your own communication behavior as a result of a consideration of this need component.

You should also better appreciate the intimate relationship between what Schutz termed interpersonal needs and the drive-reduction needs discussed by Maslow. Since these two need components intraface constantly, you can appreciate the complexity of what has been termed "motivation," whether it be the motivation underlying statements made by people or whether it be the motivation to get out and drive a racing car in a stock car race.

THE VALUE COMPONENT

As we have been discussing why people do the things they do, we have been dealing with increasingly larger components, starting out with what might be considered by some people to be so basic as to be genetically determined needs. We next considered interpersonal needs, which are "larger" in that they are entirely concerned with the inputs and outputs in social relationships and are built upon our other needs. We now reach a point at which we deal with a system that is based on the previously discussed components and more. Rokeach (1973, p. 5) defined a *value* as "... an enduring belief that a specific mode of conduct or end-state of existence is personally or socially preferable to an opposite or converse mode of conduct or end-state of existence. A *value system* is an enduring organization of beliefs concerning preferable modes of conduct or end-states of existence along a continuum of relative importance." Our primary concern is with the overall value component. The definition offered by Rokeach suggests that, in addition to any specific values we may hold regarding the way we ought to behave or the goals we ought to seek, we have an entire collection of values that are interrelated. A person's value system can include beliefs about the desirability of being honest, of obtaining wealth, of maintaining good health, etc. A value system is a person's whole collection of beliefs.

We learn values early in our lives. We are first taught values by our parents, teachers, clergy, etc. We tend to learn these values as absolute truths without questioning. Because we learn them in this way, they tend to be extremely stable and may last throughout our lives. This is not to say that we never change our value systems as we get older, but rather that value systems are highly resistant to change.

Every value we have concerns a belief we have about a goal or an action in terms of its desirability. Thus, a value is a kind of belief in which we determine that a particular kind of behavior or goal is preferable or not preferable for us. For instance, if you decide that high grades are good to work for, then you have expressed a belief that Rokeach terms a prescriptive belief. A prescriptive belief mandates certain kinds of behavior for you. On the other hand, a value of avoiding the ingestion of harmful substances into your body in order to preserve your physical well-being would be a proscriptive belief because it prohibits a behavior.

Values can refer to either end-states or modes of conduct. Values concerning our modes of conduct and moral behavior in our interpersonal relationships are called "instrumental." In addition, most of us have a set of values concerning the end-state of our life. Such goal-seeking is the mark of all systems. The values concerning acquired wealth or maintenance of good health or possession of good relationships all our lives are what Rokeach calls "terminal values."

We should also mention that values can relate to either personal or social concepts. It is possible for us to talk about things we value because they are personally preferable to us or things we value because they are socially desirable. When we talk about a value component and we're talking about something being preferable, we have to ask, "Preferable for whom?" The answer is usually that the goal or end-state is preferable either in personal or social terms.

Values can also be thought of in terms of higher- and lower-order values. This categorization is very similar to our earlier discussions of the system nature of communication and Maslow's need hierarchy. It is interesting to note that rather than relating the hierarchical nature of values to physical and nonphysical needs as Maslow did, Rokeach suggests that the most important values with the strongest effect on our behavior are those that relate to the self. In other words, if we value equality for all people in our society, this value will occupy a position of lesser importance in our value hierarchy than our value of a happy and comfortable life for ourselves. The reason why the former value occupies a position of less importance is that it is not as directly related to ourselves personally as the latter value. Thus, much of what we consider to be important is important because it more directly relates to us personally.

This hypothesis suggests that as we are observing other people's communication behavior, we should try to figure out what people are saying about themselves. We should never forget that in spite of all the protestations we may hear about unselfish behavior, all behavior ultimately relates back to self. More specifically, Rokeach suggests that our value component relates directly to self-perception. Those things that relate to a positive self-perception are the values that are of most importance to us.

When we talk with someone, it is important to always keep in mind that what we are saying may have an effect upon the other person's self-concept. For example, a simple statement criticizing a set of religious values can be disastrous when the values we are criticizing are held by the person with whom we are talking. The criticism is not perceived as objective criticism, but rather as a direct attack on the receiver's personal beliefs. This interpretation has negative implications for the receiver's self-concept and for the success of the interaction.

The Function of the Value Component

We are considering the nature of the value component because it relates directly to human communication behavior. Values affect behavior because they fulfill certain functions. Values are manifestations of human needs. Thus as we discuss the various functions of values, you should try to keep in mind our earlier discussion of the need and consistency components of motivation.

One of the primary functions served by values is to act as standards by which we can evaluate our behavior. Values also enable us to perceive and reason about the objects and stimuli in our environment. The values a person holds serve as the standards by which they evaluate and determine their responses to messages we may produce. Likewise, because values serve as standards they cause us to take stands. If we value human rights, we may take positions related to the proposed Equal Rights Amendment to the Constitution that are based upon this value. Likewise, these values can cause us to favor one political or religious ideology over another.

A second important concern in communication is the way in which values affect our presentation of self to other people. For instance, if we value logic and reason, we will probably communicate in ways that seem logical and reasonable to us. On the other hand, if we value friendship and feelings above all else, we will tend to communicate on a more personal, intimate level. Whatever way we communicate is very much a reflection of the kind of value component we have. Values enable us to evaluate ourselves and the attitudes, values, and messages of others with whom we come in contact. Although it is possible to discuss many other ways in which values can be used as standards, suffice it to say that the values we hold serve as an important yardstick by which we reason about almost all the stimuli we encounter.

The third important function of values is to help us develop general plans for our behavior. Because the value component is a reasoned organization of principles and regulations, it enables us to formulate plans about how we will behave and communicate with other people. We probably never manage to utilize all of our values at any given time and formulate all of our behavior according to them, but the overall group of values that we carry around with us helps guide our behavior toward others and our responses to others' behavior.

Motivation

Finally, one of the most important functions of values is to motivate our behavior. According to Rokeach, values have a strong motivational effect, and thus they significantly affect perception, reasoning, and behavior. This should not be surprising, since we have discussed values as being manifestations of our need component. It seems only logical that something that is related to our need component should have a significant effect on the way we behave. According to Rokeach, values are the conceptual tools and weapons we all use to maintain and improve our self-esteem. We mentioned the self earlier as an important concept insofar as values are concerned. Those values directly related to self-concept are more important than those less related to self. This fact could be no more evident than in the motivational function of values. Our values, in combination with the other motivation components, cause us to do and say those things we feel are most likely to enhance our self-perception. Our values and attitudes are directly related to our definition of self—who and what we think we are and why we think we are valuable, worthwhile human beings.

Because so much of our value component relates to the perception of self, one of the things that motivates us to change our behavior is dissatisfaction with ourselves. The more someone can point out to you in a message that what you are doing is inconsistent with a positive perception of yourself, the more likely you are to change your behavior, perception, reasoning, values, attitudes, or whatever is necessary to restore a positive sense of self-worth.

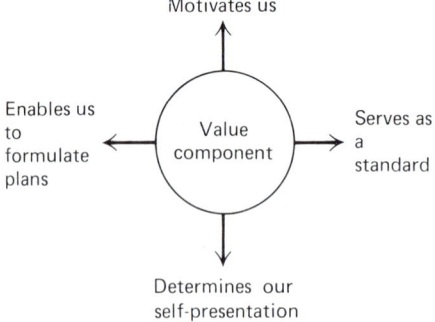

Fig. 3.2 Functions of the value component.

If it is possible in a message to show that a person's values are inconsistent with a positive perception of self or that the person's behavior is inconsistent with a professed value, then you are very likely to motivate that individual to change in order to restore consistency in his or her values, perceptions, reasoning, behaviors, and positive self-concept. For example, if you find out that someone values good health and maintenance of a youthful body and appearance, it might be possible in a message to demonstrate that overeating is a behavior that is inconsistent with that person's value of good health maintenance and youthful appearance. By pointing out this inconsistency in values, behavior, and self-perception, you create a situation in which the person will be motivated to change in such a way as to restore consistency. In this case, your objective might be to get the person to join a health club. Essentially, what you have done in this kind of message is to induce self-satisfaction. This would result in the individual's employing what Rokeach suggests is the basic principle for bringing about change. In this principle, "contradictions are resolved so that self-conceptions will, at the least, be maintained and, if at all possible, enhanced." (p. 230)

ENVIRONMENTAL EFFECTS ON MOTIVATION

Before we conclude this chapter, we must point out that as important as drive-reduction needs, interpersonal needs, consistency needs, and values are in motivation, the environment is just as important. We do not believe that the only components that make us engage in a particular behavior are inherited or learned needs and values. In addition, we must also consider the stimuli we are receiving from our environment.

The press of the outside environment on us is just as important as the existence of any need or value we might have within us. In the television production "Roots," a ship's captain was portrayed as needing a new command. He was offered a position as captain of a ship that would take some goods to England and some other goods to Africa. Then, in Africa, he would pick up slaves and bring them to America. It was the last part of this triangle that involved an action that was contrary to the Christian values he held. These values included treating people in a Christian manner and prohibiting fornication outside of marriage. During the trip, the captain was told that by bringing African natives as slaves to America it was possible to introduce them to Christianity. By accepting that point of view, the captain was able to enhance his own positive self-concept and adhere to his positive value of Christianity. When he was offered a black female with whom to spend the night, another one of his needs was satisfied—a social need, and possibly a physical need as well. By accepting the offer of the black female, he was again changing his behavior in a way that was consistent with his own needs. The important thing to keep in mind is that had he not needed the position as ship's captain to support a family and had his environment not been such as to present the opportunity to have African female slaves brought to his cabin at night, he most likely would not have changed his behavior. The values and needs by themselves would not have changed his behavior. Rather, it was the interaction of his values and needs with his environment that caused him to change his behavior and attitudes about being the captain of a slave ship and sleeping with a woman other than his wife. It is only fair to point out that even at the completion of his trip, he was still left in a considerable state of inconsistency. He was still confused and angry over what he had done. However, because the environment had facilitated and reinforced the kind of change just discussed and because his value and need components supported that kind of change, all of them interacted together to bring about a rather significant change in the man's behavior.

Motivation

This kind of interaction is true of everyone with whom we wish to communicate as well as of ourselves. The motivation for any behavior we engage in at any moment is the product of our values, needs, environment, and the other components together. It would be a mistake to try to trace the motivation for a particular behavior to any one of these things. Much research in the behavioral sciences has been somewhat confusing because it has not taken into account this interaction. Most research concerning values and needs has not been designed with the assumptions of interdependence and holism built in. However, our approach in this book, in which we view communication as a system, requires us to consider a value as one component within a system, needs as a component within a system, and the entire individual system as influenced by the environment. Because systems are characterized by interdependence and holism, it is imperative for us to consider what the interaction might be among all of these components and the environment. It is our position that what a person will do or say at any given moment is partially the result of values and needs, but also, just as significantly, partially the result of the opportunities available in the environment, the constraints placed on that person by the environment, and any other stimuli that can be received as input at any given moment from the environment.

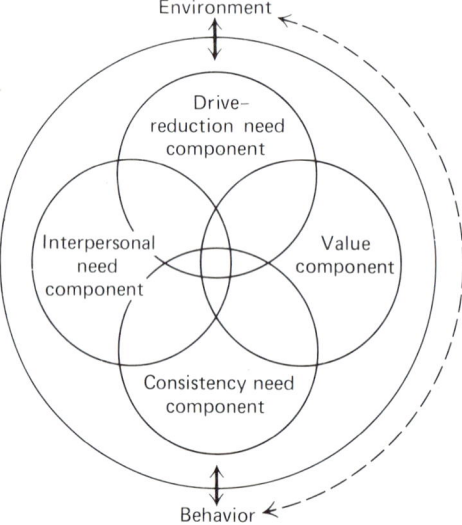

Fig. 3.3 Relation of motivational components to environment and behavior.

The logic we are employing in our discussion of motivation is the same as that underlying a set of commercials we once saw on television. Car owners were urged not to leave their keys in their cars because such carelessness would encourage youths to steal the cars and take them out for joy rides. The point of the commercial was that the value and need components that the youths already had within them might permit or motivate them to steal cars, but only if within the environment there was a car available with a set of keys in it. The point of the commercial was that the interaction of a youth's needs and values with the availability of a car in an environment could motivate theft.

As you can see from Fig. 3.3, needs and values are part of an overall intrapersonal motivational subsystem that interacts with the environment. The environment affects the need and value components and the need and value components in turn affect the way we perceive and reason about our environment. This interaction can result in a given behavior, which in turn has its effect on the environment. This reciprocity continues in a circular fashion with all components having an effect on all other components in a true example of system interdependence.

SUMMARY

At this point, we hope you are aware that we possess several different need components. These need components include genetically inherited and learned drive-reduction needs such as those discussed by Maslow, which we have classified as physical, social, and ego needs. We also have a basic need to be consistent in our attitudes and behaviors. Finally, we possess an interpersonal need component that has been discussed by Schutz, including the needs of affection, inclusion, and control. In addition to need components, we all have a value component that is intimately based on a positive perception of self. These need and value components finally intraface with each other and also with the system's environment at any given time. All of these together result in motivation for the various behaviors in which we may engage at any given time.

KEY TERMS AND CONCEPTS

AFFECTION NEEDS
CONSISTENCY NEEDS
CONTROL NEEDS
DEFICIENT RESPONSES TO INTERPERSONAL NEEDS
DRIVE-REDUCTION NEEDS
ESTEEM NEEDS
EXCESSIVE RESPONSES TO INTERPERSONAL NEEDS
FUNCTIONS OF VALUES
INCLUSION NEEDS
INTERPERSONAL NEED RESPONSES
INTERPERSONAL NEEDS
LONG-TERM MAINTENANCE NEEDS
MASLOW, ABRAHAM
MOTIVATION PROCESSING SUBSYSTEM
PHYSIOLOGICAL NEEDS
ROKEACH, MILTON
SAFETY NEEDS
SCHUTZ, WILLIAM
SELF-ACTUALIZATION NEEDS
SHORT-TERM MAINTENANCE NEEDS
SOCIAL NEEDS
VALUE SYSTEMS
VALUES

SUGGESTED READINGS

LEPPER, MARK R., AND DAVID GREENE. eds., *The Hidden Costs of Reward: New Perspectives on the Psychology of Human Motivation.* Hillsdale, N.J.:

Lawrence Erlbaum Associates, Publishers, 1978. This book contains readings that will acquaint the reader with the background of research and theory in the area of human motivation and that will provide a perspective on recent research. Some readings do relate the motivational process to communication in addition to psychological concerns.

MASLOW, ABRAHAM H., *Motivation and Personality*. New York: Harper and Row, Publishers, 1954. Although this book is almost thirty years old, it remains the most complete and, obviously, the most accurate statement of Maslow's need theory. Any student seriously interested in human motivation should read this classic.

ROKEACH, MILTON, *The Nature of Human Values*. New York: The Free Press, 1973. This book, although written for the advanced reader, is an excellent explanation of values and value systems. The book is based on Rokeach's research as well as that of other scholars. In addition, Rokeach has accomplished a very difficult integration of vast amounts of research from related areas of study.

4 Perception

Understanding human communication systems requires an understanding of how we perceive people and messages. We don't ever see things the way they are but rather interpret events around us. The process of interpreting incoming stimuli is called perception. Perception occurs in human communication as we become aware of the credibility, attractiveness, and personality of communicators. In addition, we also interpret the messages we receive; our interpretation, in turn, determines our acceptance and rejection of the messages. The perception subsystem intrafaces with the motivation and reasoning subsystems to form the intrapersonal processing subsystem through which we receive inputs and transform them into outputs.

Perception

Have you ever seen an optical illusion? If you wonder why you see something that isn't "really there," you are questioning the process of perception. Consider Fig. 4.1. You may see either a young lady looking in a mirror or a skull. Whichever image you think you are seeing, you are really seeing the same thing either way. The difference is what you perceive.

Although Fig. 4.1 is visual, we can have similar kinds of illusions with sound, taste, touch, or any other stimuli we receive. Why is this so? Most of us have been brought up to believe that "seeing is believing." We really think that what we are inputting at any given moment is the reality in front of us. Actually, we transform or interpret the sensations we receive.

Fig. 4.1 Lady and the skull.

One of the most startling examples of seeing not being believing has to be the television picture. Many of us watch television, assuming that what is in front of us are moving pictures. Actually, a television set displays only a dot of light that is traced along 525 lines every 1/30th of a second. The only thing that is really on a television screen at any given split second is a dot of light. In addition, we go to movies and think we are watching a continuous moving image in front of us, when, in fact, there are 24 different pictures flashed on the screen each second. We "interpret" the physiological phenomena in front of us in both cases as "moving pictures."

In addition to interpreting our sensations, we also have to learn how to interpret what is in front of us. In the photograph of the boy and the girl, who is closer? If you have answered that the girl is closer than the boy, we must remind you that neither is closer. Both are figures on a flat page and are, therefore, both the same distance from you. However, because you have learned over time that objects producing a larger image on the back of your eyes are closer than objects producing a smaller image, you interpret the picture in front of you to represent the girl as standing closer to you than the boy. There are people in nontechnological cultures who have not learned to perceive depth in photographs through prior experience as you have learned.

PHOTO BY CAROLE DUGAN

Perception

It is important for us to realize that all of the sensations a system receives at any given moment must be transformed. The physiological reception of light, sound, heat, etc. must be interpreted for the human system to exist in its environment. We never see things the way they are. We can only see things the way we perceive them. Perception is the process of organizing random stimuli received from the environment about us, transforming them, and attaching meaning to them. Perception is the intrapersonal processing component that prepares inputs for the reasoning component.

The study of perception is very important in communication. It is important because all messages, communicators, and communication contexts must be interpreted and perceived. It is not possible to listen to a person speak and hear exactly what that person says. What we really do is listen to the person speak and hear what we interpret. We are always faced with the necessity of interpreting inputs and attaching meanings. As we discuss the perception component, we will be talking about the inputting process from the model of human communication presented in Chapter 2. Because all stimuli must be inputted before they can be processed, it should be obvious that the perception component is basic to the human communication system because it affects both inputting and the other intrapersonal processes of motivation and reasoning. Until we understand the way people perceive messages and communicators, it is next to impossible for us to fully understand the other intrapersonal processing components. All the intrapersonal processing components are inseparable. They constantly intraface with one another. You must recognize and understand how the perception component intrafaces with the others in order to understand the human communication system.

THE PROCESS OF PERCEPTION

There have been several approaches to the study of perception. Rather than consider them all, we would like to discuss some basic principles of perception that have considerable empirical support and that are accepted by most behavioral scientists.

Before discussing these principles, we will briefly mention an approach to perception that is no longer in favor or accepted today, but that clarifies through contrast the approach we will be using. It is called the *structuralist approach*, and it views perception as a process in which all of the inputs received by individuals are combined in an additive manner into a single input. Thus, someone adopting the structuralist approach would assume that as we are perceiving a person we would receive, among other perceptions, a visual perception of height, an auditory perception of voice, and perceptions of various attitudes and values the person holds. Each of these separate inputs would then be combined into an overall perception of the individual. A person adopting the structuralist approach would assume that by simply adding these separate inputs together we would have the total perception of the person.

In recent years, however, research has suggested that a perception is more than the sum of its parts, as implied by the concept of holism discussed in Chapter 2. There is evidence suggesting that we cannot add up separate inputs to form a whole perception. This finding has led to greater acceptance of what has been called the *Gestalt approach* to perception. The Gestalt approach to perception assumes that we perceive perceptual wholes. This means that when a person is first introduced to you, you don't simply perceive all of the separate parts of the individual and then put them together. Rather, this approach suggests that you have an overall global perception of the individual that includes all of the separate perceptions but ends up being more than the separate perceptions added together.

Try to think of your very best friend. If you were to attempt to describe this person to someone you would, no doubt, start out by using the structuralist approach. You would probably try to describe his or her height, weight, color of hair, attractiveness (or lack of it), voice quality, interests, activities, values, and beliefs. Having described all of these individual parts of your friend, could you now say you have described your friend? Probably not. For most of us, to describe a friend would require that we go considerably beyond these individual components of appearance and behavior. To describe a close friend requires that we go beyond the sum of the parts because our perception is more than the sum of the separate parts. You would not expect someone to recognize your friend solely from a structuralist description.

This necessity to go beyond the individual parts in describing a friend, lover, parent, or child is an example of the Gestalt approach to perception. This approach helps explain our reactions to communicators and messages. Frequently, we react to much more in a communication situation than is suggested by the individual components.

Basic Principles

There are six principles of perception that we will consider at this point. Three principles are derived directly from the Gestalt approach to perception and three are consistent with it. As we consider these principles, we hope you will remember that the perceptual element is only one part of the inputting process in communication. Everything discussed in this chapter must be related to the other elements, components, and subsystems within the entire human communication system, such as motivation, reasoning, and outputting.

Proximity In political campaigns a common behavior, which you have probably observed many times, is that of one politician's having his or her photograph taken with another politician. Inevitably, the first politician wants such a picture because it will be perceived positively by the voters. This is an example of a politician's trying to take advantage of the principle of proximity, a concept first articulated by Gestaltists relative to perception.

The principle of proximity suggests that things located or grouped close together tend to "go together" or are perceived as "perceptual wholes." Thus, politicians who are seen standing next to each other or shaking hands in a picture are perceived by those looking at the picture as somehow linked together. This is a good example of "GILT by association."

"GUILT by association," on the other hand, is the case of one politician's digging up a picture of an opponent in the company of someone of low repute. This device is not unusual, and sometimes it is used to call into question the credibility of political opponents. The strategy here is that by associating

Perception

through proximity our opponent with someone with a negative image we reduce our opponent's credibility. If you will look at the photograph of the party, you can see that in a room with several people, those people who sit close together are perceived as pairs. We have already discussed the effect of two people being seen together as providing either a "guilt" or a "gilt" by association/proximity. This is important to keep in mind when communicating. The people with whom we are in close physical proximity are the people with whom we are linked. Likewise, within a message, it is wise to keep in mind that any two parts of the message that are close together will tend to be associated with each other. Finally, a message that people hear immediately before or immediately after our message will be linked perceptually to our message. This effect is sometimes helpful, but in some cases it can be a problem.

PHOTO BY CAROLE DUGAN

Good form Another principle of perception associated with the Gestalt school of thought is good form. Good form occurs as we naturally perceive a whole in something. One example of good form is two straight lines that continue in a given direction. Another example is two half-circles that are opposing each other and thus are perceived to form an entire circle. The circle is the good form in this case. Finally, good form can be perceived when something is incomplete but its complete form can be discerned. This phenomenon is called "closure" and occurs as we perceive the good form inherent in the parts. In Fig. 4.2, the house is formed from dotted lines. Closure occurs and we perceive the entire form of the house.

In communication, the principle of good form is used whenever we strive for balance or symmetry in messages. We hope that the balance, or symmetry, of the message will result in our message being perceived as a whole. For instance, in public speaking the principle of symmetry is emphasized frequently. We talk about a speech being balanced. Another example of closure, or good form, occurs in our own conversation when we suggest to someone that he or she can "guess the rest" or "read between the lines." We can also leave a conclusion unstated after we have presented all the evidence. We are inviting our listeners to employ closure to reach the conclusion implied in our message.

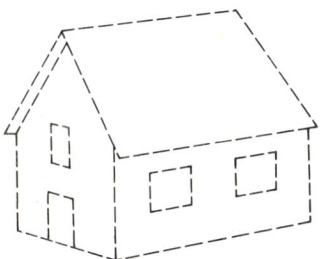

Fig. 4.2 An example of closure.

Order Another principle frequently associated with the Gestalt approach to perception is order. We live in a world in which we receive essentially random inputs from any number of sources in a nonordered, chaotic fashion. The concept of entropy discussed earlier assumes this natural pattern toward disorganization. Disorganization is not easy to cope with. If there were no order in our perception of the world, we could not predict the weather, the way people will behave in various situations, or even if the water will go up or down when we turn a waterglass upside down. What enables us to make all of these predictions is our perception of order among the stimuli that we receive as inputs into the system. We order our perceptions to combat entropy.

Just as unpredictable behavior in people is confusing, so also are messages confusing when they have no order. No doubt when you were in high school you wondered why teachers spent so much time in talking with you about how to organize essays and speeches. The organization of messages is taught because teachers know that people will impose order in their perception of a message if it is not already there. Most of us in communication feel that a message will be more effective if it is well organized because it will provide order for our receivers. An organized message is one that is more easily perceived by listeners and readers than an unorganized message. We might also add that because people will attempt to order sensations they are receiving and their perception of those sensations, we have more control over how our messages are perceived if we organize them and impose our own order on them to begin with. This action is preferable to our allowing the recipients of our messages the option of imposing whatever organizational scheme they wish on those messages.

Our earlier discussion in the preceding chapter of the need for consistency is probably related to this perceptual principle of order. A major reason why we desire ordered perceptions (just as we need to have attitudes and behaviors con-

Perception

sistent) is our need for consistency, which is ultimately related to our need to survive in what seems to be a random world. We feel that it is threatening, or dissonant, to perceive the world about us as unordered, just as it is dissonant for us to perceive inconsistency within ourselves. We said in Chapter 2 that the human communication system was antientropic. A great part of antientropism results from our need for consistency, which is expressed as the principle of order for the perception component.

Categorization Because we receive so many different stimuli all the time, we need a way to structure these inputs. One of the most striking aspects of the intrapersonal perception component is its tendency to impose structure or categories on incoming stimuli. By categorizing everything we see, hear, and feel, we are able to develop a standard for ourselves by which we perceive the world. Rather than perceiving every stimulus as unique, we group inputs into categories. We should point out that our language plays a significant role in this categorization process. Rather than processing all incoming stimuli separately, we think and talk about the existence of "women," "men," "dogs," "cats," "conservatives," and "liberals" rather than a specific woman, man, dog, cat, conservative, or liberal. Category words enable us to predict (to some extent) that since we have encountered one "dog" previously, the next time we encounter a member of the same category we can expect similar types of behavior.

Categorization is not simply descriptive; it is also evaluative. A person thinking of the category "dog" probably does so in terms of positive or negative as well as descriptive characteristics. We have known several children who at impressionable ages have had unfortunate encounters with a dog; they have perhaps been bitten or scared by a dog. As a result of these experiences, they have developed a category, "dog," which for them has negative associations. As a result, all future dogs they encounter are included in the same category and the negative associations result in behaviors of fear and avoidance. It is important to keep in mind that we all generalize in much more complex ways than this example suggests. It is common for us to develop categories regarding "conservatives," "liberals," "Democrats," and "Republicans" that completely determine the way we respond to a person once we have placed that person in one of these categories. Although our categories are not always accurate, we nevertheless continue to classify stimuli because past experience has convinced us that these categories usually help us predict events in our environment.

Remember that our category system is very much related to our past experiences and associations as well as to the language systems we have learned. The category of precipitation that we call "rain" is positive for some people and negative for others, depending on their past experiences with rain and their past environments. The two of us live in a part of the country in which we receive less than 12 inches of precipitation a year. Therefore, "rain" for people in this part of the country has extremely positive associations, and we are happy to receive it. There are places in the world where there is so much precipitation that "rain" is almost dreaded.

Our past experiences and even the language we learn have a significant effect on our categorization process. In the chapter on verbal communication we will be discussing the important relationship between the way we perceive the world and the language we use to categorize things within our environment.

The language we learn has a significant effect on the way we perceive the world about us. In turn, the experiences we have significantly affect the way our language develops. There is a circular relationship between our language and our past history and experiences. Each has a significant effect on the other, according to the perceptual principle of categorization.

Stabilization One of the fascinating principles developed by Hastorf, Schneider, and Polefka (1970) is that in addition to imposing structure and developing categories by which to perceive our world, we also attempt to *stabilize perceptions within these categories* as we develop them. You have often experienced this principle in your relationships with other people. After you developed a perception of someone, he or she subsequently did something that was inconsistent with your perception. Such a circumstance is not easy for us to handle because of our need for consistency. We frequently become upset when people do not behave according to our categorization of them because we wish our perception of them to remain the same. We strive for perceptual stabilization. In fact, we sometimes keep it stable by misperceiving the things that are actually going on about us. We know of a colleague who perceived one of his friends to be an honest person. When his friend on one occasion committed a dishonest act, our colleague continued to perceive his friend as being an honest person. Thus, our colleague maintained a stable perception of his friend, even at the cost of being unable to accurately perceive actual behaviors engaged in by the friend.

A physical example of the principle of perceptual stabilization might occur when someone is walking toward us from cross a wide field. When we first look at the person, the physical image on our retina is very, very small. As the person walks closer to us, the image becomes larger and larger. At no time do we think the individual is actually growing in size. Rather, we maintain a stable perception of the person's height, but we interpret the change in size of the image on our retina as indicating a change in distance. When the retinal image is small we perceive the person as being far away, and as the image gets larger we interpret that phenomenon to mean the person is getting closer to us. Perceptual stabilization allows us to impose order on our environment and satisfy our need for consistency. We also use this principle to maintain the consistency we have already developed among this perception and others.

Decoding Several times in this chapter we have mentioned the necessity of imposing structure on our view of the world as we interpret incoming stimuli. Many communication models refer to a process called "decoding." Decoding is the process by which we assign meaning to the various inputs we perceive. We determine that "cold" (whatever the physiological sensation we experience may be) is either good or bad, helpful or dangerous, and so on. If we live in Alaska, we may decode "cold" as being dangerous. If we live along the equator, "cold" may be decoded as a welcome relief. In both cases, we associate meanings with the sensation we call "cold." This type of decoding can be thought of in terms of micromeanings, or those meanings that we decode based on our individual or personal categorization of stimuli. When we decode, then, we assign individual meanings, or micromeanings, to input stimuli.

Of equal importance in decoding are macromeanings, or meanings concerned with relationships among different categories, stimuli, and structures. Not only do we need to determine that we have a category of things called "food," but we also need to decode the relationship that exists between food and us, as well as the relationships that exist among various types of food. We might parenthetically add that for many years the importance of the relationships among different kinds of food was overlooked by many people, with the result of poor nutrition. For our own survival, it is important that we decode as well as perceive these relationships so that we may deal with them. In the example of foods, it is important for us to realize that if we eat nothing but carbohydrates or nothing but protein, we can have nutritional problems.

The preceding example is not directly related to communication, but there are many situations in which the perceptual decoding of relationships is a vital part of the communication process. Unless we decode the meaning of the relationship between men and women in our society as well as the micromeanings concerning each category, it is quite possible for us to engage in communication behaviors with members of the opposite sex (and for that matter even sometimes with members of our own sex) that are counterproductive. In our country, as in many other societies, there has been a tendency to identify males as superior, intelligent, and strong, and women as inferior, unintelligent, and weak. Although we do not personally agree with these meanings attached to the male and female categories, they are commonly decoded in our country. Even with recent movements to change such meanings we are still faced with them.

An important part of understanding those meanings and how to communicate with men and women in our society is a knowledge of the relationships that exist between the categories of men and women. In our society, women are generally assumed to be in a subordinate relationship to men. Because of this perceived relationship, men and women have developed communication output patterns that are necessary to understand in order to work effectively with members of both genders. For instance, it has been observed that when a male talks aggressively, "takes charge," and initiates action, it is considered acceptable communication behavior in our society. A male who behaves in this way is perceived very positively. A woman who engages in the same kinds of communication behaviors, however, is often perceived negatively by both males and females. She is considered masculine rather than feminine, as well as too aggressive.

An understanding of the macromeanings in our society provides considerable insight into how people will respond to our communication behaviors. Males and females sensitive to these relationships will probably develop communication patterns that will enable them to accomplish their objectives without violating the expectations and norms of society and will thus take advantage of these macromeanings. Males and females who do not have a sensitivity to these relationships may violate norms and thus displease other persons in our society. We hope no one will interpret this discussion as suggesting that we don't believe women should be aggressive. Quite to the contrary, we find many of our more aggressive students of both genders to be refreshing. However, it is important for all of us to realize that these relationships do exist and to understand them in order that we may effectively cope with and interact with those around us.

PERSON PERCEPTION

The most important component of a human communication system is the individual. Because people make up our communication systems, it is important to understand how we perceive people. As you think about your own personal relationships with other people or as you consider how you perceive people talking on television, what makes you decide about the kind of person each one is?

The judgment you make about another person has a significant effect on the way you receive their messages. It is of considerable interest to those of us involved in communication to find out how we form our impressions of other people and how they, in turn, form their impressions of us. The following discussion will focus on the way we develop our perceptions of other people, which in turn has implications for the ways in which other people form their impressions of us.

Perceiving Communicator Intent

As we observe other people engaging in behavior we assume that they intend to do the things we see them doing. Although our assumption may seem thoroughly reasonable, the problem with it is that we suppose others are doing what they are doing for the reasons *we* infer. When you see someone eating broccoli, you probably assume they are doing so because they like it. But that may not necessarily be the case. Some people eat broccoli for reasons totally unrelated to taste preferences. They may eat broccoli because it is served to them by someone they do not wish to offend. Or they may eat it because they think it is good for their health. The important point is that we make inferences about other people's intentions every day whenever we perceive them engaging in various behaviors.

We probably make these assumptions about other people's intentions because it satisfies our need for consistency. It would be a very confusing world indeed if all of the actions we could see other people engaging in were unrelated to their intentions and preferences, because we would then have no explanation for our observations. Because of our need for consistency, we assume that intentions and behaviors must also be consistent for others. This assumption is probably reasonable in most cases. Although the evidence is mixed concerning the relationship of attitudes and intentions to behaviors, there is support for the proposition that most people do things because they want to and/or because they feel it satisfies some need. As we pointed out in the chapter on motivation, there are many different factors that motivate an individual at any given moment, but we can assume that the behaviors we see generally result from some set of individual intentions.

These assumptions we make about other people's intentions are very important to understanding the human communication process. Because we believe that people behave according to their preferences and intentions, we most often assume that if they say something, they must believe it. Likewise, most of us assume that if people smile at us, they must like us. We also infer that if people avoid us, they must not like us. We assume that if a person touches us, that person feels affection for us. Why do we make these judgments

Perception

about people? What is the process by which we infer things about people and thus develop our perception of them?

We usually don't base an overall perception about an individual on one given behavior. If, for example, we hear a man say that a mother should stay home with her child during the first two or three years, we are not usually inclined to make the judgment that the man is prejudiced against women. This one behavior is generally not enough for us to make that inference. However, if we later see the same man refusing to hire a woman for an executive position in his business, we then observe him monopolizing a conversation with a woman by never allowing her an opportunity to make a comment, and we finally overhear him expressing opposition to women doctors or lawyers, we begin to infer that this person has negative intentions and attitudes toward women.

This process of inferring intentions from observed behaviors and developing an overall perception of an individual based on observed consistencies among several different behaviors is important to our understanding of the communication process. When we observe people who consistently interrupt others we can infer a couple of things. We may infer that this person has no sensitivity to conversational norms. We may also infer that this individual has no respect for other people's opinions. If we observe an individual telling a lie several times, we may infer that the person is dishonest. This process of assigning conscious or unconscious intentions to observed behaviors can result in any number of perceptions of people as communicators. We might keep in mind that because our communicative acts are behaviors to which people can assign intentions, these acts will significantly affect the way we are perceived by others.

What is the first impression that each of these people makes on you?
PHOTO BY CAROLE DUGAN

Forming Impressions

Have you ever been told that it is important to make a good first impression on people? This is fairly sound advice. The first impression we make on people is long-lasting and requires many experiences to overcome. If the first impression we make on a person is important, then the question for us becomes "How do we make impressions on other people and how do other people make impressions on us?" Two theories used by psychologists to explain impression formation are the trait approach and the implicit personality theory approach.

Trait approach The trait approach suggests that as we perceive a person we observe that person's honesty, friendliness, aggressiveness, etc., and then put these traits together in an additive fashion to form a total impression. This approach to impression formation is an outgrowth of the structuralist view of perception mentioned earlier. Early studies by Asch (1946) indicated that if our perception of one trait of a person changes, our overall impression of that person changes. These early studies would typically use a set of adjectives to describe an unknown person, holding all of the adjectives constant except for one (i.e., "cold" might be one adjective changed to "warm"). Asch found the warm/cold continuum to be what he called a "central trait." A central trait was one that he considered to have a greater effect than most other traits on our overall perception of an individual. Although there was some partial support for the trait approach to impression formation, today there is a more commonly accepted approach called implicit personality theory.

Implicit personality theory Although the trait approach is similar to the structuralist view of perception, the approach of implicit personality theory is more consistent with the Gestalt view. We perceive people as entire systems, and our perceptions are based on the inferred intentions already discussed. When we meet someone, we observe behaviors such as smiles, frowns, statements, and silences. From all of these behaviors taken together and from any consistent patterning we form impressions of various sorts. As a result of these impressions we begin to develop a total picture of the person, which serves to explain the observed behaviors. This explanatory picture is our own private personality theory that explains the particular individual for us. We may develop a notion that "this person is shy and withdrawn," or that "this person is aggressive, outgoing, and dynamic." We store away and hold these private personality impressions for every person we know.

From our implicit personality theory we develop a set of predictions. Whenever we see a person for whom we have an implicit personality theory, we expect them to behave consistently with that theory. We expect the person we classify as shy and withdrawn to behave quietly and in a reserved manner whenever we are around. If you have perceived someone as a "happy person," you are somewhat surprised if on any given day you discover that person simply sitting quietly, without a smile on his or her face. It is so surprising to us when we discover a friend of ours violating our expectations that we frequently ask, "What's wrong?" We believe in our implicit personality impressions. We expect them to correctly predict the way people will behave. When people don't behave according to our predictions, we experience confusion. We have to resolve this dissonance so we may say to ourselves, "Well, maybe that's not a happy person. Maybe I was wrong." Or we may instead say, "That's a happy person who is just not smiling." In the first case we revised our private personality impression of the person, while in the second case we decided that we were wrong in the way we perceived the individual.

Our need for consistency is so great that when the observed behaviors of a person are contrary to our implicit personality impression, we may actually distort our perception of the observed behaviors in ways that will make the behaviors and our private personality impression consistent. This distortion may occur when we consider a person to be honest and then observe that person engaging in a behavior that is dishonest. Frequently, we develop rationalizations for the behavior we have observed. We may repress the behavior so we don't remember it. Sometimes we distort the behavior so that we are unable to perceive that the individual actually did engage in it. We will resort to any of these tactics to make our implicit personality theories and perceptions consistent.

Some people are very good at inferring intentions from other people's behavior and have fairly accurate private personality theories for the people they know. You may be one of these people, and you may have discovered that it doesn't take you very long to develop a valid impression of another person. You may instead be a person who has a difficult time in forming accurate perceptions of other people. Several factors appear to significantly affect our ability to develop accurate perceptions of other people's personalities, including our own interpersonal attitudes, the role relationship, perceptual biases based on prior information, and our own moods and motivations at any given moment (Argyle, 1969).

We can also think of these private personality impressions as stereotypes that we have of other people. Ordinarily, when we use the term *stereotype* we are referring to large groups of people. For instance, some people have stereotypes of professors and some people have stereotypes of used car dealers. However, it is also possible to stereotype an individual's behaviors. Having observed a number of behaviors, we develop an overall picture of the kinds of behaviors we expect from a person. We can stereotype a person as gregarious, shy, honest, or dishonest. We go through four steps when we are making use of implicit personality theories (Brooks and Emmert, 1980).

1. We observe an individual's behavior.
2. We make a generalization based on the observed behavior.
3. We make an inferential leap to an implicit personality impression.
4. From this impression, we stereotype the behaviors we expect from that kind of person.

Self-fulfilling prophecy One of the more interesting implications of implicit personality theory is the circular nature of these impressions. After we have developed our stereotype for a person, we have a set of expectations regarding that given person. Because we have these expectations, we frequently communicate with that person in ways that are consistent with our expectations. This communication behavior can, in turn, cause the other individual to respond to our messages in ways that are consistent with our expectations. A full cycle is thus completed, which is called a "self-fulfilling prophecy."

One of the best examples of the self-fulfilling prophecy concerns students in a small college town. In a small college town, professors and students have a significant impact on the community. It is also true that merchants and police officers can develop negative attitudes toward students and professors because of their impact on the town. In watching students interacting with merchants and police officers in a small town, it has been our observation that if the students believe there is hostility toward them they behave in ways that cause merchants and police officers to react negatively toward them (the traditional town/gown conflict). We have observed students being excessively aggressive in department stores and grocery stores simply because they assume that the people who work there don't like them. As a result of the aggressive, hostile behavior the people who work in the stores do end up not liking the students and treating them badly. The point of this example is that the stereotype developed by the students in their own minds can cause them to behave toward people in ways that then cause the other people to respond according to the students' expectations.

One of the obvious conclusions to be drawn is that we perceive people according to those inferences we make from our observations of their behaviors. Subsequently, we perceive their behaviors according to our perceptions of them, or the impressions we have formed of them. This process is circular and yet we must emphasize that it happens. It is an important part of the human communication process, and it has a significant effect on our interpersonal relationships. The self-fulfilling prophecy significantly affects intrapersonal processing within any human communication system.

Cultural effects We have already mentioned that background and past experiences have significant effects on the way we perceive events and people. We pointed out that people who have never before been exposed to photographs find it impossible to perceive depth in a photograph, as in those illustrated earlier. Likewise, children who have grown up in deprived homes and experienced poverty perceive coins to be larger than do children who have grown up in affluent homes. Different people can experience the same physical phenomenon in front of them and yet, because of their varying backgrounds and experiences, they will "see" and "hear" very different things. The old cliche "tell it like it is" would be more accurate were we to rephrase it as "tell it the way our culture tells us to see it."

Nowhere is the effect of background and culture more apparent than in the way we perceive people. In one study, white students at a major American university were found to perceive black students as emotional, defiant, hostile, argumentative, aggressive, and critical. These same students also perceived Mexican-Americans as emotional, argumentative, sensitive, straightforward, and talkative, and Japanese-Americans as intelligent, courteous, industrious, quiet, soft-spoken, and reserved. The communication characteristics of each ethnic minority, in the eyes of the white students, were significantly different from group to group (Ogawa, 1971). The white students had stereotyped the ethnic groups in different ways. In addition, the self-fulfilling prophecy probably conditioned the way in which the white students communicated with people from these various groups when interacting with them, thus insuring behaviors consistent with the stereotypes. After interaction with someone from another cultural group, many people find that their expectations and stereotypes have been confirmed because of the self-fulfilling prophecy.

Lest you think that our attitudes and stereotypes don't have this strong an effect on us, take a look at Fig. 4.3. This figure was used in a classic study by Allport and Postman (1947). In this study, a procedure similar to the old parlor game of "rumor" or "telephone" was used. Some subjects in the study were asked to view the picture and then to describe it to other subjects. The latter subjects then described what they heard to others, and so on. White subjects tended to see the black man standing up as holding a razor blade. They perceptually shifted the razor to the black man's hand, and they perceived him as hostile. In addition, white subjects tended to emphasize the interracial aspects of the picture more than did black subjects. Blacks, on the other hand, tended to ignore the interracial nature of the picture. It is interesting to note that black subjects tended to ignore, repress, or somehow overlook the fact that the black man in the picture was better dressed than the white man. Such perceptual distortion on the part of these black subjects suggests a poor development of self-esteem—one of the by-products of the long history of discrimination against blacks in this country.

This picture and the results of the study by Allport and Postman are very illuminating in that they show us how strong an effect our stereotypes and our implicit personality theories have on our perceptions of people and interpersonal situations. It should be apparent by now that the role perception plays in the communication process is a significant one.

We would also like to point out very briefly that although most of us may be aware of the cultural differences among ethnic groups, we are much less

Fig. 4.3 Allport and Postman picture.

From *The Psychology of Rumor* by Gordon Allport and Leo Postman. Copyright 1947 by Henry Holt & Co., Inc. Renewal © 1975 by Holt, Rinehart and Winston. Reprinted by permission of Holt, Rinehart and Winston.

likely to recognize that there are other cultures in America that also play significant roles in our person perception. Although it isn't always recognized, males and females constitute very different cultures in our society. Males and females often have very different experiences as they grow up. Girls, for example, are often dressed in ways that prevent them from climbing trees and playing ball. Boys, on the other hand, are seldom taught to cook, iron, and sew, and they are thus at a disadvantage when they get out on their own. Males and females are taught different values, and as a result they constitute what could be considered separate cultures, although obviously there is an overlap and commonality between them. The differences in the ways in which men and women perceive situations and words are important. These differences should not be forgotten when communicating from one gender to another.

Other cultural differences in our society that we should remember relate to the differences among age groups. People who were reared during a war have different outlooks on life and different perceptual sets than people who were reared during more peaceful times. Children who grew up during the demonstrations, riots, bombings, and assassinations of the 1960s have perceptions different from those who grew up during the relative tranquility of the 1950s.

Religious groups also constitute major cultural subgroups. We cannot deny differences in values and perceptual outlooks that exist among different groups such as Mormons, Catholics, Jews, Moslems, Protestants, Calvinists, Baptists, and Moonies. We do not mean to imply that any one of these groups is more right than the others, but rather that because of a number of value and theological differences, perceptions are developed that are very different from one group to another. In addition, if you consider that there are also many agnostics and atheists in the country who are different from the other religious groups, you begin to realize the complexity of communication between and among members of these various groups. Topics such as birth control, abortion, capital punishment, divorce, welfare, and the Equal Rights Amendment are perceived differently as a result of different cultural backgrounds based on religious affiliation.

In the communication process, our perception of other people is greatly affected by cultural differences. The words, issues, and examples used in messages by various people will be perceived in very different ways, depending on the cultural background of both the sender and receiver of the message.

Credibility As we pointed out in Chapter 1, Aristotle was one of the first people to realize the importance of person perception for communication. He used the term "ethos" to refer to the way an audience perceives a speaker. Today, we refer to the same phenomenon as "communicator credibility." Credibility refers to the way in which a communicator is perceived by people receiving the communicator's messages. We speak of credibility in terms of the extent to which we trust and respect another person, and even in terms of how much we think that person is exciting to be around. Many factors are involved in our overall perception of communicator credibility, but there seems to be considerable agreement that we can break down credibility into various components. There appear to be three components that together make up our perception of a person's credibility. These components are competence, trustworthiness, and dynamism.

When we say that there are three components of credibility, we are in essence adopting a kind of structuralist view of person perception. In other words, we mean that we are attempting to break down an overall holistic perception into its component parts and to suggest that the overall perception, or credibility, is the result of adding these components together. Actually, our perception of an individual's credibility is probably an overall response, or a holistic perception. The components of credibility are the major elements in our perception of credibility, and these components probably are combined in our own minds in various ways of which we are not consciously aware. Please keep this in mind as you read the discussion of these components.

When Aristotle first spoke of ethos, or ethical proof, he explained that it included the honesty and expertness of a speaker. The competence component refers to expertness. When we make a judgment as to the abilities, knowledge, and/or education of a person, we are assessing the competence factor. Interestingly enough, many different things about a person's behavior can cause us to perceive that person as more or less competent: age, language, clothing, use of evidence, and education, among others. All of these contribute to our perception of an individual's expertness. Often we can, during communication, change other people's perception of our competence by making sure they know about our education or by using evidence from highly respected sources.

When Aristotle discussed the importance of honesty, he was concerned with what is today called the *trustworthiness component* of credibility. An important factor in our perception of someone's credibility is trustworthiness, or how honest we perceive the individual to be. This dimension includes a moral judgment as well. A communicator's "goodness" and ethics, and possibly even some elements of the social confidence we have in the communicator, are all included. Is this person comfortable to be around? Do we enjoy interacting with this person? We feel that the social confidence we have in the communicator is an important part of credibility. We have often observed that people will overlook someone's incompetence if the person is perceived as possessing good character. Probably one of the best examples of this phenomenon is our relationships with doctors. Most of us are not really qualified to determine whether a doctor is a "good" doctor or not. It is not uncommon, however, to hear people refer to their doctor as "excellent." Statements like this one probably reflect a high degree of trust based on interaction with the doctor and on other factors unrelated to the doctor's ability as a physician. Sometimes, in addition to our response to a doctor on the trustworthiness dimension, we also respond on the dynamism dimension.

The way we perceive a person in terms of that person's energy level and responsiveness to us is referred to as the *dynamism component*. In many situations we want our friends, leaders, and others with whom we interact to be dynamic, responsive people. We don't want doctors who constantly look tired, run down, and passive. Rather, we want them to be active, dynamic, and responsive to us. Part of our judgment of their dynamic quality may result from what they say, but we suspect that most of our judgment results from observation of nonverbal factors. These factors include handshakes, energy level in the voice, eye contact, touching behaviors, and others. These are obviously communication variables that we can manipulate while we are talking with someone. We would suggest that you have it in your power at any time to increase other people's perception of you in terms of this dynamism component and thus possibly to have a more positive effect on the way your credibility is perceived.

These three components comprise a whole perception of a person's credibility. How they are combined, we are not really sure. We do know, though, that it is possible to break down overall perceptions of credibility and consistently obtain these three components. The credibility of any communicator, whether that person be someone you are responding to or yourself when you are talking to other people, is an important part of the communication process. Any message you produce will be received and accepted more positively by listeners if they perceive your credibility positively. The more competent, trustworthy, and dynamic you are perceived, the more effective you will be in getting your messages accepted.

It is quite reasonable to suggest that all of us should make a conscientious effort at introducing elements into our messages that will increase perceptions of competence. Likewise, if only to maintain a positive perception of your

Perception

trustworthiness, it is of considerable practical benefit for you to be honest and fair in your treatment of other people and not to introduce deceptions into your messages. Finally, you should try to avoid the trap of being passive and tired-looking when you talk with people. You have it in your power to communicate in ways that result in people perceiving you positively. Some of your perceived credibility is based on your background and what people know about it. Some of it is based upon your past behaviors and what people know about them. And obviously much of your perceived credibility is the result of what you do while you are communicating. Never forget that credibility is a perceived quality rather than an absolute quality, and at any time you have the chance to increase the perception of your own credibility.

Do you trust your doctor? If so, why?
PHOTO BY CAROLE DUGAN

Perceived attractiveness Frequently when we talk about how attractive a person is, we discuss it as though it were a quality that resides in the person. However, like credibility, attraction is perceived by observers; it does not inherently exist within a person. This fact is not so surprising when you consider that someone can be frequently considered attractive by some people, but not by others. Likewise, when you stop to consider the standards of attractiveness as they vary from culture to culture, it becomes apparent that attractiveness is a relative quality that must be perceived.

Attraction is an overall positive or negative response of one individual to another. In communication, more attractive people are more likely to be believed. In this respect, attractiveness is very closely related to, if not a subset of, credibility. As with credibility, we perceive attraction in component parts (McCroskey and McCain, 1974). The components, or dimensions, of interpersonal attraction are somewhat similar to both the need areas discussed in Chapter 3 and the components of credibility. The three components of attraction include a *social-liking component*, a *task-respect component*, and a *physical appearance component*.

The *social-liking component* concerns the extent to which we think we can enjoy an interpersonal or a social relationship with the perceived person. The degree to which we would like to have this person in our circle of friends, how well we think we know that person personally, and how much we would like to meet that person are all concerns involved in the social-liking component. When we make a comment such as "I like John" or "I like Susan," we are expressing this component of interpersonal attraction. When we perceive a communicator in terms of the social-liking component or the trustworthiness component of credibility, we make this judgment in response to our own social or interpersonal needs.

The *task-respect component* of attraction is a combination of our judgment of the individual's overall competence and our judgment of the person relative to a work situation. It involves a judgment about the extent to which we think we can accomplish a task while working with that person, how much we feel we can depend on the person, and whether that person is a fast or a slow worker, among other concerns. When we say, "Charlie is a good worker," we are expressing the task-respect component of interpersonal attraction. The more competent we think an individual is, the more likely we are to respond positively to that individual. This kind of judgment is related to our own esteem, feelings of competence, and the expertness or competence dimension in communicator credibility.

The *physical appearance component* of attraction has to do with looks. The extent to which we think someone is good-looking, sexy, fashionably dressed, and well-groomed is involved in our judgment of physical attraction. The comments "Sam is an attractive man," and "Jane is a good-looking woman" reflect this component of interpersonal attraction. It is interesting to note that our judgment of someone's physical attractiveness has a significant effect on the development of our implicit personality theories, which we discussed previously. The more attractive a person, the more intelligent and more honest we believe that person to be. Likewise, the less attractive a person, the less we expect in terms of intelligence, honesty, and warmth. It must be apparent that it is in our best interest as communicators to attempt to project as attractive an appearance as possible so that we are judged positively on this dimension. The physical appearance dimension of attraction is very likely related to our physical needs and the dynamism component of communicator credibility.

Perception

It may be that the dimensions of attraction discussed here are partially the result of the types of people studied. Research investigating this phenomenon has by and large been conducted with students in college. Consequently, we think it possible that the results may be more work- or task-oriented than in nonwork settings.

A major factor that causes us to see people positively in terms of these three components is our tendency to perceive similarities between ourselves and others. The more we think people are like us, the more positively we perceive them. Similarity is usually called "homophily" and dissimilarity is called "heterophily." These two terms refer to the degree of perceived similarity that we feel between ourselves and another person. We determine how similar we are to another individual in terms of the attitudes, values, background, and physical appearance of that person (McCroskey, Richmond, and Daly, 1975). The more similar we perceive someone's attitudes, values, family, socioeconomic background, and physical attractiveness are to ours, the more attracted we will be to that person. Because the same holds true of others' perception of us as communicators, it is to our advantage, whenever possible, to find common ground between ourselves and other people. When discussing attitudes, values, and background, we should make apparent in our messages those things we have in common with the people we are trying to influence. In addition, it is to our advantage to use those items of dress and grooming that will enhance our appearance in order to increase our perceived attractiveness, as long as we don't deviate too far from those we are trying to affect.

The ways in which attraction functions in the communication processes will be discussed further in Part IV of this book. Suffice it to say, at this point, that attraction does play a role in the communication process, and it is to our advantage to achieve a positive perception of our attractiveness whenever possible in order to make ourselves more effective communicators.

MESSAGE PERCEPTION

Of considerable interest in the study of human communication is the way messages are perceived. The message is a primary focus of those disciplines concerned with communication. There are two major concerns in message perception. The first is the way we select the messages we chose to perceive. This aspect will become more important when we discuss mass communication, although it is of concern in all human communication systems. Second, we will consider how we perceive messages once we are exposed to them.

Selectivity

What makes you decide to listen to another person's message? If there are speeches being presented on campus that are open to the public, what determines whether you will go or not? We are selective in the way we expose ourselves to messages. Three phenomena that explain our decision in this regard are selective reception, selective perception, and selective retention.

Selective reception Obviously, we don't pay attention to all of the messages available to us. Selective reception refers to the decision we make to listen or not to listen to an available message in our environment. An important factor in this decision appears to be the degree to which we agree with the message. We choose to listen to messages with which we believe we are already in agreement. This is a strange statement to make in a world in which we talk about being open-minded. It is not so strange, however, when you think back to our need for consistency. Because of our need to be consistent, we tend to want to hear messages that are in agreement with our own beliefs, attitudes, values, and previous information. Political candidates have known this for years, but they are now making better use of the knowledge on radio and television. Seldom does a politician schedule one-hour speeches on radio and television. Rather, 30- or 60-second spots are inserted into programs people are already watching. This change in political advertising has taken place because politicians recognize that if a potential voter does not already agree with them, they are very likely to turn off a speech coming from someone with whom they are not in agreement. By slipping in short commercials during programs or station breaks between programs, the politician hopes that viewers will listen to the message, even though they don't agree with it, because they are watching something else that is consistent with their value systems.

Selective reception does not just happen with the mass media. We have seen people walk out of rooms when a discussion starts to take a direction that is not consistent with their beliefs and attitudes. No doubt you have had that experience yourself. One of the major problems in communication is simply how to get someone to listen to us when we are presenting a message that is not consistent with that person's belief system. The only possible answer is to sandwich it into something else that they do find acceptable and/or phrase our message so that it does not seem to be extremely contrary to the person's belief system.

Selective perception What happens when we hear a message that is not consistent with our belief system? As you might expect, given our discussion of the need for consistency, we experience discomfort. When we experience dissonance in response to a message that is inconsistent with our belief system, we often reduce the dissonance by distorting the message we hear. One of the best examples of this kind of distortion occurred in 1964 at the Republican National Presidential Convention. Barry Goldwater, a senator from Arizona, who had just been selected by the Republican party to be its presidential candidate, made a statement in his acceptance speech that was contrary to the beliefs of many of his own supporters. The statement was: "Extremism in the defense of liberty is no vice." This statement could be construed to endorse riots, bombings, and demonstrations, just as long as they were in the name of a good cause. When interviewed, many of his supporters perceptually distorted the statement unconsciously in their own minds so that they stated to interviewers that he had actually never made the statement in his speech. By doing so, they reduced their dissonance and were able to continue to support Senator Goldwater as a presidential candidate. This same pattern is not uncommon in everyday life. If someone makes a statement with information that might ordinarily produce a negative perception of a close friend or relative, we may perceptually distort the statement in order not to perceive the negative implications.

One of the implications of our selective perception is that we cannot always be certain of the kinds of information we are receiving from other peo-

Perception

ple. We may ourselves be distorting their messages. Likewise, it is not easy to present unwanted information to a person without that person's distorting it. One of the pieces of advice we would suggest is that whenever you are faced with the necessity of giving someone bad news, you may want to be highly repetitive or redundant in your message. By repeating the bad news in different words several times, it becomes more difficult for the receiver of the message to distort it.

Selective retention Let's assume for a moment that in spite of our best efforts to avoid exposure to information we don't want to hear (through selective reception as well as selective perception and distortion), we are nevertheless exposed to a message that is inconsistent with our beliefs, highly redundant, and so clear that it is very difficult, if not impossible, to distort it. What do we do then? The answer lies in a defense mechanism called "repression." Repression consists of our forgetting events we don't want to remember. If the information received is damaging to our self-concept or inconsistent with information we strongly believe, or if it is simply something with which we do not agree, we are less likely to remember it than if it were supportive of our self-concept, consistent with prior information, or in agreement with our opinions. This phenomenon is called selective retention.

As difficult as it may be to believe, we have a capacity to forget things that are dissonance-producing. At a major university, one of us observed another professor in the department who often missed classes and department meetings. This professor was ultimately denied tenure by the department, and one of the reasons cited was the frequently missed classes and meetings. However, the professor seemed unaware that he had indeed missed the classes and meetings. He had selectively excluded memories of those past experiences and behaviors that were inconsistent with a positive view of himself as a professor. It would have been uncomfortable, if not damaging, for the professor to have considered himself irresponsible or untrustworthy. Therefore, rather than remembering these past failures, the professor selectively retained only positive past behaviors.

Because people are capable of selective retention, it is important for us as communicators to develop messages that have sufficient redundancy, vividness of examples, and clarity of language so as to make them difficult to forget. Obviously, selective retention is a subconscious process that one engages in to protect one's self-concept and need for consistency. It is difficult to construct messages that will prevent many people's tendency to engage in this selective process. Obviously, we will not always be able to foil others' selective processes, so it may be necessary for us to repeat messages at intervals so as to reinstate information in the receptor's mind after it has been repressed.

Social Judgment Involvement

Probably one of the most interesting theoretical developments in the behavioral sciences in recent years has been the social judgment involvement approach of Sherif (1961, 1965). This approach to communication behavior has much to offer us in our understanding of the way messages are perceived. Although the model developed by Sherif is not, strictly speaking, a perception theory, a significant part of its content is concerned with message perception. We will, therefore, briefly discuss those aspects of Sherif's model that are ordinarily used to explain "attitude change," but our primary concern with this model will be its implications for message perception.

To give you an idea of what Sherif's approach is all about, try to think of the concept of height. What do you consider tall or short? If you had a friend who was six feet two inches tall, would you perceive that person as being tall or short? The immediate response of many people would be "Of course, six-foot-two is above average; therefore, the person is tall." But suppose your friend asked you to meet at a gym for a game of basketball, and when you showed up, you found the school's basketball team standing around your friend. At that point, your friend might not seem very tall. In fact, your friend might seem short.

The point of this discussion about height is central to the social judgment involvement approach. *We perceive things relative to an anchor point in our own minds. An anchor point is a standard that we have developed through experience. We judge incoming sensory experiences based on this anchor.* In the example above, the anchor point that we would ordinarily use to judge height would be the average height of the hundreds and possibly thousands of people we have met throughout our lives. As we go through life meeting people and observing how tall or short they are, we begin to develop in our own minds an average that becomes an anchor by which we judge the height of other new people we meet. We perceive not only the nonverbal characteristic of height relative to the anchor we have developed from our past experiences but also other communication variables such as attractiveness, trustworthiness, intelligence, speaking fluency, and—the object of Sherif's concern—the position taken in a message.

Have you ever considered what makes you agree or disagree with another person's statements? Likewise, have you ever wondered why people accepted or did not accept what you had to say to them? It should be apparent from our discussion that an important determinant of our agreement or disagreement with another individual is how we perceive the message we are listening to. If we are listening to a political candidate and we perceive the position in his or her message as being consistent with our own beliefs, attitudes, and values, we are more likely to accept the message than if we perceive the position as being inconsistent with our beliefs, attitudes, and values. This observation makes simple common sense. Most of us have known for years that we should not expect atheists to agree with sermons preached on Sunday morning and that we should not expect Republicans to accept points made by a Democrat. But let's go a little further and consider the basic principles of the social judgment involvement model so that we can better understand the process underlying what seems to be common sense.

Try to picture a continuum that runs from a point representing those extremely in favor of abortion to a point representing those extremely opposed to abortion. We could place anyone who has ever thought about the issue of abortion at all somewhere on this continuum. Some would be closer to the positive end of the continuum, in which case they would support abortion. Others would be closer to the negative end, in which case they would oppose it. Further, consider that we could divide this continuum into nine equal spaces so that it would be possible to consider someone who was extremely in favor of abortion as a 1 and someone who was extremely opposed to abortion as a 9. At this point, we have in Fig. 4.4 what many behavioral scientists would call an attitude scale. The person's attitude would be that point on the continuum with which they most agree. Thus, we could call someone a 2, a 7, or a 5, depending on how they felt about the issue of abortion.

Fig. 4.4 An attitude scale.

The social judgment involvement approach has gone beyond the simple placement of an individual at one point on a continuum. Sherif's model suggests that all of us have not only a point on a continuum that we find most acceptable but also another point that we find most unacceptable. Thus, if an individual is a 1 and extremely in favor of abortion, we would most likely expect that the most unfavorable position on the continuum would be a 9. These two points, according to Sherif, could be considered "anchor points" for an individual's attitude toward abortion. These attitude anchor points develop over the years through acquisition of information and experiences. They serve as the basis for judging and perceiving messages concerned with the attitude under consideration.

If person A, who is extremely in favor of abortion, hears a message from anyone regarding abortion, person A perceives that message relative to the positions that he or she finds most acceptable (i.e., 1) and most unacceptable (i.e., 9). Obviously, this is an extreme example. Most of us aren't clear out on the end of the continuum on many issues. But we hope that this extreme example is parallel to the earlier one we used concerning height. Because person A has anchor points of 1 and 9 regarding acceptable and unacceptable positions, a message that falls at position 4 on this continuum may not be perceived by this individual as a neutral or moderate message. Just as a group of extremely tall basketball players could make someone who is six feet two inches tall look short, an extreme anchor point of 1 could make a "moderate message" about abortion appear to be antiabortion to someone who is extremely in favor of abortion. This is one of the problems that moderates have in our society. When a moderate speaks out, the extremists inevitably believe that the person is a traitor or maybe even the enemy.

One of the most striking examples in recent history of this problem of misperception was Dr. Martin Luther King. Dr. King, a Nobel-Prize-winning civil rights leader, was frequently hated, feared, and vilified by other blacks in this country for being an "Uncle Tom." He was perceived as an "Uncle Tom" because the speeches he gave were, if we are to be objective, relatively moderate. His messages were never extreme. To the black extremists who were advocating a separate black nation or wholesale murder of white people, Dr. King's messages were perceived as totally unacceptable and almost "antiblack." At the same time that Dr. King was being rejected and vilified by

Message Perception

black extremists, white bigots were also castigating him. They considered him to be a revolutionary of the worst sort, and they feared him greatly. Again, although King's messages were "moderate" by most standards, to anyone extremely prejudiced against blacks he seemed to be a revolutionary agitator. From the perspective of today, if you examine Dr. King's messages in light of the times in which he was active, he will appear to be moderate in his speaking. However, to those on opposite ends of the spectrum, Dr. King appeared to be opposed to their respective points of view because he took moderate positions that did not seem moderate to them, *relative to their own attitude anchor points* on the issue of racial equality. The explanation for this kind of misperception is suggested in Fig. 4.4.

Latitude of acceptance In addition to a point on a continuum that is most acceptable to us, there are several other positions that are also acceptable even though they are not our most preferred positions. Those positions that are most acceptable to us, and others that are also acceptable to us are called our "latitude of acceptance." In his research, Sherif discovered that any message that was perceived as falling within an individual's latitude of acceptance was accepted by the individual. This finding suggests that even if our use of language, nonverbal messages, and credibility are not necessarily ideal, if the major thrust of our message is perceived as falling within a person's latitude of acceptance, it will be accepted.

Latitude of rejection In addition to points on a continuum that are acceptable to us, there are also points that are unacceptable. There is always a position that is most unacceptable, as well as other positions that, although less objectionable, are still not acceptable to us. The most unacceptable position, plus any other objectionable positions, constitute the "latitude of rejection." Sherif's research suggests that any message that is perceived as falling within the latitude of rejection will always be rejected by the receiver. Even if the message is well-presented and well-worded and the source has high credibility, it will still not be accepted by the receiver.

Latitude of noncommitment The area between the latitudes of acceptance and rejection is termed the "latitude of noncommitment." These are positions that are neither unacceptable nor acceptable to listeners. You should not infer from the term noncommitment that messages falling within this area would be neither accepted nor rejected. In all likelihood, persons receiving messages will perceive them as falling within the latitudes of either acceptance or rejection. There are occasions, to be sure, when people cannot decide and thus neither accept nor reject a message. But we suspect that in most cases messages are perceived to be either in the latitude of acceptance, near the most acceptable position, or in the latitude of rejection, away from the most acceptable position. Thus, it is usually to the advantage of a communicator to attempt to formulate messages that fall within or near the latitude of acceptance.

Assimilation and contrast effects Sherif also discovered that any message falling *close* to the latitude of acceptance would be perceived as acceptable. This perception of a message as more acceptable than it really is, because of its closeness to a person's anchor point, is called the "assimilation effect." This is an important concept of message perception. We can take advantage of the assimilation effect when speaking with people. It is not always necessary for us to formulate a message that falls within the latitude of acceptance. The assimilation effect can cause the message to be perceived as acceptable, even though by "objective standards" it may be a bit outside the latitude of acceptance.

Although the assimilation effect is important to communication, probably even more important is the "contrast effect." The contrast effect is the opposite of the assimilation effect. The contrast effect causes a message to be perceived as unacceptable, even though by "objective standards" it may be a bit outside the latitude of rejection. Once a message is perceived as falling within the latitude of rejection, there is no way through communication that we can have the message accepted. By definition, a message perceived by a listener as falling within the latitude of rejection is rejected, regardless of the various communicative skills of the message sender. The contrast effect can be thought of as a process in which a message, through the process of perception, is contrasted away, or perceptually shifted, from the most acceptable position of the receiver. As we discussed in the example of Martin Luther King, someone who presents a seemingly moderate message may discover that some listeners find the message unacceptable and reject it because of the contrast effect. The contrast effect is a phenomenon that communicators should attempt to avoid. When preparing a message, we should be very careful to analyze thoroughly the latitudes of acceptance and rejection of potential receivers of our message so that we can place our messages either within or near the latitude of acceptance, not in or near the latitude of rejection. In so doing, we will attempt to take advantage of the assimilation effect and avoid the consequences of a contrast effect.

Involvement We would like to make one final comment regarding message perception and the social judgment involvement approach. Sherif and subsequent researchers have frequently observed that there is a pattern that occurs fairly consistently regarding the *size* of the latitudes of acceptance and rejection. For persons who are highly "ego-involved" with an issue, the latitude of rejection appears to be much wider than it is for persons who are not highly "ego-involved." The highly ego-involved person is one who has a strong interest in a topic. A highly ego-involving topic for an individual is one that is strongly related to the individual's needs, values, and self-concept and thus of significant importance to that individual. Thus, we could guess that persons who are Catholic, Mormon, or members of Right-to-Life organizations would be highly ego-involved with the previously mentioned topic of abortion. Presenting a message perception and the social judgment involvement approach. Sherif and point of view. The reason is that any message that could be construed as defending abortion would very likely fall either right within their extremely wide latitude of rejection or certainly close enough for a contrast effect to occur. In either case, the message would be rejected.

On the other hand, persons with low ego-involvement in an issue tend to have narrow latitudes of acceptance and rejection. These people have a wide noncommitment area. Thus we do not have some of the problems of the contrast effect that we experience with highly committed or ego-involved persons.

If you will think back to the discussion of Martin Luther King and the reaction of white bigots and black extremists to his speeches, it should become apparent that Dr. King was unsuccessful with these extremist groups because of their wide latitudes of rejection and probable contrast effects. It is not surprising to learn that the groups that he had the greatest success with were those of moderate blacks and moderate whites who may have had smaller latitudes of acceptance and rejection and were thus more able to perceive his moderate messages as acceptable.

One of the points we should make in this discussion of message perception is that whether you explain the perception of messages through the selectivity model or whether you employ a social judgment involvement model, it is apparent that messages are not received but perceived. The importance of the perception process comes down to a very basic fact that many communicators are not willing to face. What you say or what you mean to say is not nearly as important as the way it is perceived by someone. We never tell it like we hear it; we tell it the way we *perceive* it. All of us perceive according to our prior values, attitudes, and beliefs. Therefore, whenever we try to repeat something we have heard, it is important for us to take into account our frames of reference that might possibly affect the way we perceive messages. Likewise, as we are trying to talk or write to other people, we should formulate our messages with the frames of reference of potential receivers in mind. We should then attempt to anticipate the various kinds of distortion, assimilations, and contrasts that may occur as people receive our messages. We must be willing to face the fact that our messages will be avoided, forgotten, distorted, perceptually shifted, and contrasted away from the position we are taking if our receivers do not agree with us. It is important for us to figure out ways of constructing messages that can be perceived as similar to the beliefs, attitudes, and value systems of the people to whom we are communicating. Above all, the importance of ego-involvement and the link of the message topic to self-concept should never be forgotten. As we discussed in the chapter on motivation, we ultimately will arrange our beliefs, perceptions of messages, and perceptions of people in ways that will positively reinforce our self-concept. This factor should be remembered in the construction of messages. It is our self-concept and those of others that will ultimately determine how latitudes of acceptance and rejection develop. Self-concept also determines how people engage in selective perception and social judgment processes.

SUMMARY

In this chapter, we have discussed the inputs received by all people from their environment. It is apparent that we do not see the world as it is, but rather we see it through our own perceptual filters. These perceptual filters are based on all of the factors of motivation and past experience previously discussed. These factors significantly affect the ways we perceive people and the ways we perceive messages. Underlying the perception of events, people, and messages is the need for consistency. This need results in our attempting to obtain order in our perceptions in many ways.

Our perceptions of communicators are usually thought of in terms of credibility and attractiveness. Both of these qualities are perceived; they do not exist absolutely in the communicator. Finally, messages are perceived relative to anchor points by which we can selectively distort the messages we receive.

KEY TERMS AND CONCEPTS

Anchor Point
Assimilation Effect
Categorization
Communicator Credibility
Communicator Intent
Competence Component
Contrast Effect
Decoding
Dynamism Component
Gestalt Approach
Good Form
Implicit Personality Theory
Involvement
Latitude of Acceptance
Latitude of Noncommitment
Latitude of Rejection
Macromeaning
Micromeaning

Order
Perceived Attractiveness
Perception
Person Perception
Physical Appearance Component
Proximity
Selective Perception
Selective Reception
Selective Retention
Self-Fulfilling Prophecy
Social Judgment Involvement Approach
Social-Liking Component
Stabilization
Stereotype
Structuralist Approach
Task-Respect Component
Trait Approach
Trustworthiness Component

SUGGESTED READINGS

Jones, Russell A., *Self-Fulfilling Prophecies*. Hillsdale, N.J.: Lawrence Erlbaum Associates, Publishers, 1977. This book provides an excellent overview of the research concerned with interpersonal perception and prior expectations. The "self-fulfilling prophecy" discussed in this chapter and other chapters of our book is presented in great depth in this book.

Schneider, David J., Albert H. Hastorf and Phoebe C. Ellsworth, *Person Perception, Second Edition*. Reading, Mass.: Addison-Wesley, 1979. This extremely readable book concerns the ways we perceive people. There is a brief review of theories of perception and a very complete and up-to-date review of research in the field.

Sherif, Carolyn W., Muzafer Sherif, and Roger E. Nebergall, *Attitude and Attitude Change*. Philadelphia: W.B. Saunders Company, 1965. This was the first and remains the major statement of the social judgment involvement approach to attitudes. It is an excellent statement of the way message perception relates to the holding of prior attitudes.

5 Reasoning

Our description of the intrapersonal processing elements of the human communication system is almost complete. We have discussed what motivates the system and how the system perceives informational inputs from the environment. We will now discuss how the system transforms the stimuli it receives from these two sources into outputs. In the human communication system we call this transformation process *reasoning*. We reason to understand our environment in light of our motivations; this process in turn helps us to remain an open system and survive. Reasoning also helps us maintain motivational and perceptual consistency. The stimuli that we perceive in our environment and that act as a basis for our reasoning are called evidence. We use evidence to draw inferences or conclusions about the world around us and about how we should respond or output to our environment. Perhaps the most significant barrier to reasoning is its dependence on motivation and perception. It is the intraface between the three intrapersonal processing elements that accounts for the strengths and weaknesses of each.

Reasoning

Red Skelton once did a wonderful sketch in which he played "Freddie the Freeloader." Freddie was hungry and saw people being served in a restaurant. His hunger motivated him, and his perception of the food only increased his desire to obtain food. He had to figure out a way to get it, however, since he also perceived that he was broke. The ways he attempted to get food, including begging, flirting, and stealing were hilarious and pointed out the importance of reasoning as an intrapersonal processing element. In this final chapter on the intrapersonal communication processing subsystem, we discuss the ways in which human communication systems draw conclusions based on their perceptions and motivations. This process is called reasoning. Reasoning is the final stage of communication input processing. By the time the reasoning process is completed, the human system is ready to begin outputting information or behavior. The term "reasoning" is often associated with its more common cousin, "thinking." For the purpose of this text, these terms will be considered to be the same. As with Freddie the Freeloader, our survival often depends on our ability to think or reason.

WHY PEOPLE REASON

We have seen that communication itself is anti-entropic and that the more communicatively active the system, the more open it is and the more likely it is to survive. It is our desire to understand our environment that keeps our system open. An opening system is one in which old ideas and concepts are constantly updated. A closing system, on the other hand, is one in which the desire for understanding has begun to cease and in which the system is no longer searching for new and updated inputs.

However, even an opening system eventually determines that there are many more possible inputs from the environment than it is capable of perceiving. Therefore, it learns to filter its perceptions. What we choose to filter out and what we choose to process are based on the conclusions we draw through reasoning. Remember that we defined reasoning as conclusions based on our motivations and perceptions. What we have, then, is a circular process in which our perceptions and motivations cause us to reason through to certain conclusions, which in turn act to structure future perceptions and motivations.

A primary criterion by which we draw our conclusions about our internal and external world is consistency. As we discussed in Chapter 3, human beings seem to have an innate need to be consistent. Reasoning is the means by which they attempt to remain consistent. People reason, then, to understand their perceptions and motivations and to maintain consistency in their perceptions and motivations. It is the need for consistency that can also cause systems to begin closing because of the fear that new inputs may be inconsistent. A number of theories have been developed to explain this need for consistency.

Dissonance Theory

The importance of the need for consistency is illustrated by Festinger (1957) in his theory of cognitive dissonance. Festinger points out that individuals strive for consistency between (1) their various inputs, (2) their various outputs, and (3) their inputs and outputs. For example, if you perceive yourself as a Democrat you will attempt to structure your voting behavior so that you vote for few, if any, Republicans. You will also attempt to filter out all inputs that do not agree with your political beliefs, and you will keep your outputs consistent with what you believe to be the principles of the Democratic party. Filtering, in other words, will occur in both the inputting and outputting subsystems.

Festinger replaces the word "consistency" with the more neutral term "consonance" and the word "inconsistency" with the term "dissonance." He uses the term "cognition" to mean "any knowledge, opinion, or belief about the environment, about oneself, or about one's behavior" (Festinger, 1957, p.3).

The term cognition thus refers to both motivations and perceptions as they are used in this text. In these terms, reasoning can be considered the process by which we draw conclusions based on our cognitions in order to reduce dissonance and achieve consonance.

The fear of creating dissonance directly affects the reasoning process. The effect that dissonance, either felt or anticipated, will have on the reasoning component is related directly to the amount of dissonance. Some inconsistencies are perceived as not very important and as creating little dissonance, and therefore they have little effect on reasoning. For example, say that you are a Democrat. Say that you subscribe to a local newspaper, even with the knowledge that it tends to support Republican candidates. However, since it is the only newspaper in town, this inconsistency is not very troublesome to you. But take another hypothetical example. Anticipating that a particular piece of land will be rezoned, you invest money in it, and then the local Democratic candidate for mayor comes out in opposition to the rezoning. This situation can produce potentially serious inconsistency and much dissonance for you, especially if you end up voting for a Republican in order to salvage your investment.

The main factors determining the amount of dissonance that will occur are the number and importance of the cognitions involved. If the only two cognitions that conflict for you are political affiliation versus land investment, then the amount of dissonance will be less than if a number of other cognitions are also involved such as friendship with either of the candidates and/or their supporters, other campaign issues, and so on. The importance of the cognitions is equally as influential as the number in determining the amount of dissonance. If you have most or all of your money tied up in the land investment, the dissonance will be much greater than if you have invested only a small amount.

According to Festinger, there are four ways in which you may handle such inconsistency or dissonance, as illustrated in Fig. 5.1. First, you might alter the reasoning that caused the cognitions to be inconsistent. You might reason that you knew the investment was risky when you bought the land and that sometimes such investments do not work out. Second, you might change the behavior that caused the dissonance. You might vow that you will never again invest in anything that might become a political issue. The other behavior change, if the investment is important enough, would be simply to vote for the Republican and perhaps even work to get the Republican elected. Third, you might attempt to change the environment. You might visit the Democratic headquarters and attempt to change the candidate's mind about opposing the land rezoning. Finally, you might add other cognitions that would relieve the inconsistency. You might discover other issues about which you and the Republican agree, and you might therefore determine that in this case voting for a Republican is not so bad. "Besides, isn't it only the ignorant who always vote a straight party ticket?"

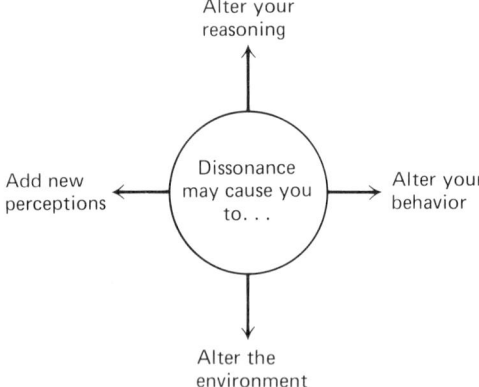

Fig. 5.1 Ways of reducing dissonance.

One of the major problems with Festinger's dissonance theory is that he does not offer us a method of predicting which of the four means of reducing dissonance will be chosen. Festinger seems to imply that all four methods are equally probable. Even though dissonance theory did not appear first historically, we have chosen to discuss it before the other consistency theories because we feel it is the most complete and the most directly relevant to reasoning. It is by far the most widely accepted of the consistency theories.

Other Consistency Theories

An early examiner of the consistency principle was Fritz Heider (1946). He developed what has become known as balance theory. Balance theory suggests that if you judge X to be of potential benefit to your welfare, you cannot at the same time judge Y (which is also judged to be of benefit) and X to be antagonistic to one another and still maintain a stable or balanced cognitive structure. According to Heider, X and Y may be things, people, the products of people, or the characteristics of people. Some examples of balanced and unbalanced situations are given in Fig. 5.2. They reflect positive (+) and negative (−) orientations of X, Y, and person (P).

An unbalanced situation, according to this theory, causes the person (P) to change his or her reasoning regarding X, Y, or the relationship between X and Y. This theory is very simple but clear in defining consistency and inconsistency. It does not, however, deal with the strength of attitudes, the possibility of changing one's reasoning regarding more than one element, or the prediction of which option for regaining consistency will be chosen.

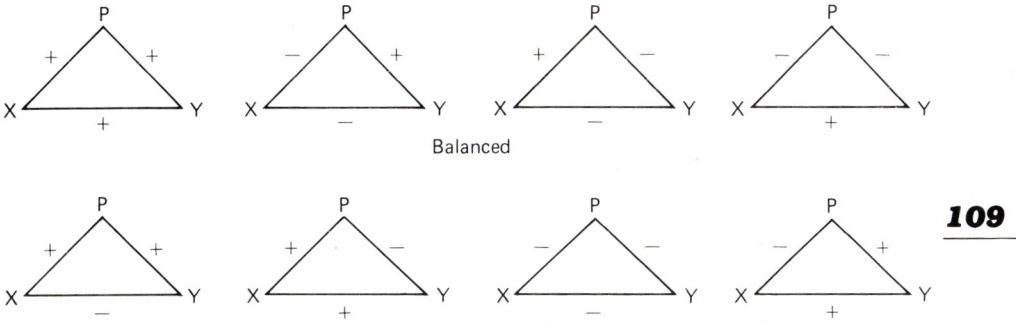

Fig. 5.2 Examples of balanced and unbalanced situations.

In 1953, Theodore M. Newcomb used Heider's balance theory to develop some propositions concerning dyadic communication. He believed that the tendency toward balance is characteristic of interpersonal as well as intrapersonal systems. He suggested that the orientations that two people have toward one another affect how they perceive a third entity. If the two people perceive each other positively, the likelihood is increased that they will perceive the other entity similarly. When the situation is unbalanced, a pressure develops for one of the pair to change. Otherwise, the interpersonal relationship will deteriorate. The attempt at change usually involves the use of communication. According to Newcomb, the decision about which orientation will be changed is determined by the strength of the bond between the two people involved and the strength of the attitude of each toward the third entity. As you might expect, the weaker attitude will be the most likely to change.

Osgood (1955) attempted to improve on the consistency theories of Heider and Newcomb. He predicted changes in orientation similar to those of Newcomb. He, like Newcomb, suggested that when an unbalanced perception changes to a balanced one, it is the less extreme position that will be changed. His theory was called congruity theory. Through the use of attitude measurement scales, Osgood was able to quantitatively predict the direction of attitude change. He also suggested that more than one attitude might be changed. Osgood's *congruity theory* has many advantages over Heider's and Newcomb's theories, but it also has some weaknesses. It allows only for changing the reasoning, not the environment, and it also does not account for the bond between the other person and the third entity. Moreover, it measures only one person's attitude strength.

HOW PEOPLE REASON

Understanding and consistency explain why people reason. Now we will explore how they reason. Before we begin a complete discussion of how people reason, we will first examine the nature of the data we use as the basis for drawing reasoned conclusions. These data come primarily from our perceptions of

Reasoning

the environment and are usually termed evidence. Evidence must be inputted into or perceived by the system before reasoning can take place. It is important to realize that not all evidence is qualitatively equal. Some types of evidence are better than others.

Classifications of Evidence

Various authors have tried to classify evidence in many different ways. Some suggest that you should differentiate between first-hand and hearsay evidence, that is, evidence that you directly perceive yourself as opposed to evidence that someone else perceives and tells you about. An example might be taking a test drive in a new car you are thinking about buying (first-hand evidence) as opposed to having someone who already owns such a car telling you how well it runs (hearsay evidence). Other authors like to classify evidence on the basis of whether it is written or unwritten. In a court of law, for example, written evidence is considered to be better than unwritten evidence. Still others choose to differentiate between general and specific evidence, general evidence being more inexact as to amounts, names, and sources. "Authorities say that insulating your home will help save energy" would be an example of general evidence. On the other hand, the following statement is an example of specific evidence: "The Department of Energy suggests that improper insulation can cost you up to 40% loss of heat in your house, and therefore you should check to see if you have the current insulation standards of R-38 for ceilings, R-18 for walls, and R-19 for floors (R value indicating ability of a material to prevent heat from passing through it)."

The preceding categories represent just a few of the ways in which evidence has been classified. They illustrate the point that all evidence is not equal in quality. Whenever feasible, you should attempt to find evidence of the highest quality and quantity possible on which to base your reasoning.

Types of Evidence

There are four basic types of evidence: observations, examples, statistics, and testimony. It is through the use of one or more of these types of evidence that we are able to draw reasoned conclusions. As you will see later in this text, the use of evidence does not guarantee the truth of a statement. All four types of evidence must be tested before they can be considered truthful.

Observations We are using the term "observations" here as it is used by Berlo (1960, pp. 219-225) to refer to a sentence that can be labeled as either true or false. We use this term instead of the term "fact" because of the problems inherent in the latter. The word "fact" carries the implied meaning that it is true. If we say that facts are true, we run into problems because (1) truth is relative and (2) some facts are neither true nor false but just "are." When we say that truth is relative, we mean that something may be true for one person at one particular time but not true for someone else at another time. At one time, many of us believed that Santa Claus was a "true" person. In the same way, at one time almost everyone believed the planets and stars revolved around the earth. A fact, then, is true only as long as someone believes it is true.

Debate is one way for college students to learn the value of evidence.
PHOTO BY CAROLE DUGAN

The second problem with the term fact is that it refers to physical reality. Physical reality either exists or it does not exist. It is not true or false. A pencil is not true or false; it just is. On the other hand, statements *about* physical reality can be true or false. These statements are often labeled "statements of fact" or "observations" as we have done here. Observations, then, are not facts but are statements of fact or about facts. The key term is "statement"—a belief about the nature of physical reality that provides us with observational evidence. Such statements require no authoritative support, and yet they are the most powerful form of evidence. Observations can be first-hand, that is, made on the basis of personal perception, or they can be hearsay, that is, made by someone else.

Examples An example is a situation that shows what other situations are like. Throughout this text, we have tried to provide examples to illustrate various comments we have made about human communication. Examples help us illustrate, classify, dramatize, and support our comments. People generally like examples, especially if the example illustrates and reinforces a statement that they already believe to be true. Examples are much less effective when they are the only type of evidence offered to prove a point. In this instance, an example must be so typical that other examples will immediately come to mind. Examples must be significant by relating directly to matters that the reasoner believes to be important. Finally, when examples are the only form of evidence used, they must be free from obvious weakness or else they can easily be attacked. People tend to prefer examples over other less vivid types of evidence.

Reasoning

Statistics One can think of statistics as simply a large number of examples. Even though statistics are logically stronger than examples, they do not seem to have the same appeal for the receiver. Think, for instance, about the commercials you have seen on television for the United Way. The commercial often shows a handicapped child, tells a little about the child, and finally shows the child being helped by the United Way. At the end of the TV spot, some statistics might be presented on how many people were helped by the charity. However, this presentation takes up only a brief portion of the message. The makers of the commercial realize that one good example is probably more effective than a large number of statistics. Logically, statistics should be more effective, but emotionally, the example works better, even though it does not necessarily prove that the problem is widespread.

COURTESY OF UNITED WAY OF AMERICA CAMPAIGN

There are some important matters that must be taken into account when using statistics as evidence. You must be aware of the source of the statistics. It is a very simple matter for a biased source to mislead you with statistics. In a great many cases, the source from which you get your statistics is not the source that collected them. A newspaper, for example, can very easily miscopy or misinterpret statistical information reported from another source. The statistics we hear are often combinations of figures and interpretations with relevant information left out. A survey of how people might vote in a future election would be more accurate if conducted with registered voters than with all citizens. In many cases this information is not reported. Even worse, we are sometimes treated to such oversimplifications as "Our ABC/CBS/NBC poll shows that Candidate X will beat Candidate Y in the upcoming election," with no indication if the survey results were even close.

Testimony The form of evidence least preferred by receivers is testimony. We use the term testimony to refer to the opinions of experts or authorities about a subject. The best type of testimony is a direct quotation from the authority. The quality of the authority is often very hard to judge. Even authorities often make offhand guesses. In order for testimony to be considered valuable, the evidence on which the statement is based and the reasoning behind the conclusion should both be stated. In other words, your tests for your own evidence and reasoning should also be used in determining the acceptability of the testimony of others.

FORMS OF REASONING

Once you have gathered and tested evidence, you are ready to draw some conclusions from that evidence. This is the process we have defined as reasoning. Many authors refer to this process as *inference* because drawing inferences is the main object of reasoning. We infer conclusions based on evidence. A common definition of an inference is that it is a prediction about the unknown made on the basis of the known. Our inferential ability allows us to identify relationships among pieces of evidence and to draw conclusions based on those relationships. It is to be hoped that the analysis of evidence and the inferences we draw from that analysis are rigorous and logical rather than imprecise and illogical. Whether the inferences we make are logical or illogical will depend in great part on the form of reasoning we use and on how we use that form of reasoning.

In the introductory chapter, we pointed out how important the various approaches to reasoning were to the development of the communication discipline as well as to all intellectual thought. We introduced at that point the two major forms of reasoning that have dominated our history: deductive reasoning and inductive reasoning. The deductive pattern dominated almost all of human intellectual thought until the Renaissance, when the inductive form of reasoning challenged for equality. In this section we will examine both the inductive and deductive forms of reasoning as well as a newer model developed by Toulmin (1958), which combines many of the best features of both the inductive and deductive forms.

Deductive Reasoning

Deduction is probably the oldest known form of reasoning. The first systematic examination of deductive reasoning was done by Aristotle. His system of deduction involved the use of premises to lead to a conclusion. He demonstrated that if the premises were true and the relationship between them were valid, then the conclusion had to be correct. He suggested that reasoning serves two purposes: (1) the proving of certain conclusions and (2) the development of new conclusions from agreed upon premises.

In the deductive reasoning process, the premises are always much more general in nature than the conclusion. For example, in Aristotle's classic example of deduction (All men are mortal [premise]; Socrates is a man [premise]; therefore, Socrates is mortal [conclusion]), we can see that the two premises represent rather more general information than the conclusion, which applies to a specific case. Thus, deductive reasoning is defined as the drawing of conclusions about a specific case from general principles. The general principles from which we deduce specific conclusions are often called generalizations. An even simpler definition of deduction, then, might be "going from generalizations to specifics."

The model often used to illustrate an instance of deductive reasoning is called a *syllogism*. Aristotle's classic example cited above is a syllogism and is most commonly written in the following manner:

All men are mortal. (Major premise)

Socrates is a man. (Minor premise)

Therefore, Socrates is mortal. (Conclusion)

All syllogisms contain two premises and a conclusion. Very often, however, one of the premises is unstated. When this is the case, the syllogism is called an *enthymeme*. The enthymeme is a very commonly used form of deductive reasoning. The statement "Socrates is mortal because he is a man" would be an enthymeme derived from the above syllogism. Enthymemes make it difficult to analyze the quality of the reasoning that is being used because the listener must supply the missing premise. What premise is missing in the statement "You will be a good communicator because you are reading this book"? Think about it. Do you think you could write the syllogism on which this enthymeme is based? If you proposed the following, you would be correct.

Anyone who reads this book will be a good communicator. (Missing premise)

You are reading this book. (Minor premise)

Therefore, you will be a good communicator. (Conclusion)

Simply recognizing a syllogism is not enough. You must also determine if the premises are accurate and if the relationship between them is valid. In our previous section on evidence, we discussed the means by which one can determine the relative truth of a statement. We must now look at the types of valid and invalid relationships between premises. The important point to remember here is that the truth or falsity of a deductive conclusion is independent of the relative validity of the syllogism. It is quite possible to have a valid syllogism with a false conclusion. In such a case, one or both of the premises would have to be false. In the example concerning the reading of this book, we ourselves are unwilling to say that the statement "anyone who reads this book will be a good communicator" is absolutely true or that the conclusion is absolutely true, yet the syllogism is valid. We do believe that if the term "better" were substituted for "good" in the syllogism, it would be both true and valid. Some might even argue with that, but we hope not.

The type of classical syllogism that we have been discussing is called a *categorical syllogism*. This type of syllogism has several rules that determine its validity.

1. It can have three and only three statements: a major premise, a minor premise, and a conclusion.
2. It must deal with three main terms or ideas (i.e., mortality, man or mankind, and Socrates). These terms or ideas are labeled the major term (mortality), the middle term (mankind), and the minor term (Socrates).
3. The middle term must be all-inclusive in one premise (i.e., it must follow a word like "all," "every," "any," "no," or "nothing"). Terms like "some," "many," and "often" are not all-inclusive.
4. If one premise is negative (i.e., with terms like "no," "not," or "nothing"), then the conclusion must also be negative.
5. A valid conclusion is impossible with both premises negative.

There are two other types of deductive reasoning that were added by logicians after Aristotle. The first of these is the *disjunctive syllogism*. This type of syllogism has as its major premise an "either/or" statement. Such statements might be: "We will either do the homework or we will go out to get pizza"; "The light is either on or off"; "Either the Democrats or the Republicans will win the election." The minor premise affirms or denies one part of the major premise, and the conclusion then affirms or denies the remainder of the major premise. An example of a disjunctive syllogism is the following:

Professor X is either teaching or in her office. (Major premise)

Professor X is not in her office. (Minor premise)

Therefore, she is teaching. (Conclusion)

Using the same major premise, we can derive other possible valid conclusions:

Professor X is in her office. (Minor premise)

Therefore, she is not teaching. (Conclusion)

Professor X is not teaching. (Minor premise)

Therefore, she is in her office. (Conclusion)

Professor X is teaching. (Minor premise)

Therefore, she is not in her office. (Conclusion)

The only two rules that apply to a disjunctive syllogism are (1) that the two choices be mutually exclusive and (2) that the two alternatives be all-inclusive. If Professor X sometimes taught a course in her office, then the choices in the major premise would not be mutually exclusive. If it were possible that she could be someplace else, then the two alternatives would not be all-inclusive. In our example, then, the syllogism is invalid because both possibilities exist. In the case of a light switch, such a syllogism would be valid because a light cannot be both on and off and there is no third alternative.

The third common type of deductive reasoning is the *hypothetical syllogism*. It follows an "if . . . then" pattern for the major premise. In a hypothetical syllogism, the "if" clause is called the *antecedent* and the "then" clause is called the *consequent*. The following is an example of a hypothetical syllogism with the antecedent and consequent labeled.

> If you complete a college degree (antecedent), then you should be able to get a good-paying job (consequent).
>
> You will complete a college degree in June. (Minor premise)
>
> Therefore, you should be able to get a good-paying job. (Conclusion)

In a hypothetical syllogism, the minor premise either has to confirm the antecedent or deny the consequent. Denial of the antecedent or confirmation of the consequent is invalid. In the example above, having a good-paying job does not mean that one has a college degree.

The biggest problem with the deductive form of reasoning is that it is difficult to use in everyday situations. One rarely considers statements that fit a rigid, all-inclusive, either/or, or "if . . . then" pattern. When we do have such situations, deductive reasoning provides an excellent test of the validity of the reasoning. A second weakness of deductive reasoning is that the conclusion provides nothing new over what is contained in the premises. It only makes the information explicit. The greatest value of deduction is in providing an ideal model of how our reasoning should work, but when we attempt to apply this model too strictly, we find it difficult. It is like trying to apply very strict codes of moral conduct to all situations. They do not always fit. Finally, you must always remember that logical validity and truth are independent of one another.

Inductive Reasoning

Inductive reasoning is much more flexible than deductive reasoning, and it allows one to go beyond the information contained in the premises or reasons. Whereas in deductive reasoning one goes from generalizations (premises) to specific cases (conclusions), in inductive reasoning the process is reversed. In inductive reasoning, one moves from specific cases to generalizations. In order to be valid, however, the conclusion of induction must account for all of the cases. With the inductive reasoning process, we not only account for the known cases but we go beyond them to similar but unknown cases. We all use inductive reasoning without really being aware of it. For example, when we negotiate higher salaries, we probably generalize from the inflation rate for the past several years. If you have studied under a professor for two courses and have felt you learned a lot, you assume that you will probably learn a lot in this professor's other courses. The key word in those two examples is "probably." Unlike deduction which is based on certainty and validity, induction is based on *probability*.

Probability suggests that an inductive conclusion is not guaranteed but that it is likely. Probability allows for the possibility that the conclusion will be wrong. In our discussion of evidence we talked about examples as a form of evidence. Inductive reasoning is often called "reasoning from example." The same problems that arise from the use of examples as evidence also apply to reasoning from example. One must be constantly aware of the number of instances represented, the typicality of the examples, the significance in terms of size and scope, the timeliness of the example, and the number of contrary examples. Thus the more timely, the more typical, and the greater the number of examples used, with few opposed examples, the greater the probability that an induction based on the example(s) will be reliable. The goal of inductive reasoning is reliability, that is, a conclusion that has a good chance of being correct.

Scientific induction strives to express the probability or reliability of its conclusions through the use of statistics. Using the terms we have already introduced, we could define the scientific method as a form of inductive reasoning that draws conclusions called hypotheses and theories from specific cases or examples and then tests those conclusions through research studies, which utilize a form of probability testing called statistics. You may have heard of the term ".05 level of significance." This term simply means that for every 100 examples covered by a theory or hypothesis, you probably will find fewer than 5 contrary cases. A scientist who finds more than 5 contrary cases or a probability greater than .05 will reject the conclusion as unreliable.

Because of its reliance on probable rather than absolute conclusions, induction is more applicable to many of the situations that occur in day-to-day life. Therefore, it is used more often than deductive reasoning. However, the fact that inductive reasoning does rely on probable rather than absolute conclusions suggests its major weakness. If you do not look at or make a statement about all of the specific cases but look at only a few examples and generalize to the rest, you can never be sure of the absolute validity of your conclusion. One of the nice things about deductive and inductive reasoning is that they are complementary, that is, we can combine them and try to eliminate the weaknesses of both. Toulmin developed what has come to be called an inferential pattern of reasoning even though, as we have seen, all reasoning is inferential or uses inference. It is a contemporary approach to the process of reasoning that has much to offer to students interested in improving their reasoning ability.

Inferential Reasoning

Inferential reasoning, as developed by Toulmin, was designed to aid the student of argument. However, we believe that its uses go far beyond the original purpose. We believe it is useful as an aid to reasoning for any purpose. We hope that each of you will study the model we are about to present with the goal of understanding it so thoroughly that you will be able to mentally visualize and use it to analyze all communicative inputs.

Toulmin starts out with three basic model elements: data, claim, and warrant.*

---

*The following four diagrams are reprinted from *The Uses of Argument* by Stephen Toulmin by permission of Cambridge University Press. © 1958.

Reasoning

Data ─────────→ Claim
         │
      Warrant

By *data*, Toulmin means what we have called evidence. The *claim* refers to our concept of a conclusion. The *warrant* is the underlying assumption that relates the data to the conclusion; it is very similar to the major premise of a syllogism. Toulmin offers the following example to prove the claim that "Harry is a British subject."

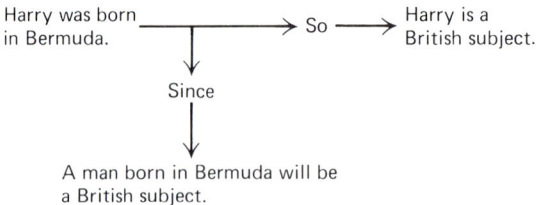

The terms "so" and "since" are added in order that the argument can be read: "Harry was born in Bermuda (data), *so* Harry is a British subject *since* a man born in Bermuda will be a British subject." The warrant is the logic that connects the data to the claim. Any argument needs, at its very minimum, these three elements. It is possible to have more than one piece of data and more than one warrant without violating inferential reasoning. It is also possible to read the diagram by starting with the warrant: "A man born in Bermuda will be a British subject, and Harry was born in Bermuda, so Harry is a British subject." Thus far it looks a lot like a syllogism, doesn't it?

All persons born in Bermuda will be British subjects. (Major premise)

Harry was born in Bermuda. (Minor premise)

Therefore, Harry is a British subject. (Conclusion)

Just as it is possible to leave one of the premises unstated (an entheymeme) in a syllogism, it is possible to leave out the warrant in inferential reasoning. As Toulmin suggests, ". . . the warrant is, in a sense, incidental and explanatory." This is why he differentiates data and warrants, that is, data must be explicit in the argument but warrants can be implicit.

The last three parts of the Toulmin model are the backing, the qualifier, and the rebuttal.

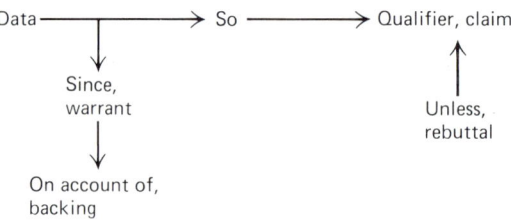

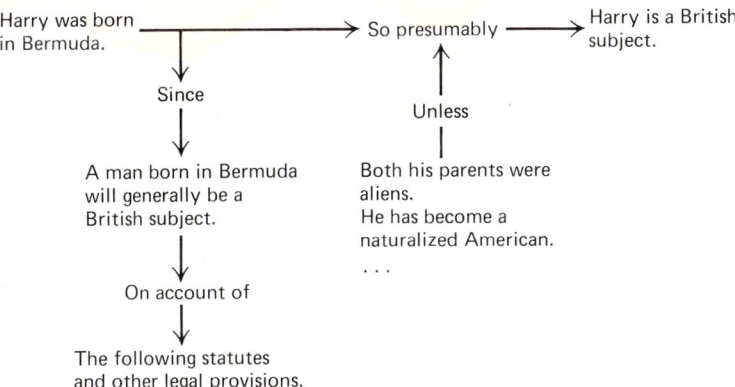

The qualifier and the rebuttal are very similar in that they both refer to the claim. The qualifier comments on the probability or reliability of the claim, while the rebuttal offers possible conditions whereby the claim would not be accepted. Even with these two elements, one could still question this reasoning on the basis of the warrant; therefore, backing is added to the warrant. Such backing can be either more logic or more evidence. Can you now read in sentence form the entire argument for claiming Harry's British citizenship from the diagram? Give it a try.

Inferential reasoning is probably the most useful of the three forms for students, but it is also the hardest to master. It can provide some very helpful insights and is useful in a wide variety of situations. For example, it can help you analyze the inputs you receive by allowing you to break them down into their basic elements and examine the evidence, logic, and reasoning that lead to the conclusion. You can check each separate part. As a communicator, it allows you to construct reasoned arguments by first deciding on your claim, then on the evidence by which you will support it, then on the warrant with its backing, and finally on the various rebuttal and qualifying statements. Inferential reasoning is valuable because it grows directly out of its two predecessors, deductive and inductive reasoning.

FALLACIES OF REASONING

Up to this point, we have discussed why and how people reason through the use of evidence and logic. We have tended to focus on correct reasoning that leads to correct conclusions. At this point, we will turn to those pitfalls of reasoning that lead to incorrect conclusions. These snares are called *fallacies*. Conclusions based on one or more fallacies should not be accepted. Yet it is very easy to be fooled by a fallacy because it gives the appearance of correct evidence and reasoning. Speakers use fallacies both intentionally and unintentionally, and thus a receiver should constantly be on the lookout for the following fallacies of reasoning.

We believe the best contemporary discussion of the fallacies of reasoning is that of Kahane (1976). Kahane divides fallacious reasoning into two basic categories: (1) reasoning that is fallacious because it is invalid and (2) reasoning that is fallacious even though it is valid. In other words, the validity of an argument is not a guarantee of its correctness. Fallacies can occur in both valid and invalid reasoning. This distinction relates directly back to the one we made earlier between validity and truth. Its importance will become clear as we discuss reasoning fallacies.

Fallacies in Invalid Arguments

1. *Appeal to Authority* is the fallacy based on the type of evidence we earlier called testimony. Testimony can become fallacious when there is an improper appeal made to the authority or expert, for example by implying that because a person is an expert in one field, he or she is an expert in all fields, or by assuming that authorities can never be wrong or disagree. Reasoning based on these or any of the other testimony problems discussed earlier is likely to be fallacious.

Kahane further divides the appeal to authority fallacy into two variations: popularity and traditional wisdom. The *popularity variation* assumes that public opinion is a form of authority and that if a large enough number of people believe something, it has to be true. We demonstrated this fallacy in our earlier discussion of the once popular belief that the planets and stars revolved around the earth. The corollary to this fallacy is that unpopular ideas must be wrong. Yet this belief is utterly foolish in light of the fact that most great ideas were unpopular at one time. For example, at one time the idea of recognizing mainland China was unpopular until President Nixon visited China and recognition became perceived as popular and advantageous.

The second variation of the appeal to authority fallacy is called *traditional wisdom*. This fallacy appeals to history as an authority. It suggests that the past has been free from mistakes and that what has been done traditionally should be our guide for the present and the future. If our government had succumbed to this fallacy, we might still have slavery, child labor abuse, and dirt roads. There is nothing wrong with looking to the past for guidance, but it should not be accepted as an authority.

2. *Provincialism* is the fallacy that only the familiar can be right and that anything foreign is wrong. This fallacy is also called "narrow-mindedness." The voter who will consider only those candidates for state and federal offices who are from his or her district is demonstrating this fallacy. The "ugly American" who is unwilling to learn about another culture is also practicing provincialism. Loyalty to one's own possessions, group, and culture is good and natural in light of our need for consistency, but it is not a guarantee of truth.

3. *Irrelevant Reason* is a fallacy easy to understand but often hard to spot. It is the use of evidence that does not directly apply to the conclusion. The following is an excellent example of this fallacy.

> The fallacy of *irrelevant reason* was committed on a wholesale basis by the Democrats during the Johnson administration and Republicans during the Nixon administration. In reply to charges that the United States had no business in Vietnam, either morally or to

satisfy our national interests, politicians during that period frequently replied that such talk only prolonged the war by making the enemy believe that America's will to fight was declining. This reply in all likelihood was true, but it was utterly irrelevant to the question of our justification for being in Vietnam (Kahane, 1976, p. 14).

You will also find that some of the other fallacies we will discuss could also fall under this broad classification. One is more likely to find irrelevant reasons in inductive and inferential reasoning than in deductive reasoning because they are easily spotted in the syllogism.

4. *Ambiguity* is the use of words or phrases with more than one meaning or with an unclear meaning so as to mislead. Our language is filled with such ambiguous words and phrases. A current advertisement for a major oil company suggests that the company is making only a very small profit after all other costs are taken out of earnings. The ambiguity lies in the terms "profit" and "costs." The ad suggests that payment to shareholders is a cost, whereas many others would call it a profit. Most of the ambiguity in our language is relatively harmless, but we should be on the alert for the kinds that lead us to a fallacious conclusion.

5. *Slippery Slope* is the fallacy that one action inevitably leads to another and that once the first step is taken, you must take all the other steps. This is like the beginning skier who does not know how to stop or is afraid to even try and so goes from the top of the mountain to the bottom, gaining speed all the way. There are two ways in which this fallacy is commonly used. First, one may object to an action because of all the consequences. Someone might have used this reasoning to object to President Carter's Camp David meetings between the leaders of Israel and Egypt in 1979, citing the fact that all other hostile countries will want to do the same thing.

In reasoning, as in skiing, once you start down a slippery slope, there's no turning back.
PHOTO BY CAROLE DUGAN

A second form of this fallacy occurs when the justification for the first step is also used as justification for all the other steps. This reasoning is often used with regard to freedom of speech and of the press. Some say that people should be able to say or to print anything they like, regardless of whether the information is true or false and regardless of how many people get hurt because of it. However, the United States Supreme Court has ruled that the first amendment is not a license to say or to print anything. The Court has reasoned, as you should, that sometimes a first step does lead to other steps, but sometimes it does not. Like the smart skier, you should know when and how to stop on a slippery slope.

6. *Ad Hominem Argument* is the fallacy of attacking an argument by attacking the person who put the argument forward. There are many examples of the ad hominem argument. In politics, it is often labeled "mud slinging." "You can't believe anything Robert Redford, Jane Fonda, or Ronald Reagan says about politics because they're all just actors!" "Joan Kennedy couldn't be a good First Lady because of her personal problems." "You can't trust anyone over thirty."

A variation of the ad hominem argument is *guilt by association*. This is the fallacy that people are no better or worse than those with whom they associate. This fallacy became a national pastime during the McCarthy Era, when people could be labeled "Communists" if they were seen talking to a member of the Communist party, if they belonged to suspected organizations, or even if they made their living in the same manner as someone labeled a Communist. This fallacy works in reverse in the form of "character witnesses." The reasoning goes that if one can be guilty by association, one can also be innocent by the same criterion. "The boy's father is a minister; he couldn't have robbed that store." This is an example of the "gilt" by association we mentioned in Chapter 4.

The ad hominem argument and its variations may or may not be fallacious. The characteristics of the arguer and his or her associates might be important factors to take into consideration, but they do not, in and of themselves, make the argument true or false. Just because Pope John Paul II is not Italian is no reason to assume that anything will change in the Catholic Church any more than if he were Italian.

7. *Two Wrongs Make a Right* is the fallacy that because someone else does some evil, it is all right for us to do it too ("All people cheat on their income tax"). A good example of this fallacy is to be found in those Republican supporters of Richard Nixon, who defended the financial tactics of the Committee to Reelect the President by saying that "Democrats do the same thing." That statement may or may not be accurate, but it does not justify the behavior. It is similar to the statement, "If I don't do it, somebody else will." Yes, they probably will, but if the action is wrong, it doesn't make you right.

In many organizations this fallacy is so common that it becomes the standard operating procedure (S.O.P.). In many companies such dubious practices as ignoring customer complaints, using office equipment for personal purposes, overcharging, and outright lying have become S.O.P. A builder we know actually orders 10% more lumber than he needs because he "expects" his workers to walk off with some and his neighbors to make "midnight raids." Somebody has to pay for that lumber.

8. *Tokenism* is the fallacy of misleading by making a small number seem larger or by making a part of something seem to be the whole thing. This fallacy was and is practiced extensively by organizations to meet Equal Employment Opportunity (EEO), Title IX, and Environmental Quality standards set by the government. These organizations make token efforts to hire minorities or women and to meet standards set by the government, and they claim that they are doing all they can. This same pitch is used by many "get rich quick" advertisements that present quotations from persons who have "made it." This is a fallacy only when a token is made to appear to be more than it really is.

9. *Hasty Conclusion* is the fallacy of presenting insufficient information to justify the conclusion. Notice that we are not dealing with the quality of the evidence with this fallacy, but only with the quantity. We have dealt with the question of quality of evidence in previous fallacies like the ad hominem and appeal to authority fallacies. Remember that when we talked about inductive reasoning, we said that the specific cases cited to justify a conclusion had to be sufficient in terms of both quality and quantity. When quantity is missing, we have the fallacy of a hasty conclusion. As the name implies, such conclusions have the appearance of occurring because of a time problem (hasty), whether time is a problem or not. The old saying "act in haste, repent at leisure" relates directly to this fallacy. An amusing example is "Chicken Little," who went around telling friends that the sky was falling after he was hit on the head by an acorn.

10. *Questionable Classification* occurs when given the available evidence, we make an incorrect classification. At one time we used to classify many countries and people around the world as "backward," "primitive," or "savage." These faulty categorizations were often based on the information that was available. We have since discovered that a more accurate classification is "underdeveloped," a term suggesting that a given people may not have all of our benefits and advantages but that they may be equal or superior to us in other ways. As we discussed in Chapter 4, we like to classify things and people because it makes thinking about them easier, but we must be constantly on guard to be sure that we have enough evidence to make proper classifications.

11. *Questionable Cause* refers to the act of suggesting that one thing is the cause of something else on the basis of insufficient or inaccurate evidence. We all like to determine the causes of things, but we must be very careful when we do so. One of the main attacks on the proposed Equal Rights Amendment (E.R.A.) is that it will cause divorces and force women to work. We should be very careful about such reasoning, since incidents of divorce and of women's working are growing even without the E.R.A.

This fallacy is quite common among inexperienced researchers, who imply "cause-effect relationships" based on research that merely proves a relationship between two variables. Teachers in most beginning research classes are quick to point out that there are several reasons other than cause-and-effect why variables might correlate with one another. Two of the most obvious reasons are (1) that the correlation might be an accidental or chance occur-

Reasoning

rence and (2) that it might be caused by some third element that has not been examined. You must be very wary of assigning causes or believing causal statements.

12. *Questionable Analogy* is the term we use to refer to the problems discussed earlier in using the analogy as evidence. You will recall that an analogy suggests that because two things have certain characteristics in common, they will also be alike in other characteristics. As we said earlier, you must constantly be aware of the dissimilarities as well as the similarities between the items in the analogy. Any analogy will work only up to a certain point.

These twelve invalid fallacies conclude the list that we will present in this text. There are many others, but these twelve appear to us to be the most significant. However, they do not mark the end of our discussion of fallacious reasoning since a fallacy does not have to be invalid. We now move on to those fallacies in which the argument or reasoning is valid but in which the conclusion is still incorrect.

Fallacies in Valid Arguments

1. *Suppressed Evidence* is the omitting of evidence that is unfavorable to one's argument. This omission is quite common in much of the reasoned argument one hears. It is so common that communication scholars have developed a whole line of research on the effects of *one-sided and two-sided* arguments. They have discovered, for example, that a one-sided message (one in which the evidence is suppressed) works best when the receivers are initially receptive to the message and when they are not likely to hear opposing arguments. Such an approach seems to condone this fallacy. These researchers are, of course, looking at communication purely from the point of view of the sender and the effect of the message. From the perspective of the receiver, such a one-sided message is obviously a fallacy that one must guard against.

2. *Questionable Premise* is the name given by Kahane to any fallacy in which one accepts a premise that is questionable or that is insufficiently supported in arriving at a conclusion. He lists six variations of this fallacy: unknown facts, questionable evaluation, straw man, false dilemma, begging the question, and inconsistency. Each of these could easily be labeled as a fallacy in and of itself, but since Kahane treats them as subclasses of the questionable premise fallacy, we will also.

There are two classes of *unknown facts*, those that are unknown to anyone (such as how many stars and planets there are in the universe) and those that are known to someone, but not to the person committing the fallacy. We are interested only in this second form of the fallacy in which the fact is knowable. Perhaps the most common form of this fallacy is the attempt to use premises based on another's personal facts. Such a premise might be that "political candidate X is only supporting an issue in order to win the election." Only candidate X would really know the factual reason for his or her support of the issue. The premise is based on an unknown fact, but we see such premises in many political statements leading to the conclusion that one should not vote for a candidate. You should constantly be on the lookout for facts that are claimed but not known. This fallacy ties in closely with our earlier discussion of facts, statements of fact, and observational evidence.

Whereas the fallacy of unknown facts deals with factual statements, *questionable evaluation* deals with statements of value or value judgments. When individuals make personal evaluations, such as saying something is "good" or "bad," they are making value judgments. They are telling us something about themselves, not about the object being evaluated.

Some texts suggest that all statements can be classified as facts, inferences, or value judgments. We have already discussed facts and inferences in this chapter. Value judgments are the evaluations we assign to facts and inferences. If you said, "This is a good textbook," it would be a value judgment based on your evaluation of the book. It says something about you and your evaluation process. Someone else might not think it is a "good" textbook. You should be sure not to confuse facts and values based on judgments or evaluations.

It is very tempting to suggest at this point that we should never accept value judgments or evaluations as logical premises at all. We cannot go that far. Judgments and evaluations made by experts are often the best premises available and should be used in the reasoning process, but be on your guard and be aware that it is easy to commit the fallacy of questionable evaluation.

The third variation of the questionable premise fallacy is called the *straw man*. An arguer who twists an opponent's argument to make it more vulnerable to attack or who attacks weaker rather than stronger opponents is practicing the straw man fallacy. In a recent Wyoming campaign, one candidate attacked another as being "owned" by interests from outside the state like major oil and coal companies. By itself, this statement would have been classified as the fallacy of ad hominem that we discussed earlier. But the attack did not stop there. Each issue on which the two candidates differed was twisted by the candidate who was making the attack to look as if his position would benefit the people and as if his opponent's position would benefit only the outsiders. The candidate who was being attacked in turn used the second form of this fallacy and attacked one of his opponent's key aides and the party chairman rather than the opponent himself. Since both candidates were using this fallacy it was O.K. Right? Wrong! Or, specifically, two wrongs did not make a right. By the time these two candidates quit throwing fallacious arguments at one another, there were very few issues of any substance left on which the voters could make a reasoned decision.

The fourth subcategory of the questionable premise fallacy has several names. It has been called the *false dilemma*, *either-or*, *dichotomy*, and *black or white* fallacy. It involves reducing the number of possible alternatives on any question. In most cases, the final number of alternatives that remains is two, hence the use of the terms "either-or" and "black or white." The false dilemma fallacy is a method of oversimplifying an argument. The "America—love it or leave it" bumper sticker is one of the better examples of this fallacy. It leaves no room for those who attempt to improve those things they find wrong with America.

If you will remember, the major premise in a disjunctive syllogism must always be an "either-or" statement. If such a premise is really not a true

Reasoning

dichotomy, that is, if its terms are not truly mutually exclusive, then the false dilemma fallacy applies. Many false dilemma fallacies occur as the major premise in a disjunctive syllogism.

Begging the question is the fifth form of the questionable premise fallacy. We beg the question whenever we fail to support every claim. The inferential reasoning model demonstrates the importance of data, warrants, and backing in an argument. When these are missing, the arguer is begging the question. Evidence is an extremely important part of reasoning, and reasoned conclusions should be drawn only when evidence is available to support every questionable issue.

Inconsistency is the last subcategory of the questionable premise fallacy. Inconsistent premises can occur in many ways. Premises can be inconsistent within the same argument, between arguments separated in time, or in the same argument made by different spokespersons. Inconsistency can also occur in the conclusions arrived at from similar premises. The last and perhaps most crucial form of inconsistency is that of saying one thing and doing another. We have already discussed the need for consistency as one of the motivations for reasoning in the first place. As receivers of communication, we desire to be consistent, but in order to accomplish a purpose, senders of messages are often intentionally inconsistent. Politicians will often say different things to different audiences and at different times to accomplish some goal, such as getting elected. There is nothing wrong with changing one's mind. It is sometimes just as destructive to never change (even in the face of much new evidence) as it is to be inconsistent. It is the motive or intent of the inconsistency that is important. When a person has a legitimate reason for changing a position or for being inconsistent, there is no fallacy. As a matter of fact, Kahane suggests that if you label this behavior as the fallacy of inconsistency, you are guilty of a fallacy yourself (i.e., *false charge of fallacy*). When a person's motives are to mislead the listener into incorrect conclusions, then the fallacy of inconsistency applies.

This completes our list of fallacies of reasoning. We have spent a considerable number of pages on these fallacies because we believe it is important for a student of communication to be able to reason well and to identify fallacies of reasoning both in inputs received and outputs transmitted. It might seem from this chapter that effective reasoning should not be hard to accomplish, yet we constantly make mistakes in our reasoning. Why does this happen? We will conclude this chapter by trying to answer that question.

BARRIERS TO EFFECTIVE REASONING

There are any number of reasons why we draw incorrect conclusions based on information available to us. One of the most important is not understanding the reasoning process itself—how and why it operates; the types, strengths, and weaknesses of evidence; the forms of reasoning and the fallacies of reasoning. Most teachers assume that we pick this understanding up as a by-product of the learning process. Therefore, they don't teach it as a subject in and of itself. We have tried to give you some of this information. If you carefully study what we have presented in this chapter, we believe your reasoning ability will improve. But that is not enough. We all make reasoning mistakes, so there must be something else involved in addition to knowledge.

That "something else" is directly related to the way in which our motivation, perception, and reasoning components intraface with one another. These components are inseparable, and as such they serve both to add and to detract from the efficiency of one another. As we said at the beginning of this chapter, our reasoning is the product of both our motivations and perceptions. We need to think about what has been said concerning motivation and perception and to try to relate that to how we reason.

We said that people are motivated by four factors: drive reduction components, consistency components, interpersonal need components, and value components. The drive reduction need component causes us to engage in reasoning and behavior that will reduce the felt need or drive. Our physiological, safety, social, esteem, and self-actualization needs can each predominate at any particular time.

These different needs can have very different effects on our reasoning. When we are experiencing a short term maintenance need, we are more likely to draw a hasty conclusion because of the immediacy of the need. It must be reduced in a hurry or serious problems can occur. We are much more likely to make reasoning mistakes when our evaluation is based on those needs than when it is based on a long-term maintenance need.

Our consistency need also plays a very important role in our reasoning. As we mentioned in the first part of this chapter, it plays a very positive role in determining why we reason at all. It also has a negative effect on our reasoning in that it affects our perceptual component and causes us to distort our percep-

Reasoning

tion of reality in order to maintain consistency. How this distortion of perception takes place through selection and filtering is discussed fully in the preceding chapter. We distort our perceptions in order to categorize and to maintain consistency. This distortion has a tremendous effect on our reasoning. We cannot reason very well if the data on which we base our conclusions are distorted. No matter how much we know about evidence, we cannot use it if we do not see it or hear it or if we distort it.

Our reasoning is also affected by our interpersonal need component. Our desire to control others, to be affectionate with others, and to be included by others affects our reasoning. Our reasoning will be effective only when we obtain the proper levels of these interpersonal needs. When we are deficient or excessive in our responses the reasoning behind those responses will tend to be fallacious. We will rationalize our behavior with fallacious reasoning.

Perhaps the most important explanation as to why we do not always reason well is because of our value component. We value people and things to the point where they become more important than correct reasoning. These values get all mixed up with the data, claims, warrants, and backing. We tend to hang on to these values in the face of strong contrary evidence. We want to deceive ourselves to protect our "self". The one thing that overrides reasoning is protection of one's self-concept.

Reasoning is usually associated with public communication, but it is important in all contexts.
PHOTO BY CAROLE DUGAN

SUMMARY

In this chapter we have focused on the basic elements and types of reasoning. We have explained that people reason in order to understand their environment and to maintain consistency between their perceptions and motivations.

Reasoning is the process by which we transform the stimuli from our perceptions and motivations into communication outputs. We have defined the stimuli on which we base our reasoning as evidence. The four main types of evidence discussed in this chapter are observations, examples, statistics, and testimony. Each type of evidence has its strengths and weaknesses, and high quality reasoning demands an ability to determine quality of evidence.

Reasoning is very similar to the processes of thinking and inference. Each process involves the drawing of conclusions based on evidence. We have identified the three main forms of reasoning as deductive, inductive, and inferential. Deductive reasoning goes from the general to the specific and relies on the syllogism and enthymeme as its basic structures. The three types of syllogisms are categorical, disjunctive, and hypothetical. Inductive reasoning is based on probability and is the basis of the scientific method. Inferential reasoning is a combination of induction and deduction. It involves the use of data, warrants, claims, qualifiers, backing, and rebuttal. The use of reasoning, evidence, and logic for purposes of communicative advocacy is often termed argument or argumentation.

We have discussed various fallacies and barriers to effective reasoning. We divided the reasoning fallacies into those that occur as part of invalid arguments and those that occur as part of valid arguments. We have pointed out the fact that the validity of an argument or of reasoning is no guarantee of the correctness or truth of the reasoning or argument. We concluded this chapter by stating that the major barrier to effective reasoning is not the use of fallacies, but the effects of motivation and perception on the reasoning component. Because the three intrapersonal processing elements are interdependent, they tend to influence one another both positively and negatively. Our motivations and perceptions often act to prevent us from reasoning properly. The intraface relationship causes as many problems as it solves. Without the intraface of these three intrapersonal processing elements, however, the human communication system could not survive, let alone bring us to the advanced state of civilization we enjoy today.

KEY TERMS AND CONCEPTS

Ad Hominem Fallacy
Ambiguity Fallacy
Appeal to Authority Fallacy
Backing
Balance Theory
Barriers to Reasoning
Begging the Question Fallacy
Categorical Syllogism
Claim
Conclusion
Congruity Theory
Consistency
Data
Deduction

Disjunctive Syllogism
Dissonance Theory
Enthymeme
Evidence
Examples
Fallacy
False Dilemma Fallacy
Hasty Conclusion Fallacy
Hypothetical Syllogism
Inconsistency Fallacy
Induction
Inferential Reasoning
Invalid Reasoning Fallacies
Irrelevant Reason Fallacy

Reasoning

Major Premise
Minor Premise
Observations
Probability
Provincialism Fallacy
Qualifier
Questionable Analogy Fallacy
Questionable Cause Fallacy
Questionable Classification Fallacy
Questionable Evaluation Fallacy
Questionable Premise Fallacy
Reasoning
Rebuttal

Slippery Slope Fallacy
Statistics
Straw Man Fallacy
Suppressed Evidence Fallacy
Syllogism
Testimony
Tokenism Fallacy
Truth vs. Validity
Two Wrongs Make a Right Fallacy
Uknown Facts Fallacy
Valid Reasoning Fallacies
Warrant

SUGGESTED READINGS

Ehninger, Douglas, and Wayne Brockriede. *Decision by Debate*, 2nd ed. New York: Harper and Row, Publishers, 1978. An extremely interesting and up-to-date book on argument and reasoning. Of special interest to those who want to read more on reasoning are Chapters 3 (Perspectives on Argument), 4 (A Unit of Proof), 5 (Evidence), 6 (Warrants), and 7 (Criticizing Units of Proof). This text also puts a great deal of emphasis on the use of reasoning through debate.

Gilbert, Michael A., *How to Win an Argument*. New York: McGraw-Hill Book Company, 1979. An easy-to-read, contemporary book designed to make you more critical in your reasoning. Some of the chapter titles will give you an idea of how reasoning is approached in this book: "What Are We Arguing About?" "Zen and the Art of Argument," "What's Going On Here?" "Ring Around the Argument," "Three Sneaky Moves," and "Equal Rights for Equal Arguments." This book teaches you how to argue and to persuade people outside of the formal debate format.

Toulmin Stephen, Richard Rieke, and Allan Janik, *An Introduction to Reasoning*. New York: Macmillan Publishing Company, Inc., 1979. This is a rather formal text designed to teach a student about rationality and criticism as well as the Toulmin model of inferential reasoning. The text also discusses the fallacies of reasoning. The importance of reasoning in such fields as law, science, the arts, and business are also discussed. This book is for anyone who intends to continue a serious study of the reasoning process.

III

COMMUNICATION INPUTS AND OUTPUTS

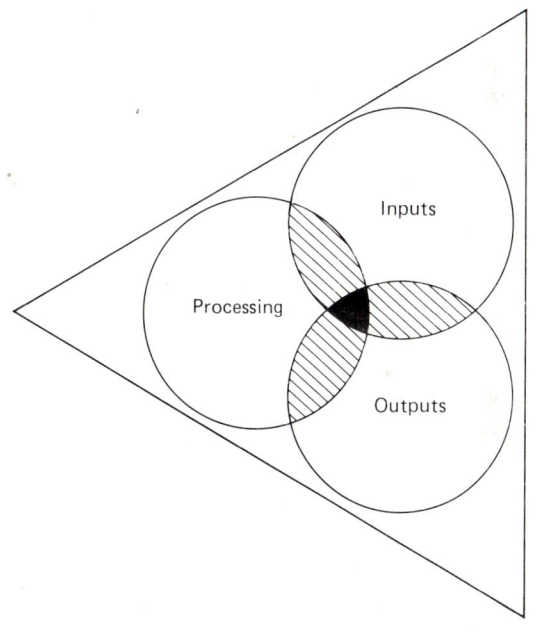

6
Verbal Communication

A primary distinguishing characteristic of human beings is the use of spoken symbols. With the exception of nonverbal communication, our other language systems such as mathematics, sign language, and music are derived from spoken language. Our power to use abstract spoken symbols enables us to talk about the past, present, and future; to communicate about classes of events; and to manipulate the world about us. Our language is composed of two subsystems: vocabulary and grammar. Our vocabulary consists of words for which we have learned arbitrary meanings. Our grammar includes the rules for using the words in our vocabulary. Our language system is derived from our culture and our environment and, in turn, affects our perception of culture and environment. Thus, language can both create problems and serve as a powerful tool for us.

Verbal Communication

In this chapter and the next two chapters, we will discuss the input and output components represented in our communication model. In order for us to communicate with another human being, we must provide outputs that the other person can receive as inputs and to which he or she can respond after processing. The two output abilities possessed by human beings have been termed verbal and nonverbal communication. What you probably imagine when you think of verbal and nonverbal communication are language (or words), gestures, facial expressions, and the like. When the average person is trying to use a word to express an idea, that person is making use of the output ability referred to as *verbal communication* or language. Likewise, when we notice an expression on someone's face and interpret it to reflect sadness or happiness, we are responding to the output ability that is called *nonverbal communication*. Both of these subsystems together comprise the input and output components of every human communicator and are essential to communication. In this chapter, we will focus on the use of verbal language and the role it plays in the communication process. In the following chapter, we will focus on nonverbal communication and the role it plays within human communication systems. Finally, in Chapter 8 we will examine the physiological aspects of the input and output components, as well as how they develop and how they can be improved.

THE POWER OF LANGUAGE

Central to the communication process is the use of verbal language. Much of the progress made by human beings throughout the centuries can be traced to the power of verbal language. Verbal language allows us to bind ourselves to the past and to the future and to develop abstract concepts. These two characteristics make language very powerful.

Time-Binding Power

The centrality of language to the communication process should be fairly obvious to most people if they think about it. Try to imagine yourself explaining a past event to a friend without the use of words. It would be rather difficult, wouldn't it? The ability to use language in order to explain past events is one characteristic that makes human beings unique. We can talk about the past and, more importantly, we can learn about the past by talking about it. Today, in the 1980s, it is still possible for us to "interact" with people such as Aristotle, Plato, and others who lived hundreds and even thousands of years ago. We can learn from these people. We can learn from their mistakes as well as from their accomplishments. Through language, we can enjoy the company of people who are long dead. General semanticists call this characteristic of language its *time-binding* capacity. This term means that we can, through language, bind ourselves to another time. We can receive messages from people who lived in the past. Although nonverbal communication is extremely important in human communication, it is evident that we cannot, through gestures or facial expressions, talk as easily to someone about an event that has occurred in the past as we can through language.

In addition, we can bind ourselves to the future. As the two of us have been writing this book, we have faced the interesting task of trying to anticipate future events and people. We have tried hard to use examples that will be relevant a year, five years, and longer from the time we write them down. Although neither of us expects it, it is always possible that one or both of us may die two or three years from now. Although mentioning this may seem a little morbid, it is an interesting thought to consider because, in essence, it means that we are able to output messages to people in the future even though we might not be alive when the messages are read. From the time this book is published, there is a way for us to communicate with people in the future. We could output nonverbal messages to people in the future through the use of film or pictures, as we do with home movies, but the types of messages that we can bind to the future through nonverbal means are limited.

Abstraction Power

What do we mean by an abstraction? *Abstraction* refers to the process of categorizing stimuli based on selected attributes. If you will recall, in Chapter 4 we indicated that a part of the perception process included the categorization of incoming stimuli. As long as we don't categorize, we remain at a very concrete, nonabstract level. The further we get away from the physical world, the more abstract we are. As long as we stand in front of our office building at our university and call it "Ross Hall," we are at a very low level of abstraction. However, when we put it in the category of "office building" and refer to it as an "office building," we have just moved one step up what Hayakawa (1964) called an abstraction ladder. We can move another step up the abstraction ladder by referring to our office building no longer as "Ross Hall" or "office building" but as a "building." By placing the physical object in front of us in a category that includes more objects we become more abstract. Whereas the real object in front of us constitutes 100% of the phrase "Ross Hall," it represents only a small fraction of the word "building" because this word includes additional objects. Because we are more abstract and more removed in terms of abstraction levels from all of the physical objects that are contained in our category, we are able to talk about the abstract concept of buildings more easily. Yet we have lost the identifying characteristics of the individual objects within our category. Unlike verbal communication, nonverbal communication often operates at a lower level of abstraction.

Language permits us to talk about high-level abstract ideas and concepts. It is possible to explain the concept of "equal rights for all citizens" to someone through the use of words. It would be very difficult to explain this same concept through the use of gestures or facial expressions. Love is both an abstract concept and a concrete feeling. As we will discuss more completely in the next chapter, it is true that communicating the feeling of love that we have for another person to that person is ideally accomplished nonverbally rather than verbally. It is easier for us to express most of our emotions nonverbally than verbally because the actual feelings are very low on the abstraction ladder. A red face, tense body, and clenched fists express anger much more effectively than a three- or four-sentence statement. Likewise, the words "I love you" carry very little meaning for most of us compared with a soft touch, a caress, a direct look,

Verbal Communication

and a low voice. Behaviors of this nature convey the emotion of love much more effectively than a paragraph, or even an essay, in which we try to express our feelings.

Expressing an emotion nonverbally is not the same thing as *discussing* the abstract concept involved. Pick someone whom you do not love and try to imagine yourself explaining love to that individual without words. It is next to impossible. The reason is that the *concept* of love is a higher-level abstraction. As long as we are concerned with concrete concepts at a lower abstraction level, it is possible to communicate them to another individual nonverbally. What gesture do you use to describe "democracy" to someone? What facial expression conveys "time-binding" or "abstraction" to another human being? The answer is that there are none. Thus, to discuss a highly abstract concept requires words, because words themselves are abstractions.

Ross Hall can be labeled many ways at different levels of abstraction.
PHOTO BY CAROLE DUGAN

It is extremely important to relate the language subsystem back to the intrapersonal processes discussed in Part Two of the book. As we have said, all subsystems intraface with each other and have significant effects on each other. We would like to especially emphasize the relationship of language's powers of abstraction and categorization with the intrapersonal subsystems of perception and reasoning. It is difficult to imagine reasoning existing without verbal communication. Language provides us with the ability to develop categories, which we employ in using evidence and reasoning. In addition, the ability to develop categories and to abstract is intimately related to the way we perceive the world. We categorize all incoming stimuli. This is a language-based process, highly dependent on the abstraction power of the language system used by the individual and on the categories present in it.

Thus far we have discussed language in an abstract sense. However, language is something that exists only when it is used. In human beings, a striking characteristic of language is that it is spoken, although there are other ways of using language. At this moment you are reading language as it is written in a book. Spoken language is a naturally occurring phenomenon in human beings. With very little and sometimes with no help from their parents, children manage the complex tasks of learning word associations and generating complex sentences necessary for speech.

Manipulating our environment so that we might survive within it requires that there be a means of communication. Language is our means. The idea that language is unique to humans is probably not acceptable if we use a broad definition of language. However, the notion of *spoken language* as unique to humans is more acceptable (Dance, 1975; Adler, 1975). One characteristic, the ability to speak through the use of a verbal symbol system, is apparently unique to human beings. We would further suggest that without this characteristic it would have been difficult, if not impossible, for our species to have survived as it is today.

The least we can say is that speech/language is important to us and possibly critical to our survival. As we consider characteristics of language, please keep in mind the power of spoken language in human communication. Please also remember that although other forms of language such as writing can be elevated to great levels of eloquence and effectiveness, they are still derivatives of this very basic and possibly this most human of all acts: speech communication.

WHAT IS LANGUAGE?

Although we have talked about language, its importance, and the role it plays in our lives, we have not yet defined it. Language is a system of symbols that allows us to relate sounds and written words to meanings in ways that facilitate the influencing of other human beings.

A *symbol* is something that can stand for something else. It can be a word. In the language of music notation, notes stand for finger patterns on violins, clarinets, or trumpets, and therefore they are symbols. Symbols are used to catalog things in the world. This discussion is consistent with our earlier treatment of perception in which, you may recall, we talked about the necessity of attaching meaning to our perceptions. The way we attach meaning is through the use of symbols in language. It is sometimes difficult to determine whether we need symbols to provide meaning for the physical perceptions we have, or whether we need physical perceptions to provide meaning for the symbols we use. It probably works both ways and we do both.

Language is also potentially self-reflexive (DeVito, 1970). At first glance, this statement may seem intimidating, but self-reflexiveness in language simply means that we can use language to talk about language. Right now, as you are reading this book, we are employing written language to talk about spoken language. In your communication class, when your professor is lecturing or when the class is discussing the characteristics of language, you are again employing the characteristic of self-reflexiveness.

Riccillo and Liebig (1977) suggest that in order to better understand spoken language we must think in terms of three different types of competencies that they consider components of the spoken language system: linguistic, communicative, and cognitive competencies. *Competency* refers to "... the underlying knowledge of a language an ideal-speaker/listener has to generate" (Riccillo and Liebig, 1977).

Linguistic Competence

Linguistic competence refers to the knowledge people have about the relationship of their language to sounds and meanings. This concept relates to our understanding of how sounds and meanings are associated and how they are used to produce speech. The actual production of language is what Dance (1975) refers to as that essential characteristic in human beings that triggers the conceptualization process and that enables us to develop mentally as human beings. This essential characteristic is speech communication.

Communicative Competence

This component of the spoken language system has to do with a knowledge of the norms that are associated with interaction. How do we know what words are appropriate and what words to avoid? How do we know when to talk about sex and when not to? This knowledge is what is called communicative competence.

Cognitive Competence

Cognitive competence is related to our ability to organize, generate concepts, and think. We can think of it as a combination of the intrapersonal processes of perception, motivation, and reasoning, coupled with the symbols present in our language system.

Riccillo and Liebig go on to suggest that there is an intrafacing among these three competencies to produce an area of overlap that we call speech behavior, speech communication, or syntactic speech. Cognitive competence and linguistic competence overlap. The language we possess and our knowledge of it affect and are a part of the way we think and develop concepts in relationships. Likewise, the overlap between linguistic competence and communicative competence suggests a similar kind of interaction between our awareness of conversational norms and the language we possess. Finally, the overlap between cognitive competence and communicative competence suggests that our awareness of appropriateness in interaction has an effect on the way we think about things and the way we conceptualize. The overlap area suggests that the actual production of sounds also affects the way we think, the way we understand language, and the way we are aware of rules of appropriateness. The phrase "making love" and our associations with it significantly affect the way we think about the reality it represents, and vice versa. Likewise, the phrase effects the way we accept or reject the norms concerning the appropriate times to talk about the reality behind the phrase. This awareness in turn affects our cognitions about the phrase, as well as our associations with it. All of these responses to and awarenesses of the term "making love" mutually affect one another, just as they affect the speaking of the phrase, which likewise affects them.

To be sure, this is a very complex set of relationships, but one that will be important for you to keep in mind as we proceed throughout the rest of the chapter to discuss the way we use language and the way it works. At this point, we will now consider four characteristics related to language: vocabulary, grammar, the spoken nature of language, and its relationship to conceptual development.

THE VOCABULARY COMPONENT

We probably cannot legitimately speak about human language apart from speech. The tone of voice, volume, rate, and pitch used in producing speech are all integral parts of spoken language. It has been the custom, however, for many years to discuss the words used during speech separately from the acoustic behavior of the speaker that accompanies the words. We do this first of all because it is difficult to talk about them all at once and still have material that makes sense. Second, research has tended to be conducted separately on these nonverbal vocal characteristics. The nonverbal characteristics that accompany the production of words are referred to as vocalics, or paralanguage, and will be considered in the next chapter on nonverbal communication. Realizing that we should keep these vocal factors in mind, we will now discuss some of the characteristics of language.

Our Word Pool

Verbal language systems are composed of at least two subsystems. There is a "pool" of meaningful symbols or words that is called a *vocabulary* on which we can draw at any time. There is also a system of rules and regulations for employing those words and combining them in meaningful ways; this system is called *grammar*. In this section we will discuss vocabulary, and in the next section we will focus on grammar.

Symbolization *Signs* bear a real relationship to the things for which they stand. Symbols do not. An example of each might help make this point clearer. If we observe someone with a runny nose, the runny nose is a sign of a cold or an allergy. It is directly related to the thing it "signs." On the other hand, the word "chair" has no direct relationship to the thing it represents. We could just as easily call it a "bloch." It is an arbitrary designation. Whenever we use a word to stand for something else arbitrarily, we have employed the *symbolization process*. There is no direct relationship between the symbol and the thing the symbol stands for. How we have come to use symbols to represent things can be questioned, but it is true that none of our words in and of themselves have meaning. The meaning is in the people: Words don't mean; people do. You and I carry around within us associations that, when taken together, are meaningful for us.

Verbal Communication

Associated meaning There is not complete agreement among scholars as to how we learn words, but a learning theory approach to word meaning is one of the most defensible explanations available. This position suggests that words become meaningful for us through a very complex process of association. That words are learned through association should not mislead you into thinking that learning them is a simple process. It is not a simple process of one object being paired with one word, thus producing meaning. This might be true initially, but over time we have many associations and pairings of a word with various events so that we ultimately have a very complex combination of associations. Your first association with the word "water" may have occurred when you were a baby and you were placed in a bath. Your mother or father may have splashed the water, all the while saying "water." Many babies enjoy this process if it is approached positively, and they develop positive associations with it. As you continue to grow, however, you began to discover that water could come to you in a glass and that you could drink it and feel good when you were thirsty or hot. In other words, you began to have multiple associations with the word "water." As you continued to grow older and move about in the world, you discovered that water could fall out of the sky and make you wet and uncomfortable—another association with water. If you are like one of us, you may have grown up next to a river that periodically overflowed its banks; therefore, you also associated water with the destruction of homes and the enrichment of farmland. Then, too, you may have experienced the pleasures of boating, and you associated these with the word "water." Likewise, you may have enjoyed swimming, or you may have had a scare in which you almost drowned. Either experience could have provided an association with the word "water"—one positive and one negative. Thus for the single word "water" you have many associations, all of which you combine in your mind to form a meaning when you hear or see the word "water."

Our association with the word "water" begins at a very early age.
PHOTO BY CAROLE DUGAN

As a result of this process of association, we can discuss two different types of meaning for words: *denotative meaning* and *connotative meaning*. *Denotative meaning* is the definition of a word which you find in dictionaries. The definition supposedly does not involve any subjective, emotional associations with the word. It is considered by some people to be the "objective" meaning of a word.

The way we arrive at denotative meanings is interesting. Have you ever thought about how dictionaries are written? The people who write dictionaries collect samples of language from books, radio, television, magazines, and the like to determine from the context in which a given word occurs what meaning is being employed. In other words, they try to abstract the meaning of words from the context. The most common meaning that they uncover is listed as the first definition of a word in a dictionary. The second most common usage is the second definition. It should be obvious from this practice that what is written in a dictionary could be considered an "average" meaning of each word. There is the most common average meaning, the second most common average meaning, and so on. Each of these meanings includes emotional associations, although the emotional associatons are those that are common rather than unique.

The *connotative meaning* of a word is not found in dictionaries because it is personal. The connotative meaning of a word includes all of the personal associations and emotional responses that one particular individual has toward a word. If you have warm and happy associations with the word "home," when you hear the word "home" you respond positively and warmly. The connotative meaning of this word is, for you, all of those responses you have. One way to distinguish between denotation and connotation is simply to remember that denotation is a meaning based on the use of a word by many people, whereas connotation is an individual response to a word. However, both involve associated meanings.

Arbitrary meanings In our discussion of how we learn meanings we have said that there is no inherent meaning in the words themselves. This fact is sometimes very difficult for many people to accept, because the idea that words have no meaning is not consistent with the many experiences we have had of observing people argue about what a word "means." We can all recall being told by someone at one time or another what a word means. Unfortunately, because of these experiences, we come to think of words as "having meaning." In addition, because we have learned a given language and because we are so familiar with that language, we tend to think that everyone's experience is the same. This erroneous conclusion can easily mislead us into thinking that words have consistent meanings. Because we learn meaning through association, each of us has different experiences with words, although fortunately for the sake of communication, most of us have many fairly common experiences as well. These common experiences leave us with some similar, though not identical, meanings/associations for many words that enable us to interact with each other successfully much of the time.

One of the best known approaches to the explanation of the arbitrary nature of meaning was developed by Ogden and Richards (1946). They created what is called a *triangle of meaning*, a version of which you see in Fig. 6.1. In order to have word meaning, a *reference process* has to occur. The reference process within our minds is part of our symbolization ability in which we make one thing stand for something else. In Fig. 6.1, the *referent* is the object we make the word stand for. In this particular case, the object is the building in which we live. This object exists physically in the environment; we can touch it, walk around it, and look at it. In addition, we use a *symbol* to indirectly represent, or symbolize, the object. In this particular case the symbol is the word "house." Any arbitrary symbol could be used to stand for that physical object, as long as there is agreement among those with whom we communicate. Finally, we make the connection, that is, we associate the object with the symbol through the reference process. This process goes on inside our heads and is the result of all of the associations we have had between physical objects such as those we live in and arbitrary words such as "house." Over time, we build up these arbitrary associations, and they are what Ogden and Richards mean by our reference process.

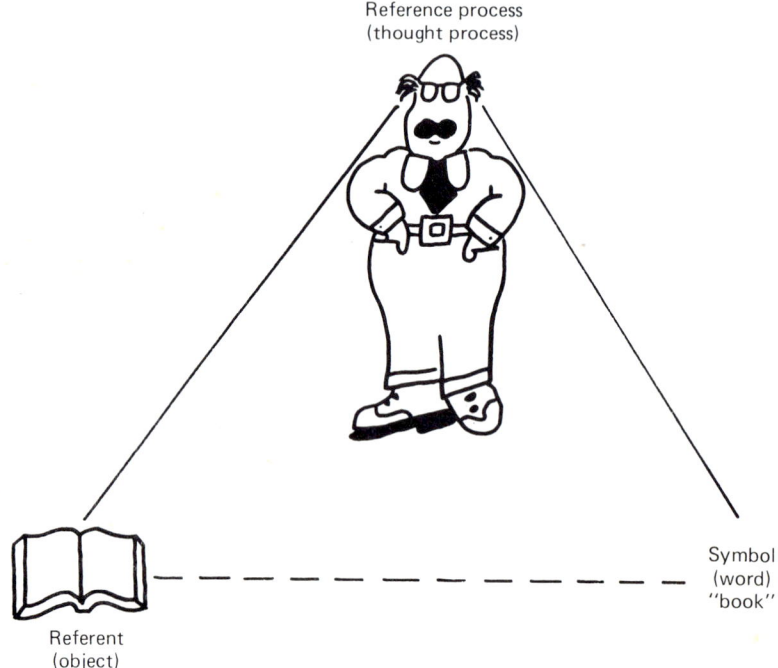

Fig. 6.1 Triangle of meaning.

The reference or symbolization process is one of the things that gives language such power. It is this ability to indirectly represent the world about us through the use of arbitrary symbols that enables us to verbally manipulate our world without actually having to physically manipulate it. By manipulating it symbolically we are able to solve problems and to create new ideas and philosophies. The symbolic process can also cause us many problems. Because there is no direct connection between the words and the things they represent, we can become very argumentative and experience conflict with other people. We have gone through associational processes different from theirs, and we have arrived at different meanings for words. Later in this chapter we will discuss many language problems that we can trace back to the arbitrary meanings of words.

Structural meaning In the chapter on perception we discussed the distinction between micromeanings and macromeanings. We said that micromeanings involve the interpretation, naming, or categorization of objects and living things in the world. The micromeanings we were discussing in that chapter are analogous to the symbolization process, the naming of an object through the use of a word. As they relate to the acquisition of meaning, the symbolization and association processes are an important aspect of language. However, it would be difficult to go through life if the only thing we could do was to name objects. This is not to say that our language would have no meaning, but rather that there would be much missing from what most of us are used to saying and hearing. Macromeanings provide meaning for words beyond the symbolization process.

Macromeanings show how different things connect and relate to each other. In language, we derive and create macromeanings for words through the structure of the language itself. We don't intend to get into an in-depth discussion of the structure of language or the rules of grammar. Probably, if you are like us and most people we have ever known, you hated having to study grammar when you were in high school. Some of you may have diagrammed sentences and learned the various parts of speech such as nouns, verbs, prepositions, and direct objects. Many people think grammar is a waste of time. Since we already know how to speak, why in the world should we bother to learn how to name the parts of speech? It is our belief, however, that a better understanding of language helps us to use it better. Also, an awareness of language structure helps us express some word meanings better.

Some languages have structures very different from ours. This book is written in English. However, not all languages have the same structure as English. Have you ever thought about the fact that in English we consistently place the verb toward the beginning or somewhere in the middle of a sentence? German is not like that. In German, the verb frequently falls at or toward the end of a sentence. Thus, if you are reading or listening to someone speak a very long German sentence, you have to wait a long time before you discover the verb. It has always seemed to us that this aspect of German has a significant effect on what the sentences mean. You must retain many words in your mind and then establish the relationships when the verb finally comes. This necessity should force you to listen and assign word meaning differently than you do in English.

There are some languages that have no future tense. This is an interesting problem, isn't it? In English, we can talk about tomorrow. We can also talk about September 25, 1990 at 4:00 p.m. Eastern Standard Time. It is an interesting notion that we could make an agreement to meet someone at a particular place at a particular hour many years from now. People using a language with no future tense cannot do this.

Verbal Communication

Different languages, because of their structure, have different ways of handling gender. Are you aware that some languages consider objects in our world to be masculine, feminine, or neuter? In our language, the articles "the" and "a" have no gender. We don't talk about a female table or a male house, but if we turn once again to German, we will discover that words are modified by a feminine, masculine, or neutral article. The word "the" in German is "der" (masculine), "die" (feminine), or "das" (neuter). These three words translate into English as "the," but in German there is an added meaning that results from the association of gender with words that are genderless in English.

We also derive word meaning from language structure in another way. We concern ourselves with coordinate conjunctions in our language because they can result in a meaning that links two ideas in our minds. In the phrase, "It rained on Bill and Suzie" the conjunction "and" results in our perceiving Bill and Suzie as a unit, a couple. When two people are linked by the word "and," you are more likely to perceive them as a couple.

It has been said that we can never say the same thing twice in different words. Likewise, we would suggest that you cannot say the same thing even when you use similar words in different sentence structures. Some of you may recognize the difference between the sentence "Mary hit Jimmy" and the sentence "Jimmy was hit by Mary." In the first sentence, the verb is in a form that is referred to as the *active voice*. In the second sentence, the verb is in a form that is referred to as the *passive voice*. Quite apart from naming the verb characteristics, in both sentences we are "saying the same thing." However, by rearranging the words and using a different sentence structure the meaning is altered slightly from one sentence to the next. The emphasis in the first sentence is on Mary as the active hitter. The emphasis in the second sentence, however, has shifted from Mary to Jimmy. In the second sentence, the person who was hit is the focus of the sentence. Thus, simply by changing the structure of a sentence we can alter the meaning of the words because we have altered the structural context in which the words occur.

The more sensitive we can become to the way the majority of people use language structure and the more we can adapt to and use similar kinds of structure, the less likely we are to have our words misunderstood. At least we will be able to use a sentence structure that helps make our words mean similar things to us and to others.

Contextual meaning We have discussed the arbitrary character of meaning and have suggested that we learn to associate meanings with words over time. An interesting implication of this association process is that we also associate words with other words. The other words that surround a word also impart meaning to that word. We acquire meaning from the *context* in which a word is used. Have you ever had an experience in which you have asked a friend, "What does 'X' mean?" To which your friend has replied, "How was it used?" Sometimes, if it is a written use of the word, your friend will ask to see the sentence in which it is used. People ask the context in which a word is used because even if they don't know the precise "meaning of a word," they can deduce the meaning by examining the sentence or the paragraph in which it occurs. They accomplish this task by examining the other words around it, plus the structure of the sentence. Picture yourself encountering the following sentence: "Joe jumped into the softly trickling skleem and felt the cool, refreshing drops of skleem on his body." You probably can guess that the word "skleem," which you have never encountered before in your life, is, first of all, what we call a noun. You can also deduce that "skleem" is a word that refers to what we call "water." You arrive at this deduction by observing the way the word is used in the sentence. The structure of the sentence suggests that "skleem" is a noun; we have certain forms we follow in our language and the location of the word in that sentence relative to other words suggests that the word refers to an object or a thing in Joe's world. Second, because of the associations you have with the other words in the sentence as well as with the word "water," you gain further contextual meaning of the word "skleem" from these words with which "skleem" is associated.

Contextual meaning has practical implications for us because we always have some clues as to what people mean, simply from the context in which their words occur. In addition, although we may have a specific meaning in mind for any word we speak or write, if we associate the word with other words in a sentence it may "change in meaning" for the listener because of the associations the listener has with the other words surrounding it. Many of us have encountered a situation in which we say something to somebody, and the person to whom we are speaking provides feedback indicating that what he or she has "heard" is very much in conflict with what we have "said."

The context in which a word occurs has a significant effect on its perceived meaning. In addition to the context that words provide, even the context of the situation in which the language is being used can affect our interpretation. Thus we would suggest that if we wish to be more effective communicators, it is important for us to always be sensitive not only to individual words and their meanings but to the way these words relate to other words and to the situations in which they occur.

Components of meaning In our discussion of vocabulary, we have focused on the way we acquire meaning. We have also discussed the way meaning affects us when we communicate. The concept of meaning itself is a very difficult one on which to reach agreement because it is not something we can directly examine. People have attempted to study meaning, however. Probably one of the most impressive approaches to the study of meaning was undertaken by Osgood, Suci, and Tannenbaum (1957). These men devised an instrument by which they could measure the meaning we have for words. What they actually did was to measure the associations we have with various words. This approach, of course, is another way of talking about meaning.

The process they used to measure meaning is very complicated, but to give you an idea of what they were doing we can show you what one of their typical measurement instruments would look like. They constructed what they called a *semantic differential*. These paper-and-pencil tests were devised to differentiate semantic meanings between words and for the same words. A typical semantic differential would include the word being measured at the top of the page, as in the example in Fig. 6.2. Here the word is "mother." Underneath this word, there would appear a number of bipolar adjectival scales. As you can see in the example in Fig. 6.2, the adjectives are the kind with which we are very familiar in everyday language usage. People receiving this scale would be asked to indicate the degree to which each adjective applied to the term at the top of the page for them. For instance, in the example used here, if the term "mother" were perceived as extremely good, the person would mark the blank closest to the word "good." Each person would be expected to go through the entire form marking the appropriate blanks to indicate how the various adjectives applied to the term being measured.

MOTHER

Good	___	: ___	: ___	: ___	: ___	: ___	: ___ Bad
Soft	___	: ___	: ___	: ___	: ___	: ___	: ___ Hard
Fast	___	: ___	: ___	: ___	: ___	: ___	: ___ Slow
Optimistic	___	: ___	: ___	: ___	: ___	: ___	: ___ Pessimistic
Strong	___	: ___	: ___	: ___	: ___	: ___	: ___ Weak
Passive	___	: ___	: ___	: ___	: ___	: ___	: ___ Active
Cruel	___	: ___	: ___	: ___	: ___	: ___	: ___ Kind
Heavy	___	: ___	: ___	: ___	: ___	: ___	: ___ Light
Excitable	___	: ___	: ___	: ___	: ___	: ___	: ___ Calm
Painful	___	: ___	: ___	: ___	: ___	: ___	: ___ Pleasurable
Large	___	: ___	: ___	: ___	: ___	: ___	: ___ Small
Hot	___	: ___	: ___	: ___	: ___	: ___	: ___ Cold

Fig. 6.2 Semantic differential.

Osgood, Suci, and Tannenbaum used a mathematical procedure in their research to find out if there were any patterns in the way people responded to words generally. They discovered a consistent pattern that suggested that we do have associations regarding words. These associations are composed of three components: an *evaluation component*, a *potency component*, and an *activity component*.

The *evaluation component* consists of a pattern of associations represented by scales such as "good-bad," "optimistic-pessimistic," "kind-cruel," "pleasurable-painful," and "important-unimportant." In other words, one of the components in our associations for words includes an overall evaluation in which we are responding either positively or negatively to the word.

The *potency component* consists of a pattern of associations represented by scales such as "hard-soft," "strong-weak," "heavy-light," and "large-small." In these adjectives, we find an overall theme of power employed in our responses to words.

The *activity component* consists of a pattern of associations represented by scales such as "active-passive," "excitable-calm," "fast-slow," and "hot-cold." These adjectives appear to be related to the dynamic qualities we associate with a word.

Our interest in this particular line of research is the finding that associations, or meanings, of words break down into dimensions, or components. This means that we can consider the evaluation, potency, and activity dimensions as "building blocks" of meaning. For any given word, we respond along at least these three dimensions. These three kinds of responses, put together, largely explain the associations we have for a word.

What is of special interest to us in this consideration of language is that the evaluation dimension by itself accounted for more of the measured associations than the potency and activity components combined. That finding is of considerable importance because it suggests that the meaning of words for most people is largely evaluative in nature. Words that seem very unemotional to us can be highly emotion-producing for another person. The reason they might seem unemotional to us is because our response to them may be somewhere toward the middle of the evaluation dimension. For another individual, the response may be at one end or the other of the evaluation dimension, resulting in an extremely positive or negative response. This finding might suggest explanations for the many situations in which we find ourselves talking with an individual and discover that we have used language that is a "turn-off" for the other person, in spite of the lack of negative or positive implications for us. That's not a usual occurrence, but it is one that happens often enough for it to be a problem.

The way we begin to respond to words on these dimensions is a result of past associations. Along the evaluation dimension, the word "professor" may be a negative concept for some of you because you have had unfortunate experiences with people called "professors." These experiences would cause you to respond negatively to the word "professor." For the two of us, however, the word "professor" is one we respond to positively because we are professors and because we have had positive experiences over time with the word "professor."

In regard to potency, on the other hand, the word "professor" may be a very powerful concept for you because professors are the people who "have the power" in your interactions with them. They are the ones who give grades and control interactions in class. As professors, we, on the other hand, may view the term as much less powerful than you do because we are faced with the position of having department heads, deans, vice-presidents, and presidents in positions superior to ours. Therefore, we don't feel nearly as powerful as many students perceive us to be. Likewise, in these days of restricted budgets, decreasing enrollments, and precarious job positions, we might perceive, as many other professors might, that the word "professor" is less powerful than you might.

Finally, in regard to the activity dimension, we can recall that when we were students, professors actually seemed to be rather passive, quiet, inactive individuals. The reason was that our primary associations with them were in their offices or classrooms. In the classroom, they were obviously working indoors in a very quiet manner, lecturing and talking with people. This role is not nearly as active, for instance, as that of a football player. Likewise, when students encounter professors in their offices they frequently find them sitting, reading books, or writing at their desks. All these activities are perceived as passive. Thus, on the activity dimension, you may perceive professors as more passive than active. As professors, however, our experience includes associations of hurrying from one part of campus to another in order to make classes on time, going from classes to various meetings with students all day long, talking on the phone to colleagues across the country, and going off to conferences that are full of hustle and bustle at which we present papers, listen, and have meetings. Of course, there's the personal side of our lives in which we do things ranging from swimming to skiing to trailbiking to simply going out for a social drink. Because of these associations, we tend to perceive professors as being on the active end of the activity dimension.

A professor's self-image is frequently very different from a student's perception of him.
PHOTO BY CAROLE DUGAN

We hope you can see from this discussion of the term "professor" that a professor and a student could perceive the word very differently on each of the three dimensions of meaning. The differences in perception result from different experiences and associations with the word. Remember from our earlier discussion that meaning is in the heads of individuals encountering the word and that the different experiences can cause us to respond very differently in regard to each of the meaning components.

We hope this discussion has suggested not only that words can be broken down into meaning components by a paper-and-pencil measurement technique but that these components of meaning have implications for us as we communicate with other people. We can begin to think and analyze other people's possible responses to words in terms of these components, as they relate to our listeners' experiences and possible associations. This discussion should also suggest that because the associations we have cause us to respond in very different ways along these meaning dimensions, we should never assume that other people are going to respond to words identically as we do. Rather, we should at all times attempt to be sensitive to the differing ways in which people can respond to words along these three dimensions of meaning.

THE GRAMMAR COMPONENT

We indicated earlier that our language system is composed of two language subsystems: a vocabulary and a grammar. We have also to some extent discussed the effect of grammar on meaning. Many of you have probably thought of grammar as referring only to the placement of words in sentences or to what we earlier defined as linguistic competence. We are also defining grammar as the way we use language in interaction or as what we earlier defined as communicative competence. We will discuss the first type of grammar in this section and the second type in the following section.

In our discussion of communication systems in Chapter 2, you may recall that we talked about the importance of regulation in any communication system. Regulation is critical to our effective use of any language system, and grammar provides for the regulation of language. The following sentence doesn't make a whole lot of sense: "But wall skiing hit sky bullet cold more skidded." The reason it doesn't make sense is that it is not a sentence according to the grammar of our language system. It is a collection of words from our vocabulary, for which we have separate associations. However, the sentence itself has no meaning because the words do not relate to each other according to any set of rules with which we are familiar. As in all communication systems, there must be some regulation of the language components in order to produce meaningful utterances. If we think of all the words in a sentence as the component parts of a language system, then a system of rules must be available to determine how those components relate to each other. That system of rules is what is called "grammar." Grammar is important because without it we would all be going around uttering single words and hoping that people would have similar meanings for these words in their heads. And even if the meanings of our words were similar to another's, we would never be able to talk about relationships and the way things in our world go together or don't go together.

Sentence Structure

Probably the most important function immediately obvious to us when we consider grammar is the way it relates to sentence structure. In order for a sentence to be meaningful, the words within that sentence must be structured according to commonly accepted rules so that the sentence is intelligible to us. Grammar provides the format for us as we put words together within sentences so as to be sure the structure of our sentences makes sense to other people. In

English, an overall pattern that we tend to follow is that the subject, or the thing we are talking about, is usually followed by the verb, or the action engaged in by the thing we are talking about. The verb is then followed by an object, or the thing that is acted upon by the subject. In addition to this overall pattern, we have appropriate places within a sentence at which we can place adverbs, adjectives, clauses, and prepositional phrases. It is important to note that there is an overall structure that most of us recognize as appropriate and that most of us use when we speak and write. Grammar determines that structure. We learn the rules of grammar as we grow up, even though we don't necessarily learn them formally. Even though we may not be able to identify and name various parts of speech, we do internalize this grammar and employ it when we produce sentences.

As we will see in Chapter 8, children of five or six have already learned the grammar necessary for producing thousands of sentences that they have never heard before. They don't just memorize things and learn things. Given their vocabulary, they learn rules that enable them to generate brand-new sentences that they've never before encountered in their lives. All of us do this every day. We do it to a degree that is almost startling. How often do you actually repeat yourself? How often do you actually repeat word-for-word sentences that you have uttered before? If you pay close attention to yourself on any given day, we think you will find that it is not a very common occurrence. We have no idea exactly how many new sentences a person may produce in his or her lifetime, but we suspect it would be a very impressive figure indeed. Keep in mind that we all learn this set of rules of our own language system that we use in conjunction with our vocabularies to produce meaningful speech.

The grammar component doesn't tell us what is "right"; rather, it tells us what is acceptable and understandable by other people. Grammar is not a set of rules that it is illegal to disobey. Rather, we can think of it as a set of norms that we follow because the sentences we produce when we follow these rules are more often understood and more often have the effect we wish than when we don't follow the rules. Nobody will put us in jail for failing to learn and follow the rules of our grammar; however, we will become more ineffective in our interactions with other people if we don't learn and follow these rules.

Word Appropriateness

Another part of grammar has little to do with sentence structure. The rules of appropriateness are also part of our grammar. You can easily think of a number of subjects and words you know that should not be used in certain contexts. It has long been suggested that "vulgar" four-letter words are not appropriate in mixed company. Even though adults of both genders are quite aware of the existence of the words (and have probably used them), we still follow a norm that prevents us from using them in that circumstance. There is evidence that this norm is changing today.

Another changing language norm concerns the use of gender-related words. Today we are beginning to develop a number of rules regarding the use of gender-related language that are different from those of the past. In years past, we could have written this book using the pronouns "he" and "him" throughout the text. You may notice that we often employ pronouns of both

The Grammar Component

genders such as "she" and "he" and "him" and "her." We do so because many feel that having gender inherent in a word can condition people to think about members of both sexes in different ways. Thus, we now find the concern with words such as "policeman"—no longer an acceptable term because there are also "policewomen." We now talk of "police officers." We are now advised to avoid using either the word "man" or the word "woman" as suffixes or prefixes in job titles. We are urged not to say "businessman" or "businesswoman" but to refer to "business executives" or "managers." We try to avoid terms such as "workman" or "foreman" and to use terms like "laborer," "employee," and "supervisor." Even the term "paperboy"—a role both of us played at one time—has evolved into "paper carrier."

For many years, English grammar did not include the prohibition of using gender-laden language. As with our earlier discussion of German articles, English grammar infused gender with concepts. Why this should have been the case is not certain, but we suspect it may have reflected a societal reality in which women were excluded from many professions and jobs throughout our country. The language merely reflected that fact. Today, as women are moving into many positions and careers that had previously been closed to them, it is possible that the concern with language may be a reflection of these changes in the workplace.

A similar example of a change in the rules of appropriateness concerns words referring to racial groups and people of different colors. The term "boy" was used in the South, especially by white males, to refer to black males of any age. It was a derogatory term in many respects and tended to put down the black man. This term is no longer acceptable. Because it is an offensive term, one would run a risk (if one were white) of using the term "boy" in front of blacks. Possibly we now have within our grammar a norm of not using that term any longer. Likewise, terms such as "redskin," "chink," "polack," and "jap" are all considered inappropriate for use in polite conversation today. About the only times these terms occur any longer in conversation is when we find people joking among friends who will accept this kind of language or when there are extremely hostile situations in which the words are used as expletives in place of obscenities.

We hope you can see from this discussion of gender and language and racism and language that there are many rules you have learned as you have grown up that govern the kinds of words you will use in various situations. Isn't it interesting, for instance, that while eating meals at the table, you don't talk about bodily excrement or graphically describe injuries involving blood and gore? Moreover, you never discuss parties and tell jokes when you are at a funeral. If you do, many people will consider your conversation to be in poor taste and a violation of rules of appropriateness. These rules, which are part of our grammar, govern our interaction every day. They determine the topics we elect to talk about and the words we will use to talk about those topics. These things are governed by many situational factors, but most of us have grown up learning the norms we must follow in order to interact effectively.

All of these rules together govern when and how we are supposed to produce spoken language. They are all a part of our grammar. It is important for us to become sensitive to these rules, because when we violate them and speak at the inappropriate time or when we use inappropriate words or topics, we are perceived negatively and are likely to be less effective when communicating with another person. It is not just polite to learn the grammar of sentence structure, appropriateness, and turn-taking. It is crucial to effective communication.

LANGUAGE AND THOUGHT

As we said earlier, the language process involves the creation of categories that we employ to represent the world about us. This is accomplished through an association, or reference, process. Because we use language to represent the world, many people think that our language significantly affects our perception of the world and the way we think about the world. The best known statement relating to the effect of language on thought and perceptual processes is the Sapir-Whorf hypothesis (Whorf, 1956). Benjamin Whorf, influenced by his professor, Edward Sapir, developed a theory in which he suggested that the language system we learn determines what we can think about and the way we will perceive events about us in the world. As a fire-insurance engineer, Whorf noticed that welders in a plant were prone to bring their lighted welding torches close to gas tanks that were labeled "empty." From this observation he reasoned that they did so because the word "empty" determined the way they perceived the gas tanks. This situation was unfortunate because an "empty" gas tank may be as dangerous, if not more so, than one full of gasoline. An empty gas tank is full of more flammable gas fumes.

We experienced the effect of language on perception when we moved to the Rocky Mountain region from the American Midwest. One of us grew up in the Midwest and the other in California. The words we had for snow were essentially "wet" and "dry" (unless you want to include "clean" and "dirty"). Wet snow is a heavy kind of snow that causes tree branches to bend down, electric lines to snap, and similar occurrences, whereas dry snow is a gentle, light snow that does not pack into a snowball very well because the flakes don't have enough moisture to stick together. After moving to Wyoming, we were introduced to a number of different kinds of mountain snow conditions in which snow was referred to by different names. Some skiers can identify a half-dozen different kinds of snow. We must admit that prior to experiencing these different types of snow, we noticed only the two kinds of snow that we had labeled "wet" and "dry." However, today we can identify several kinds of snow, such as powder, corn, and icy snow. We also have associations of what kind of maneuvers we have to execute on skis in order to remain in an upright position. In other words, as we have acquired new words that differentiate among types of snow, we now perceive different kinds of snow about us.

There is an intraface between the language system and the environment. In addition, both our environment and our language system intraface with our perceptual, motivational, and reasoning processes, discussed in previous chapters. What Whorf was attempting to describe was essentially the result of a complete intraface among the elements of the output and the processing systems with environmental characteristics. When all of these components in a human communication system intraface, they have a mutual effect on each other. Thus we find ourselves in agreement with Whorf to the extent that we believe the language system learned by an individual will certainly affect the way that individual perceives the world. It will also facilitate and affect reasoning about the world, as well as the way in which an individual is motivated. Similarly, the language system learned will be affected by these other components.

This is why we feel that many people are concerned today about sexist language and racist language, which we discussed earlier. There is a feeling that if little girls grow up in a world in which all personal pronouns in textbooks are "he" and "him," they will begin to perceive the world about them as a "male world" in which they are subordinate or merely tolerated. Likewise, if a firm is attempting to hire "salesmen," there is a concern that the use of this term might cause the perception of a woman to be less positive because she does not fit into that category. Is this a legitimate concern? We think it is, since our language affects the way we think and feel. Many of the concerns expressed today by minority groups may have considerable basis in the way we use language and, more specifically, in the way we are affected by language.

PROBLEMS IN LANGUAGE

As we communicate, we frequently have conflicts and problems in our interactions with other people because of the way we have misused words. At this point we would like to discuss a few of those problems and try to relate them to some of the concepts previously discussed.

Multiple Meaning

One of the most frequent problems results from the assumption that words have only one meaning. Given our previous discussion on this subject, it should be apparent that there are as many different meanings for a given word as there are people who might use it. However, because several of us use the same word we are sometimes fooled into thinking we are talking (or thinking) about the same thing. We might keep Lewis Carroll (1925) in mind. "'When I use a word,' Humpty Dumpty said in a very scornful tone, 'it means just what I choose it to mean neither more nor less.' 'The question is,' said Alice, 'whether you can make words mean so many different things.' 'The question is,' said Humpty Dumpty, 'who is to be master, that's all.'" Are we to allow words to master us or are we to master words? We can gain greater control over words and avoid some of the problems that result from multiple associations simply by remembering that words do have multiple meanings.

One of us once had a slight problem resulting from the multiple meanings of a word. Some of you may be familiar with the use of the word "madam" as a form of address used when speaking to a French woman who is married. You also may know that it is a "flip" way of addressing women in America. This latter use of the term is not derogatory but rather part of the light banter we engage in at one time or another with someone we like. During interaction with a secretary, one of us once referred to her as "madam." Very quickly we discovered that she was offended. Upon discussing the matter with her, we discovered that what she thought of when she heard the word "madam" was the term in American slang referring to the proprietress of a "house of ill repute." Thus when she was addressed as "madam," she did not perceive the exchange as humorous but rather as derogatory. Had we kept in mind the two different uses of the term we wouldn't have had the conflict. Once we explained to her the way we were using the term, there was never a problem again.

General semanticists, in their pragmatic approach to the use of language, suggest a very useful device to employ in regard to words that they call *indexing*. They suggest that we should remember that "madam" is not a single word, but rather that there is "$madam_1$" and "$madam_2$." Thus, we index two different meanings for the word and try to keep in mind when using or hearing that word that it could be interpreted in many ways. Remember, the ability to abstract means that we can have multiple meanings for words, and this fact gives words considerable power. Likewise, it can result in misunderstanding. The technique of indexing may be a way to keep these considerations in mind.

Another problem resulting from multiple meanings concerns the comparative statements we make. There is a communication exercise we use in workshops and classes called "how often is often." Has it ever occurred to you that words such as "big," "little," "often," and "frequently" have very ambiguous meanings? They can be interpreted in many different ways. Take the word "often." Whenever we ask our classes to indicate within a range of 1 to 100 how many times an "often-occurring" event happens, the estimates have ranged from 25 times to 75 times out of 100. The word "often" can mean many different quantities to different people in different contexts. You may begin to wonder how we ever manage to understand each other when you consider that we use terms like this every day and throughout the day in our language. In fact, you might find that it is even difficult to talk without using comparative terms. When we use these terms, we should define what we mean by them. When we hear someone use a term such as "often," "large," or "frequently," we would do well to ask them what they mean by the term. Likewise, when we use terms like these we would do well to explain what we mean by them and to provide some sort of objective basis for people interpreting what they are hearing from us.

Emotional Words

As we discussed in the section on the dimensionality of meaning, better than half of the meaning accounted for in words results from the evaluative component. This fact suggests that our language has emotional implications, even though we may not be aware of them. Is the word "old" a descriptive term? To many of us it is, until someone applies it to us. Although perhaps not many people have called you "old" yet, you may already have found out that little children consider you old. Within the next five to ten years, you will experience people who are your current age calling you "old." At that point, "old" will not sound good or neutral to you. We try to come up with acceptable ways of saying "old." No doubt you have heard terms such as "senior citizens," "elderly persons," or "golden agers." All of these terms are attempts at agreeable substitutes for an expression that may carry some unpleasant emotional connotations for older citizens.

Language Intensity

There are positive and negative elements in every word as well as potency and activity components, and when you put all of these together you can come up with something we call *language intensity*. Look back at Fig. 6.2. The farther away we get from the midpoint on that measurement instrument, the more intensely we are perceiving the word (no matter which end of the continuum we are marking). If somebody says to you, "I have a bad cold today," how does that compare with the statement "I have a terrible cold"? How about "a horrible cold"? In talking with our classes, we have found that "a terrible cold" is worse than "a bad cold" and that "a horrible cold" is worse than "a terrible cold." It is also our impression that these words are similar in terms of the denotative meanings we discussed earlier in this chapter. Although the words "bad," "terrible," and "horrible" might be described or defined similarly in a dictionary, they vary considerably in intensity.

It has been discovered that when we say something with which our listeners are in disagreement, we are more effective if we use words of low or moderate intensity than if we use words of high intensity. When we use words of high intensity our listeners are very prone not only to reject what we are saying but actually to "boomerang" or shift their attitudes in a direction opposite to the one we are advocating. Likewise, if listeners are in agreement with what we are saying, they are most likely to be satisfied when we use highly intense language rather than language of low intensity. The upshot of this discussion is that we should employ moderate- to low-intensity language whenever possible, unless we know absolutely that the people to whom we are speaking are 100% in agreement with what we are saying.

Meanings Change

At times, one of the hardest things to keep in mind is that meanings of words are constantly changing. These changes can occur for a couple of reasons. First, meanings of words can change because the physical reality to which the words relate or with which they are associated is itself changing. One of the best examples of this phenomenon is a child growing up. Johnny in 1980 is not the same as Johnny will be in 1985 if, for instance, Johnny is 15 years old in 1980. The difference between 15-year-old Johnny and 20-year-old Johnny is profound. Johnny grows up, becomes an adult, and is a very different individual indeed. Therefore, the meaning of the word "Johnny," in this particular instance, has changed considerably. According to general semanticists, we live in a process world in which everything is constantly changing. Although children provide one of the most graphic examples of change, all of us are changing. Both of us today are much different than we were five or ten years ago. Likewise, we can look at various friends, colleagues, and members of our family and see considerable change, if we really stop to think about it. Most often we don't notice change in people because we are around them day to day, and we live through change with them. Thus we experience change in small degrees from day to day.

Verbal Communication

1970
PHOTO BY CAROLE DUGAN

The general semanticists who call the process world to our attention suggest that, as with the indexing of words with multiple meanings, we should date words as we use them. As with indexing, dating is a mental process. We don't need to write the words down. Mentally, we should keep in mind that $Scott_{1980}$ is not $Scott_{1970}$ and will not be $Scott_{1990}$. They are all different "Scotts" even though they might refer to the same person. Many friendships and marriages have been dissolved because one person or the other in a relationship has neglected to do this kind of mental dating and so provide for change in the other person. To say that "Shirley is a wife" may have meant one thing in 1970, but it may mean something very different in 1980. Thus, we need to constantly reevaluate and keep in mind that change is always occurring.

Stereotypes

Because we can categorize with words, it is very easy to engage in a process called *stereotyping*. We can use a word such as "doctors" to represent many observations we have made about members of a group of people in the

Problems in Language

1980
PHOTO BY CAROLE DUGAN

medical profession. It is possible, then, to go from that overall abstraction of "doctor" and develop a stereotype. Stereotypes occur when we take the category that includes a number of different people or events having something in common and we make statements about the category as if it applied in the same way to all the members of the category. For instance, we might say that doctors are wealthy. Granted, we rarely find doctors starving to death in this world, but there are differences among the incomes that doctors earn each year. The statement that "doctors don't have time for patients" is a stereotype. This is certainly not true of all doctors. We have doctors who spend anywhere from a half hour to an hour per patient every time we go in for visits.

We have picked on doctors, but there are obviously many other stereotypes you have heard that are derived from the capacity of language to abstract and categorize. "Chinese people are intelligent" is a stereotype. That statement may be true of some Chinese, but it certainly is not true of all Chinese. "Jewish people are good at business." Some of our Jewish friends could no more make ends meet from month to month than the most financially incapable of our friends. "Blacks are lazy." Certainly there are some lazy people who are black, but there are also lazy people who are white, red, and yellow. We know of no racial group that has a corner on laziness. Notice that the stereotypes we have mentioned are both positive and negative.

Why do we employ stereotypes? First, as is the case with other abstractions, a stereotype is useful to us when it is accurate. A stereotype about doctors is that all doctors have attended medical school, gone through an internship, and passed state-administered exams. Fortunately, that stereotype has been true of the doctors we have encountered. If we could not assume that stereotype, it would be necessary for us to go through the process of checking out the qualifications of each doctor we go to in every new town to which we move. In truth, most of us are not capable of determining how qualified a doctor is. We do not have the medical training necessary to make what is essentially a medical judgment. Therefore, we rely on a stereotype that enables us to know how to interact with a doctor and whether to trust her or him, even though we have never met this person before in our lives. Because stereotypes can be useful to us at times and because we can frequently develop accurate stereotypes, we often fall prey to using inaccurate stereotypes. This is where our problem begins. As with other inaccurate abstractions, when we use an inaccurate stereotype we get into big trouble. A statement such as "Women don't really want to work; they would rather stay at home and take care of a house" is a stereotyped statement that can be very dangerous for us to hold, whether we are male or female.

How do we avoid stereotypes? Go back to the section of this chapter that dealt with multiple meanings and consider that the process of indexing can be useful here, too. Remember that doctor$_1$ is not doctor$_2$, that they are not necessarily the same, and that they do not necessarily have all characteristics in common. Likewise, woman$_1$ is not the same as woman$_2$. Although they may share some characteristics in common that enable us to put them in the same category (the category of "woman"), it is also true that each has characteristics that the other does not share. Thus we must be careful not to use stereotypes that treat all people, animals, or institutions as if they were the same.

Cultural Differences

The area of cultural differences is where we most frequently encounter stereotypes and an even more diabolical form of the stereotype, *prejudice*. As we approach individuals, do we wait to interact with them and find out what they are like? Or do we prejudge them and assume they are smart, stupid, lazy, cunning, or the like because of the cultural group to which they belong? When we make these prejudgments, we are exhibiting what has been called prejudice. Unfortunately, prejudice makes it almost impossible for us to cope with people on an individual basis. As a result, we are prone to overlook the characteristics of the individual, to use language that is inappropriate, and/or to do any number of things that could offend the person toward whom we might be prejudiced.

In our country, there are at least three major cultural conflicts that manifest themselves in our communication. These include the cultural gaps between generations, between white Anglo-Saxon Protestants and various ethnic groups, and between males and females. We are willing to grant that some people don't think of these groups as distinct cultures, but we believe that the notion of cultures suggested by Richard Porter (1972, p. 3) very clearly defines these different groups as separate cultures.

> **When I use the word culture, I am referring to the cumulative deposit of knowledge, experience, meanings, beliefs, bias, attitudes, religions, concepts of self, the universe and self-universe relationships, hierarchies of status, role expectations, spatial relations, and time concepts acquired by large groups of people in the course of generations through individual and group striving.**

Many people think of culture in racial terms. They think of groups such as German, Spanish, and American. Porter's approach to culture includes what has frequently been referred to as *subcultures*. Subcultures are frequently considered smaller cultures within large cultures, without any connotation of substandard or subordinate groups. We mention the cultural conflicts between generations, between WASPS and ethnics, and between males and females because all of these cultural conflicts have a way of manifesting themselves in the way people communicate.

Young people in America talk a language different from those who are older. The new "in" terms vary from year to year. These language changes appear to be a defining characteristic of whether you are "part of the group" or not. Words currently acceptable to today's youth may be totally unknown to older groups.

The differences between white Anglo-Saxon Protestants and other ethnic groups such as blacks, Chicanos, Indians, Japanese, and Chinese-Americans are probably more obvious to many people. At one time, we were taught that America was the "melting pot" of different cultures. The more predominant view today among anthropologists and sociologists is that we have not been a melting pot but rather that we have tended to be a country in which multiple cultures and different languages have existed side by side. Languages such as Black English Vernacular are significantly different from those spoken by the majority of white Anglo-Saxon Protestants. Although many English teachers in public schools once believed that the language spoken by black children in urban ghettos was a substandard form of English (or incorrectly spoken English), linguists have now discovered that it actually is a distinct and valid language in its own right. Black ghetto English exists with its own vocabulary and its own grammar, just as Standard American English. Today, the black person who has grown up learning both Black English Vernacular and Standard American English has accomplished a task parallel to the mastering of both English and Spanish. Such a person should be considered bilingual.

We most often refer to men and women as being part of the same culture. If you reconsider Porter's definition of culture, you can see that men and women in our country have had very different experiences, associations with words, beliefs, biases, attitudes (especially concepts of self), role expectations, and the like. Because two different cultures defined by gender exist in America, many of the problems between men and women in our country can be traced to cultural differences that are manifested in language misunderstandings. Who could ever suggest that the word "abortion" has the same meaning for a man as it does for a woman? "Abortion" is something that can happen to a woman, but not to a man. Likewise, words like "pregnancy," "menopause," "prostate trouble," "impotence," and the like are all words that have significantly different meanings for people, depending on their gender. When we discuss public policy concerning abortion or birth control, or whenever men and women attempt to talk with each other, it is apparent that there are monumental problems present in their differing uses of language that arise from cultural differences.

We should always attempt to keep in mind the effects of cultural differences on language. These effects are pronounced for both verbal communication, as we have discussed, and for nonverbal communication, as we will discuss in the next chapter. We hope that you will also be sensitive to cultural groups that don't appear to be different from yourself at first glance.

IMPROVING LANGUAGE EFFECTIVENESS

Having learned of the complexity of language, its power, and its misuses, along with the various problems just discussed, we might feel as if we should give up since language is an impossible tool for people to use. The facts don't support that point of view. Language has been a very useful tool by which human beings have built considerable accomplishments. Although it is true that we have had wars, fights, and personal tragedies that have resulted from the misuse of language, it is equally true that human beings have made considerable progress from those days when we lived in caves and beat each other over the head to solve our problems. Language is a two-edged sword that can be employed to create problems as well as to solve them. There are four basic suggestions we would make to avoid problems in language usage.

Moderation

Always try to be moderate in your use of language. Extreme statements and terminology and highly emotional and intense language tend to be threatening and work against the acceptance of our ideas by other people. It may sound like a cliché to suggest moderation. However, not only does common sense suggest moderation as a reasonable way to use language but also language research in the social sciences. Except for unusual situations, whenever you are making a choice between the use of extreme language and the use of moderate language, choose the moderate approach. Rather than speak of "the most horrible" gas bill, speak of a gas bill "that appears to be excessive."

Use Feedback

We employ feedback to determine when there are misunderstandings and when our message is not getting across as we intended. Always feel free to ask if people are understanding the message and use all of the feedback (both verbal and nonverbal) you can get from your listeners to determine your effectiveness as a communicator. Once you discover misunderstandings through feedback, it is usually possible to correct them. If you don't discover the misunderstanding, it is impossible to correct it.

Audience Analysis

For years, public speaking teachers have suggested to would-be orators that they carefully analyze their audiences prior to speaking to them. This suggestion may see absurdly simple, but it is amazing to contemplate the number of people who don't follow this basic rule of thumb in everyday communication situations. The politician preparing to give a public speech recognizes the importance of figuring out what kind of people he or she is about to address. Likewise, when one of us has to give a speech to a club or civic group we tend to understand the necessity for thinking a little bit about the people to whom we are going to talk. However, all too often when we are meeting people in a social situation or when we are just talking with friends, we tend to forget that it is just as important to analyze these people from the same kind of perspective as the public speaker. We need to consider these people's age, gender, ethnic background, and educational level. We need to consider experiences they have had that can leave them with various word associations. We should consider all these things in an effort to predict the way they may react to our use of language. The better we can predict their responses, the less likely we are to encounter problems as we talk with them.

This analysis should be conducted from the point of view of the dimensions of language we mentioned earlier. We can never know for sure exactly how a listener will respond. However, the more we can relate a person's background to the way that person is going to respond to a word on the evaluative, potency, and activity dimensions of meaning, the more likely we will be able to choose a word that will not offend but that will affect the individual in the way we wish. There are obviously no guarantees, but a very careful and conscientious attempt to understand our listeners is always in order when we are about to communicate. This attempt involves more than simple armchair analysis. Sometimes it might be wise to pick up a book and do some reading. For instance, if you are aware that you are going to be interacting with people of a specific group, it is wise to find out about that group. We do have the opportunity to anticipate these interactions.

Observe All Output Systems

Throughout this book we've discussed the importance of remembering that all components and subsystems within human communication systems relate to and affect each other. Most specifically, we have suggested that there is an important intrafacing of all components. Nowhere can this be more important or more evident than in our input/output systems. As we have discussed, it is almost impossible at times to separate what is popularly called "verbal communication" from what is called "nonverbal communication." Both are components within our input/output systems. Verbal and nonverbal language systems intraface with each other. There are elements common to each. Fur-

Verbal Communication

thermore, the way one is performed affects the way the other is performed. The vocalics we use, such as tone of voice, volume, and the like, significantly affect the way in which the words we have selected are perceived by our listeners. Likewise, the words we select to communicate affect the way in which our facial expressions, gestures, and even our posture are perceived by people with whom we are communicating.

We can use language more effectively if we never forget this intimate relationship between verbal and nonverbal language. Many communication misunderstandings result from a lack of awareness that these language systems work together and have a significant effect on each other. The more sensitive we can be to this relationship, the less likely we are to produce messages in which the verbal and nonverbal components contradict each other or in some way detract from each other.

SUMMARY

One of the primary distinguishing characteristics of human beings is the ability to produce spoken language. There appears to be no other animal on earth that possesses this primary tool for survival. Our spoken language is an extremely complex system comprised of both nonverbal and verbal components. The verbal component can be broken down into two subsystems: vocabulary and grammar. Within our vocabulary are words that have acquired meaning through an association process. These meanings are arbitrary, arrived at through language structure, and they have dimensional components. Our grammar is a system of rules that governs the way we structure sentences, determine appropriateness, and even take turns during conversation. The spoken language that we learn evidently has a significant effect on the way we think and the way we perceive our world.

Finally, there are any number of language problems that we all encounter. These problems result from the abstract nature of language and the constant change in the world in which we live. They can more effectively be overcome through the moderate use of language, the use of feedback, and audience analysis, and by never forgetting that verbal language is a part of an overall input/output system consisting of both verbal and nonverbal components. The next chapter will focus more extensively on the nonverbal component of input/output systems.

KEY TERMS AND CONCEPTS

ABSTRACTION	EVALUATION COMPONENT
ACTIVITY COMPONENT	GRAMMAR
COGNITIVE COMPETENCE	INDEXING
COMMUNICATIVE COMPETENCE	LANGUAGE INTENSITY
COMMUNICATIVE MEANING	LINGUISTIC COMPETENCE
CONNOTATIVE MEANING	POTENCY COMPONENT
CONTEXTUAL MEANING	PREJUDICE
DENOTATIVE MEANING	REFERENCE PROCESS

REFERENT
SAPIR-WHORF HYPOTHESIS
SEMANTIC DIFFERENTIAL
SENTENCE STRUCTURE
STEREOTYPING
STRUCTURAL MEANING

SUBCULTURES
SYMBOL
SYMBOLIZATION
TIME-BINDING
TRIANGLE OF MEANING
VOCABULARY

SUGGESTED READINGS

HARDY, WILLIAM G., *Language, Thought and Experience*. Baltimore: University Park Press, 1978. This book contains a statement and analysis of most of the major theories of language. Hardy places these theories in their historical perspective and provides his own insights. Each essay on each theory provides the reader with a good overview of the theory discussed.

HOWELL, RICHARD W., AND HAROLD J. VETTER, *Language in Behavior*. New York: Human Sciences Press, 1976. This book provides a linguistically oriented introduction to language for the serious student. Its major asset is its focus on language as it is *used*. This should be a very useful book for any student of human behavior who is pragmatically oriented.

WHORF, BENJAMIN LEE, *Language, Thought, and Reality*. Cambridge, Mass.: M.I.T. Press, 1956. John B. Carroll edited this collection of Whorf's essays. It is an excellent statement of the Whorfian hypothesis discussed in this chapter.

7

Nonverbal Communication

The verbal input and output channel is extremely important to the human communication system, but it is not the only channel that humans employ. We communicate with one another in many nonverbal ways such as gestures, tone of voice, posture, the clothes we wear, and the ways we touch. In this chapter, we will explore this aspect of human communication. Most of us are not conscious of the nonverbal channels we will be discussing in this chapter. After reading this chapter, you will be able to relate the way we communicate nonverbally to what you have already learned about the way we communicate verbally. All of the various human communication channels are interrelated to one another.

The input/output processes in human communication systems are not restricted to verbal language. The term most commonly applied to the other channels used by humans to communicate is *nonverbal*. The nonverbal communication channels are no less important to human communication than verbal communication. Nonverbal communication refers to ways other than words whereby we communicate and receive meaning. Some of the nonverbal channels by which we communicate include our use of gestures, tone of voice, head or other bodily movements, posture, facial expressions, eye behavior, proximity, spatial position, bodily contact, body orientation, and personal artifacts. In this chapter we will discuss each of these nonverbal communication behaviors and illustrate the ways in which they relate to interaction, interpersonal attitudes, emotion, and personality. First, we will discuss the interrelations between the verbal and nonverbal communication channels.

VERBAL VERSUS NONVERBAL COMMUNICATION

Nonverbal messages cannot be studied in isolation. In order to understand their importance, we must look at them holistically relative to the other aspects of communication, especially verbal language. The nonverbal channel most often complements the verbal channel. Nonverbal communication can also contradict, repeat, regulate, and even substitute for verbal messages. Nonverbal communication is primarily *analogic* while language is primarily *digital*. Analogic means that the code elements generally are continuous and natural. A natural code utilizes symbols that resemble what they are designed to represent. For example, if you shake your fist at somebody, that nonverbal gesture bears a close resemblance to the type of behavior you intend toward that person (i.e., a fist fight). An analogic code is also continuous; in other words, we receive our nonverbal meanings all at once. The process of shaking our fist communicates a whole meaning by itself; we do not usually shake our fist and then proceed to pound our chest, fall to the ground, and pretend to be knocked out. The shaking of our fist communicates the whole message all at once. Language, on the other hand, is a digital code; this term designates that it is made up of code elements that are discrete and arbitrary. Verbal messages are arbitrary because we have assigned certain meanings to certain words by chance. Verbal messages are also discrete. We receive a verbal message by understanding the meanings of a series of letters and words, each of which is separate and distinct from those coming before and after it. We understand language because we have memorized how our particular vocabulary and grammar work.

Verbal and nonverbal communication channels differ in other ways as well. First, we communicate nonverbally from the moment we are born, whereas we develop verbal communication much later. There is considerable speculation that some of our nonverbal communication ability is inherited, even though we know that most of it is learned. We will discuss the development of both the verbal and nonverbal communication channels in the following chapter. Second, verbal communication is less universal than nonverbal communication. If you go to a foreign country you will find that you will be able to communicate to some extent with persons whose language you do not understand through the more universal nonverbal communication channels. Finally, verbal communication is a more intellectual activity than nonverbal communication, which represents a more emotional activity. In other words, we verbally communicate abstract ideas and concepts, often in the third person, but our nonverbal messages are more directly related to our own personal and concrete feelings and emotions.

It is only recently that communication specialists have begun to look at the nonverbal channels carefully, and we are just beginning to understand their potentialities and interrelationships with verbal communication. Many of the early investigators of nonverbal communication were surprised to discover that people tend to believe messages that flow through the nonverbal channels more than messages that flow through the verbal channel when the two are in conflict. They believe the reason for this phenomenon is that most of us realize that the verbal channel is more under conscious control and that many of the nonverbal channels are not. We are less likely to lie nonverbally than we are to lie verbally. When you are purchasing a new or used car, for example, and the salesperson is telling you about all of the good features of the car, you will probably be looking at the salesperson's eyes, gestures, and other nonverbal channels to determine if he or she is telling you the truth. If you see some nonverbal behavior that indicates you may not be getting accurate information, you will most likely believe the nonverbal message over the verbal one. We must constantly be aware of the relationships between verbal and nonverbal communication. Each facilitates the other and both are necessary parts of the input/output components of human communication systems.

CHARACTERISTICS OF NONVERBAL COMMUNICATION

Nonverbal meaning is perceived holistically. One of the most common mistakes people make is to assign too much meaning to a single nonverbal behavior. Authors of popular books on nonverbal communication often make this mistake. They assume, for example, that because you have your arms folded across your chest, you are being defensive. In fact, you might just be cold. An informed student of nonverbal communication soon learns to look at more than one cue before making a judgment about the meaning of a nonverbal message. All nonverbal cues are highly interdependent and need to be studied together as a whole system of communication. A person who makes a judgment based on a single nonverbal cue is like a quack medical doctor who tries to diagnose a disease by looking at only one symptom. In addition to looking at all of the nonverbal cues that accompany one another, the sensitive observer will also analyze the setting in which the cue occurs, the time at which it occurs, its duration and frequency, and the culture or subculture in which it occurs. A person holding out a thumb means something completely different if he or she is standing alongside the road or behind home plate at a baseball game. This warning about not assigning a single meaning to a single nonverbal cue is cited in almost every textbook on nonverbal communication, but it is still the most abused rule of all.

Nonverbal Communication

The same nonverbal cue can have different meanings, depending on the circumstances.
PHOTO BY CAROLE DUGAN

Nonverbal communication operates on both the conscious and unconscious levels. We usually do not communicate through language accidentally, but it happens all the time nonverbally. An often quoted statement about nonverbal communication is that "One cannot not communicate." This statement implies that our nonverbal behavior is interpreted by others whether we consciously wish it or not. Just because a person is sitting down and is silent does not guarantee that a meaning is not being assigned to this scenario by someone. Nonverbally, and perhaps unconsciously, this person might be saying, "Don't come near me; I don't want to talk to anyone." We might pick this meaning up because the person is hunched over, with face hidden. There are many degrees of consciousness in nonverbal communication, ranging from very intentional messages to completely subconsciously motivated behaviors. It takes much training to become sensitive to the entire range of nonverbal cues.

Nonverbal cues are often misinterpreted. Assigning too much meaning to a single cue is one kind of misinterpretation. R.P. Harrison (1974) suggests two other ways we can misinterpret nonverbal cues. The first he calls *missed cues*. A missed cue is one that we simply are not aware of at all. The cue is available, but the receiver either does not see it or filters it out. The second way people can misinterpret nonverbal cues is called a *miscue*. A miscue occurs when a receiver is aware of the cue but fails to assign accurate meaning to it. Let's assume that three people are interacting. At one point, the speaker looks up at the ceiling for a moment while talking. If one of the receivers happens to be looking away at the time the nonverbal cue takes place, it is a missed cue because it is not perceived. If the third participant sees the speaker looking at the ceiling and interprets it as an attempt to collect his or her thoughts when it is really a sign of boredom, it is a miscue. It is important to distinguish between these two types of mistakes. Both can be reduced through nonverbal communication training.

Nonverbal communication is regulated by the social system. Society has determined that some types of nonverbal behavior are appropriate for certain situations and others are not appropriate. Some of the *societal norms* governing nonverbal behavior are written in books of etiquette and similar sources. Others are learned and understood from those around us as we grow up, although they are not necessarily stated overtly. We learn very early in life, for example, that we must stand up straight, pay attention, and generally behave submissively in the presence of persons who are older and/or of higher status. These norms were developed originally by the dominant members of the social system and are maintained through social pressure and persuasion. Persons who break the "rules" are rejected.

Perhaps the best way to discover what norms govern nonverbal communication is too break a rule deliberately. This is a commonly used research method in nonverbal communication. An interesting experiment you might try is to break the norm regarding eye behavior when approaching a stranger. The rule seems to be that we can look at a stranger from a fairly long distance, but as the stranger gets closer we should no longer stare. Try looking directly at a stranger as he or she approaches you. What is the reaction? By experimenting and observing reactions for yourself, you will learn some interesting facts about how nonverbal communication is rule-governed.

Many of the early nonverbal communication textbooks devoted a chapter to each of the different nonverbal cues. There were chapters on facial expressions, gestures, and so on. This arrangement encouraged students to view the various types of cues as independent and unique. Students found it difficult to understand the interdependence of nonverbal cues and to take a holistic perspective when nonverbal communication channels were presented in this manner. More recent texts have begun to take a process- or systems-oriented perspective by discussing the various types of cues relative to the types of messages they communicate. We will use this approach. In the following sections we will discuss each nonverbal channel relative to the functions it performs, such as regulating interaction, displaying interpersonal attitudes, communicating emotion, and presenting ourselves to others.

NONVERBAL COMMUNICATION AND INTERACTION

When two or more individuals come together as part of a communication system, many nonverbal cues occur as part of the interaction along with the verbal symbols. Some of the most important nonverbal channels that operate during interaction are vocalics, facial expression, eye behavior, head and hand movement, touch, posture and orientation, and proxemics. Since this is the first section in which we will be talking about each of these cues in detail, we will define each cue as it comes up in the discussion.

Vocalics

As we discussed in Chapter 6, we have many vocal outputs and inputs other than the words we speak. These other vocal outputs and inputs are called vocalics, or paralanguage. Vocalics includes such vocal outputs and inputs as vocal range, articulation, resonance, dialect, word rhythm and tempo, coughing, sighing, swallowing, groaning, yawning, "um," "uh-huh," pauses, silences, and all forms of verbal disruptions or nonfluencies such as stutters, omitted words, and incoherent sounds. In interaction, these cues play an important role, especially timing, pitch, and loudness, which are called the *prosodic features* of the voice. The words you speak can change in meaning depending on how rapidly or slowly they are spoken relative to one another, the pitch level at which they are spoken, and how loudly or softly we speak them. For example, a sentence can be either a question or a declarative statement, depending on whether the pitch rises or falls at the end. Try saying the sentence "You are feeling well," first as a statement, then as a question. What happened to the pitch of your voice? Now try saying the same sentence a little more loudly and notice how the received meaning might change. Now try varying the timing between the various words. The meaning will change once more. In a communication interaction, the other aspects of vocalics can also be as meaningful as these prosodic features.

The vocalic aspects of an interaction play an extremely important role in determining the final outcome of the interaction. The words we use to communicate to one another provide only part of the meaning perceived by a receiver. Think of the difference in meaning that comes through when you hear a person talking and when you read the words spoken by that person in written form. This is most noticeable when reading and hearing the text of a speech. Much of a speaker's credibility is determined by the paralanguage that accompanies the verbal message. Vocalics is one of the most important nonverbal communication channels that occurs during interaction.

Facial Expression

During interaction, the most observed area of the body by both the speaker and listener is the face. Our facial expression includes all of the features of our face other than our eyes, which are a special channel in and of themselves. Our forehead, eyebrows, nose, cheeks, and mouth are all capable of communicating nonverbal information. In interaction our facial expressions are constantly changing, regardless of whether we are speaking or listening. Most people seem to feel that our nonverbal feelings are most easily recognized through our facial expressions. They look for wrinkles on the forehead, smiles, frowns, grimaces of various sorts, and many other forms of facial expression. Actually, the facial channel is one of the worst places to discover a person's "true attitude" because it is a nonverbal channel over which people have considerable conscious control.

Early in our childhood we were taught to manipulate our facial expression to conceal our real feelings. We discovered that during certain situations, social norms demanded that we learn to mask, intensify, deintensify, or substitute emotions and feelings as portrayed on our face. Because our facial expression was so often regulated, we learned how to control it very well. We learned how to be "poker-faced," for example. This is not to say that facial expression has no value in interaction, but rather that we should beware of trusting it too much. Our faces reveal the messages we want others to believe. They are not necessarily accurate messages. We consciously use our face to help us communicate our verbal message. We may wink, for example, as we say something to show that it is not to be taken seriously.

One type of facial expression that does not seem to be under as much conscious control as some of the others is called *micromomentary expressions* (MMEs). These facial expressions, which last approximately two-fifths of a second, represent a momentary lapse by an individual. While trying to maintain control of our facial expression, we sometimes slip and let our real feelings show through for a brief moment. Have you ever noticed when someone is lying to you that for some reason you begin to get the impression that he or she is lying? You don't really know how you recognized the lie because MMEs occur so quickly they are almost subliminal (below the level of conscious awareness). It is hard for us consciously to look for these facial expressions, but careful attention to the faces of others during interaction will often be rewarded with a kind of intuitive feeling regarding their "true" feelings. When observing the facial channel during interaction, be aware that the messages you receive on that channel are almost as consciously controlled as those on the verbal channel, except perhaps for the MMEs.

Eye Behavior

The main communicative aspect of eye behavior is that of who or what we are looking at and for how long. Our eyes provide a nonverbal communication channel that is important not only during interaction but also before the interaction begins and after it ends. By establishing eye contact, raising eyebrows, and smiling, people indicate that they are interested in communicating. This pattern seems to be a universal greeting. Such facial and eye behavior helps set the interaction climate, even before the participants begin to talk. Leavetaking is also marked by various forms of eye behavior. We can signal a readiness to halt the interaction by looking around and closing or unfocusing our eyes. Have you ever noticed the behavior of children who are being disciplined? They seem to go into a trance and their eyes seem to have an invisible film that comes over them. This is the point at which the parent usually says,"Are you listening to me?" The answer in most cases is "No!" Such children are ready to leave the interaction. They have closed that communication channel. The eye behavior that takes place after the final words have been said in any interaction is a final summary of how the interaction has gone and the likelihood of further interactions in the future.

Eye behavior is also important *during* interaction. Kendon (1967) suggested four main kinds of functions of eye behavior during interaction: cognitive, monitoring, regulatory, and expressive. The *cognitive* function refers to such eye behavior as breaking eye contact in order to mentally clarify thoughts and properly prepare the verbal message. The *monitoring* function relates to obtaining feedback. During an interaction, the speaker and listener look at one another or relevant other objects in the environment (a map, slide, conversation piece, piece of paper, etc.). Monitoring occurs when at least one of the participants is looking at the other. In most interactions, it is the receiver who looks most often at the speaker in order to monitor the nonverbal message channels. The sender of the message looks at the listener when seeking feedback as to how the message is being received. The *regulatory* function of the eyes tells when we should be outputting and when we should be inputting messages. We can signal that the communication channel is available by looking at the other person without speaking. This signal usually occurs at the end of an utterance. This is our nonverbal means of asking the other participant if he or she wants to speak. On the other hand, we can suppress speech by certain kinds of threatening stares. Mutual gaze and threats of this sort often take place when a listener attempts to interrupt the speaker. Finally, eye gaze can serve an *expressive* function by signaling the degree of involvement by either the speaker or the listener. If we are interested, we will maintain eye contact. If we are highly involved in the interaction, our eyes can express many things to a sensitive receiver. We can learn much about an interaction by watching the eyes of the participants. When, where, and how people look at one another are important before, during, and after interaction.

Head and Hand Movements

Human communicators move their heads and hands often during interaction. Some of these movements occur consciously, while others take place unconsciously. Almost all of them can have meaning. Hand movements tend to be used most often by the speaker, while the listener tends to use head movements. Perhaps the most common head movements used by listeners are the nod of agreement (up-and-down head movement) and the head-shaking of disagreement (sideways movement back and forth). There are, however, many other head movements that can accompany language, such as the cocking of the head in puzzlement, usually accompanied by a frown. The listener uses head movement to provide feedback for the speaker.

Hand movements serve many message functions for speakers during interaction. They punctuate what is spoken, as when we say, "I have three points to make today" and hold up three fingers. They can emphasize speech, as when we bang our fist on the table while speaking. They can illustrate what is being said, as when we say, "The dog is about so tall" and hold our hand level above the floor. Some people do not seem to be able to speak without using their hands. Sometimes people use hand gestures that have no real relationship to what is being said in order to indicate the intensity of the message, such as shaking their hands rapidly to express excitement.

It is hard to imagine that human interaction could take place without head and hand movements. Paul Ekman and Wallace Friesen (1969) developed five categories to distinguish among different types of gestures: emblems, illustrators, adaptors, affect displays, and regulators. *Emblems* are consciously controlled gestures that have fairly commonly agreed upon meanings in a particular society. They often have a verbal meaning, such as the "OK" signal. *Illustrators* are all of the nonverbal gestures we use to accompany our verbal communication. If we indicate a specific direction verbally and also point in that direction, the act of pointing illustrates the words. *Adaptors* are self-touching gestures often used during periods of high nervousness or anxiety. We can touch our own skin (called a *self adaptor*), or we can touch our clothing or some other object like a pencil (called an *object adaptor*). Adaptors are old habits that are usually below our level of conscious awareness yet are meaningful to persons who know us well. *Affect displays* are all of the gestures that reveal something about our emotional state. When we are happy, we sometimes raise our hands in the air. When we are sad, we frequently cover our eyes. We have gestures to express most of our emotions. *Regulators* are gestures that help us control interactions. Head nods, for example, are used by a listener to encourage a speaker to continue. The Ekman/Friesen classification scheme gives us a way to identify the type of head and hand movements taking place as we interact with others.

Body Posture and Orientation

During any interactive encounter there is considerable postural movement. We shift from side to side, we cross and uncross our legs, and we lean forward or back. Some of this movement relates to the comfort of the interactors, but much of it also has communicative value. A person who sits or stands rigidly generally communicates attention and subordinance. In most conversations it is the higher-status or dominant participant who normally assumes the more relaxed posture. However, relaxed posture can also communicate boredom or other similar feelings. Postural shifts seem to occur at periods of transition, or when we have a strong reaction to something that has been said. Sideway leans can signal disbelief or hostility to what is being said. We will lean forward when we want to begin or maintain speaking. Have you ever noticed that when a speaker is finished, he or she leans back and the next person to speak often leans forward? These are nonverbal cues, along with vocalics and eye behavior, that allow conversations to progress with a minimum of overtalk and interruptions. This is our way of alternating turns. It is an established interaction pattern understood by almost everyone.

The ways people position themselves relative to one another is called *bodily orientation*. Orientation is usually determined by the relative position of our shoulders to the shoulders of the other person. A vis-a-vis orientation, in which two people are facing each other directly with their shoulders squared to one another, usually communicates a desire not to be interrupted, especially when accompanied by direct eye gaze and little or no eye wandering. As the shoulders of the participants grow farther apart at one side and begin to form a V shape, at least one of the participants is beginning to communicate less interest in the interaction.

Body posture and orientation changes do not occur as often in interaction as some of the other nonverbal channels just discussed, but when they do they usually signal a major change in the nature of the interaction. They tend to indicate more general and more slowly changing aspects of the relationship such as the general atmosphere of the interaction, major topic shifts, anxiety or discomfort on the part of either participant, or the beginning or end of the interaction. Being able to detect these broader changes is just as important as understanding the more fleeting aspects of interaction.

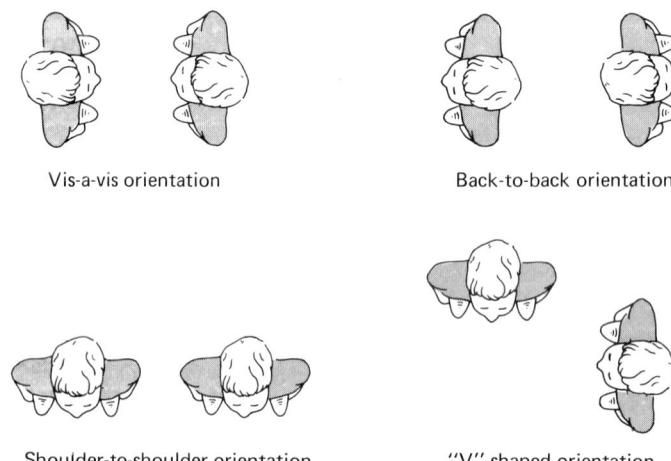

Fig. 7.1 Body orientations.

Proxemics

The final area of nonverbal communication that directly relates to interaction is *proxemics*, the way in which people perceive and use space. People who study proxemics are interested in architecture, color, sound, lighting, movable objects, territory, density, seating arrangement, and many other aspects of space. There are many ways in which space affects interaction. The first is the environment in which the interaction takes place. For example, who possesses the interaction space is important. People are usually more relaxed and willing to talk freely if they are interacting in their own territory. The color of the interaction area, the way the furniture is arranged, the temperature, other objects in the area, and hundreds of other things have the potential to affect the interaction.

The most important aspect of space and interaction, however, is what has been called *interaction distance*. Edward Hall (1959) classified interaction distance into four zones, based on the type of verbal communication that would probably be taking place. The first zone is called the *intimate* zone (9 to 18 inches) within which intimate conversations take place, usually by means of a whisper or very soft voice. The *personal* zone (18 inches to 4 feet) includes types of interaction that are somewhat less intimate but still close. The third zone is *social-consultative* (4 to 12 feet) and includes most business interac-

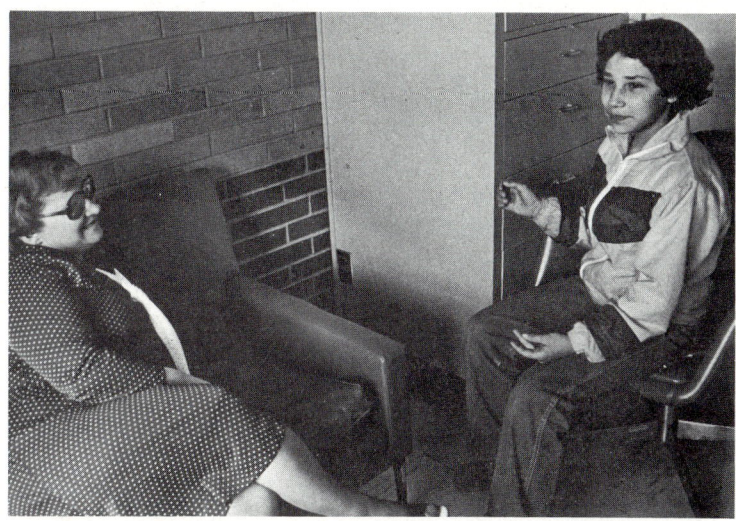

Body posture, orientation, vocalics, and eye behavior are all important nonverbal aids in interaction.
PHOTO BY CAROLE DUGAN

tions. Here, a louder voice is needed and more impersonal topics are usually discussed. The final zone is *public* (12 feet and above) and includes all of the types of public communication such as speeches, forums, and lectures. Interaction distance can shift, although usually only slightly, during an interaction. Changes in interaction distance usually correlate with the degree of friendliness or hostility in the interaction. Proxemic cues have a very important role to play in all types of interaction. We are just beginning to discover how important that role really is.

Interrelationship of Verbal and Nonverbal Interaction Channels

In the beginning of this chapter we said that we cannot look at any nonverbal cue in isolation. We can only understand these cues if we look at them holistically. Perhaps the best way to look holistically at the interrelationship between verbal and nonverbal interaction channels is to provide an extended example. As we go through this example, see if you can spot the interrelationships for yourself. This example supposes that you are going to visit one of your professors in her office to get a homework assignment for a day on which you missed class. This is a pretty clear-cut situation. There should not be too many channels needed, right? Wrong! Let's look at all of the possibilities.

You knock on the professor's open door, see her sitting at her desk, and ask if she has time to talk with you. Because it is the professor's office (or territory) and you are asking to enter, she has a proxemic advantage over you. You would probably make your request in a fairly soft voice to show respect for the professor's status. Because your request is a question, the pitch of your voice would rise on the last syllable. If the professor is working, she may not look at you right away or answer you for the first several seconds. This lack of eye contact and silence make you anxious because they signal that perhaps you have come at the wrong time. Perhaps you should have checked her scheduled office hours. After what seems like an eternity, the teacher looks up and makes eye contact with you. She smiles slightly and points to a chair. Your anxiety decreases slightly because you have been greeted in a somewhat warm fashion and your request for an interaction has been accepted, even though the professor has yet to say a word.

I hope she doesn't ask me why I missed class.
PHOTO BY CAROLE DUGAN

As you move into the office and sit down you change your posture, bodily orientation, and interaction distance. These changes also signal a change from the greeting stage to the main body of the interaction. As you sit down the professor returns her eyes to the material she was working on when you knocked. This behavior tells you that it is not yet time to begin talking. While you wait, your mind unconsciously notes the fact that you are sitting on one side of the desk while the teacher is on the other side. This proxemic feature establishes a business-like atmosphere and predetermines that the interaction distance will be in the social-consultative zone. When the professor looks up and establishes eye contact, she is signaling you to speak. You say that you missed her class and need to get the homework assignment. She frowns slightly and asks why you missed the class. At this point, she also leans back in her chair and shifts to one side so that she is no longer facing you directly (vis-a-vis). All of these things taken together warn you that the interaction climate has changed and that she does not appreciate students' missing class. You had better have an acceptable excuse or you will lose some credibility in her eyes.

Nonverbal Communication and Interaction

Well, she asked.
PHOTO BY CAROLE DUGAN

She doesn't buy my story.
PHOTO BY CAROLE DUGAN

Things could have been worse.
PHOTO BY CAROLE DUGAN

As she asks you the question her eyes monitor your nonverbal reaction to the question. You drop your eyes to collect your thoughts and also signal that you do not feel very good about missing the class. You try to make your facial expression communicate sadness about missing the class, but you are not really too sad because you had one of your best skiing days when you missed the class. You know the professor will not buy your skiing story so you tell her that you overslept. She's pretty sensitive, however, and notices that you shift your posture, fidget with your clothing, jiggle your leg, and have a slight quiver in your voice as you answer her question. She smiles slightly, turns back to orient herself to face you directly, and, resting her arms on the desk, she leans forward as she tells you the homework assignment for the day you missed. Her voice is stern and is a bit louder than usual as she tells you the assignment, and somehow you know that she did not buy your story. You give a little smile and nod as she tells you the assignment in order to thank her nonverbally for not pressing your excuse and for giving you the homework assignment. Because of her behavior, you are able to maintain your dignity in what could have been a much more awkward situation. You try to maintain eye contact with her as you verbally thank her, and you try to make the timing of the words indicate that you really do appreciate her attitude about the whole matter. You both maintain eye contact as you get up to leave, but to your surprise she also gets up and comes around the desk to establish a personal distance zone. You begin to feel much better as she does this, and you both head for the door. She touches you on the shoulder and tells you in a friendly voice to try to get to class from now on. You smile and nod your assent. You now feel very relieved. From your viewpoint, the interaction has been successful because you got the homework assignment and also maintained your credibility in her eyes (at least you think you did).

This whole interaction would have taken probably no more than five minutes, but in that short time every one of the nonverbal channels we have discussed was involved. Each channel contributed something important to the interaction. In order to understand all of the dynamics of the interaction, however, you would have had to perceive it as a whole, as a group of interrelated verbal and nonverbal messages. Some of the messages were conscious and some were not. The channel that was most difficult to describe in this story was the vocalic; there would have been a lot more of it in this situation than we described. The feeling you left with in this interaction may have been accurate or it may not have been. In this story we shifted away slightly from the nonverbal channels of interaction to the nonverbal cues of interpersonal attitudes. The purposes of these nonverbal cues are so similar, however, that it is often difficult to keep them apart, as you will see in the following section. The interpersonal attitudes of the two participants about one another at the end of this interaction could have been very different if even a few of the nonverbal cues had been slightly different. In this situation, as in most interactions, the words spoken were only a part of the whole communication event that took place. They were highly interrelated with all of the other nonverbal communication channels. No one channel provided all of the necessary information. Instead, the participants had to be aware of all of them at once.

NONVERBAL COMMUNICATION AND INTERPERSONAL ATTITUDES

Nonverbal cues are especially effective in communicating emotions and interpersonal attitudes. The difference is that interpersonal attitudes are directed at another person while emotions are not necessarily other-oriented. If the nonverbal cue is merely indicative of the feelings one has about oneself, that feeling is called an emotion. We will deal with this topic in the following section.

Interpersonal attitudes refer to the feelings we have about another person, usually someone who is more or less in direct contact with us. We have already discussed some aspects of interpersonal attitudes in the previous section on nonverbal communication in interaction. We will now go into greater detail. The important nonverbal cues that can communicate interpersonal attitudes are facial expression, eye behavior, bodily posture and orientation, touch, personal artifacts, and proxemics. As you can see, most of these channels have already been introduced in the preceding section. However, different features of these channels are relevant to interpersonal attitudes.

Much effort has been devoted to determining the most important interpersonal attitude dimensions that can be communicated through nonverbal channels. The three dimensions that are best documented are those derived by Mehrabian (1972); these include immediacy, power, and responsiveness. These dimensions are very similar to the interpersonal need dimensions of affection, control, and inclusion mentioned in the chapter on motivation. The *immediacy dimension* refers to how much we like or dislike one another. This dimension is commonly represented as a continuum ranging from "liking" on one end to "disliking" on the other. This dimension correlates with our interpersonal need for affection. The *power dimension* relates to the degree of status or control we feel that we have over another person. This dimension is commonly represented as a continuum ranging from "dominance" on one end to "submission" on the other. This dimension correlates with our interpersonal need for control. The *responsiveness dimension* refers to the amount of interest in, or reaction to, one person by another. This dimension is commonly represented as a continuum ranging from "active" on one end to "passive" on the other. This dimension correlates with our interpersonal need for inclusion. In discussing the following nonverbal cues that communicate interpersonal attitudes, we will relate each to one or more of these interpersonal attitude and need dimensions.

Facial Expression

Since facial expression is probably the least trustworthy nonverbal cue, it is quite possible for us to communicate interpersonal attitudes such as friendship, submission, and active interest in our face when our true attitudes are just the opposite. If we had not developed this ability, we would not be able to function effectively in our society. Just think of what kind of grade you might get in a very dull college class if you were not able to appear interested. How long would a person be able to maintain a pleasant work environment if he or she did not appear friendly to other coworkers, whether they were truly liked or not? Such nonverbal behaviors should also be taken "with a grain of salt" and carefully documented by observing several other nonverbal indicators of the same dimensions.

Facial expressions of immediacy include various forms of smiles and frowns that communicate liking and disliking for the other person. Power and responsiveness are more often communicated by the face in conjunction with the eyes. People differentiate smiles and frowns of the various interpersonal attitude dimensions by means of the eye behavior that accompanies them.

Eye Behavior

Our eyes carry somewhat more power as communicators of interpersonal attitudes than our faces, especially if some of the less obvious aspects of our eye behavior are examined. One example of how a person's eyes can communicate responsiveness and immediacy is *pupil dilation*. The pupils of our eyes dilate when exposed to weakened intensities of light, but they also do so when we are aroused by another person positively or negatively and/or our interest in that person is heightened. This aspect of nonverbal communication often seems to go unnoticed by Americans, although not by members of touch-oriented, close-proximity cultures such as those of the Middle Eastern countries. In order to observe changes in pupil size, persons in those cultures operate more often in an intimate spatial zone, even with strangers. They stand close enough to see pupil dilation and they use it to judge interpersonal attitude. We can observe pupil dilation only with close friends with whom we share the intimate spatial zone.

There are other types of eye behavior that communicate interpersonal attitudes but do not demand such a close proxemic relationship. Examples include the amount of gaze that takes place and the type of eye behavior involved. People tend to look more at persons they like, at dominant persons, and at persons in whom they are actively interested. If, for example, you walk into a group discussion that is in progress, you can tell who the dominant individuals are, whether they are talking or not. You can do this by carefully observing whom the other participants sneak peeks at during the discussion. They are trying to determine the reaction of the dominant person. The dominant individual will in turn look more at the other participants and will tend to break mutual gaze last. This increased gaze is a form of controlling threat by which the dominant individual maintains power. Another type of eye behavior, often called flirting, is a means by which people communicate interest in persons of the opposite sex. The traditional example of such behavior is winking, although much more subtle forms of signaling friendship and interest also exist. Simply breaking eye contact will signal disliking, submissiveness, and rejection. Used in conjunction with facial expression, eye behavior is a fairly powerful communicator of interpersonal attitudes.

Body Posture and Orientation

The most commonly communicated interpersonal attitudes for body posture and orientation are immediacy and power. We have already discussed the vis-a-vis orientation, which indicates friendship and interest. Scheflen (1972) suggests that there are two types of friendship and interest signals, which he calls *courtship* and *quasicourtship* behavior. The first involves many nonverbal cues, including many types of postural and orientation behaviors. Such cues as slow seductive postural shifts, increased muscle tension, intimate direct orientation, and uncrossed legs all relate to courtship and sexual attraction. On the other hand, quasicourtship behaviors indicate that friendship, not sexual courtship, is desired. The same nonverbal cues are used, but not to the same degree. Quasicourtship is a form of passive immediacy, while courtship behaviors indicate active immediacy desires.

Another way in which we can communicate immediacy and responsiveness through posture and orientation is called *response matching*. This means that people who like one another or are responsive to one another will imitate or copy the nonverbal behaviors of one another. For example, if one person is sitting back or crossing the legs or leaning sideways, the other person will do the same. Response matching can also occur with other nonverbal channels such as head and hand movements and vocalics. This kind of response matching is often seen in close family relationships, such as that of a husband and wife who develop the same nonverbal mannerisms. Response matching can develop over years of close involvement or in a relatively short time with someone for whom you have strong positive feelings.

We communicate the power dimension of interpersonal attitudes very effectively through posture and orientation. If, from a distance, you see two people communicating and one of them is standing in an erect and stiff manner while the other is more relaxed, who do you think would have the power or dominance over the other? If you said that the relaxed person probably was the most dominant, you would be correct. A person sitting or standing very straight and proper is generally communicating submissiveness and respect for the other. Persons who believe they have status and power over another will assume a more relaxed and casual posture. A relaxed posture can also signal disinterest or dislike, but in those cases the eyes of the person will also clue you in; they will wander and look away from the other person. In the control situation, the dominant person will usually look at the submissive person.

Response matching often signals similar thoughts and attitudes.
PHOTO BY CAROLE DUGAN

Posture and orientation can be very important communicators of all three interpersonal attitude dimensions. We have mentioned only a few ways in which such communication is accomplished; you can no doubt think of some others.

Touch

Perhaps the best way of communicating both positive and negative interpersonal attitudes is through bodily contact. Both the frequency and duration of touch can be indicators of friendship and interest. Touch can also be the most extreme indicator of hostility, rejection, and dominance—slapping, kicking, punching, etc. One other way in which dominance is communicated through touch occurs when the dominant person touches first and most often. Dancing, holding hands, and embracing are all signs of immediacy. To illustrate the importance of nonverbal communication versus verbal communication in this regard, think about the difference between saying "I love you" and embracing someone you love. The bodily contact provides a much more effective and longer-lasting expression of interpersonal attitudes than the words. Touch operates at the extremes of the interpersonal attitude dimensions. When we touch people, we either strongly like them or strongly dislike them; we feel either very submissive toward them (kissing feet, etc.) or very dominant over them.

Our most effective means of expressing affection is through touch.

PHOTO BY CAROLE DUGAN

Personal Artifacts

A personal artifact is something a person wears such as clothing, rings, necklaces, political buttons, watches, corsages, lipstick, eyeglasses, eyebrow shadow, earrings, and similar accessories. A wedding ring can signal that a person is not available for courtship, while in Hawaii a flower behind the right ear can signal availability. Whenever we accept a personal artifact from another person or whenever we give such a token to another, we signal strong liking of and interest in that person. Going steady and engagements usually involve the exchange of such personal artifacts.

Clothing can also indicate the power dimension. Uniforms establish a person's role in society and the power that goes with it. A person wearing a police officer's uniform is signalling a form of dominance over the average citizen. In the military, stripes and emblems also indicate power. By wearing a suit, males indicate formality and a form of dominance. A T-shirt or blue-collar shirt indicates less power. What you wear will also affect how others perceive you. There is no doubt that we either consciously or unconsciously communicate interpersonal attitudes by the personal artifacts we choose to put on.

Proxemics

Finally, we communicate our interpersonal attitudes through our use of space. We try to get in close proximity to people we like and maintain greater distances from those we dislike. Proximity and eye contact are related in this respect. We tend to have less eye contact in an intimate zone and more eye contact in a public zone. It has been suggested that this variation occurs because eye contact and proxemics are alternative ways of communicating immediacy. We use one or the other, but not both at the same time. Perhaps there are other similar relationships between interpersonal attitude cues that we have yet to discover.

An interesting aspect of proxemics that relates directly to interpersonal attitudes is what has been called *personal space*. Personal space refers to that invisible "bubble" we seem to carry around with us and claim as our own. For example, when we sit down in a chair next to someone, we usually adjust the distance between the two chairs. If we are sitting next to someone we like or are interested in, we sit closer than if we dislike that person. If we become interested in someone we will attempt to decrease personal space, but if the other person does not feel the same he or she will step back. If we are walking down a street, we have a certain distance behind, next to, and in front of us that we feel is "ours," and anyone who invades that space is perceived negatively. Dominant persons like to have a larger space given to them, whether it be personal space or territory. They like large offices and often sit apart from others in groups. Our personal space demands change, depending on the time of day or night, the temperature, who we are with, and many other situational factors.

The preceding examples are only a very few of the ways in which we communicate our interpersonal attitudes nonverbally. Our attitudes toward others are closely related to our own interpersonal needs. We attempt to satisfy our inclusion needs by being nonverbally responsive to others. We try to relate our control needs to our nonverbal power behaviors. Most of us have strong affection needs, so we try to establish a climate of immediacy nonverbally. Some of us have stronger needs in a specific area than others, but we all try to relate our needs to our nonverbal behaviors. Our interpersonal attitudes are closely related to our emotions, which we will discuss next.

COMMUNICATING EMOTION NONVERBALLY

Emotions refer to states such as anxiety, depression, happiness, and so on. Emotions are temporary and are not necessarily directed at someone or something specific. In any study of the ways in which people communicate emotions, we must be constantly aware of the emotions of the receiver as well. Miscues very often occur regarding communicated emotions because the receiver is also frequently in an emotional state that filters and biases his or her perceptions. Everyone has such emotions, but we do not all react in the same way to them.

Fig. 7.2 The six primary emotions.

In most of the research that has been conducted regarding the nonverbal communication of emotions, six basic emotions have been isolated as the ones most commonly identified. They are happiness, surprise, anger, sadness, fear, and disgust. You should remember that these emotions are cognitive rather than physical phenomena. Physiologically, there does not seem to be much difference between extreme happiness and extreme sadness. Your heart rate, blood pressure, perspiration index, and other physiological features will go up no matter what type of emotion you are feeling. We give names to our emotions like happiness, contempt, or surprise based on the circumstances we associate with the emotion. In much the same way, we are able to assign meanings to the nonverbal cues of emotions that we receive from others. The main cues that indicate emotion are facial expression, eye behavior, hand and leg movement, vocalics, and, to a lesser extent, posture and personal artifacts.

Facial Expression

Our face is the primary channel for displaying our emotions, or at least the emotions we would like others to think we have. Much early research was conducted regarding parts of the face as indicators of emotions. The results of this research indicated that different parts of the face communicate different emotions. For instance, we communicate happiness around the mouth area and surprise in the forehead area. However, later evidence has tended to suggest instead that emotional patterns involve the whole face. Investigators have found that the six basic emotions manifested in the face seem to have universal understanding. This finding may suggest that, in part, our facial patterns could be genetically determined rather than just learned or imitated. For most of us, the face is still the main focus of our attention when we want to determine another's emotions.

Determining emotional states from the face is still a difficult chore. As we said earlier, the face can mask, intensify, deintensify, or substitute emotional displays for the real emotions. You can also blend the emotions that are displayed on your face. The slightest change in your facial expression can make a large difference in what another person will perceive. The better you know someone, the better you will be able to judge that person's emotions from his or her facial expression. Regardless of all that we know about our ability to consciously control the expressions on our face, most of us will continue to look to the face for cues concerning the emotional state of another.

Eye Behavior

Besides pupil dilation, which we mentioned earlier, there are two facets of the eye behavior channel that seem to indicate emotion. The first is the avoidance of eye contact. This behavior seems to be associated with the emotions of guilt, shame, and embarrassment. When you are embarrassed, you do not want to make eye contact with anyone. You may often bury your head in your hands to make sure you do not see anyone or that anyone sees you. Children will immediately bring their hands up to cover their eyes when they have been caught doing something they were not supposed to do. Eye blink rate also varies with states of emotional arousal. People blink their eyes more when they are in a high state of emotional arousal than when they are more relaxed.

The reason that more is not known about the relationship between eye behavior and the six basic emotions is because so little research has been done in this area. There is some reason to believe that a definite relationship exists between the eyes and the basic emotions. At least one study (Nummenmaa, 1964) has suggested that the most accurate recognition of emotions is found around the eyes, particularly in regard to emotions like pleasure and anger. More research is needed to confirm and expand this finding.

Communicating Emotion Nonverbally

Children in many parts of the world cover all or part of the face when embarrassed or self-conscious.
PHOTO BY CAROLE DUGAN

Hand and Leg Movements

Many people attempt to hide their emotions. There are, however, certain gestural cues that can give them away. These are called *leakage cues*. The best area to find leakage cues is that of the feet and the legs. The second best area is the hands, while the least reliable area is, you guessed it, the face. People who are highly aroused will often give themselves away by shaking their feet or hands, even though their faces remain relaxed. You are probably familiar with novice public speakers whose hands shake while speaking because of nervousness. A person would do well to look for rapid and random hand and leg movement to determine if others are experiencing strong emotion.

Another example of how gestures show emotion is that of *displacement activities*. We have also earlier identified these as gestural adaptors. They include such behaviors as scratching, touching oneself, or playing with clothing or objects. These behaviors usually indicate negative emotions such as anger, fear, contempt, and frustration. Many people have their own idiosyncratic or personal gestural displacement activities that display emotion. These can be detected by someone who is familiar with that particular individual. For example, we know someone who constantly runs her hand through her hair when she becomes agitated or frustrated. This is not a behavior used by a great many people, but for that woman it is very revealing, if you know her.

Vocalics

Next to facial expression, the best indicator of emotion is vocalics. The speed at which a person talks, the pitch level used, the loudness of the utterances, and the number and types of hesitations and nonfluencies that appear can all indicate various emotions. When we get excited, most of us begin to talk louder and faster. There seem to be some common vocalic features that indicate what emotion is occurring. A common research experiment is to have someone try to display the six emotions mentioned earlier while reading from a telephone book. Listeners seem quite capable of distinguishing the various emotions displayed. Psychologists have, in recent years, started listening for nonfluencies and pauses to determine a patient's emotional level. The more nonfluencies and hesitations that occur, the more emotionally aroused they find the patient to be. Filled pauses ("uh," "um," and "ah") indicate anxiety and boredom, while unfilled or silent pauses indicate anger and contempt.

Posture

Our posture communicates emotions to a certain extent, but not to the degree of the other nonverbal cues already discussed. It is possible that posture indicates the intensity of emotion rather than the type of emotion. When you feel a great deal of emotion, your posture begins to show it. For example, you can be mildly sad or angry with little change in posture, but when your anger or sadness reaches a high intensity you begin to move in some characteristic fashion. If you are very sad, you may hunch over and shake uncontrollably. If you are angry, you may tremble but also take on an upright and rigid posture. Random movement such as pacing may also come into play during periods of fear, anger, and disgust. Posture is a secondary, not a primary, indicator of emotion. We use it to double-check emotional levels discovered through other channels.

Personal Artifacts

People often dress to display a certain emotion. For example, a woman recently widowed will wear black clothing to express her grief. People who are happy will very often pick out clothes for that day that are bright and made of light materials. Other personal artifacts may also reflect emotion. A woman, for example, might not put on any makeup in the morning if she is unhappy or angry. At one time, "smile buttons" were worn by many people to express their emotional state and to encourage others to adopt the same emotion. Currently, T-shirts with pictures or writing on them are often used for the same purpose.

Up to this point, we have discussed how nonverbal communication channels operate to facilitate interaction, to signal our interpersonal attitudes, and to display our own emotions. We are sure it has become obvious to you that there is considerable overlap among the various messages of nonverbal communication channels. The same nonverbal channel can express messages for more than one of the purposes we have discussed. It is impossible to determine the purpose of any nonverbal behavior until you have examined it relative to all of the other message channels. The same thing is true for the area with which we will deal next—personality expression through nonverbal channels.

NONVERBAL COMMUNICATION AND PERSONALITY

Whereas your emotions and interpersonal attitudes are more or less fleeting states, your personality is ongoing. Our personalities are developed very early in life through identification with our parents, friends, and life experiences. Once established, it is very hard to change our personality. People in our society frown on those who blatantly express their personality, even though it is essential to communicate our own personality and determine the personality of others if interaction is to be effective. In order to communicate this information, we have developed methods of sending and receiving it nonverbally. This information guides us as we deal with one another. In most cases we try to present our personalities in the best possible light. We want to create a favorable impression. In some cases, our attempts to create a favorable impression actually help modify our personality.

Our personality is in part derived from our own *self-image*. We all have an image of ourselves that we developed very early in life, and in many cases this image is very idealized. People who are bald may see themselves as having hair. People who are short may picture themselves as being taller than they really are. We usually picture ourselves as being dressed the way we did when we felt we looked our best. Our self-image affects how we behave, both verbally and nonverbally. We attempt to make our personality and our self-image match, and we express our self-image and personality nonverbally. The areas that relate most directly to personality are physical appearance, personal and public artifacts, and vocalics.

Physical Appearance

Perhaps the most important way we express our personality nonverbally is through our physical appearance. There are many widely accepted stereotypes that accompany various physical-appearance characteristics. When we see people who are heavyset, we very often jump to the conclusion that they are soft-hearted, affectionate, soft-tempered, contented, generous, cooperative, relaxed, and jolly. On the other hand, we tend to think that thin people are tense, self-conscious, serious, withdrawn, introspective, and meticulous. We reserve all of the finest characteristics for people who are neither fat nor thin. We see them as energetic, competitive, active, optimistic, enterprising, efficient, and confident. These people tend to get higher grades, better jobs, and are generally better liked than their excessively fat or excessively thin counterparts.

You probably are aware that hair length has a significant effect on the way people perceive you. We cannot make very many changes in our body build, but we can easily change our hair styles and lengths. We wear our hair the way we do in order to communicate something about our personalities. Hair styles change rather rapidly, but they usually reflect certain personality stereotypes.

Other physical-appearance characteristics for which our society has personality stereotypes include weight, height, skin color, facial contours, and various types of scars and blemishes. Like body build, many of these physical-appearance characteristics cannot be easily changed, although we try to do so with elevator shoes, diets, and plastic surgery. When possible, we attempt to manipulate our perceived personalities by changing our physical appearance. Often, in changing our physical appearance we also change our actual personalities. There are many accounts of people who have undergone complete personality reversals after plastic surgery. As a nonverbal channel, physical appearance functions primarily to reflect personality.

Personal and Public Artifacts

Our dress and personal artifacts are easier to change than our physical appearance, but they have no less value in communicating our personality. A very interesting but somewhat dated study by Aiken (1963) demonstrated this point very effectively. After surveying 160 women, he found that those who preferred "decoration" in clothing tended to be conforming, sociable, and nonintellectual. Those who wore clothing for "comfort" were self-controlled and extroverted. "Interest" in dress correlated with compliance, stereotypic thinking, social consciousness, and insecurity, while a "conformist" attitude toward clothing related to social conformity, restraint, and submissiveness. Finally, "economy" in choice of dress positively correlated with responsibility, alertness, efficiency, and precision. Whether consciously or subconsciously we dress to express our personalities, and we generalize about the personalities of others by how they are dressed. The same holds true for the personal artifacts we wear. Rings, necklaces, watches, buttons, pins, makeup, and so on all can communicate part of our personality.

Public artifacts are all of those things we own or rent but do not carry on us that also have communicative value. The first time you walk into someone's house or room, you immediately get an impression of the personality of the person who lives there. If the house is neat and clean, you classify the person as efficient, careful, hard-working, and organized. The types of pictures or posters on the wall also communicate to you as do the type of furniture, the presence or absence of plants, animals, or knick-knacks, and hundreds of other things. A person who owns a big, expensive car is stereotyped as having a personality different from a person who drives a Volkswagen. With the variety of public artifacts available to all, we tend to choose those that will reflect the self-image and personalities we believe we have or would like to have.

Dress and other artifacts are important nonverbal cues in all parts of the world.
JOHN DUGAN PHOTO

Vocalics

When you receive a telephone call from someone you do not know, you immediately draw certain conclusions about that person just from the voice. You judge the person's age, sex, body type, race, social class, and, perhaps even the person's occupation. From these judgments, you assign a certain personality to the caller. Evidence suggests that general agreement can be obtained from vocalic cues on such personality characteristics as forcefulness, aggressiveness, realism, and boldness. Americans prefer people with fairly deep voices. We tend to believe, for instance, that males with high-pitched voices are effeminate. A person's accent significantly affects our determination of that person's personality. A southern or eastern accent immediately makes you think of personality stereotypes associated with southerners and easterners, unless, of course, you also have such an accent. People will very often make a conscious attempt to deepen their voice or get rid of an accent if it does not fit their own

What impression do you have of the occupant of this office? Upon what did you base your opinion?

PHOTO BY CAROLE DUGAN

self-image. On the other hand, some people will attempt to perfect an accent in order to fit an image they have of themselves as intellectual, distant, and superior.

We have been talking in this section about nonverbal cues relating to personalities as stereotypes. Many of these stereotypes actually do have some basis in past experience. They may also have validity because they have been carefully chosen to reflect our personality or at least to reflect the kind of personality we would like to have. It may also be that a self-fulfilling prophecy occurs regarding nonverbal characteristics and personality. For example, since many people expect fat persons to be jovial, they may treat them in ways that, through interactions, cause fat people to behave in a jovial manner. It seems safe to say that, in part, you can put some confidence in the relationship between nonverbal communication and personality if you are careful in your inferences. Our personalities and self-images are often products of our unchangeable physical and vocal characteristics. Personality cues are also interrelated with the nonverbal cues of interaction, interpersonal attitude, and emotion.

SUMMARY

As we mentioned at the beginning of this chapter, nonverbal communication channels are at least as important as our verbal communication channel. We have suggested that verbal and nonverbal channels of communication seem to be designed to accomplish somewhat different purposes. We have also pointed out that nonverbal communication works on both the conscious and unconscious levels and is often regulated by the social system.

Nonverbal communication is important in interaction itself as well as in communicating interpersonal attitudes, emotions, and personality. We would like to conclude, however, with the same warning we made throughout this chapter: You should be very careful not to jump to conclusions based on one nonverbal cue. You can learn this lesson only when you consciously begin to become aware of the nonverbal cues that exist around you and to develop your nonverbal sensitivity. We will talk about how you can develop your nonverbal sensitivity and we will discuss the physiology and development of nonverbal and verbal communication in the following chapter.

KEY WORDS AND CONCEPTS

- Adaptors
- Affect Displays
- Analogic Code
- Body Orientation
- Body Posture
- Conscious vs. Unconscious Communication
- Digital Code
- Displacement Activities
- Emblems
- Emotion Cues
- Eye Behavior
- Facial Control
- Facial Expression
- Hand Movements
- Head Movements
- Holistic Nature of Nonverbal Communication
- Illustrators
- Immediacy Dimensions
- Interaction Cues
- Interaction Distances
- Interpersonal Attitude Cues
- Leakage Cues
- Micromomentary Expressions
- Miscue
- Missed Cue
- Personal Artifacts
- Personal Space
- Personality Cues
- Physical Appearance
- Power Dimension
- Prosodic Features
- Proxemics
- Public Artifacts
- Pupil Dilation
- Regulators
- Response Matching
- Responsiveness Dimension
- Self-Image
- Societal Norms
- Touch
- Verbal vs. Nonverbal Channels
- Vocalics

SUGGESTED READINGS

Burgoon, Judee K. and Thomas Saine. *The Unspoken Dialogue: An Introduction to Nonverbal Communication.* Boston: Houghton-Mifflin Company, 1978. This text intentionally shies away from the cue-based approach. The authors take a basically functional approach to the study of nonverbal communication. They focus on information transfer, persuasion, decision making, cohesion, social solidarity, and impression formation as functions of nonverbal communication. The text tries to stress the interrelationship and interdependence of the various nonverbal communication cues. Only two chapters are devoted to examining each of the cues individually. Unique chapters deal with the various approaches that have been taken to nonverbal communication study, and there is an excellent chapter on the individual, subcultural, and cultural differences that occur in nonverbal communication usage.

KNAPP, MARK L., *Nonverbal Communication in Human Interaction*, 2nd ed. New York: Holt Rinehart and Winston, 1978. This text is one of the most complete and up-to-date books available on nonverbal communication. The text takes a cue-based approach to the subject; that is, each cue is discussed in a separate chapter. The focus of this book is on the research findings relating to each type of nonverbal cue. The text also features several excellent chapters that are not cue-based: Basic Perspectives, Developmental Perspectives, Observing and Recording Nonverbal Behavior, and The Ability to Send and Receive Nonverbal Signals. These chapters are especially important because they deal with subjects that are often neglected by other nonverbal communication texts.

LAFRANCE, MARIANNE, AND CLARA MAYO, *Moving Bodies: Nonverbal Communication in Social Relationships.* Monterey, Calif.: Brooks/Cole Publishing Company, 1978. This text is listed as one of the suggested readings because it takes a somewhat different approach from either of the other texts listed above. This text attempts to provide more explanation and interpretation of nonverbal behavior. After two basic chapters, the book discusses what nonverbal cues tell us about an individual's psychology (emotional expression, personality, and psychopathology), relationships between people (attraction, aggression, status, and influence), and finally, how these cues fit into the larger social system (rules, rituals, development, gender cues, and cultural cues). The authors provide some remarkable insights into how and why nonverbal communication works as it does.

8

Sending and Receiving Mechanisms

In this final chapter of our discussion of the elements and relationships that make up the human communication system, we will discuss several aspects of communication that we have been unable to examine without prior discussion of the elements and how they interrelate with one another. The three major sections of this chapter include (1) the physiological aspects of human communication, (2) the development of human communication, and (3) our sensitivity to human communication. This chapter also serves the purpose of reuniting the elements we have discussed previously in order to reassert that human communication must be understood as a whole and not simply as the sum of its parts.

Sending and Receiving Mechanisms

The model of the human communication system that we have been developing throughout the preceding chapters will be completed in this chapter. We will discuss the entire system: how it works, how it develops, and how we go about assessing and improving communication sensitivity. It is in this chapter that we will attempt to reunite the various elements of the human communication system that we have examined in isolation in previous chapters. By the end of this chapter you should be more fully aware of the interdependence and holism in human communication systems. We will begin by examining the physiology of communication. We will then explore the various theories of human communication development. Finally, we will discuss the nature of communication sensitivity, how to assess it, and how to improve it.

THE PHYSIOLOGY OF HUMAN COMMUNICATION

In order to understand the physiology of human communication, you must understand the human nervous system. The human nervous system involves the brain, the spinal cord, and the nerves that extend throughout the body. The various sense organs of sight, smell, hearing, touch, and taste respond to the stimuli in the environment and allow us to process the various inputs we perceive. Our nervous system controls the output mechanisms such as speech, facial expressions, gestures, posture, and other mechanisms by which we output messages to others in our environment. The human nervous system accounts not only for the input and output mechanisms but also for the various processing elements of motivation, perception, and reasoning.

Nerves run from the brain and spinal cord to the muscles and organs all over the human body. Our nervous system sends messages from the nerve endings to the brain and from the brain to the various nerve endings. The nervous system is made up of cells, as are all other parts of the body.

The several billion nerve cells or neurons in the human body are all connected to one another. It is the nervous system that accounts for the intrafacing of the input, output, and processing elements. It is this intraface of the three elements that we represent in our model as overlapping circles. The neurons receive stimuli from another neuron, the brain, a receptor organ, or an effector organ, and they then pass it on.

Receptor organs account for message inputs, and effector organs account for message outputs. *Effector organs* are usually muscle cells that control various output mechanisms; these organs include the vocal cords, lips, tongue, arms, legs, face, and eyes. The only output mechanism we will discuss in detail in this chapter is the speech mechanism, but all these mechanisms work in approximately the same way. The effector organs contract or expand the muscles to produce movement of the various body parts that we have learned to use to create messages.

Our *receptor organs* include the five senses of sight, smell, hearing, touch, and taste. Each of these receptor organs works somewhat differently. We will discuss each of the organs briefly in the following sections. The most marvelous part of the whole human nervous system is the brain. Our brain accounts for the intrapersonal processing elements of motivation, perception, and reason-

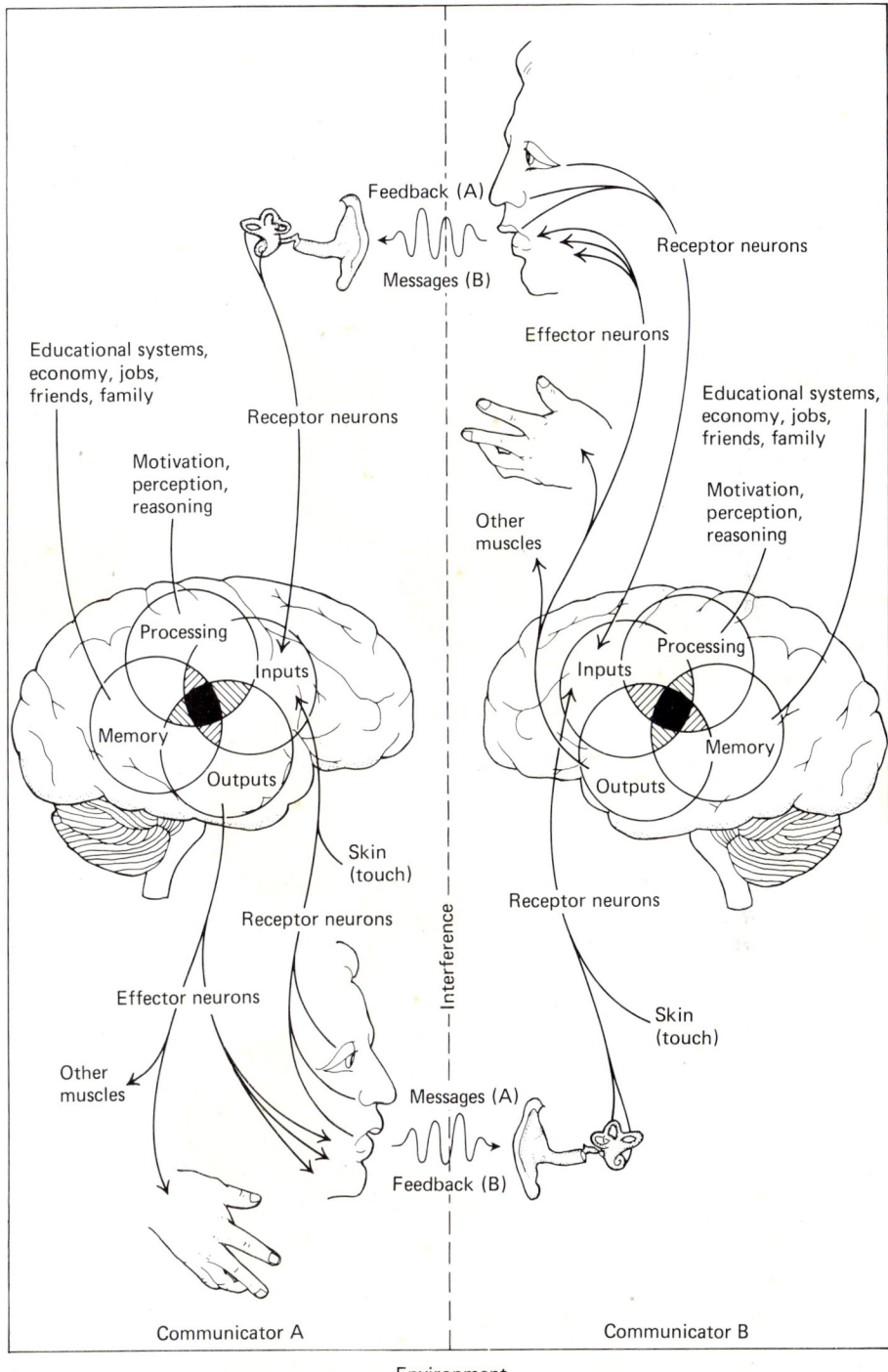

Fig. 8.1 Physiological representation of the Emmert-Donaghy model of dyadic communication.

Sending and Receiving Mechanisms

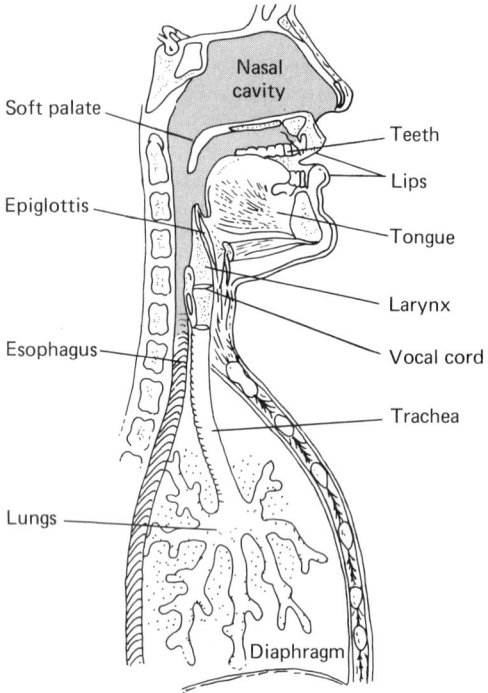

Fig. 8.2 The speech production mechanism.

ing. Our brain also stores information necessary to make these elements operate effectively.

To put the entire human communication process in perspective, let's look at our original model in physiological terms. Figure 8.1 presents the Emmert-Donaghy model in terms of the neurophysiology involved. You will notice that the brain of each communicator accounts for the processing as well as the memory necessary to make the processing work. The effector and receptor organs are connected to the input and output centers of the brain. These three aspects of output, input, and processing intraface through the nervous system. It is impossible for any of these elements to operate properly without the others. We begin our discussion of the physiological aspects of this communication system with the speech chain.

The Speech Chain

Most of you probably know a little bit about how we produce the sounds others hear. You know that we move our lips and tongue to produce words and that the words are carried by the air as vibrations. Some of you also probably know something about the voice box and vocal cords. But if asked to explain exactly how we produce sounds, you would probably be unsure of yourself. The same is probably true of your knowledge of sound reception or hearing. You know it is done with the ear and you have probably heard of the eardrum, but beyond that, you are stumped. We will now discuss the process, or chain of events, that links a speaker's brain with a receiver's brain. Peter B. Denes and Elliot N. Pinson (1963) call this process the *speech chain*. They indicate that there are three levels involved in the speech chain: the linguistic level, the physiological level, and the acoustic level. The speech chain accounts for verbal inputting and outputting and the vocalic aspect of nonverbal communication.

The *linguistic level* refers to the selection of words, phrases, and sentences that will make up a message output by the speaker and a message input by the listener. We have discussed many of the factors that go into this linguistic process in the preceding chapters. The *physiological level* refers to the mechanisms involved in the transmission and reception of sound waves. The sound waves themselves are part of the *acoustic level*. In this section, we will discuss the physiological level of the speech chain.

Speech production The effector organs used in speech production are the lungs, windpipe, larynx, throat, nose, and mouth. Figure 8.2 illustrates the location of each of these parts. As we exhale air from our lungs through the windpipe, we can cause our larynx, which contains the vocal cords, to close off or restrict the air. When we are not talking, the air moves freely past the vocal cords. When the vocal cords restrict the air, a "buzz" is created that is transformed into words through the use of the teeth, tongue, lips, nose, and mouth cavity. These other parts that help to transform the vocal "buzz" into different sounds provide *resonance*. It is the resonance that allows us to create the different sounds necessary for speech. This is obviously a very oversimplified discussion of speech production, but it should at least help you understand how we produce speech outputs.

Hearing Figure 8.3 presents a view of our hearing mechanism—the ear. Sound waves come into the ear canal and vibrate the eardrum. The area behind

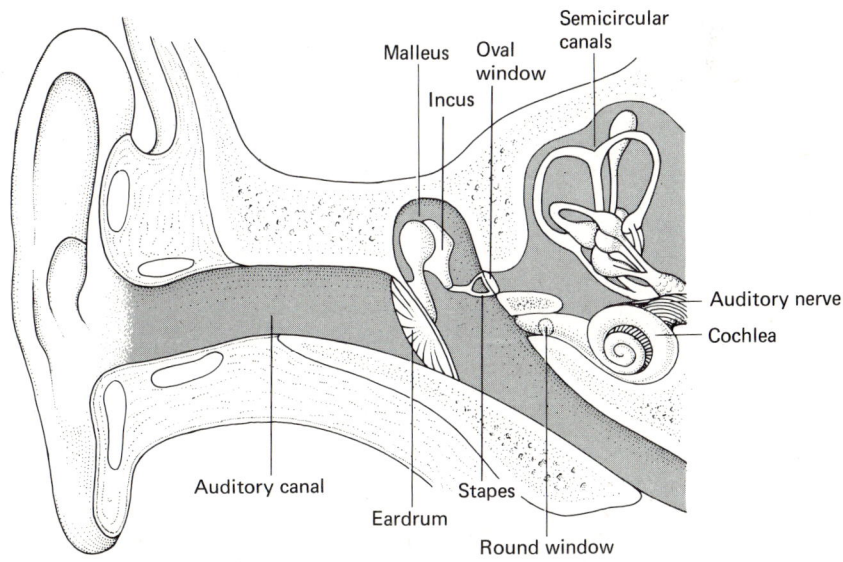

Fig. 8.3 The speech reception mechanism.

Sending and Receiving Mechanisms

the eardrum is called the middle ear. The middle ear contains three bones that connect the eardrum to the oval window. These bones transmit the sound wave vibrations from the eardrum to the oval window and amplify the sound. They also protect the inner ear from extremely loud sounds. The area behind the oval window is called the inner ear. The purpose of the inner ear is to transform the vibrations of the middle ear bones into nerve impulses that can be interpreted by the brain. This transformation is done through a system of cavities. The main cavity is called the *cochlea* and is shaped like a snail's shell. The inside of the cochlea is extremely complex, but basically what happens here is that a large number of hair-like cells are bent in various ways as the vibrations of the oval window are transmitted through fluid. The movement of these hair cells triggers the fibers of the auditory nerve, which produces electrochemical pulses that proceed to the brain.

Other Receptor Organs

In the preceding chapter on nonverbal communication, we pointed out that we use all of our senses for message reception. These senses include not only the speech chain but also the channels of sight, smell, taste, and touch. We will examine the physiology of each of these senses before we discuss the development and sensitivity of our communication input and output mechanisms.

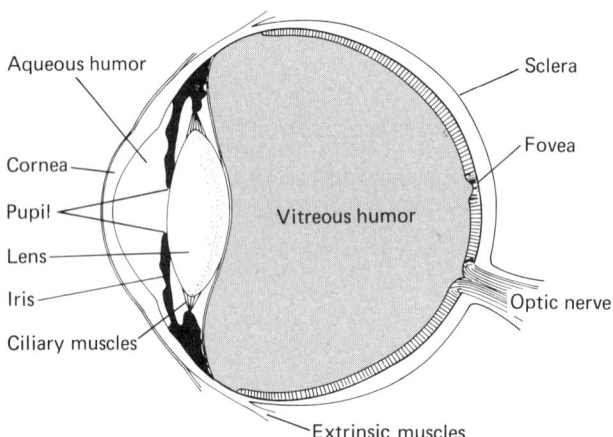

Fig. 8.4 The visual reception mechanism.

Sight As you know, the mechanism we use for sight is our eye (see Fig. 8.4). We have already discussed this input channel somewhat in our chapter on perception. Like our sense of hearing, our sense of sight can overcome great distances. Touch and taste require actual contact with the stimuli, and smell requires that the nose contact odor-causing particles.

Vision occurs when light rays pass through the cornea, pupil, lens, and vitreous humor and finally reach the retina. Light-sensitive cells of the eye's retina cause electrochemical impulses to be sent to the brain. The other parts of the eye pictured in Fig. 8.4 are basically for the eye's protection. As the light-sensitive cells respond to the light that strikes them, they form an image much like the dots that form an image on a TV set. The image, which is upside down and reversed, is carried to the brain through the optic nerve that is attached to these cells. The brain interprets the picture as right side up, and we "see."

Smell Smell is a less important means of communication in human systems than in other animals. Many animals get most of their inputs through the sense of smell. Human beings in some cultures such as those in the Mideast also use smell extensively for communication purposes. Smell occurs when tiny gas and vapor particles in the air come into contact with the olfactory nerve cells in the lining of the nose. Liquid from the nasal lining keeps these nerve cells damp so that particles that strike them will dissolve in the liquid. The chemicals in the liquid cause the olfactory nerve cells to respond. The olfactory nerve cells create electrochemical messages that travel to the brain, and we smell. Even though our sense of smell is not highly developed for the purposes of communication, it is still very sensitive. We can often smell one part odor in one million parts air. However, our sensitivity to odors does not last long. We "get used" to a smell after only a few minutes, but we will become sensitive again to a new smell.

Taste Smell is very closely related to taste. Many tastes are blends of smells and tastes. If you hold your nose, it will be difficult to differentiate an onion from an apple. The physiology of taste also functions much like that of smell in that particles are dissolved in liquid next to the nerve endings. In this case, the nerve endings are mostly on our tongue but also in other parts of the mouth cavity. These nerve endings are called taste buds. They are small pits in the mouth into which the liquid containing the chemicals and dissolved particles runs. Again, electrochemical impulses are created that travel to the brain through the nerve. We have four basic taste reactions: sweet, sour, salty, and bitter. Other "tastes" are combinations of these four.

Touch Touch is one of our most basic and important means of communication. Our sense of touch occurs because of nerve endings in the skin. Touch, along with warmth, cold, and pain, is called a cutaneous sense. The nerve cells that account for touch are called tactile corpuscles and are of several types. One type is found near hair, another in hairless areas of the skin, and still others below the outer layer of the skin. When the shape of these corpuscles is changed, an electrochemical impulse is sent to the brain. Nerve endings for warmth, cold, and pain are also distributed throughout the skin and mucous membranes. Scientists estimate that there are three or four million pain points (nerves), one half million touch points, 15,000 cold points, and 16,000 warm points on the body.

Sending and Receiving Mechanisms

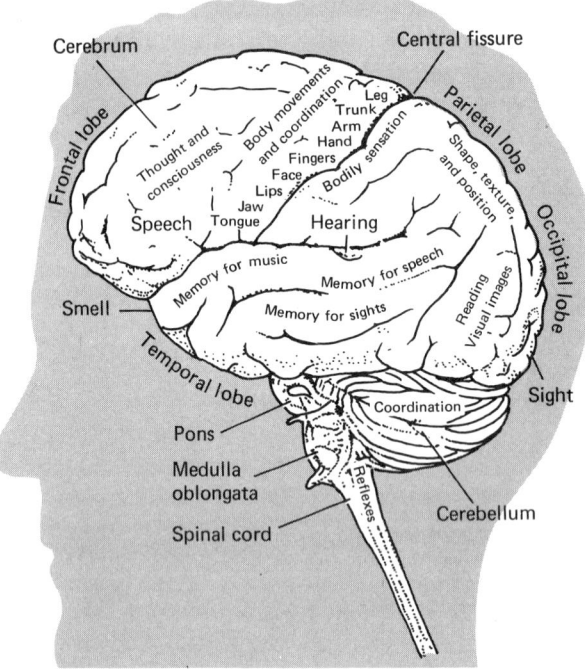

Fig. 8.5 The human brain.

The Brain

All of the various input neurons controlling the receptor organs end at the same place, the human brain. The output neurons controlling the effector organs also begin in the brain. This mechanism is beyond belief in its complexity. Scientists are still puzzled over many aspects of the human brain. Figure 8.5 presents a simplified picture of the brain. As you can see, the brain is simply a large bulb that sits on the upper end of the spinal cord. A complete discussion of the brain would take much more space than is appropriate in a communication text, so we will focus only on the brain processes that are important to human communication. Input messages from many of the receptor organs end up behind the central fissure at the top of the brain. Impulses from our ears are received by the brain at the top of the temporal lobe. The occipital lobes receive the pictures sent from our eyes. The areas for smell reception are under the temporal and frontal lobes. Most of the effector organs are controlled from the area of the brain just above the central fissure. The largest part of the brain is concerned with the intrapersonal processing elements of motivation, perception, and reasoning, as well as memory and speech. The temporal lobes are primarily concerned with certain memories. Speech is located in parts of the frontal, temporal, and parietal lobes. The importance of speech as a survival tool can certainly be demonstrated by the amount of space in the brain devoted to its functioning.

The location of the intrapersonal processing elements in the brain is a little more difficult to pinpoint than the location of the input and output mechanism controls. The major site in the brain that seems to account for most intrapersonal processing is called the forebrain. It consists of the cerebrum, which lies toward the top and front of your head, and the diencephalon, which lies in the center of the brain (not pictured in Fig. 8.5). The diencephalon contains the hypothalamus, which plays the major role in our motivation and emotion, and the subthalamus and thalamus, which connect the hypothalamus with the other parts of the brain such as the cerebrum and cerebellum. Reasoning is found primarily in the cerebrum, while perception is located near the various sensory reception sites. Memory areas are located in the midbrain, which includes the occipital and temporal lobes.

As we said, scientists have a long way to go before they fully understand how the brain works. They are continuously finding out more and more about the brain that relates directly to communication. Our perceptual sensitivity, for example, seems to be determined by portions of the temporal lobe. Researchers have found that stimulating one part of the temporal lobe will cause the organism to become more open and sensitive to inputs by allowing a greater number of signals to be processed. On the other hand, stimulating another part of the temporal lobe will cause the organism to close down the input channels and restrict information processing to a limited number of signals. These processes account in great measure for perceptual filtering as a means of coping that does not demand any behavioral action (Pribran, 1971). Such selectivity relates directly to the interference portion of our model. The above is just one example of why communication specialists should become more familiar with the physiology of the human communication system.

We hope you will go back and carefully look at Fig. 8.1 once more. Everything we have talked about in this book thus far can be related to this model. Needs, values, person and message perception, consistency, evidence, reasoning, vocabulary, grammar, meaning, stereotyping, feedback, interpersonal attitudes, emotion, personality, and all the rest are there if you think about them. The model will also tell you much about the systemic nature of human communication. Interdependence, holism, goal-seeking, transformation, regulation, hierarchy, differentiation, and all the rest of the characteristics of systems are implied in Fig. 8.1. The figure would have been too cluttered and confusing if we had tried to put all of this in it. Having come this far with us, however, you can now most likely determine most of the connections by yourself and see how it all fits together. You can do this because of that marvelous instrument called the brain. It is the core of the human communication system. We will now move on to discuss how we develop our input and output mechanisms and how they can be improved.

THE DEVELOPMENT OF HUMAN COMMUNICATION

Our receptor and effector organs were not necessarily designed to produce messages. We evolved our verbal and nonverbal symbol-using capacity. The evidence seems to support the conclusion that our ancient ancestors had

Sending and Receiving Mechanisms

nonverbal communication skills before they had verbal ones. However, of more interest to most communication students than how we developed our communication capabilities historically is how each individual learns to communicate. In her fascinating book on verbal and nonverbal language development, Wood (1976) suggests a three-component model represented in Fig. 8.6. The components are input, child's equipment, and output.

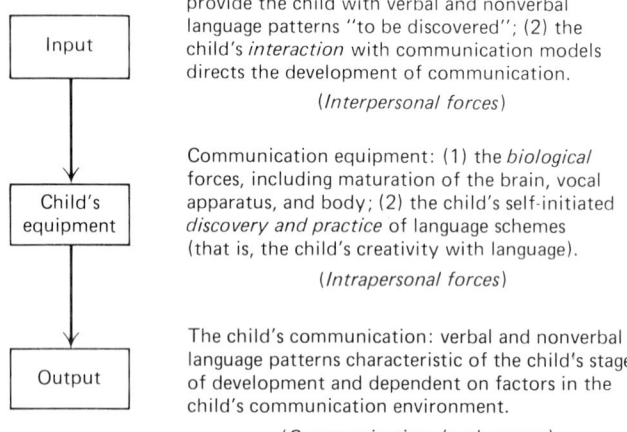

Communication data: (1) *communication models* provide the child with verbal and nonverbal language patterns "to be discovered"; (2) the child's *interaction* with communication models directs the development of communication.

(*Interpersonal forces*)

Communication equipment: (1) the *biological* forces, including maturation of the brain, vocal apparatus, and body; (2) the child's self-initiated *discovery and practice* of language schemes (that is, the child's creativity with language).

(*Intrapersonal forces*)

The child's communication: verbal and nonverbal language patterns characteristic of the child's stage of development and dependent on factors in the child's communication environment.

(*Communication development*)

Fig. 8.6 Model of communication development.

Barbara S. Wood, *Children and Communication: Verbal and Nonverbal Language Development*, © 1976, p. 42. Reprinted by permission of Prentice-Hall, Inc., Englewood Cliffs, N.J.

The Child's Equipment

We start in the middle of the model with the child's equipment because we find it easier to understand the whole process from there. Every child brings certain qualities and capabilities to the process of communication skill development. These include the physiological mechanisms described earlier such as the brain, effector and receptor organs, and the nervous system. Also included in this category are the child's intrapersonal processing elements, motivations, reasoning abilities, and perceptual skills. A major disagreement among persons interested in communication skill development involves the biological equipment available to a newborn child. The debate revolves around the question of whether or not a child has an inborn or innate predisposition to communicate or whether communication skills are totally learned through the child's contact with the environment. We will call the former proposition the nativist position and the latter the environmentalist position.

Nativist position The nativists propose that children have the innate capacity to acquire verbal and nonverbal communication skills. In other words, a child is prewired to use symbols in a systematic and rule-governed manner.

The major disagreement among nativists is whether or not there is any environmental influence necessary for the child to be able to communicate. One set of nativists says "no" and cites evidence suggesting that children without any communication stimuli from their environment will still develop communication skills, even though their language may not be understandable to others. The second group of nativists also maintains that the child is prewired for communication, but this group believes that some environmental "trigger" is necessary as a catalyst to set the innate capabilities into action. Both agree, however, that once the innate mechanisms begin to operate, it is seemingly impossible to interfere with them or to stop them. The nativists point out that all children tend to develop communication skills at almost exactly the same rate or according to the same schedule, regardless of the environment in which they find themselves.

Environmentalist position This position suggests that all language development can be explained by learning theory or environmental influence. It states that children learn language because they discover that it helps them to satisfy their needs. Each time a child is fed, the mother or father may say "Here's your milk." The baby begins to associate the word "milk" with the bottle. As children babble, they begin to repeat words that have a pleasurable association in their minds. Babbling the word "muck" gets the child the bottle, and it is learned as a symbol for the object. This is often called the *imitation-reinforcement* model of communication development. In order to explain unique or novel communication behaviors on the part of the child, the environmentalists suggest that the child generalizes those stimuli that have been reinforced to new situations. This explanation has been rejected by some in the communication development area because the concept of stimulus generalization is usually limited to cases where the child can recognize a similarity between the input situations. The nativists contend that this is not always the case for language. This explanation also does not take into account the fact that our language has many words and nonverbal cues that have more than one meaning, depending on the context—words and nonverbal cues that would take more time to identify than is usually necessary for the child. Finally, it has been found that children who can not talk and thus have no imitation or reinforcement can still understand rather complex instructions. For these reasons, we presented in Chapter 6 a model of association to explain the way people learn meanings for words. All of this evidence tends, then, to suggest that the imitation-reinforcement model of the environmentalists is useful in explaining verbal and nonverbal language development at later ages, but that by itself it does not necessarily account for early communication acquisition. Probably the most complete explanation of communication acquisition draws on elements from both the nativist and environmentalist positions.

Physiological development Besides innate prewiring and environment, children must also have the proper neurophysiological development before they can communicate. One example of the interrelatedness of physiological and communication skill development is the fact that children are able to utter the "p" sound prior to the "m" sound. Many parents have noted that a baby will use a word that sounds like "papa" before he or she uses the word "mama." When this happens, parents often conclude that this utterance signals a closer attachment to the father than to the mother. In reality, it is merely a result of physiological development.

The milestone event in verbal language development occurs when children begin to form sentence-like structures, shortly before their second birthday. At this point, the child's brain has undergone tremendous development. The number of neurons in the brain has increased greatly, and at about the age of two the cerebral cortex enlarges significantly. It has been speculated that the occurrence of these two events at 24 months or so is more than mere coincidence. At this same point, the child begins to gain other advanced motor skills as well, such as eating with a spoon. There has been very little research on the nonverbal communication abilities of children under the age of five. Many have noted the importance of touch, eye gaze, facial expressions, and paralanguage at the early ages, but they have failed to really isolate the point at which various nonverbal input and output abilities develop. Someday we hope researchers will examine nonverbal development in conjunction with verbal development. We suggest that the age of two might also be significant for nonverbal communication development.

Another physiological aspect of language development involves the effector and receptor organs. Newborn children have a much more fully developed hearing apparatus than speaking apparatus. In the very young child, the larynx cannot produce all of the language sounds and the tongue is so large that it is incapable of modifying air flow properly. The ear functions adequately at birth. An example of this phenomenon is cited by Miller (1967). He tells of a conversation with a little girl named "Lisa," who pronounced her name as "Litha." When Dr. Miller also pronounced her name as "Litha," she continued to correct him until he said "Lisa," at which point she responded "That's right, Litha." She heard her name as it should be pronounced, but her effector organ would not let her pronounce it correctly herself.

Wood (1976) suggests that a child's gender role is also established at about the age of two. At this age, children begin to take on either male or female nonverbal behavior patterns. Such things as hip movement, arm and posture positions, and other nonverbal behaviors that differentiate men from women develop at approximately 24 months. The child has developed a bodily readiness for nonverbal communication at that point. The physiology of the human communication system, then, has important implications for understanding not only how we communicate but also how and when we develop our communication skills.

Motivational forces As all of you know, children have boundless energy. They are constantly exploring their world and especially those things they do not understand. This energy is another intrapersonal force that the child brings to the process of communication skill development. Children will practice verbal language for hours. They will go over and over a sentence in an effort to improve their grammatical skills. Weir (1962) studied her son Anthony's practice sessions and discovered that he negated sentences, used various verb tenses, and made declarative sentences into questions and back again. He had a building-up exercise that went from "the block" to "the yellow block" to "look at the yellow block." He also broke down sentences in the same way.

The Development of Human Communication

Prior to the age of two, the child is able to communicate nonverbally.
PHOTO BY CAROLE DUGAN

Children are also extremely creative in developing their language. They attempt to find the rules that cover specific utterances and to apply those rules. They learn prefixes, suffixes, plurals, and tense in this way. "I goed home" is an example of a common suffix rule discovered by a child that turns out to be wrong only because some of our rules have exceptions. Eventually, through trial and error and reinforcement, the child will discover the exceptions as well as the rules. Children are highly motivated to learn language.

Environmental inputs In addition to the skills the child possesses, inputs from the environment are necessary for communication development. Our prewiring requires trigger samples of the language for the child to use as models on which to base new output attempts. Once children have language samples, they need someone on whom to try out new outputs. This gets us back to the imitation-reinforcement model. People in the environment provide models for children to imitate and from which to learn. These same people act as reinforcers who tell the children when they are correct and when they are wrong. Friends and family are usually the persons who help children in this regard. Children try to learn the systematic rules of both verbal and nonverbal communication.

In our middle-class American culture, the mother is the primary model. The child learns such communication skills from mother as body movements, eye behavior, personal space, vocalization, and facial expressions, as well as words and grammar. Take eye contact, for example; each child must learn certain display rules about when to look another person in the eye and when to avert gaze. A child will smile at a mask with two dots for eyes but will not smile at a real person who has his or her eyes covered. The child has learned that a smile is appropriate only when the other person is looking. This nonverbal communication rule is learned by the second month of the child's life and probably results from the very early eye contact experiences between the child and the mother. Mothers are not the only possible models. In other cultures, a grandmother is the recognized model. Or, if both parents work, a sibling or a babysitter might serve this function. As we get older, teachers serve as our models. These models provide reinforcement for both the content and the form of our communication.

In addition to serving as models, the people in the child's environment must interact with the child. The child must learn more than rules of grammar. The child must learn about the flow of conversation. This interaction also allows the parent, friend, or relative to extend the child's vocabulary. Needs, beliefs, attitudes, values, personality, perception, and reasoning are also developed through imitation and reinforcement. All of these aspects of human communication become interdependent during these formative years. The communication system is developed only if the models are willing to respond to the child with comments, new ideas, questions, and evaluations.

We have already pointed out that children tend to develop language at about the same rate, regardless of the culture or the environment. Such factors as socioeconomic and ethnic background, size of family, and absence of parents do not seem to have much effect on the child's language development, although these factors may determine whether a child learns standard American English or some other language system. The child still develops communication abilities in the same progressive manner. Some may progress more slowly at one point or another, but they tend to catch up later.

On the other hand, a child's environment is not unimportant in input, output, and processing development. As we said before, parents and others provide the child with examples of communication. Bernstein (1972) suggests that the communication style of the child's models (usually the family) can have a definite effect on verbal and nonverbal language development. He perceived two basic family forms that can affect the child. The first is called the *person-oriented* family. Such a family has an open role system whereby each member is allowed to play various roles at different times. In such a family, the child and the adults are allowed much more freedom to make judgments and express opinions. The desire is for each family member to develop to their fullest potential. The models in such a family use what is called an *elaborated code* to explain statements and to provide reasons for them. Such a code allows for subtle differences in meaning and is analytical and abstract. Children in such families exhibit sophisticated motivation, perception, and reasoning processing components, as well as highly developed input and output mechanisms.

Very often the earliest model the child has is the mother.
PHOTO BY CAROLE DUGAN

Bernstein calls the second basic family form *position-oriented*. Position-oriented families have a highly differentiated role structure. The role of parent is much different from the role of child, and communication is less open because of such boundaries. The models talk much differently to one another than to a child. Messages sent to the child are rather simple and brief, with a more rigid syntax and a narrower vocabulary than the messages sent in the person-oriented family. Bernstein calls this type of communication a *restricted code*. Children in such a family do not learn to handle subtle, analytic, or abstract language and concepts, and hence the other interrelated human communication system components also become less fully developed. This is not to say that the elaborated code is any better than the restricted code for communication purposes, but the former does allow the child to reason by permitting a wider range of ideas and meanings. Environment does, then, have an important role in communication skill development. The family example above is only a sample of how the environment influences the human communication sytem.

Communication outputs Until the age of about seven or eight, a child's verbal output is very self-centered. Piaget, a noted Swiss child psychologist, calls this verbal output *egocentric speech* (1955). The child looks at everything from his or her own point of view. The child fails to take into account that the receiver may have a different point of view and thus believes that everything communicated is totally understood. At about seven or eight years of age, the child begins to develop *socialized speech*. According to Piaget, this development signals that the child is adapting himself or herself to the receiver. A child's nonverbal communication follows much the same pattern. In terms of personal space, for example, the child seems to have little or no spatial "bubble" that is off-limits to others and tends to behave in the same manner toward others. Children will grab, climb on, pull, and interrupt you, regardless of whether you are talking to them or to anyone else. Children communicate both verbally and nonverbally as if they were the only persons of any importance. They do so until they become socialized. This socialization process means the child is beginning to modify outputs based on the feedback received from people in the environment.

Up until this point, the child has used environmental feedback to develop what we called *linguistic competence* in Chapter 6. The child learns linguistic competence relatively early, that is, the underlying linguistic rules of grammar and meaning. The other rules of communicative competence such as staring, interrupting, distance, facial expression, and various paralanguage characteristics (i.e., linguistic performance) take much longer to learn. We call these rules *display rules*. They are also taught to us by our society through our models. In many ways, communication output development never ceases as we grow older. It seems to be just a matter of developing greater and greater sensitivity to both verbal and nonverbal communication. In this way, we can honestly say that we never stop in our communication skill development until the day we die. In the next section, we discuss how we can continue to evolve our human communication ability by developing greater sensitivity in both the input and output processes.

COMMUNICATION SENSITIVITY

By now it should be obvious that not all people are equally sensitive to communication inputs and outputs. In part, this is because each person's neurophysiological system and communication skill development are unique. Knapp (1978a) suggests four other factors that account for communication sensitivity: motivation, attitude, knowledge, and experience. *Motivation* refers to the greater desire some people have to improve their communication sensitivity. Perhaps their jobs depend on it, or perhaps something in their personal life has created a need in them to improve their input and output skills. Like the child discovering language, there has to be some motivation to develop and maintain communication sensitivity. *Attitude* refers to the feelings one has about one's communication skills. Some people just give up because they think they have poor skills and don't have a positive attitude about improving them. You cannot improve your communication sensitivity without a positive attitude. *Knowledge* is pretty self-explanatory. You need to know something about the skill you want to improve. Much of our knowledge about communication has come from our environmental models. Some of it is accurate; some is not. Your knowledge level of accurate information must be fairly high to improve your communication sensitivity. Finally, *experience* plays, perhaps, the most important role in developing communication sensitivity. Just as we said in regard to children's language development, communication cannot be learned without interaction with other people. These people provide models, guidance, and feedback for skill development. The imitation-reinforcement model is just as important for adults as it is for children. The greater the variety of communication experiences, the more sensitive you will become. The person who experiences a wide range of ideas and meanings communicated in analytical and abstract terms with subtle differences will develop a more elaborated code and be more sensitive to the entire human communication system.

At this point, students often ask if it is possible to become too sensitive to communication. The implication is that too much sensitivity can have negative consequences. We might begin to see and hear meanings that are not really there, or we may use our knowledge to manipulate people. This argument has been advanced for centuries. It is one reason why people in the past have burned books, censored the media, and the like. We find it hard to believe that anyone will become too sensitive to communication. There may be times when you will "read" something into a message that is not there, but this is also part of developing sensitivity, that is, being sensitive to which messages are meaningful and which are not. People may try to manipulate us, and we may try to manipulate others, but these behaviors have little to do with sensitivity. They *are* concerned with your ethical and moral standards or those of others. There are many skills that can be destructive in the hands of an unethical person. For most of us, there is little danger of becoming too sensitive to the communication around us. We are too busy just trying to develop an acceptable level of communication sensitivity.

Developing Verbal Communication Sensitivity

We all begin at different verbal and nonverbal sensitivity levels, but we all have some sensitivity, or we would not be able to communicate at all. Most of us are beyond 18 years of age, so we have a fairly high degree of communication competence; that is, we are fairly familiar with the grammar, syntax, and vocabulary of our language. We are still, however, learning the linguistic performance aspects of verbal communication. Skill development in this area involves speaking, listening, reading, and writing. Although all are vitally important to linguistic performance, we are not prepared in this text to focus our attention on the latter two aspects of reading and writing. Much of what we have to say about listening and speaking will also relate to the other two areas, but you will have to make the connections on your own. We will discuss the skills of speaking and listening separately, but they relate closely to one another. We will point out the interrelations as we come to them.

Speaking Much of our discussion in the preceding chapters concerned the development of sensitivity to your own message outputs. All of us have some idea as to how good or bad we are as speakers, but we are not sure if this image of our communication abilities is correct. Many people go to T-group or sensitivity training sessions to help them become sensitive to themselves as communicators. In a sensitivity training group, the various members of the group tell each other openly and honestly how they feel about themselves and

Sending and Receiving Mechanisms

the others in the group. This is one way of becoming sensitive to how your outputs are perceived by others. People have had to go to these extremes, because others do not often honestly and directly tell them what they think of their outputs. They do not want to hurt another's feelings. There are, however, some people around you who will give you this information. These are your good friends and relatives. These are often the same people who originally served as your models and helped you develop linguistic competence. Sometimes we tend to assume that we know how others perceive our outputs. In other words, we become intentionally insensitive to our speaking abilities. Because we seem to get along all right when communicating, we cut off this form of feedback. We need to reopen these channels. We can become sensitive to our own speaking abilities primarily by being alert to the information others give us about ourselves. Some of this information will be verbal (if encouraged), but most will be nonverbal.

Another way of developing sensitivity to your own speaking behavior is through the use of audio or videotape recordings. We often use this technique in college courses and training programs. For most of us, such an experience comes as a real shock. Such equipment allows us to see ourselves as others see us and critically analyze our verbal skills. You must work to improve this area of communication sensitivity. Or you can take the easy way out by not even trying, but you will then continue to make the same mistakes in your speaking.

Listening Speaking is not the only verbal communication skill that we tend to neglect. Most of us have little information about the quality of our listening. This is not unexpected, however, since even specialists in listening know little about it other than its physiology. Audiologists specialize in testing hearing and problems, but few people know much about listening. Hearing is only one part of the listening process. Barker (1978) proposes that listening is a four-stage process involving hearing, attention, understanding, and remembering. If you will think back to the chapter on perception, we discussed how selectivity can enter into any one of these stages and thus affect perception or listening.

Hearing refers to the physiological process discussed earlier in this chapter; it involves sound waves that stimulate the receptor organ and the movement of the electrochemical impulse to the brain. *Attention* is the process of the brain's deciding either to perceive the auditory impulse or to reject it (i.e., select it out). *Understanding* occurs when the brain attaches a meaning to the impulse—a meaning, it is to be hoped, that is intended by the sender. Finally, *remembering* is the act of storing the stimuli in the memory area of the brain. Although this memory function is often neglected by communication specialists, it is extremely important because it has a direct effect on future intrapersonal processing.

There are many misconceptions regarding the listening process that affect our sensitivity to it. The first of these misconceptions is that listening will happen naturally and that all the receiver has to do is to relax and let the sound waves enter the ears. In other words, listening is seen as a passive rather than an active process. The sensitive listener realizes that message reception is a very difficult and tiring job that requires much effort. Many people are poor listeners because they do not want to put out the effort necessary for good listening. A certain amount of motivation is necessary for sensitive listening.

Think back to the various courses you have had in the past. When you were interested in a course and anxious to understand the material, your listening improved and came almost naturally. When you weren't very interested in a course, you had to work at listening.

A second misconception about listening ability is that it is primarily determined by intelligence. Intelligence does have something to do with listening, but not as much as most people think. Motivation and experience in listening are much more important. Early language development patterns, especially the orientation of your family, can play a major role here as well. In fact, listening sensitivity is a combination of many factors, with intelligence being only one. People who consider themselves to be highly intelligent make a great mistake if they assume that they need little training, experience, or motivation to listen.

The next misconception is that good listeners simply register the information presented as if they were tape recorders. Listening is much more than simply recording words and facts. The physiology of the brain shows that we can handle incoming stimuli five to ten times faster than most people can speak. When given a choice of adjusting the rate of incoming verbal messages, most of us choose a much faster speed than the normal speaking rate. If we merely recorded the incoming messages, we would still have a lot of time to waste. Many poor listeners use this time to daydream or to think of things other than the incoming verbal stimuli. Sensitive listeners use this extra brain capacity to analyze and to expand on the input, but they do not let their mind wander off to unrelated topics. They look for the meanings behind the words, how they all fit together, and how the message fits their particular circumstances. This is where the active part of listening comes in. And this is why listening is such hard work. Sensitive listeners must force themselves to keep their mind on the message.

There is another tactic utilized by poor listeners that is related to the poor use of extra time in listening practices. This tactic involves using the extra time to rehearse a response to the speaker's message. In other words, if you are such a listener, you make up arguments or plan what you will say when your turn comes to speak, rather than make sure you have heard the speaker's message accurately. We find this to be one of the most commonly practiced habits of insensitive listeners. Rogers (1961) found this practice to be so prevalent that he developed a technique to prevent it. He suggested that before one person (the listener) can respond to the message of another, the listener must repeat the message to the speaker's satisfaction. This technique would force the receiver to be sure that the message was fully understood. You might try this suggestion as one way of improving your sensitivity as a listener.

In addition to daydreaming and preparing a response, there is a third way in which many poor listeners use extra thinking time: They allow themselves to be distracted by some other stimulus in the environment. Some of the common stimuli that distract listeners include the speaker's unique delivery or language usage such as an accent or mispronunciation of a word, some nonverbal mannerism of the speaker like a tick of the eye or jingling of keys, or some other object or sound in the environment such as the sound of an automobile or an airplane. Sensitive listeners force out such distractions. Again, this is hard work, but it must be done. A professor, for example, must not be tempted to look at papers or books while listening. You will notice that many good listeners actually move away from their work areas in order to avoid such temptations.

Sending and Receiving Mechanisms

Any distraction, including the photographer's camera, can reduce your listening ability.
PHOTO BY CAROLE DUGAN

The final misconception about listening is that we can develop sensitivity only through experience and not through training. Many people feel that their daily listening experiences are all they need. Just because you listen does not guarantee that you will do it well. "Practice makes permanent" poor listening habits, as well as good ones. Bad listening habits will not change without conscious effort. You can improve your listening sensitivity without formal training, but you must at least be aware of what you are doing right and wrong in order to accomplish this goal. If you take the preceding comments to heart and make a conscious effort to avoid listening pitfalls, your sensitivity will improve. But it will be hard work. For many people, formal training is the only way to become a sensitive listener.

Developing Nonverbal Communication Sensitivity

Just as there are some people who are more sensitive than others to verbal communication, there are also some people who are more sensitive to nonverbal communication. It is just as important to the communication process that we be sensitive to the nonverbal cues that others use to express their interpersonal attitudes, emotions, and personality as it is to understand the words people use to express their ideas. The process for developing nonverbal sensitivity is essentially the same as the process for developing verbal sensitivity. It is based on the imitation-reinforcement model. We imitate those people around us whom we admire. We adopt many of their nonverbal behaviors as our own. We then get feedback or reinforcement as to how well or poorly we are performing the various nonverbal cues. For instance, we may learn to flirt by watching an older brother or sister flirting. We then try a flirting behavior with one of our own friends and receive either positive or negative feedback by the way they respond to us. If the nonverbal cue results in a date, we have learned the behavior and have become more sensitive to how our nonverbal behavior affects other people. The same process occurs for improving our nonverbal receiving sensitivity. We will perceive another person's nonverbal behavior and interpret a meaning. We then act or respond in a certain way, based on the meaning we have attributed to that person's behavior. Depending on how the other person responds to our response, we either confirm our interpretation or reject it and form a new meaning. We do this until we get positive feedback, at which point we have increased our nonverbal sensitivity.

Perhaps the biggest problem in developing nonverbal reception sensitivity is the fact that so much of nonverbal behavior is unique to one person. There are unique aspects of verbal behavior as well, but not so many. People in the same cultures tend to use words in approximately the same way. Obviously, no word will have exactly the same meaning for any two people because, as we said before, meanings are in people, not in words. However, we do have much more commonly accepted meanings for verbal communication than we do for nonverbal communication. Because so much of nonverbal behavior is unique, receivers are forced to develop a sensitivity to the individual who is producing the nonverbal cues as well as to the cues themselves. If we have problems with verbal messages, we at least have a dictionary that will tell us the most common meanings of a word. We do not have a dictionary or any similar reference for the most common meanings of nonverbal cues. We learn the meanings of nonverbal messages totally through feedback, and obviously some people learn them better than others. Perhaps by analyzing the types of people who are more sensitive to nonverbal messages we will have a clue as to how we can improve our own abilities.

The most consistent finding regarding nonverbal sensitivity is that women are much more sensitive to nonverbal communication than men. This is true for both sending and receiving ability. There have been many theories that have attempted to explain why this is true, but the one we accept relates to the traditional stereotypes or roles of males and females. Our society seems to tell women in some very subtle and some not-so-subtle ways that they are to be more social-emotional, while men are to be more task-oriented and rational. Women are to be "people-oriented," and men are to be "thing-oriented." This social-emotional or person-oriented prescription for women implies that they should be more sensitive to the feelings of other people, and, by extension, to the nonverbal behavior of others. If this is part of the socialization or gender-role training of women in our society, it could account for the greater sensitivity of women to nonverbal cues.

Nonverbal sensitivity does not seem to be related to verbal sensitivity. People who score high on vocabulary or IQ tests based on verbal ability do not necessarily score better on tests of nonverbal sensitivity. There is some evidence that persons with high verbal sensitivity may actually be less sensitive to nonverbal communication. This finding would suggest that sensitivity to one or the other mode of communication may cause a deficiency in the other. It is still too early to make this claim, however. We just don't have enough information.

Other factors that seem to account for nonverbal sensitivity are age, personality, and occupation. A person's race seems to have little to do with nonverbal sensitivity. Children improve their nonverbal sensitivity until about the age of twenty to thirty, when the sensitivity level seems to reach its maximum. People who are outgoing, well adjusted, and egalitarian are usually more popular and nonverbally sensitive. They are probably more popular because of their sensitivity level. As you might imagine, the occupations that are more skillful in sending and receiving nonverbal messages are those that have made a serious study of such behavior. These include actors, artists, musicians, and communication students. People in occupations that involve dealing with other people, like teachers, psychologists, and business persons are generally more sensitive than scientists, for example.

Women are often more sensitive to the thoughts and feelings of others.
PHOTO BY CAROLE DUGAN

Persons who are sensitive to one nonverbal channel, such as the face, are usually found to be sensitive to the other nonverbal channels. In the same way, people who are good senders of nonverbal messages are also good receivers, and vice versa. The interesting point about all of this is that not all people are sensitive to the same messages. Most people seem better able to detect negative messages than positive ones, but this ability differs according to the individual. We are probably better attuned to the negative messages because they can have more potentially harmful effects.

Now we come to the question of how you can improve your nonverbal sensitivity. Perhaps the most important factor is not to allow your emotions to cloud your perceptions of your own nonverbal behavior and that of others. People with lower levels of physiological arousal have been found to be more accurate nonverbal senders. We would guess that this is also true of receiving abilities. Like the listener who must refrain from arguing with the speaker, the sensitive nonverbal sender and receiver must not let their own feelings cause miscues.

The second factor in developing nonverbal sensitivity is being alert. We said earlier that missed cues occur when someone fails to perceive a cue in the first place. Nonverbally sensitive people are constantly alert for the cues that occur around them, as well as their own. Many of our own nonverbal messages are sent without our ever being aware of them. We think we are putting on a good front until someone asks, "What's the matter?" All of us like to think we have good "poker faces," but few of us really do. It's just as important to be sensitive to the cues we are sending as it is to be sensitive to the cues we are receiving.

There are several ways that have been devised to train people to be more sensitive to nonverbal communication. Two of these are role-playing and the use of audio and videotape. Simply learning about nonverbal communication by reading, listening to lectures, and talking about it with other people can also help develop such sensitivity. For most people, nonverbal communication is one of the least understood areas of study. We have few grammar schools and high schools that spend any time at all in training students to understand nonverbal messages. Compared with all the training we give students in speaking and writing, is it any wonder that many of us are so insensitive to nonverbal communication? Just as with verbal communication, we can improve our nonverbal sensitivity only if we have the motivation, attitude, knowledge, and experience to improve.

SUMMARY

This chapter has been devoted to three seemingly different aspects of the human communication system: the neurophysiology of the system, the way we develop communication skills, and the development of communication sensitivity. In fact, however, these three aspects are closely related, as you have discovered in this chapter. In looking at the physiology of the human communication system, it should have been made clear to you that we are concerned with a complex and truly interdependent system. Our input mechanisms of hearing, sight, smell, taste, and touch perceive and send information to the brain, which, through reasoning, combines this information with our motivations and with the previous information stored in memory to produce message outputs in the form of verbal and nonverbal behavior. We find that the physiology of human communication points out to students better than anything else why we must view this process as a whole rather than as unique and unrelated parts. None of the parts of this system can stand alone. They are so interrelated that scientists still have not discovered all the relationships.

Once we understand the physiology of communication, the process of verbal and nonverbal communication development makes sense. Our communication development is a combination of innate ability, physiological maturation, experience, and feedback. We combined these elements into the three aspects of input, the child's equipment, and output. After examining the various theories concerning how the child learns language, we came to the conclusion that the child has an innate language acquisition device but that imitation and reinforcement account for much of the child's communication development.

Sending and Receiving Mechanisms

Sensitivity to communication continues to develop even after we are no longer children. We continue to aspire to higher and higher levels of both verbal and nonverbal communication sensitivity. To do this, however, we need to be motivated, to keep a positive attitude, to acquire as much knowledge of the communication process as possible, and to practice what we have learned. We suggested some things to keep in mind that we believe will help you increase your communication sensitivity. You must remember, however, that the sensitive communicator also takes into account the environment in which the communication occurs. This is the focus of the following chapters. You now have much knowledge of the human communication system. You now need to study how these elements of inputs, outputs, and interpersonal processing manifest themselves in the environments and contexts in which communication takes place.

KEY TERMS AND CONCEPTS

ACOUSTIC LEVEL ANALYSIS
BRAIN, HUMAN
CHILD'S EQUIPMENT
CHILD'S OUTPUTS
COMMUNICATION SENSITIVITY FACTORS
DEVELOPING LISTENING SENSITIVITY
DEVELOPING NONVERBAL SENSITIVITY
DEVELOPING SPEECH SENSITIVITY
DISPLAY RULES
EFFECTOR ORGANS
EGOCENTRIC SPEECH
ELABORATED CODE
ENVIRONMENTAL INPUTS
ENVIRONMENTALIST POSITION
IMITATION-REINFORCEMENT MODEL
LINGUISTIC LEVEL ANALYSIS

LISTENING MISCONCEPTIONS
MEMORY
NATIVIST POSITION
NERVOUS SYSTEM
NEURONS
PHYSIOLOGICAL LEVEL ANALYSIS
RECEPTOR ORGANS
RESTRICTED CODE
SMELL
SOCIALIZED SPEECH
SPEECH CHAIN
SPEECH PRODUCTION MECHANISM
SPEECH RECEPTION MECHANISM
TASTE
TOUCH
VISUAL RECEPTION MECHANISM

SUGGESTED READINGS

DALE, PHILIP S., *Language Development: Structure and Function*, 2nd ed. New York: Holt, Rinehart and Winston, 1976. This book examines the syntactic, semantic, and pragmatic development of human communication. Relevant portions of the book include discussions of language as rule-governed behavior, imitation and reinforcement, language and cognitive development, social class and sex differences in language development, and measuring language development. This book is very comprehensive but still understandable to the student.

WILLIAMS, FREDERICK, *Language and Speech*. Englewood Cliffs, N.J.: Prentice-Hall, Inc., 1971. This book examines language and speech from several perspectives: acoustic, phonological, linguistic, psychological, and sociological. It is especially interesting to the student who would like to learn more about the mechanics of speech production and reception. Williams writes at a level that can be understood by a freshman or sophomore student.

Wood, Barbara S., *Children and Communication: Verbal and Nonverbal Language Development.* Englewood Cliffs, N.J.: Prentice-Hall, Inc., 1976. This book is an amazingly complete account of how children develop and use verbal and nonverbal communication. Most books on language development do not go into the nonverbal aspects of communication development, at least not to the extent that they are discussed by Professor Wood. She devotes three chapters to this aspect. There are five chapters on how children develop words, sentences, and meanings, and there are three chapters on how children communicate regardless of whether the channel is verbal or nonverbal. The final section provides parents and teachers with activities, materials, and ideas designed to help a child improve his or her communication capabilities.

IV
COMMUNICATION CONTEXTS

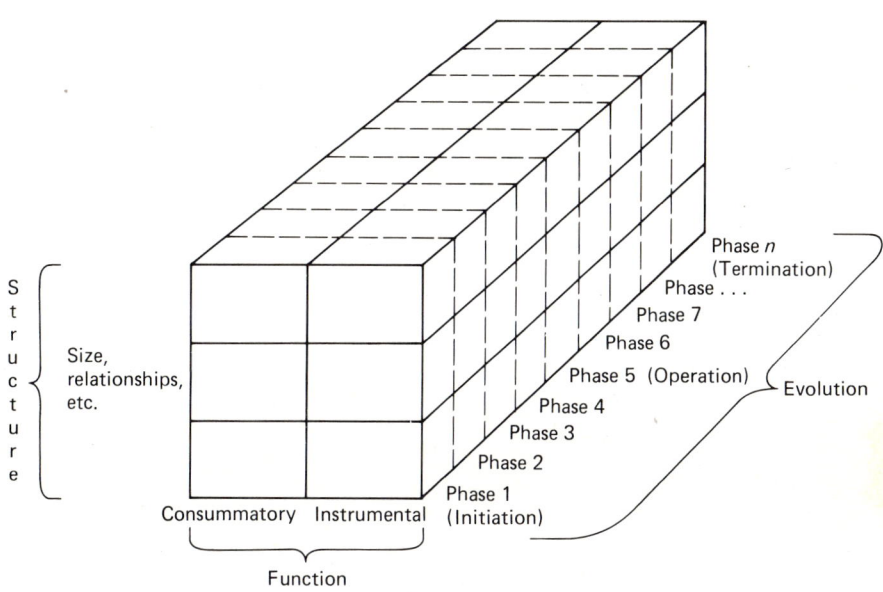

9
Context Components

In addition to discussing systems generally, it is possible to consider specific contexts. Traditionally, communication scholars have spoken in terms of five contexts: the dyadic, small group, organizational, public, and mass contexts. An understanding of these five contexts helps us to more adequately prepare for participation in communication events in these different situations. In order to differentiate among the contexts, we must consider three identifying features of any communication system: the structure of the system, the function of the system, and the evolution of the system. An understanding of these three features is a valuable aid in understanding different communication contexts.

Context Components

If you will review our discussion in Chapter 2 of the characteristics of communication systems, you will note that those characteristics apply across all systems. Thus far we have primarily focused on a generalized communication system by discussing common components, with special emphasis in Parts I, II, and III on the human being as a subsystem. As we discussed intrapersonal processing elements and communication inputs and outputs, our focus was on the way these things function as components within human beings and communication systems in general.

For many years, communication scholars have gone beyond the general study of communication and focused on different types of communication systems. Typically, courses are offered on small group communication, interpersonal communication, organizational communication, public communication, and mass communication, even though these courses appear with varying titles. Communication teachers have focused on these different areas because it has proven useful to study the systems separately. People often behave differently, depending on the nature of the system. Dyads, or human communication systems consisting of two people, operate differently from public communication systems in which one person presents a prepared, formal speech to a group of listeners. There are different concerns for communicators in each of these contexts, and the outcomes of the systems are often different. Finally, the effects of these different communication systems on the individuals involved and the skills necessary to participate effectively in each context can vary.

The term "context" has been used in several basic comunication textbooks to designate the different kinds of communication systems. The contexts we will be discussing are, in order, the dyadic, small group, organizational, public, and mass communication systems. However, in order to adequately discuss the different contexts that we will be covering in this section of the book, it is useful to consider a model with identifying features that we can use to differentiate one context from another.

How can you tell, for instance, whether the communication system you are taking part in, or observing, is a public communication system or a mass communication system? This is not an idle question, because the way you prepare to participate in either of these two contexts and the expectations you have for each should vary considerably. This will be true no matter what type of communication context you are confronting. Fisher (1975) and Gerard (1968) have suggested a basic paradigm that is useful for distinguishing among systems. They suggest that systems (1) are composed of a structure, (2) serve functions, and (3) go through a process of evolution. Structure, function, and evolution are basic to all systems, and yet differences in these features enable us to distinguish among the traditional contexts of communication. These features are illustrated in the figure on page 221. We will now discuss these three identifying features, drawing on the concepts discussed in Chapter 2. We will employ these characteristics in an analysis of the major contexts of communication discussed in the following chapters. It is our hope that this chapter will provide a framework by which you will be able to identify and distinguish among the communication contexts of dyadic, small group, organizational, public, and mass communication.

STRUCTURE

Hall and Fagen (1956) suggest that "a system is a set of objects together with relationships between the objects and between their attributes." They also define objects as ". . . the parts or components of a system . . . which . . . are unlimited in variety." When we suggested the existence of "communicators" in Chapter 2, we defined the objects, or components, of human communication systems as people who communicate. It would be possible to have a communication system in which the components were computers, but that would not be a human communication system. Thus from the perspective of viewing a human communication system the components, or subsystems, would be the people who are doing the communicating. The attributes of the components, or objects, in a system are defined by Hall and Fagen as ". . . properties of objects." Thus, attributes are the descriptive terms and characteristics we might use to define a human communicator in a human communication system. As an example of the attributes we use to define human beings, we have talked about people as part of a species, who have five senses available to them to receive inputs and who can produce speech of other symbolic language behavior. We have also described human communicators as having three intrapersonal processing elements: motivation, perception, and reasoning. In other words, the preceding sections of this book have been devoted to describing the attributes of human communication system components.

Implicit in the discussion of communication systems in Chapter 2 is the assumption that communication systems are composed of both subsystems and the relationships among the subsystems. The separate components and the relationships among them constitute what is called the system's structure. Think of the skeleton of a human being. Each separate bone and the ways it relates to others make up the structure of the skeletal system. Thus, the structure of a skeletal system is defined by both the attributes of each component and the ways in which the components relate to each other.

Physical Structure

As you can see, there are two ways in which we can discuss the structure of a communication system. First, we can consider the physical objects, the components of the system, as they exist physically in space across time. Second, we can focus on the patterns of interaction, or relationships, as a way of discussing structure.

Many of the communication contexts we will discuss in this part of the book are traditionally identified and differentiated according to the number of components within the system. This is not a difficult concept to grasp, since there is an obvious difference between a husband and wife talking with each other about their plans for the evening and a small group of five people trying to determine ways of conserving energy in a bank building. You can easily distinguish between the dyadic communication system composed of two people and the small group communication system composed of five people. Hence, one of the first characteristics we can use to identify a communication system is the structural characteristic of component quantity. As we try to consider the communication contexts that will be discussed in this part of the book,

Context Components

however, it will become obvious that the number of components in a system is not the only identifying feature of a communication context. As we have often said earlier, a system has interdependence, by which all components interrelate. Thus, in order to identify a system, we must consider more than one structural characteristic as well as the other identifying features of function and evolution.

In addition to quantity, another physical structural characteristic that is useful in identifying communication systems is whether the communication system permits face-to-face interaction between human beings or is mediated by some mechanical or electronic device(s). Communication by telephone, for instance, prevents the person who originates a message from having face-to-face contact with the person who receives the message. The structural characteristic of the presence or absence of face-to-face contact is of considerable importance. If you will consider the discussion in Chapter 7 concerning nonverbal communication, it should be obvious that any communication system that does not permit face-to-face interaction prevents the communicators from being aware of the visual channel. This observation should also suggest to you that when there is no visual nonverbal communication available to the communicators, much information is lost.

Feedback, for example, cannot function as well when the channel is mediated as it can in face-to-face communication contexts. It is impossible to adapt our message to the visual nonverbal responses of our listeners when we talk over a telephone. In face-to-face communication systems, it is possible for communicators to adapt their messages to their intended receivers while they are presenting the message. This means that we must consider very different approaches to communication when we know in advance that we will not have visual feedback during the presentation of a message. Since we will not have that information available to us while presenting our message, we must anticipate receiver responses much more accurately. The structural characteristic of whether or not face-to-face interaction is permitted in a communication system has a significant effect on the way the communication system can function as well as on the evolution of the system. If the message is mediated as in the print or electronic media, other characteristics of the medium can also have a significant effect on the message received. We perceive messages differently if they come to us through a newspaper (written words) or if they come to us through radio or television (spoken words).

The immediacy of feedback is another structural characteristic that is of considerable importance in identifying a communication system. It is frequently related to the presence or absence of face-to-face contact. Because the absence of face-to-face interaction prevents visual feedback and sometimes spoken feedback, certain communication systems (mass communication systems, for example) usually function with *delayed feedback*. The mediating characteristic of electronic and print media makes it impossible for feedback to be immediate. Producers and advertisers spend hundreds of thousands of dollars to present a message on television and then must wait days or weeks before they know whether the program or commercial was well received or not. The structural characteristic of delayed feedback is of critical importance for people working in mass communication.

Keep in mind that there are some communication contexts in which we may not have face-to-face communication but in which we do have immediate feedback. A primary example of this situation would be a telephone conversation. Two people can be talking on the telephone, engaging in dyadic communication, without enjoying the information available through a face-to-face interaction. Yet they do get immediate verbal feedback. Obviously, the more immediate the feedback in any communication system, the easier it is to adapt messages and develop new messages in response to the other people in the communication system. The more immediate the feedback, the easier it is to maintain a successful communication system.

The public communicator can adapt rapidly because of immediate feedback.
PHOTO BY CAROLE DUGAN

It is impossible for us to list all of the structural characteristics of communication systems in this chapter. We suspect that each of the identifying features of a system is well worth a chapter in and of itself. This discussion of the characteristics related to physical structure should aid you in better understanding the distinctions made among the different communication contexts to be discussed later. However, in addition to the physical structure of a system it is also important for us to consider the relationship structure in that system.

Relationship Structure

Over time, any communication system has fairly consistent patterns of interaction among its components. For instance, a father consistently has the authority to tell his children where they may and may not go, how late they

Context Components

may stay out, and with whom they may keep company. There are consistent patterns and channels of communication that regulate the relationship between father and child in their dyadic communications. Because such patterns exist, and because various links form among and between components of a human communication system, we can say that a relationship structure develops.

When we talk about physical structure, we point to human beings or to the presence or absence of face-to-face contact. When we talk about relationship structure, we mean the framework for interaction that develops as a result of how the people interact. One of the easiest ways to picture the structure that develops from relationships is to think in terms of a business, university, or any other large organization. All large organizations have a hierarchical structure that is based on the power relationships within the organization. For example, a department head in a university interacts in particular ways with his or her faculty because of formal authority. That department head likewise interacts with a college dean in consistent ways, who in turn interacts with a vice-president in consistent ways, who in turn interacts in consistent ways with the president, who finally interacts in consistent ways with a board of trustees. This is a formal relationship structure.

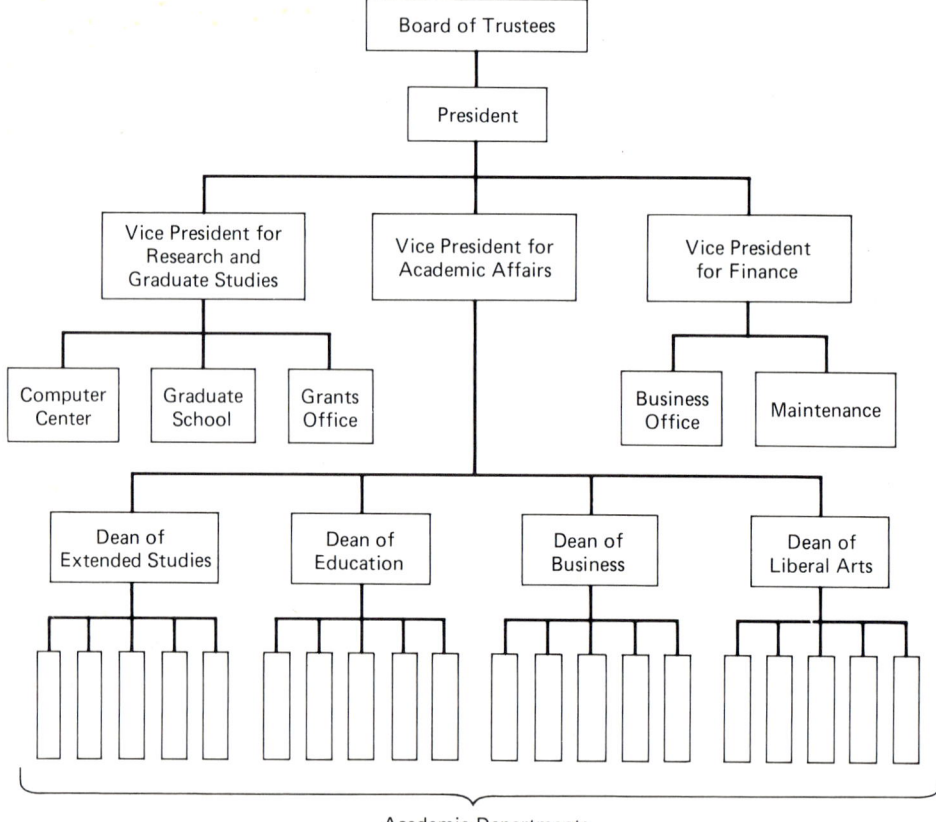

Fig. 9.1 An organization chart.

If you'll take a look at Fig. 9.1, you'll see the formal organization chart for a university. Any time you see an organization chart of this sort you can immediately perceive, at a glance, a structure built on formal relationships that are based on authority and power. If you use your imagination, this organization chart is something like the skeleton or nervous system of a human being. It involves a structure that determines the ways in which the components can and do interact with each other. It also affects the function and evolution of the system.

Relationship structure varies considerably from communication system to communication system. For instance, if we consider the relationship between a speaker and an audience in a public communication context, it should be apparent that the audience relates to the speaker in a much different manner from the way two people in a dyadic communication context relate to each other. The same kinds of power and influence cannot exist from one system to another; thus the people in these two different kinds of communication contexts communicate differently. Formal power and authority relationships between communicators are often the result of another aspect of system structure: communicator role.

Communicator role refers to the expectations others have about what the typical inputs and outputs should be for each participant in the system. The role we have in the communication system in part defines our relationships with others in the system. The roles of father, mother, son, and daughter in a family define the ways in which these people can and do interact. Given the context of any communication situation, these roles can define who can interact with whom, for how long, on what subject, and the like. These roles can determine the success or failure of a human communication system. All of us are conditioned by our roles. In small groups there are leadership roles, information-giver roles, roles concerning the task with which the group is faced, and roles concerning feelings and emotional support. These relationships are important identifying features of any communication context. It is important to recognize that the structure of communication systems can be identified by relationships established by the roles people play relative to each other.

The content of messages in a human communication system can also define the relationships among the components and in turn the structure of the system. For example, obscene content in conjunction with the role and gender of participants can determine whether or not messages will be successful. In other words, whether we are male or female and of high or low status can determine whether or not we can even interact in relation to obscene topics. Message content also significantly affects the function and evolution of a communication system. It can determine with whom we will communicate, how we will communicate, our goals, and the stages we go through to reach them. The content of messages can have a significant effect on the existence and/or continuance of a communication system.

It is interesting to note that we have certain kinds of content that we consider permissible on radio and television and other kinds of content that we do not consider permissible on these media. Have you ever noticed that some things seem entirely appropriate in a book but not on television? Likewise, material that might not be suitable for the organizational or public communication context is suitable for a dyad or small group. The content of messages in a human communication system will define the way the participants can interact with each other and relate to each other, thus defining the structure of the system as it results in relationships based on content.

Finally, the degree of formality or lack of it in a communication system often defines the relationships among the participants in the communication system. A public communication system, for example, is highly formal in nature. The very fact that people tacitly agree to sit and listen without interruption to someone who has spent time in preparing a speech suggests that there is a set of rules to this effect that everyone abides by in the public communication situation. This is one of the distinguishing characteristics of a public communication system. None of the other communication systems that we will be discussing usually occurs with this degree of formality, with the possible exception of mass communication systems.

Because of this formality, there are differences in the way people interact in the public communication context. In our country, people do not usually talk back in the middle of a speech. Rather, they wait until the end of the speech for questions and comments. However, even though they are silent, people listening to a speech provide much visual nonverbal feedback. Such feedback is part of the rules of the game, and we all tend to abide by these rules when we participate in the public communication context. On the other hand, although at times it can be formal, the dyadic context is usually an informal one. As a result, people tend to interrupt and make spontaneous comments. Nonverbal communication operates much differently, including touching, caressing, and more direct eye contact. Because it concerns prescribed relationships and ways of interaction, formality has a significant effect in determining the way people will interact from communication context to communication context.

Thus, in order to define the structure of a communication context, we cannot simply count the number of people involved or look at their physical arrangement. Rather we must consider the ways in which people relate to each other. These identifying structural features will make it easier for us to differentiate among and between different communication contexts.

FUNCTION

What does a system do? What is its purpose? When you ask these questions, you're considering the function of the system. When we talk about a pencil as something with which we draw and write, we are describing the function of a pencil. We can identify a communication context not only by its structure but also by its function. There are at least two ways to consider function in a human communication system. First, we can think in terms of the functions of the individuals in the system. Second, we can consider the functions of the whole system itself. We will consider each.

Individual Functions

Within the various communication contexts, the participants may serve different functions. One of the most obvious examples is the public communication context. To the most casual observer it should be immediately apparent that the functions served by the speaker in the public communication context are different from the functions served by the listeners. Each component does something different for the system. This is not to suggest that one is more important than the other, but rather that in a public communication system members of the audience and the speaker perform different functions necessary for the system to operate effectively.

In this example, the public speaker is usually the person who has the most control over the situation. It is the public speaker who prepares the message to which people will respond. The speaker serves the function of providing the major stimulus in the public communication context. The members of the audience serve the functions of responding to the speech, criticizing it, and accepting or rejecting it. We find similar differences in sender and receiver functions in mass communication contexts. You should not infer from these comments, however, that the functions of persons in the system are completely separate and distinct or that there is never any overlap of functions of different people in a human communication system.

We hope you can see that it would be quite reasonable to identify a public communication context through a consideration of the functions performed by the participants. Because there are functional differences in the way individuals behave in different human communication systems, we can expect the systems themselves to be different and to function differently. As we will consider in the coming chapters, each of these communication contexts has different "roles" and these differences result partially from differences in functions played by the individuals in the communication systems.

The instrumental function is primary in a business dyad.
PHOTO BY CAROLE DUGAN

System Functions

In addition to individuals' performing different functions within a human communication system, it is also apparent that from context to context, and within contexts, the function of a system itself can vary. The function served by a dyadic communication context for a husband and wife is very different from the function served by a mass communication system in which someone such as Dan Rather or John Chancellor presents the news to a group of viewers. In the marital dyad, the function of the dyadic communication context may be to enhance an affectionate relationship, whereas in the mass communication context in which news is being broadcast the function being served may be the dissemination of information to many people. Although we would not want to use this functional distinction alone to differentiate among different communication contexts, it is evident that it is one useful identifying feature by which we can make meaningful distinctions.

Aristotle first suggested that the basic functions of communication systems were to persuade, inform, and entertain. In general, however, it is possible to break down the functions of human communication systems into two general types: *instrumental* and *consummatory* (Fotheringham, 1966). The instrumental function is one in which the task—often one presented from outside the communication system—is being solved or approached. Thus, the participants in a communication system that is serving an instrumental function engage in the interaction to accomplish a goal above and beyond the pleasure derived from communication itself. An example in the dyadic context might be a customer in the loan department of a bank who is trying to negotiate a loan with a loan officer. The people communicate with each other in order to achieve a goal that can be reached only through instrumental dyadic communication.

On the other hand, two friends who are talking about the weather, a movie they have seen, or a sport in which they share an interest are communicating (though not always) primarily because they enjoy the interaction itself. The interaction itself satisfies their needs and serves a consummatory function. The consummatory function being served in this example would be the satisfaction of social needs or interpersonal needs, such as the needs for affection and inclusion. As in this example, the consummatory function served by human communication is one in which people communicate because it feels good or because the communication process itself satisfies a need or needs. In the bank example, the instrumental function is served because the participants reach a goal by communicating; they do not communicate as an end in and of itself.

At the risk of overgeneralizing, we would like to note some functional differences of contexts. A dyad most often serves the function of developing and maintaining relationships. It can also serve the function of selling. Sometimes it serves a problem-solving function. Small groups often exist to satisfy social needs, as in friendship groups or families. Likewise, small groups are frequently problem-solving groups, such as committees and decision-making groups. In the organizational communication context, we most often find businesses, government organizations, and others serving an instrumental function. On the other hand, there are organizations such as fraternities, sororities, hobby clubs, and social organizations whose communication function is that of providing pleasure for members. In the public communication context, the public speaker sometimes serves an entertainment or consummatory function by presenting after-dinner comments. Likewise, the public communication context can be used for decision-making, presenting information, and other instrumental functions. Finally, the mass communication context in its instrumental function is used to disseminate information and sell products or ideas. In its consummatory function, the mass communication context provides entertainment in the form of drama, comedy, novels, and cartoons, among others.

It should be evident that we can consider each of the traditional communication contexts from the point of view of whether the communication context is serving an instrumental and/or consummatory function. Although this distinction alone will not completely define the contexts for us, it is a useful part of an overall set of identifying features that we can use to describe and define a communication context.

EVOLUTION

Communication systems evolve and change throughout their existence. One of the best examples of the concept of evolution is a human system such as you. You include physiological and psychological subsystems that make up your overall system. When your system first came into existence, you were hardly the same as you are today. From the time we are born, we go through successive stages, beginning with the first stage of infancy. We then go through a stage called childhood, followed by the stages of adolescence, young adulthood, adulthood, middle age, old age, and finally, death. Although this is an oversimplified view of the development of human beings, it does illustrate the point that we evolve through successive stages throughout our lives and in so doing we do not remain the same person.

General semanticists have suggested that we live in a process world (Hayakawa, 1964). Everything in the world interacts with everything else in the world; thus there is constant change. Even rocks in the mountains are constantly undergoing change as a result of the wind, rain, and snow. Each of us is also undergoing change. We are born young, we grow old; we grow bigger, we grow smaller; we get sick, we get well; we exercise, we get fat. Because there is so much going on in the world that results in constant change, it is useful to think of ourselves as evolving systems. We are constantly evolving into something new as we pass through stage after stage after stage throughout our lives. Human communication systems tend to go through at least three stages in the different contexts: (1) *initiation*, in which the system is first formed and comes into being; (2) *operation*, in which the system performs its behaviors and functions; and (3) *termination*, in which the system ceases to function. In the example we have been using, you can think of birth as initiation, growing and living our lives as operation, and death as termination.

Human communication systems also go through stages parallel to these three evolutionary phases. In the dyadic communication context, these three stages have been broken down into ten stages of evolution. In the small group communication context, four specific evolutionary stages have been identified. Thus you can see that although generally the three stages of initiation, operation, and termination occur across all communication contexts, there are phases specific to the various communication contexts.

Let's take an example of a dyadic communication context—a male and female on a date. If these two individuals are attempting to develop an affectionate relationship, it is not unusual for them to go through fairly predictable stages. Initially, they experience a stage in which they try to get to know one another. Then, they probably attempt to discover common interests by talking about such topics as the weather, movies they've seen, sports they like, and so on. Next, they probably try to build on their common interests and develop their feelings toward one another a little bit more strongly. At some point, the interaction terminates, either to be renewed later or to let die.

Initiation.
PHOTO BY CAROLE DUGAN

Operation.
PHOTO BY CAROLE DUGAN

To repeat, evolutionary phases are different in various human communication contexts, although we can relate them back to the three basic evolutionary phases of initiation, operation, and termination. In order to understand what is occurring in a communication system at any given point, it is important to understand what kind of phases occur in that particular communication context and then to identify the phase in which the system happens to be at the given moment. You should also recognize that although the stages most often occur in sequence, sometimes a stage can be skipped or occur out of order. Some stages last longer than others. It is often hard to tell where one stage stops and another begins.

Termination.
PHOTO BY CAROLE DUGAN

Keep in mind that the participants in any human communication system must also change in order for the communication system to develop and reach goals. It is necessary for all persons in a small group to proceed from the stage of getting to know one another to the stage of offering ideas and arguing about them before it is ever possible for them to reach the goal of solving the problem with which they as a group are faced. Thus, in order to fulfill its function, be it instrumental or consummatory, any communication system must change, and the people in that system must change and adapt to the evolutionary phases through which the system is developing. In many different communication contexts, we have observed people who try to treat each other the same all the time because they forget that change is occurring. We have observed friendships that dissolved because there was a lack of recognition of the change that was occurring. Not recognizing those changes and the evolution of the relationship made it impossible for the members of these dyads to adapt to the evolution and communicate accordingly.

SUMMARY

This chapter should have made clear the nature of the system characteristics of structure, function, and evolution and the relationships among them. Whether there are two people or five people greatly determines how a communication system will evolve. Likewise, the number of people in a communication system will determine the kinds of goals, or functions, the communication system can strive toward. Whereas a dyad can easily serve the consummatory function of romance/intimacy, a small group of five to ten people can less probably serve that same function. Because the size of a communication system is related to the function fulfilled, we frequently constitute our communication systems according to the function we wish them to serve. Likewise, we can evolve through intimacy states more rapidly (and differently) in the dyadic context than we can in the public communication context. As is the case with other system features, the characteristics of structure, function, and evolution interact with one another. When one is changed, all are changed. We cannot, for example, change the structure of a communication system without affecting the function it serves and its evolution.

The structure, function, and evolution of communication systems are features useful in discussing and identifying the various communication contexts that we will discuss in the following chapters. No one of these identifying features alone will permit a complete identification of any communication context. It is only by considering all three of these identifying features together that we can make meaningful statements about the communication that occurs in the dyadic, small group, organizational, public, and mass communication contexts. In Chapters 10 through 14 we will discuss each of these communication contexts from both the traditional approach and the systems approach that we have been developing throughout this book. We will make use of the identifying features of structure, function, and evolution to make this discussion clearer.

KEY TERMS AND CONCEPTS

ATTRIBUTES
CONSUMMATORY FUNCTION
CONTEXT
DELAYED FEEDBACK
EVOLUTION
FUNCTION
INDIVIDUAL FUNCTIONS
INITIATION

INSTRUMENTAL FUNCTION
OPERATION
PHYSICAL STRUCTURE
PROCESS WORLD
RELATIONSHIP STRUCTURE
STRUCTURE
SYSTEM FUNCTIONS
TERMINATION

SUGGESTED READINGS

BERTALANFFY, LUDWIG VON. *General System Theory*. New York: George Braziller, Inc., 1968. Ludwig von Bertalanffy is considered the father of systems theory. This book is based on many of his earlier writings. They should help to underscore the concepts presented in this chapter.

Suggested Readings

Kuhn, Alfred. *The Logic of Social Systems*. San Francisco: Jossey-Bass Publishers, 1974. Kuhn develops his own vocabulary for systems theory and develops several concepts that are complementary to the ones developed in this chapter. His discussions of human systems at various levels should be especially useful for the student who wishes to go beyond the material presented in this chapter.

We would also suggest that you consider reading the books by Buckley and Ruben and Kim that were suggested for reading at the conclusion of Chapter 2. The systems concepts in these books are directly related to the material presented in this chapter.

10 Dyadic Communication

Dyadic communication is the first context we will explore. We have chosen this context to examine first because we believe it to be the most elementary and most directly relevant to all of the other human communication contexts. In this chapter we will explore the various structural, functional, and evolutionary facets of dyads. We will see how status differences between dyad participants can affect a dyad. We will examine the importance of openness, honesty, empathy, supportiveness, and positiveness to both consummatory and instrumental dyads. We will develop the basic differences between interviews and control-oriented instrumental dyads. Finally, we will see how, regardless of their structure, dyads go through phases of development as they progress toward their functional goal. The information we present in this chapter is important and necessary for an understanding of any of the other communication contexts.

Dyadic Communication

We begin our discussion of communication contexts with the dyad. The dyadic system is the most basic and by far the most common communication context. It is, therefore, also the most important and influential communication context. Even in larger contexts, when the dyadic relationships are satisfactory for most members of the system we usually find a healthy system. For the purposes of this book, we will define the dyadic context as any two-person communication relationship. The relationship does not have to be face-to-face. It can exist via the telephone, a memo, or letter. The participants must, however, be communicating with one another. Two machine operators who simply work near one another but do not communicate would not be considered a dyadic communication system. The communication relationship need not be verbal. If our two machine operators were to communicate nonverbally because of the loud noise surrounding them (or for any other reasons), they would form a dyadic communication system.

You can see why we say the dyad is the most frequent and important of all communication systems. Dyads are the foundation upon which larger systems are built, as well as being important in and of themselves. We cannot imagine any larger system that does not include dyadic interrelationships. In later chapters we will discuss small group, organizational, public, and mass communication systems. All of these include dyadic relationships. Many of the basic principles that are important in all of these contexts begin with the dyad.

CLASSIFYING DYADIC SYSTEMS

In the previous chapter, we discussed the common components of all communication systems. In this section, we will isolate those aspects of a dyad's structure, function, and evolution that we believe to be the most significant.

Dyadic Structure

The first and most obvious structural element of a dyad is that only two people are involved. However, for our purposes in this chapter, the important aspect of dyad structure is how the two people relate to one another. Evidence supports the proposition that one of the most important variables affecting the relationship between members of a dyad is their relative status. Significant differences occur in dyads if the participants are of unequal status, as opposed to dyads in which the participants are equal in status (or peers).

There are other aspects of dyadic structure that we could discuss, such as the norms that exist; the roles the participants are playing; the communication channels available; the proxemic aspects of the dyad; the age, sex, and race of the participants; and so forth. However, all of these aspects are much less relevant to the functioning of the dyad than the status of the participants. Therefore, we will classify dyads into only two types on the basis of their status structure: equal-status dyads and unequal-status dyads

Dyadic Function

The literature is much less clear regarding the most important functional aspects of dyads. Scheidel (1976), for example, lists what he calls only a "few examples" of the purposes of a dyad, including the loving relationship, therapeutic association, social conversation, becoming acquainted, instruction, interview, bargaining, persuasion, combat, and coercion. As suggested in Chapter 9, we classify dyadic function as "instrumental" and "consummatory." This dual classification may sound oversimplified compared with Scheidel's classification, but it has two advantages. First, it focuses on the broad purpose of the system: whether the goal of the dyad is to accomplish some action (instrumental dyad) or simply to exchange views, with any action that occurs merely a by-product of the interchange (consummatory dyad). The second advantage of this classification is that it does not exist in isolation but is interrelated with the structural and evolutionary aspects of the dyad. You will see more clearly how this interrelationship helps narrow our function classification later.

Dyadic Evolution

Evolution refers to the development of the system over time. This aspect of dyad classification has often been neglected. Much literature regarding dyads seems to assume either that dyads do not change and develop over time or that such change is relatively unimportant. We believe that both of these assumptions are far from the truth. In fact, the evolutionary aspect of dyads may be the most important of all.

We will focus on the dyadic evolutionary phases developed by Knapp (1978b). They include the evolutionary stages found in Fig. 10.1. As a dyad moves through each of these phases, it actually becomes a "different dyad" for analytical purposes. Both the structure and function of the dyad are affected as the dyad develops through each evolutionary phase.

Process	Stage	Representative Dialogue
Coming Together	Initiating	"Hi, how ya doin'?" "Fine. You?"
	Experimenting	"Oh, so you like to ski . . . so do I." "You do?! Great. Where do you go?"
	Intensifying	"I . . . I think I love you." "I love you too."
	Integrating	"I feel so much a part of you." "Yeah, we are like one person. What happens to you happens to me."
	Bonding	"I want to be with you always." "Let's get married."
	Differentiating	"I just don't like big social gatherings." "Sometimes I don't understand you. This is one area where I'm certainly not like you at all."

Dyadic Communication

	Circumscribing	"Did you have a good time on your trip?" "What time will dinner be ready?"
Coming Apart	Stagnating	"What's there to talk about?" "Right. I know what you're going to say and you know what I'm going to say."
	Avoiding	"I'm so busy, I just don't know when I'll be able to see you." "If I'm not around when you try, you'll understand."
	Terminating	"I'm leaving you . . . and don't bother trying to contact me." "Don't worry."

Fig. 10.1 An overview of interaction stages. From Mark L. Knapp, *Social Intercourse: From Greeting to Goodbye.* Copyright © 1978 by Allyn and Bacon, Inc., Boston. Reprinted with permission.

If you are able to properly classify the type and stage of development of any dyad in which you participate and if you know what to expect from that dyad's type and development stage, you will be better able to function effectively as a member of the dyad. Each of the possible dyadic types operates in a particular way, based on the combination of its structure, function, and evolution. It is, therefore, extremely difficult to look at the structural, functional, or evolutionary effects in isolation, but for the sake of clarity we will begin by trying to do just that. Later we will consider how structure, function, and evolution interact with one another.

DYADIC STRUCTURE

When two people come together to interact, one of the first things they try to determine is how they should behave toward one another. Our society has conditioned us since early childhood to base this determination on the status of the person with whom we are talking. We have been taught that we should behave very differently with persons of higher or lower status than we do with persons of more or less equal status. For example, when we are with equals we can talk much more openly. We can look them directly in the eye and touch them if we want. We are less careful in our communicative habits, both verbal and nonverbal. We don't need to stand at attention or make our grammar and pronunciation absolutely correct. In other words, we can be careless when we are part of an equal-status dyad, as can our equal-status partner.

When we are with persons of lower status than ourselves, we tend to behave in many of the same ways we behave with equal-status partners. However, we have some advantages that we do not have in equal-status dyads. We have much more ability to control what will occur in the dyad. We can dominate the discussion if we wish through the use of questions or orders. We can change the topic of discussion. We can also do many things nonverbally that our lower-status partner cannot do. We can touch the other person and be more relaxed in our posture, gestures, dress, facial expression, and so on. In other words, when we are with someone of lower status we can be ourselves, but they cannot.

Is this an equal- or unequal-status dyad? Upon what did you base your conclusion?
PHOTO BY CAROLE DUGAN

When our dyadic partner is of higher status than ourselves, we tend to behave very differently than we do in either of the first two situations. When we are the subordinate, we must conform to many restrictions. We must present the best possible image of ourselves and show the proper amount of respect for the superior. We should speak only when spoken to, lower our eyes, and follow the lead of our high-status partner. When we do say something, we are expected to distort the message to fit the expectation of the other. We cannot be totally honest or relaxed when speaking to a superior. It is hard to be ourselves when we are the lower-status member of an unequal-status dyad.

Status and Power

Status is power. In other words, one person has more status than another if that person has some kind of power over the other. One of the most complete analyses of power is that of French and Raven (1959). They have identified five different types of social power that one person can exert over another to obtain status. The first is *reward power*, or the power to give the other person something he or she wants. The reward can take the form of praise or money or affection or any number of other tangible and intangible goods. *Coercive power*, on the other hand, refers to our ability to punish the other person. Coercive power is the opposite of or a negative form of reward power. *Referent power* occurs when one member of the dyad is admired by the other member. Referent power is actually given to or bestowed on one member of a dyad by the other. *Expert power* refers to the knowledge one person has in comparison to the other. Like referent power, this is a type of status attributed to one person by the other. Finally, *legitimate power* is a status that one person formally has over another because of a position that person holds. A parent has legitimate power over a child, and a judge has legitimate power over everyone in a courtroom.

One of these forms of power or any combination of them can account for the status an individual has in a dyad. The more of such power a person possesses, the higher that person's status. In our model, we discuss only equal- and unequal-status differences, but it must be recognized that there are many different degrees of unequal status. If the status difference is only slight, then the behavior in the dyad will differ only a little from a dyad made up of equals. The behavioral differences will increase as the status differential increases. You will behave very differently when talking to a person who has only a little more expert power than you will when talking to a person (like a judge) who has total legitimate power over you.

Status and Role

A second aspect of status in dyads is closely related to power. Every person who has status in a dyad (and that includes almost everyone at some time) has a set of behaviors that apply to that status position. These behaviors are called the *status role*. The status role of a parent, for example, includes providing for the children's physical and emotional needs until they become adults. More specifically, this provision includes feeding, clothing, and sheltering them, taking care of them when they are sick, and helping them overcome problems they face as they grow older. The status role of a police officer includes preventing crime, arresting criminals, testifying in court, and many other duties. Whether any dyad is of equal or unequal status depends totally on the perception of the relationship by both participants. For a dyad to fit our definition of either equal or unequal status, the status relationship must be similarly recognized by both participants. If one party does not see the status role in the same way that the other does, a conflict will eventually arise.

Status Conflict

As you have already noticed, the term "conflict" is very important in communication. It has come up a number of times in this text and will come up throughout the remaining chapters. You will need to be alert to the different types of conflict that can occur because conflict can have many sources in human communication. Status conflict occurs when the two participants in a dyad disagree as to whether their relative statuses are equal or unequal. Perhaps the most common example of status conflict occurs in the male/female dyad.

The traditional view of a male/female dyad is that, all else being equal, the male has the higher status. A great many nonverbal cues provide evidence of the continuing influence of this belief. Many of these were discussed in the chapter on nonverbal communication. As you remember, females are expected to smile more than men; they are expected to maintain less dominant eye behaviors such as looking downward; they are expected to stand more erectly and they are expected to claim less space by keeping their arms and legs much closer to their body. These behaviors, as well as many others, are all signs of submission. Males, on the other hand, are taught by our society to display the reverse or dominant nonverbal cues. The woman who does not follow this traditional model and takes on dominant or high-status characteristics is labeled "hard," "competitive," "aggressive," and "independent"—all with a derogatory connotation. These same terms are considered positive qualities for a man. This traditional view of the male/female dyad continues to pervade our society and provides an excellent example of status conflict.

Transactional Analysis

Before we leave the topic of status, we would like to acquaint you with a popular attempt to deal with the dynamics of status relationships in a dyad. The technique is called *transactional analysis (TA)* (Berne, 1969, 1972; Harris, 1967). TA goes beyond the actual power and status of the members of the dyad and addresses the motives and feelings of the people involved. TA is intended to help us understand ourselves by analyzing the dyadic transactions we have with others.

The basic elements of TA are three ego states: Parent, Adult, and Child. According to TA, all of us have some of all three of these ego states within us. We also have an appropriate set of communication and other behaviors that we use when in each ego state, all of which probably derive from our ego needs. When in the *Parent* ego state, we are evaluative, nurturing, domineering, accusing, and critical. Messages such as "You can never do anything right" and "This is the way I want it done" are typical of the Parent ego state. When in the *Adult* ego state, we are logical, calm, inquiring, organized, knowledgeable, questioning, attentive, and understanding. Messages such as "What do you think of this idea?" and "Yes, I can see the rationale behind what you say" are typical of the Adult ego state. When in the *Child* ego state, we are a combination of spontaneity, creativity, and rebelliousness mixed with obedience, submissiveness, and quietness. Messages such as "If that's the way you want it, I quit" and "Yes, Sir, you know best" are typical of the Child ego state. You may be in any one of these three ego states while in a dyad, regardless of your status, and you may even shift ego states as the dyad develops.

When viewing a dyad, we must look at the messages of both members of the dyad to determine the type of transaction that is taking place between them.

Three types of transactions can occur: complementary, crossed, and ulterior. *Complementary transactions* are those that involve each person's understanding and addressing the correct ego state of the other. Figure 10.2 includes two examples of complementary transactions.

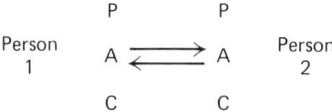

Person 1: "What do you think of that idea?"
Person 2: "Yes, I can see the rationale behind what you say."

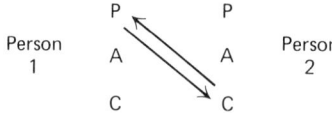

Person 1: "This is the way I want it done."
Person 2: "Yes, sir, you know best."

Fig. 10.2 Complementary transactions.

From *Games People Play* by Eric Berne, M.D. Copyright © 1964 by Eric Berne, M.D. Reprinted by permission of Random House, Inc.

Complementary transactions are usually very productive and long-lasting. Although TA does not deal with status as such, the complementary transactions diagrammed in Fig. 10.2 can be viewed in terms of status. The first example could represent an equal-status dyad and the second could represent a complementary unequal-status dyad.

A *crossed transaction* occurs when the two participants are unaware of the ego state of the other and as a result address the wrong ego states. Figure 10.3 includes an example of such a crossed transaction.

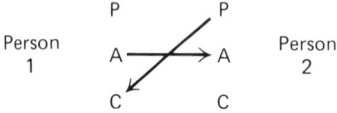

Fig. 10.3 Crossed transactions.

From *Games People Play* by Eric Berne, M.D. Copyright © 1964 by Eric Berne, M.D. Reprinted by permission of Random House, Inc.

Crossed transactions usually signal trouble for the dyad. Berne's example of the crossed transaction pictured in Fig. 10.3 is Person 1, a husband, saying to his wife, "Dear, where are my cuff links?" This is an adult-to-adult question, but the wife responds by shouting, "Where you left them!" This is a parent-to-child response. It is quite possible that a status conflict might arise from such a response. Had she responded instead by saying, "I think you left them on your dresser" or "I don't know where they are," the transaction would have been complementary (adult-to-adult or equal-status) and no problem would have occurred.

An *ulterior transaction* occurs when hidden or covert messages representing other ego states are involved as well as the obvious ones. This kind of transaction most often takes the form of a contradictory message sent through verbal and nonverbal channels. The cuff-links example presented earlier could have involved ulterior transactions, depending on the facial expression, gestures, or tone of voice that accompanied the responses. It is quite possible that even if the wife had responded "I think you left them on your dresser"—a seemingly adult response—the facial expression and tone of voice might ultimately denote the word "stupid." Figure 10.4 depicts such an ulterior transaction.

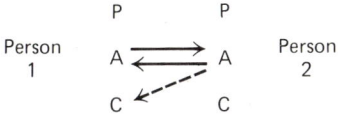

Fig. 10.4 Ulterior transactions.

From *Games People Play* by Eric Berne, M.D. Copyright © 1964 by Eric Berne, M.D. Reprinted by permission of Random House, Inc.

Ulterior transactions are the most difficult to identify and handle. You must be sensitive to all of the message channels in order to spot ulterior transactions. Very often the person communicating the ulterior message is not even aware of it. Ulterior transactions are often the first sign of a status conflict. One of the participants nonverbally indicates that he or she questions the status relationship indicated by the other.

TA is a facinating and enjoyable way of looking at dyadic communication. It makes us aware that regardless of what our actual status might be relative to another person, we can still be in any one of the three possible ego states. An unequal-status dyad can operate as if it were equal if both participants are in a complementary ego state. This fact illustrates the complexity of examining dyadic structure. Remember, status is still primarily dependent on the perceptions of the participants.

DYADIC FUNCTION

The function of a dyad refers to its purpose. We have broken down the functions of a dyad into two broad categories: consummatory and instrumental. Although, as you will see, this division is not as clear-cut as we would like it to be, it provides a distinction that is useful in classifying and understanding the functional effects of dyads.

Dyadic Communication

The Consummatory Dyad

We classify a dyad as consummatory if its main purpose is that of sharing interaction rather than making a decision or producing action of some sort. Consummatory dyads occur simply for the sake of the communicators' deriving satisfaction from the communication process itself. Many dyads actually have a combination of both consummatory and instrumental functions, but at this point we will deal with dyads as if they were purely one or the other. There are times when all of us want to get together with another person simply for the pleasure of that person's company. Such an encounter may be as brief as a simple "Hi" as you walk past the other person or as long as an extended "bull session" in your room or at a party. We all like to talk to others for the social-need satisfaction we experience. Consummatory dyads are, therefore, primarily composed of emotional or affective interactions, and we usually participate in them to satisfy social or interpersonal needs. In order for such interactions to be successful, several elements must be present. Five of these necessary elements suggested by DeVito (1976) include openness, empathy, supportiveness, positiveness, and honesty.

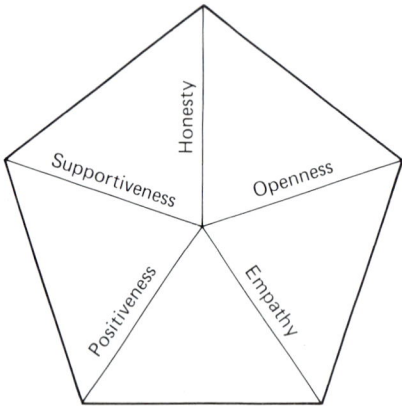

Fig. 10.5 Effective interpersonal communication.

From *The Interpersonal Communication Book* by Joseph A. DeVito. Copyright © 1976 by Joseph A. DeVito. Reprinted by permission of Harper & Row, Publishers, Inc.

Openness Openness is often referred to in basic textbooks as "self-disclosure." Both of these terms refer to one's willingness to provide another person with information about oneself that is pertinent to the encounter. Openness does not mean that you should pour out your soul to the other person, but rather that you should be willing to disclose those things that will help the other person interpret the interaction accurately. As we pointed out earlier, meanings are in people as well as in words. In order to interpret a message correctly, it is essential to know the communicator as completely as possible.

One of the more useful techniques that has been developed to express this concept is that of the *Johari Window*. The Johari Window is made up of four quadrants illustrated in Fig. 10.6.

Open self	Blind self
Known to self Known to others	Not known to self Known to others
Hidden self	Unknown self
Known to self Not known to others	Not known to self Not known to others

Fig. 10.6 The Johari Window. From *Group Processes: An Introduction to Group Dynamics* by Joseph Luft, by permission of Mayfield Publishing Company. Copyright © 1963, 1970 by Joseph Luft.

The quandrants are fairly self-explanatory. The principle is that for each person in a dyad the quadrants may be of different sizes. The goal of self-disclosure is to increase the size of the "open self" quadrant so that it resembles the following illustration.

Open self	Blind self
Hidden self	Unknown self

Fig. 10.7 Goal of self-disclosure. From *Group Processes: An Introduction to Group Dynamics* by Joseph Luft, by permission of Mayfield Publishing Company. Copyright © 1963, 1970 by Joseph Luft.

In order to self-disclose to another person, you must have a certain amount of trust in that individual. You must feel confident that the person will support you and not punish or reject you for self-disclosing. One of the ways this trust is developed is through mutual self-disclosure. You might start out by disclosing something that you feel involves little risk if the other should choose to react negatively. If the other person reacts by also self-disclosing, a self-disclosure cycle is begun, which leads to a development of trust and openness of interaction. It is much easier to develop openness in a dyad than in any other communication context, primarily because it is easier to monitor the responses of only one other person.

Honesty Honesty is the other side of openness. Whereas openness refers to you primarily as a speaker, honesty refers to you primarily as a listener. Honesty is an open reaction to the comments of others. An effective social dyad requires both openness and honesty. Both require trust as a prerequisite. These requirements do not mean that you have to agree with everything the other per-

Dyadic Communication

son says. That is not honesty. That is as dishonest as if you disagreed with everything. Honesty does not refer to the positiveness or negativeness of a response but instead refers to the truthfulness of a response. There is an old adage that says, "If you can't say anything nice, don't say anything at all." That is not good advice for promoting honesty in a social dyad. Silence and indifference are usually worse than disagreement for promoting open, honest communication.

Empathy The third quality of effective consummatory dyadic communication and probably the hardest to achieve is empathy. Empathy refers to the ability to put yourself in the other person's shoes, to feel as the other person does at that moment. Empathy is often confused with sympathy. You are sympathetic when you understand how another person must be feeling and you "feel sorry" for that person, even though you do not feel as the other person does. It is hard to empathize with others unless you have experienced the same stimuli that have affected them. It is hard for you to empathize with a person who is grieving for a lost husband or wife unless you have also lost a close loved one. All you can really do is sympathize for them. Notice we use the terms "empathize *with*" and "sympathize *for*." These terms reflect the idea that empathy implies a bonding whereas sympathy does not.

The five elements for a successful consummatory dyad are evident between these sisters.
PHOTO BY CAROLE DUGAN

A certain amount of empathy can be developed verbally through self-disclosure. Verbal descriptions are never as good as actual experiencing, but a certain amount of empathy can develop in that way. The person who has lost a loved one, for example, might disclose to you the love each had for the other through descriptions of some intimate episodes in their lives. This disclosure will allow you to project yourself into their situation and to vicariously experience their feelings, and thereby to empathize with them. We do this, for example, when we cry as the hero of a movie is crying, or when our heart beats rapidly as the star of a TV show gets into a dangerous situation. We are not having the experiences ourselves, but they are portrayed so vividly that we cannot help but empathize. Empathy is important in the consummatory dyad because it helps us to understand the other person. When we empathize, we tend to suspend judgment; that is, we do not automatically label another's behavior as right or wrong. The suspension of judgment allows us to be good and supportive listeners.

Supportiveness Supportiveness means that we will not criticize or attack our partner in the dyad. There are ways of disagreeing with another person that permit us to still be supportive of the person. Probably the best statement about how this can be accomplished is by Gibb (1961). He suggests several communication behaviors that promote supportiveness in dyads.

The first behavior that promotes supportiveness is the use of descriptive messages rather than evaluative messages. When we evaluate, we pass judgment on another. When we are descriptive, we suspend judgment. A second supportive communication behavior is *spontaneity* in our messages. Spontaneity means that you appear open and honest, with no hidden motives or deceptive strategy. In a consummatory dyad, we do not expect to be persuaded or brainwashed. When we detect a strategy behind the words of another, we become suspicious. A supportive person must appear to be open and spontaneous. The last of Gibb's supportive communication behaviors that we will discuss is *provisionalism* in our messages. Provisionalism implies an open mind willing to listen and to change an opinion. When we perceive the other person as having a closed mind and an unwavering sense of correct judgment, we become defensive.

Positiveness The last of DeVito's five qualities, positiveness, refers to the regard each member of the dyad has toward himself or herself and toward the other person. Transactional analysts refer to these attitudes as *life positions*. TA suggests four basic life positions. The first is "I'm not OK, you're OK," in which you see the other person in the dyad positively but yourself negatively. The second is "I'm not OK, you're not OK," in which you see both yourself and the other person negatively. The third is "I'm OK, you're not OK," in which you are positive about yourself but negative about the other person. The last is "I'm OK, you're OK," in which you are positive toward yourself and the other person. This last life position is the most desirable of the four and represents the type of positiveness that is necessary in a consummatory dyad. In this life position, you are willing to enter into all kinds of relationships with good expectations about your own abilities and the abilities of others. You see others and yourself as healthy, intelligent, and important individuals. This attitude allows the dyad to develop in a satisfactory manner.

As we said at the beginning of this section, the distinction between consummatory and instrumental dyads is not clear-cut. The five qualities of social dyads we have just discussed are also applicable to instrumental dyads.

however, in the consummatory dyad they take on added importance. The criteria for judging the success of the consummatory dyad are emotional and relational rather than task-oriented. It is possible to accomplish a task in a dyad without the benefit of openness, honesty, empathy, supportiveness, and postiveness, but it is not possible to have a successful consummatory dyad when these elements are missing.

The Instrumental Dyad

When the purpose of a dyad is to produce a product, reach a goal, or make a decision rather than to experience the emotional satisfaction of simple sharing, we have an instrumental dyad. It is quite possible for one member to perceive the dyad as consummatory and the other to perceive it as instrumental. Such a situation might occur at a party where one person has come for social purposes, and the other has come specifically to land a job, make a sale, or start a romantic friendship that could lead to marriage.

In this text, we use the term *interview* to refer to an instrumental dyad in which both participants are mutually involved in seeking a result through the question-answer process. We will use the term *control* to refer to an instrumental dyad in which one or both participants are attempting to influence the other toward a predetermined outcome. The latter may or may not make use of the question-answer process. This is not to say that an instrumental dyad must be either a control dyad or an interview dyad. It is quite possible that dyad participants may employ both of these forms within a single interaction. It is important, however, that the participants be aware of both instrumental communication types and the effects of each on the interaction.

Interview dyads The most important quality of the interview dyad is that neither of the participants has predetermined a conclusion. Both desire some instrumental result to occur from the dyad, and each is willing to negotiate with the other as to what the result will be. This usually involves the question-answer process to obtain and clarify information necessary to reach the goal.

An interview involves two roles that can be alternately played by either of the participants. These roles are called *interviewer* and *interviewee*. The interviewer role is assigned to the participant seeking the information, and the interviewee role is assigned to the person supplying the information. In some interview dyads these roles change often, while in others the roles remain constant throughout the interaction. As we mentioned earlier, role is closely aligned to status. In the interview, the role of interviewer is normally credited with the higher status since that person is in greater control of the interview's direction and outcome. The more often the roles alternate from one person to another, the less the status affects the interaction. It is not always the case, however, that the interviewer has the higher status. In journalistic interviewing, for example, a reporter may be interviewing a person of much greater status, like the President of the United States. In such a case, the interviewer has status in regard to the direction of the interview, but the interviewee has legitimate status that may be used to neutralize the interviewer role. In such a case, the interviewee may end up determining the interview's direction and outcome.

In journalistic and survey interviews, there is generally little status difference between the interviewer and interviewee.
PHOTO BY CAROLE DUGAN

If a formal interview is to be productive, considerable preparation must precede the interview itself. If this preparation is not done, the interview is likely to terminate without enough information or the right information being obtained. In order to prevent such an occurrence, the participants must have a clear idea of the general purpose of the interview. They must define the purpose of the interview as narrowly as possible. One of the best ways of doing this is to anticipate what you will want to know after the interview is finished. In an employment interview, such a purpose would be to pick the best person for the job. In a health-care interview, it could be either to get a general record of the person's health background or to determine the nature of a particular ailment. Whatever the general purpose, it must be defined as narrowly as possible and remain constant throughout the context of the interview.

Out of the general purpose of the interview grow the specific objectives that will accomplish the purpose. There is no "formula" for determining the specific objectives of an interview , but somehow they must be formulated because they prescribe what the questions should be, the type of question used, and the sequence in which the questions should be asked. You cannot prepare questions until you know what information you need, both generally and specifically.

The art of preparing and asking good questions is one that takes much training and many years of practice. We cannot hope to cover it completely in the space here, but we can attempt to give you some of the basics of question formulation. The first requirement of a question is that it must tell the respondent what information is desired. This is not always an easy task. It is very easy for a receiver to misinterpret the words used in the question. If the question is going to be asked of more than one person, it must be clear enough so that all or most respondents will interpret it similarly. Thus the grammar and vocabulary used must be simple and clear so that no matter what the receiver's frame of reference, he or she will make the proper interpretation. On the other hand, if the question is too simple, the respondent may be insulted.

The second requirement of a question is that it motivate the interviewee to provide the required information. Some questions will turn off a respondent; that is, they will cause the respondent to become defensive and evasive or unwilling to provide the needed information. The oversimple, insulting question is one example; others are the embarrassing, personal question or the hostile question. A question must not only tell the respondent what information is required but must also establish and maintain a supportive climate in which the respondent is motivated to provide the requested information. These goals are accomplished in part by the type of question that is asked.

There are several types of questions that can be asked in an interview. The interviewer faces several choices regarding the types of questions to be asked. The first of these choices is whether to ask for the information directly or indirectly through the use of other questions that will yield the same information. A second choice faced by an interviewer is whether to use open or closed questions. Closed questions ask for one- or two-word answers like "yes," "no," or "no opinion." Open questions allow the respondent to provide a more extensive answer. "Do you like your job?" is a closed question; "What do you think about your job?" is an open question. Open questions do not limit an interviewee's response. The advantage to open questions is that they give the interviewer information about the respondent's depth of knowledge, attitude toward the information, reasons for holding a particular opinion, and much more. The distinguishing characteristic of the closed question is that the possible responses by the interviewee are usually rather restricted and normally much shorter. In general, closed questions are used when very specific information is required and time is short. But the use of closed questions poses some dangers. With a closed question, the interviewer assumes prior information regarding the respondent's depth of knowledge and feelings on the subject, as well as the respondent's motivation to answer the questions. This is a lot to assume. Another danger of the closed question involves the introduction of bias into the interview. Bias usually occurs through the use of leading questions that encourage the respondent to reply in a desired way, or with an "obvious answer." For example, you may turn to another student in class and say, "You don't really think this is such a bad class, do you?" By asking this question, you have already indicated how you feel and what the response should be. The obvious answer is "No!" The respondent risks an argument with you by answering "yes" to such a leading question. This is not to say that only closed questions can be biased, but there is a greater likelihood for consistent bias in a closed question. With an open question, the respondent has a greater chance to clarify and amplify on a response and thus to avoid getting trapped into an obvious answer. Many interviewers employ both open and closed questions to fit the objectives of the interview, the respondent's knowledge level and motivation, the time available, and other factors.

The final step in an interview is analyzing the results. Analysis usually involves finding patterns in the responses that relate to the general purpose of the interview. The analysis stage can be rather simple or quite complex. A medical doctor may be able to analyze the responses of a patient and diagnose an ailment in a matter of seconds. For a large research or survey project, the analysis stage may take months of constant work. Regardless of its complexity, every interview ends with an analysis that relates back to the general purpose of the interview and determines the end result and success of the interview.

Control dyads A control dyad is one in which at least one of the participants has a predetermined outcome in mind for the dyad and attempts to control the interaction in the dyad to reach that outcome. As we said earlier, it is very common for a dyad to start out as an interview, but as it evolves one or both of the participants develop conclusions and attempt to force those conclusions on the other. It is important for you to be able to identify when the nature of the interaction begins to shift from interview to control. Sometimes this identification is quite easy. One of the participants says something like "Well, I think I have heard enough, and I have decided what we're going to do." In such a case, the other participant usually must go along with the decision because few people would make such a statement if they did not have the status and power to enforce it. Such a statement is seldom heard, however, even in a control dyad. The much more common situation occurs when one of the participants reaches a conclusion and attempts to indirectly influence the other to reach the same conclusion. In such a case, the undecided participant has more choice in the matter.

One of the easiest ways of identifying the change from an interview to a control dyad is to be sensitive to the kinds of questions or statements that are being made. Very often the questions asked become more and more leading. The controller attempts to condition a "yes response" by carefully selecting and phrasing questions that encourage the respondent to answer in a way that is supportive of the predetermined outcome.

In addition to the fact that leading questions are often asked in a control dyad, you should also be aware that there are often fewer questions asked. Moreover, there is a corresponding increase in the number of statements made. The participant attempting to control the dyad shifts from an "asking" to a "telling" approach. At the same time, there is also usually a shift from unbiased to selective listening. While listening, the controller begins to mentally search for arguments instead of listening to understand. Once you become sensitive to the different verbal patterns that occur in both the interview and control dyads, it will be relatively easy to identify each type and to notice where one ends and the other begins. The best way to determine the dyad type would be to get into each of the participant's heads, but since that is impossible, observing the verbal patterns is the best alternative.

Just as there are two main roles in the interview dyad, so there are two main roles in the control dyad. We will call those roles the controller and the controlled. The *controller* is the person who is attempting to infuence the other participant. The controller is the one who makes the influence attempt, and the success of a control dyad is usually analyzed in terms of his or her goal or purpose. The *controlled*, on the other hand, is the person toward whom the influence attempt is directed. Just as in the roles of interviewer and interviewee, the roles of controller and controlled may alternate during the course of a dyadic interaction, or they may remain relatively stable.

In examining a control dyad, you must be aware of the interpersonal relationship between the participants since that will have a significant effect on the controlled's willingness to accept the proposed outcome. If the participants have a positive regard for one another, dissonance or balance theory predicts that the influence attempt is likely to be successful. One of the main advantages of influence attempts in the dyad, as opposed to such attempts in other larger contexts, is that the controller can more readily manipulate his or her credibility and monitor any change in perceived levels of expertness, trustworthiness, and dynamism.

A merchant must establish credibility very quickly in order to influence a prospective buyer.
PHOTO BY CAROLE DUGAN

The second advantage a controller has in the dyad is that he or she can tailor the message for the other person. The controller can more easily spot areas of resistance and determine likely influence strategies when dealing with only one other person. This is why successful controllers often begin with an interview. The interview portion of the interaction helps them plan the message to fit a specific receiver.

A third advantage for the controller in a dyad is feedback monitoring. If the controller is sensitive to the feedback messages from the controlled, the message can be altered to obtain the most positive response. It is much easier to monitor, interpret, and respond to the feedback of one receiver than that of a group or an audience. Receivers are also more likely to give feedback in a dyad than in a larger group.

A final advantage for the controller in a dyad is in the follow-through. Once a person commits himself or herself to an attitude or behavior in a dyad, that person is likely to maintain the attitude or continue the behavior after the interaction ends. The controlled feels more committed to the conclusion reached and also feels a direct responsibility to the other participant once the proposed conclusion has been accepted. These are some of the reasons why most salespersons and other controllers like to operate in a dyad.

DYADIC EVOLUTION

Dyads, like all systems, tend to evolve and change over time. In observing this change, it is useful to think of the dyad as becoming a different system in each evolutionary stage. At the beginning of this chapter, we listed the ten evolutionary stages of a dyad. You were given not only the five stages that comprise the coming together of a dyad and the five stages that make up the dyad's coming apart but also some representative dialogue of each stage. At this point, we will discuss some of the more pertinent aspects of each evolutionary stage. You must remember, however, that all dyads do not move through these stages in exactly the same manner or at the same rate. In most cases, you will find that a dyadic relationship seems to progress systematically through the stages in the manner indicated because there are certain things that happen in each stage that affect behaviors in the following stages. Rate of movement through the stages seems to depend on such factors as previous interactions with the same partner, the amount of reward as opposed to cost, the amount of time available, proximity, individual needs, and many other factors. We will now examine how two people normally tend to evolve through Knapp's ten stages of a dyadic relationship.

Stage One: Initiating

This stage is normally rather brief, often lasting fewer than fifteen seconds. It accounts for our initial impression of our dyadic partner. Most of us are a little nervous when we first initiate a dyadic relationship. We are highly sensitive to both the verbal and nonverbal behaviors that might indicate something about the other person or about the interaction itself. People tend to be very cautious during this stage of the encounter. Our society has developed some very conventional methods of behaving during this stage. You can talk about the weather or any number of other nonthreatening matters to get through this stage. Very often we stereotype the other person during this stage.

Stage Two: Experimenting

It is hard to determine when this stage has begun and when the initiating stage has been completed. Many authors combine these two stages into one, referring to it in terms such as the formation or orientation phase. At any rate, it is during this stage that the participants in the dyad begin to search for possible similarities that will predict positive outcomes for each. They tend to exchange demographic information like names, ages, occupations, and so forth. According to Knapp, "relationships at this stage are generally pleasant, relaxed, overly uncritical, and casual. Commitments are limited" (1978b, p. 19). It is at this superficial level that we interact with most of the people around us. We progress to the following stages with only a very few special persons.

Stage Three: Intensifying

Once the two participants in the dyad have determined that they will receive acceptable outcomes from the relationship, they attempt to intensify the intimacy. This effort may begin with cautious self-disclosure. The dyad's movement into the intensifying stage is often first signaled nonverbally. The partners may begin to decrease the space between them and demonstrate courtship behaviors if one is male and the other is female. They may touch one another, smile more often, and give other friendship signals. There are also verbal behaviors that commonly occur during this evolutionary stage.

> (1) Forms of address become more informal—first name, nickname, or some term of endearment. (2) Use of the first person plural becomes more common—"We should do this" or "Let's do this."
> (3) Private symbols begin to develop, sometimes in the form of special slang or jargon, sometimes using conventional language forms which have understood, private meanings. (4) Verbal shortcuts built on a backlog of accumulated and shared assumptions, expectations, interests, knowledge, interactions, and experiences appear more often—one may request a newspaper to be passed by simply saying, "paper." (5) More direct expressions of commitment may appear—"We really have a good thing going" or "I don't know who I'd talk to if you weren't around." Sometimes such expressions receive an echo—"I really like you a lot." "I really like you, too, Elmer." (6) Increasingly, one's partner will act as a helper in the daily process of understanding what you're all about—"In other words, you mean you're . . . " or "But yesterday, you said you were . . ."
>
> (Knapp, 1978b, p. 20)

As the dyadic relationship intensifies, both persons begin to give more and more of themselves in an attempt to blend their own ideas, feelings, personalities, and behaviors. As in the first two stages of initiating and experimenting, it is often hard to differentiate this third stage of intensifying from the following stage of integrating.

Stage Four: Integrating

During this stage, the dyad continues to intensify its intimacy to the point where the two participants begin to operate as if they were one person. The participants behave as if they were controlled by the same mind. This does not mean that either or both of the participants have lost their own individual identity. In really strong dyads, each person maintains a certain distinction from the other. This distinctiveness is important for both and is a sign that the relationship is healthy. No one wants to be known merely as a subset of someone else. Each participant in the dyad must maintain some individual and personal distinction from the other.

There is no doubt, however, that during the integration stage the two participants do seem to fuse or coalesce with one another. Each participant begins to develop behaviors and feelings that are quite similar to those of the other and that are different from those of others around the two of them. Other people in their environment begin to view them as if they were a common package. You may also notice that participants in integrated dyads begin to mimic one another in terms of clothing, speech patterns, physical behavior, and so on. When the dyad is made up of a male and female, or, for that matter, even when the dyad is made up of members of the same sex, gifts such as pictures, pins, rings, records, flowers, and candy are often exchanged. We give much of ourselves during the integration stage.

When couples reach the integration stage of coming together, they adopt similar dress, behavior, and thinking patterns.
PHOTO BY CAROLE DUGAN

Stage Five: Bonding

This stage represents a formalization or public announcement of what has occurred during integration. Bonding may include such rituals as engagement or marriage. Knapp defends the act of bonding as a separate stage in the following manner:

> It is because the act of bonding itself may be a powerful force in changing the nature of the relationship "for better or for worse." The institutionalization of the relationship hardens it, makes it more difficult to break out of, and probably changes the rhetoric that takes place sans contract. The contract becomes, either explicitly or implicitly, a frequent topic of conversation. Communica-

tion strategies can now be based on interpretation and execution of the commitments contained in the contract. In short, the normal ebb and flow of the informal relationship can be, and often is, viewed differently.

(Knapp, 1978b, p. 22)

Through formal bonding, each member of the dyad is making a long-term commitment to the other. Both are saying that they intend to face the future together and not as individuals. Bonding also acknowledges that each member of the dyad is willing to abide by certain rules and regulations contained within the contract. In business contracts such as the formation of a partnership, the terms of the bonding agreement can become vitally important. Bonding is the last of the five stages that make up the "coming together" stages of dyadic evolution. Stages six through ten relate to the stages that occur when a dyad "comes apart."

Stage Six: Differentiating

Differentiating occurs when the dyad participants begin to stress their separateness rather than their togetherness. Messages begin to focus on the participant's differences rather than their similarities. The pronouns that are used are no longer "we," "us," and "our" but instead become "I," "me," and "mine." The members of the dyad begin to see that they have less in common than they might have thought they had originally. Some very strong dyads move in and out of this stage with some regularity and develop techniques for solving these differences. On the other hand, many dyads continue to come apart and progress through the remaining stages until they finally come apart completely. It is at the differentiating stage that the first signs of a split appear. It is up to the members of the dyad to determine how far they will let it go. As the principle of entropy would predict, any system will tend to continue to disintegrate unless added effort is expended to combat the entropy.

Stage Seven: Circumscribing

When the communication between participants further deteriorates to the point that only selected nonthreatening topics can be safely discussed, the circumscribing stage has appeared. Not only the quantity but also the quality of messages between the participants becomes noticeably different.

> **Familiar phrases typical of this stage include: "Don't ask me about that"; "Let's not talk about that anymore"; "It's none of your business"; "Just stick to the kind of work I'm doing and leave my religion out of it"; "You don't own me and you can't tell me what to think"; or "Can't we just be friends?" The last example is a suggestion that prescribes a whole new set of ground rules for permissible topics in the interaction.**

(Knapp, 1978b, p. 24)

It is not too late to reverse the negative entropy, but at this stage even more effort would be required. At least during this stage the two participants are still talking to one another even though the communication has been circumscribed.

Stage Eight: Stagnating

During this stage, verbal communication cuts off almost completely except for the most basic messages. Each of the members of the dyad assumes that he or she "knows" what the other person is thinking and how communication would develop, if initiated. Thus, neither attempts to say anything. Most of the communication that does take place during this stage is nonverbal. The participants "say" what they are thinking through facial expressions, eye behavior, and gestures. In many cases, these take the form of a blank expression, a cold stare, or a shrug, respectively. Some dyads remain at this stage for a long period of time because of other constraints such as children or an agreement that would hurt both if a complete separation should take place. Dyads that do not have such constraints move very quickly through this stage to complete termination. You will sometimes find persons in this stage who still hold out hope that the relationship may yet be saved. In order to reverse the process, something must be done to get the members of the dyad to begin talking to one another again. Before any relationship that has reached this point can be saved, some form of sincere dialogue is necessary because the next step after communicative separation is spatial or proxemic separation. And at that point, reconciliation becomes almost impossible.

Stage Nine: Avoiding

Avoiding is an attempt to eliminate even nonverbal communication since most nonverbal communication requires at least visual contact. Avoiding need not imply physical separation, however; one form of avoiding is treating the other person as if he or she did not even exist. During this stage, messages can begin to get very blunt. "Shut up," "Get away from me," "I don't want to see you any more," "I'll pretend you're not even here, and you do the same" are all examples of the type of conversation that can take place. It's kind of a "don't call me, I'll call you" stage. At this point, the relationship is pretty much over. It would take a major change by both parties to reverse the trend at this point. Sometimes it is the stark and real knowledge of what life is really going to be like without the other person that provides that major change, but in most cases this reality has been anticipated in the preceding stages and therefore does not come as a total shock.

Stage Ten: Terminating

This is the end of dyadic evolution. All dyads must at some point terminate. They can terminate without ever going through the other stages of coming apart, such as when one of the participants moves away or dies. Often, however, termination is a result of going through each of the stages mentioned previously. Termination can be a result of a gradual evolution through each of the preceding stages, or it can come very quickly. The communication that takes place as part of termination depends on the status and personalities of the participants, the nature and length of the relationship, the medium through which the conversation takes place (telephone, face-to-face, or letter), and many other factors. Wilmot suggests that termination need not be a bad thing but can have certain rewards.

> The rewards of dissolving a relationship are as varied as the reasons for staying in a relationship. First of all, a termination of a relationship will allow the participant to "start over." A person who has terminated a love relationship or a close friendship has space in her or his life for new intimates. Often, you find someone else who "fits" better—who shares more of the same values, responds more fully to you as a person, and generally provides more rewards. . . . Termination allows one to correct errors in the previous relationship by removing relational shackles. It is often a choice between "saving yourself" and "saving the relationship." A relational termination can allow one to grow and change in ways that would not be possible with a continuing commitment to the first person. In a new relationship, new parts of the self can become activated. . . . The decision to terminate an important relationship has both costs and rewards, with the rewards coming out stronger for at least one of the persons. Terminations happen because one of the partners expects positive value from it. While the "left" person sometimes harbors hopes that the leaver "will return to her senses," the leaver often does not return because, even with the pain, the breakup is a positive step.
>
> (Wilmot, 1979, p. 168)

This concludes our presentation of the stages of dyadic evolution, but it does not conclude our discussion of dyadic evolution. We have intentionally excluded from our discussion of the stages any presentation of the role of conflict in dyadic evolution. As dyads progress through each of the preceding stages, conflict can and should be a part of the process. In the following section, we will present a brief analysis of the types of conflict that can arise in any communication context, the positive and negative aspects of each type of conflict, and how conflict can be managed in order to allow human communication systems to evolve in a productive manner.

DYADIC CONFLICT

The term *conflict* is often perceived as something bad that should be avoided at all costs. We don't perceive this term in that way at all. As a matter of fact, we believe people should actually seek to engage in certain forms of conflict. We must first, however, define what we mean by conflict and the various forms of conflict. The term conflict as it is used here refers to any form of incompatibility that leads to a clash. We have already used the term conflict to refer to both role and status incompatibility. Neither role nor status incompatibility involves conflict unless there is a clash between the roles of one participant or between the two participants as to whether they have equal or unequal status. If there is no clash, there is no conflict.

Conflict Types

There are two basic types of conflict of concern to us in dyadic communication systems: content conflict and interpersonal conflict. In the case of *content conflict*, the clash is restricted to matters of substance; that is, the participants conflict over the pertinent topics or issues involved. This is what Coser (1956) calls *realistic conflict*; that is, the participants restrict themselves to conflict that helps them move toward the instrumental goal of the interaction. In *interpersonal conflict*, the participants may agree with one another regarding the communication content, but they have conflicting or negative orientations toward one another. This leads to what is called *affective* or *unrealistic conflict*—the type of conflict that often leads to system termination. It is a very destructive type of conflict.

Conflict Intensity

When we break down the two types of conflict, we often find that they represent various levels of intensity. The lowest level of conflict intensity is called *controversy*. Controversy occurs when participants perceive that a conflict exists, but they feel they can resolve the conflict through rational and peaceful procedures and continue to interact. The second level of conflict is called *competition*. At this level, participants perceive the only possible resolution to the conflict to be that one person wins and the other loses. Athletes engage in this form of conflict. The participants do not want to destroy one another, but they know that only one person or team can win. The highest level of intensity is *combat*. The intent here is not only to win but to destroy the opponent. A fist fight is an example of combat. Both controversy and competition can lead eventually to combat. However, the reverse is also possible; that is, conflict at the combat level can be managed in such a way that it can be reduced to competition or controversy, or even to a peaceful relationship. Before we discuss the ways in which conflict can be managed, we need to examine the values of conflict. Up to this point, it may appear that conflict is bad and should be avoided at all costs. As we said earlier, this is not the case.

Value of Interpersonal Conflict

There are many dyadic situations in which conflict has both a productive and functional purpose and should be encouraged. Both content and interpersonal conflict can be valuable to dyadic evolution. Interpersonal conflict can serve to increase participant involvement and can help to develop a deeper level of trust that in turn can lead to openness, honesty, empathy, supportiveness, and positiveness. An absence of conflict is often a sign of apathy toward the communication relationship. Conflict serves to increase the total amount of interaction, and increased interaction reflects participant involvement. If the participants are involved in the interaction they will usually express the underlying hostilities that typify interpersonal conflict. If these hostilities remain buried and unspoken, they may continue to produce negative effects. If they are expressed, they can be dealt with by the participants. Incompatibilities cannot be resolved if they are not discussed openly. This is a problem in the circumscribing, stagnating, and avoiding stages of a dyad. A clash must occur for the conflict to be resolved. Successful communicators develop techniques for managing interpersonal conflict as it arises. But such resolution can be achieved only if the interpersonal incompatibility is expressed. This does not mean that the participants should manufacture interpersonal conflict where none actually exists. However, they should be encouraged to express such conflict when it does exist.

Value of Content Conflict

Content conflict also has a number of positive values, if we measure the success of communication in terms of the quality of the substantive result and not in terms of the interpersonal aspect. Substantive or content conflict tends to produce greater effort, more ideas, and a higher-quality product. Conflict produces greater effort because it gets the participants more involved and stimulated. When we are in conflict with others, we work harder to develop data, warrants, and backing to support our claims. With this increased effort also come more ideas. The conflicting participants attempt to develop compromise or integrated solutions to the conflict. Frequently, the result of content conflict is a higher-quality product. It also usually takes more time to arrive at an outcome. Conflict stimulates critical thinking by all participants. The outcome that survives these critical tests is usually of higher quality. It is for these reasons that we want you to view conflict as an important and necessary part of the evolution of human communication. To achieve these values, however, the participants must know how to manage the conflict that does arise in order to make it work for them rather than against them.

Conflict Management

Many communication texts speak of conflict "resolution" rather than conflict "management." We see these two phenomena as being rather different. To resolve a conflict is to get rid of it. As we said above, we do not think it is always advisable to get rid of conflict. A certain level of content and interpersonal conflict is functional and should be maintained, not resolved. The trick is to manage the intensity and the focus of the conflict. Those people who talk about conflict resolution focus on such things as terminating the dyad, victory by one person over the other, compromise, negotiation, integration, and the like. These are all possible ways of reaching a peaceful relationship, and they may be desirable in some situations but not in others.

Conflict management assumes that the participants see conflict as a necessary and important part of human communication. It assumes that conflict will occur and that the communicators will try to limit its potentially destructive effects and encourage its beneficial effects. Conflict management assumes that conflict can never be totally resolved and that it will occur over and over again in the various evolutionary stages in altered forms. Interaction usually does not stay in one message area for very long. Statements are introduced, discussed for a period of time, and then dispensed with, only to rise again later in the discussion. This is especially true of statements that provoke conflict. Changing to a new topic is one way of managing conflict. It provides a cooling-off period. If the statement that provoked the conflict is important enough, it will reappear; if not, it will be lost.

Conflict, if managed correctly, can be healthy to a dyadic relationship.

If the conflict statement reappears, it must then be managed directly. The participants must decide the nature and extent of the conflict. They do this by trying to discover the roots of the conflict. It is important at this point that each person attempts to understand the other person's point of view as completely and accurately as possible. If either person is practicing selective listening, it will be hard to keep the conflict from becoming destructive. One of the most difficult things to do in communication is to listen objectively during a conflict period. This is especially true of interpersonal conflict. Objective listening can be accomplished only if you practice the techniques of listening discussed earlier.

Once each participant understands the other's point of view, both may realize that a conflict no longer exists. If conflict does still exist, the participants may be ready to explore possible ways of continuing the interaction in light of the disagreement. The conflict will remain but the participants can attempt to work it out. They begin to search for decisions that will be acceptable to both of them jointly but not totally satisfactory to either. This type of behavior occurs during the integrating stage of dyadic evolution. Dyads begin the coming-apart process often because they are unwilling to work out these mutually satisfactory decisions in light of the conflict that is occurring. The participants are unwilling to listen to one another and to deal with conflict directly. Conflict management requires both verbal and nonverbal communication. It is not easy to manage conflict, but it must be managed if people are to remain together. It would not be completely inaccurate to say that the coming-together stages of human communication relate directly to developing ways of managing conflict, while the coming-apart stages result from an inability to make use of the conflict that does arise. Evolution and conflict are intimately interrelated. To understand one, you must understand the other.

INTEGRATING DYADIC STRUCTURE, FUNCTION, AND EVOLUTION

We have outlined in a very general way the importance of a dyad's structure, function, and evolution. We have also indicated that the structure, function, and evolution of a dyad are highly interrelated. Although we do not have the space to discuss all of the interrelationships individually, we would like to discuss some of them so that you will be able to make some predictions about the other interrelationships on your own.

We will first examine the consummatory dyad and how it changes on the basis of its structure and evolution. We defined the consummatory dyad as one in which the participants share meanings and understanding rather than some instrumental purpose. We said that the criteria for judging the success of a social dyad were emotional, or affective, and that they were based on the openness, honesty, empathy, supportiveness, and positiveness that exist between the participants.

These five characteristics of successful consummatory dyads are much easier to accomplish when the dyad is equal in status than when it is unequal. Unequal-status dyads are prone to defensive, careful, and often distorted interaction. These kinds of interaction are contrary to all of the principles of success in consummatory dyads. In order for an unequal-status dyad to be successful, extra care must be taken in the initiating and experimenting stages. The high-status member assumes almost total responsibility for establishing an open, honest, supportive, positive, and empathic dyadic climate. The high-status participant must be willing to self-disclose and to open himself or herself to the person of lower status. A low-status participant cannot force an open climate unless the other permits it. This fact puts considerable pressure on both participants. Thus you seldom find unequal-status consummatory dyads that get beyond the experimenting stage. People prefer to socialize with equals because there are fewer pressures involved. People usually find equal-status consummatory dyads more attractive than unequal-status consummatory dyads.

The effects of unequal status are also felt in the other stages of dyadic evolution. If the high-status participants choose, they can use role, power, and status to force any interpersonal and content conflicts to be resolved in their favor. In a consummatory dyad, we are concerned primarily with interpersonal conflict, in which at least one of the participants does not like the other. Very often the inequality of the status is the reason for interpersonal conflict in consummatory dyads. The very fact that the other person has a higher status is often the reason for differentiating and circumscribing on the part of the subordinate. This coming apart may result from the tendency of low-status participants to perceive crossed and ulterior transactions.

When such incompatibility does arise, it is often circumscribed or remains at a low intensity and thus may not be recognized. When this is the case, it cannot be managed effectively. The superior often gets the mistaken impresssion that there is no conflict or differentiation when in fact there is. High-status people are constantly faced with the problem of identifying those persons who really have a positive orientation toward them and those who are negatively oriented but refuse to make their feelings known. Remember Ebenezer Scrooge, who found out how people really felt about him only when he dreamed he was dead? Participants in unequal-status consummatory dyads do not get involved, and the trust level is never very deep. It is very easy for them to grow apart.

With equal-status consummatory dyads, however, the situation is much different. It is easier for peers to self-disclose, open self, and share meanings. Much of this is due to the ease with which they can empathize with one another. It is hard to feel and to integrate with a person when that person holds a status that is outside your experience. In an equal-status dyad, the initiating phase is usually much stronger and will carry the dyad through the other stages of coming together. The participants are each willing to express conflicts that occur and manage the conflicts as they occur. Participants are willing to deal with one another on an adult level. In the unequal-status dyad, it is quite common for the high-status participant to patronize the other (parent ego state) or at least to appear to be doing so. This attitude may lead to crossed and ulterior transactions on the part of both participants. Members of an equal-status consummatory dyad can recognize and manage their conflict and are thus more apt to evolve completely through all the positive stages.

Instrumental dyads have all of the same problems that consummatory dyads have but they also have the problem of accomplishing a substantive goal. Unequal-status dyads are generally instrumental, because about the only time people of unequal status remain in a dyad is when they are attempting to accomplish an instrumental goal. In an instrumental dyad, the low-status participant is much more willing to accept a parent-to-child transaction. All of these characteristics seem to be reflected in both interview and control dyads. In each case, it is usually the person of higher status who acts as the interviewer or the controller. These roles are the natural outgrowth of the high-status position.

In an interview dyad, the high-status person usually determines the general purpose, objectives, and questions to be asked. This person also analyzes the results of the interview. There may be more closed questions in an unequal-status dyad. The advantage to an interview between persons of equal status is that it is easier to establish a productive climate. Just as in the consummatory dyad, persons of equal status are more willing to answer questions honestly and fully. The interviewee does not feel threatened.

In the control dyad, there is little change due to the status structure. The controller acts much the same, whether he or she has any power and status or not. One of the skills necessary for successful controllers is the ability to establish either referent or expert power in the absence of reward, coercive, or legitimate power. In an unequal-status control dyad, the high-status participant can have any or all of the five types of power. Therefore, such a person can be more direct in his or her influence attempts. This is usually not done, however, because although the desired outcome may be achieved in this fashion, the follow-up is less likely to be as successful. For that reason, it is often hard to differentiate between an equal- and unequal-status control dyad.

The most interesting facet of the control dyad, regardless of the status of the participants, is its evolution. Much has been written about the evolution of successful instrumental communication, often called persuasion. The steps involved in persuasion are often labeled differently by various authors. One common classification is that of receiving, focusing, associating, and resolving (Scheidel, 1967). The theory suggests that one must first get the other person to remain in the dyad (receiving). Then the controller must focus the receiver's attention on the instrumental goal or message including the data, warrants, and backing, as well as the claim. The associating phase occurs when the actual influence attempt either succeeds or fails. The controller must convince the controlled to accept the proposed outcome. This goal can be accomplished by associating the proposed outcome with something or someone already favored by the controlled. In other words, the controlled's ideas must somehow be associated or brought into line with the controller's ideas. The final phase of resolving occurs when the controller tries to solidify the now accepted outcome and to prevent the controlled from reverting back to his or her old beliefs.

The similarity between this process and the evolution stages already mentioned seems fairly obvious. During the initiating and experimenting stages, the participants establish a rapport that prevents them from terminating the dyad. During the intensifying stage, the controller attempts to focus attention on the message. If the controlled has an incompatible outcome in mind, conflict and differentiating are likely to occur. The integrating stage includes portions of association as the controller attempts to get his or her outcome accepted. The actual acceptance of the message comes in the bonding stage if the controller is successful in warding off all of the controlled's arguments. Finally, reinforcement occurs during bonding. It is through reinforcement that the controlled resolves in his or her own mind the acceptance of the controller's proposal.

An interview evolves in much the same fashion. The interviewer and interviewee orient themselves to one another. This orientation is often accomplished with some very open, indirect, and nonthreatening questions. As the interview begins to focus on its specific objective, conflict may occur. This is especially true, for example, in an appraisal interview in which the interviewer and the interviewee may disagree as to what is considered good and bad performance. If there are differences of opinion, they need to be resolved by the two participants before bonding can occur. The outcome of the interview then needs to be reinforced in order that the participants will not change their minds later and begin to come apart.

We have only begun to scratch the surface of all the facets of a dyad's structure, function, and evolution. As we said at the very beginning of this chapter, the dyad is the basic building block on which the other contexts rest. You will see constant similarities between the structure, function, and evolution of the other contexts and those we have discussed in regard to dyads.

SUMMARY

In this chapter, we classified the structure of a dyad on the basis of the status of the participants. Status is related both to the power held by an individual and to the individal's role. We cited five basic types of power: reward, coercive, referent, expert, and legitimate. Forms of status conflict that can develop in dyads were mentioned. We used as our overall example of such conflict the parent, adult, and child ego states and the complementary, crossed, and ulterior transactions described in transactional analysis. These are certainly not all of the structural aspects of dyads on which we could have focused, but we believe them to be the most important and useful in relation to the function and evolution of dyads.

Dyads can be said to have many different functions, but we broke them down into two: consummatory functions and instrumental functions. Some dyads are primarily consummatory while others are primarily instrumental. There are consummatory aspects of instrumental dyads, but not necessarily instrumental aspects of consummatory dyads. The five aspects of a dyad's consummatory function were identified as openness, honesty, empathy, supportiveness, and positiveness. We identified two basic types of instrumental dyads: the interview dyad and the control dyad. In an interview dyad neither participant has a predetermined outcome, whereas in a control dyad at least one of the participants does have a predetermined outcome. We talked about interview roles, purposes and objectives, question types, and analysis. We also identified control dyad roles and demonstrated how a dyad can be used by one participant to control the instrumental outcome. Dyad functions are usually very complex, involving aspects of interview and control as well as consummatory functions. It is important to determine a dyad's function(s) before you can understand either the structural or evolutionary aspects.

We discussed why dyads come together and/or come apart. There are ten stages through which any dyad may evolve. The initiating stage accounts for the initial impressions dyad members have of one another. Once the dyad participants have tentatively committed themselves to the dyad, they begin to experiment and to intensify the intimacy and communication that take place. The dyad members then integrate with one another, both giving up some of their own individuality in order to accommodate the other person and to give the dyad a personality of its own. The bonding stage is the final expression that the dyad has come together. If at some point the dyad starts to come apart, it goes through another series of stages beginning with a recognition by the participants that there are some important differences between them. If the differences cannot be worked out, the participants begin to circumscribe these areas of disagreement, and both the quantity and quality of their communication diminish. Eventually the dyad reaches a stagnation stage in which almost all communication is stopped. At this point, the members of the dyad begin to avoid one another physically as well as communicatively. Usually, the dyad will soon terminate unless there are constraints that act to hold the dyad together.

We showed how conflict plays a vital role in dyads coming together as well as in coming apart. We identified two main types of conflict as content conflict and interpersonal conflict. We tried to show how both could be used to benefit a dyad as well as to harm it. The object is to manage the conflict as it occurs by facing it directly and working it out together. Dyads that manage their conflict are usually stronger for it and have less chance of coming apart and terminating.

In the last section of this chapter we emphasized the interrelationships between a dyad's structure, function, and evolution. We pointed out that you must understand all three aspects of any dyad before you can truly say you understand the dyad. We especially do not want you to think that you now know all there is to know about dyads. We want you to be on the lookout for other processes that are relevant to dyadic communication as we progress through the other contexts. We also hope that you will interrelate the ideas presented in the preceding chapters to gain a more complete understanding of the ways dyads operate.

KEY TERMS AND CONCEPTS

Avoiding Stage
Bonding Stage
Circumscribing Stage
Closed Questions
Coming Apart
Coming Together
Complementary Transactions
Conflict Intensity
Conflict Management
Consummatory Dyad
Content Conflict
Control Dyad
Crossed Transactions
Differentiating Stage
Dyad
Dyadic Conflict
Ego States
Empathy
Equal-Status Dyads
Experimenting Stage
Honesty
Initiating Stage
Instrumental Dyad
Integrating Dyadic Components

Integrating Stage
Intensifying Stage
Interpersonal Conflict
Interview Dyad
Interview Techniques
Interview Types
Johari Window
Life Positions
Open Questions
Openness
Positiveness
Power
Role
Stagnating Stage
Status
Status Conflict
Supportiveness
Terminating Stage
Transactional Analysis
Types of Power
Ulterior Transactions
Unequal-Status Dyads
Values of Conflict

SUGGESTED READINGS

Evans, David R., Margaret T. Hearn, Max R. Uhlemann, and Allen E. Ivey. *Essential Interviewing: A Programmed Approach to Effective Communication.* Monterey, Calif.: Brooks/Cole Publishing Company, 1979. There are several good books on the market that discuss the theory of interviewing. We have suggested this text, however, because it is programmed and allows you to improve your skills without necessarily taking a formal course. The authors also present many ideas related to developing nonverbal as well as verbal sensitivity. The book will help you improve your ability to listen and to perceive accurately, to reflect both feelings and content in interaction, to confront others, to self-disclose, and much more. By the time you finish this program, you can hardly help but become more effective in your interpersonal relationships.

Knapp, Mark L., *Social Intercourse: From Greeting to Goodbye*. Boston: Allyn and Bacon, Inc., 1978. This book has a very simple purpose stated by the author: "This book is about the way people communicate in developing and deteriorating relationships." While pursuing this simple purpose, Knapp touches on almost all of the important aspects of human communication. Most of the situations described are dyadic in nature. The author makes a valiant attempt to prescribe possible ways of improving dyadic interaction. After reading this book, you should really understand why we say that dyadic communication is the building block of all the other communication contexts.

Wilmot, William W., *Dyadic Communication*, 2nd ed. Reading, Mass.: Addison-Wesley Publishing Company, 1979. This is probably the most complete text available concerning all of the various aspects of dyadic interaction. The author discusses self-image, perceptions of others, and the unique aspects of a dyadic relationship. Chapter 5 on relational intricacies is especially interesting. Like the previous suggested reading, Wilmot offers several prescriptions for improving your own communication in dyads and other contexts.

11
Small Group Communication

The study of communication in a small group context is a natural outgrowth of what you have just learned about the dyad. We define small groups as consisting of three to approximately fifteen people. There are two types of small groups: public and private. It is the private small group with which we are most concerned in this chapter. The similarity between dyadic and small group communication is best reflected in the similarities in their structure, function, and evolution. The main structural variable is, again, status. As with dyads, we divide small group function into consummatory and instrumental. When you study the phases of small group evolution, you will find that they, too, have much in common with the stages of dyadic evolution mentioned in the preceding chapter. The same basic structural, functional, and evolutionary principles in the dyadic context are found in the small group context, but the addition of more interaction participants often alters the nature of these princples, as you will see when you read this chapter.

The major difference between the dyad and the small group is the number of people involved. This structural difference, however, carries with it a host of ramifications for the function and evolution of groups. Whereas we defined the dyadic context as any two-person communication relationship, we will define the small group as any communication relationship involving three to about twelve or fifteen persons. This upper limit is rather arbitrary. The term "small" implies that the members of the group can communicate with one another without the need of a formal structure such as parliamentary procedure and without feeling inhibited by group size. We have found that twelve to fifteen people is about the upper limit for a productive discussion that does not need a formal structure to guarantee that each person will be heard. However, this number can vary from group to group.

In this chapter, we will first discuss the difference between private and public groups. Second, we will briefly analyze the nature of the three-person small group and the unique characteristics that make it somewhat different from both the dyad and other small groups. After this brief orientation, we will examine small group structure, function, and evolution in the same basic format developed in the preceding chapter. This organization will allow you to note the similarities and differences between the dyadic and small group communication contexts.

PUBLIC DISCUSSIONS

Small group discussions can be either public or private. Although we will primarily be concerned with private groups, it is important that you be able to recognize the public forms of small group communication as well. The most common forms of public discussions are the panel discussion, the symposium, and the forum. The main purpose of all public discussions is to get information to the public. You have probably seen many *panel* discussions on television. These involve a group of people, usually experts or authorities, who air their views on some particular issue and exchange ideas with one another. They do not necessarily intend to arrive at any decision. A *symposium*, on the other hand, is a much more formal procedure related to public communication. The participants in a symposium usually have previously prepared speeches. The topics they discuss are assigned to them ahead of time, and the presentations of all the participants form a common theme. Finally, a *forum* differs from the panel and symposium only in that the audience is allowed to participate.

These are not the only formats for public discussions, but they give you the general idea. Public discussions are so termed because there is an audience present. Although some public discussions attempt to make the audience think that a "real" discussion is taking place, the actual purpose is usually to inform or to persuade the audience. The discussion becomes a form of public communication, and the skills needed to participate in public discussion are those that will be discussed in Chapter 13. Therefore, we are not going to discuss public small groups in this chapter.

Private small groups do not usually involve an audience. The interaction is focused on the other participants rather than on an audience. It is with the private small group discussion that we will be concerned throughout the remainder of this chapter.

The main purpose of public discussion is to get information to a large audience.
COURTESY OF NBC'S MEET THE PRESS

THE TRIAD

Our definition of the small group included three-person groups, or, as they are commonly known, triads. The triad, however, is somewhat different from other small groups. Triads are unique in that they possess some of the characteristics of the dyad and some of the characteristics of the small group, but they really do not fit into either context. The aspect of the triad structure that makes it unique from either the dyad or the small group is the enormous potential that exists within it for two of the members to "gang up" on the third. This potential for members to unite together against other members shows up in larger small groups as well, but in those groups an individual at least has some opportunity to find a sympathetic ear. In a triad, no such opportunity exists. If you will think back on your own experiences with triads, you will probably recall that in many cases one of the members was left out. The triad member who discovers that he or she is in a minority either leaves the group or attempts to attain equal status.

One of the most common ways of obtaining equal status with the other two triad members is to conform to their ideas. This severe conformity pressure subverts the normal evolutionary development of the group by forcing premature decisions. Premature decisions are those reached before all of the concerned parties have had a chance to express their honest feelings. The triad members' purposes often change in light of this potential for extreme conformity pressure. They seek partnerships with one another rather than working toward the group's general purpose. This is not to say that we want to define triads as a context other than the small group. Except for this one difference, triads seem to share most of the other structural, functional, and evolutionary characteristics of small groups. It is probably best to think of the triad as a special form of small group.

CLASSIFYING SMALL GROUPS

The classification scheme we developed in the previous chapter on dyads will be generally maintained in this chapter. We will include two characteristics of group structure: the equal-status group and the unequal-status group. In the case of groups, this distinction is not quite as clear-cut as it was in dyads. In almost every small group, there are some status differences among participants.

Again, we will divide the functional aspects into consummatory and instrumental. The instrumental function will be used with approximately the same meaning as in the previous chapter, but we will define the consummatory function somewhat differently. Consummatory groups, as we define them in this chapter, refer to those groups in which the primary purpose revolves around the social-emotional aspect of the group. Such groups include sensitivity groups, "T" (training) groups, therapy groups, and primary groups. Some scholars prefer to classify sensitivity and therapy groups as instrumental rather than consummatory because they sometimes do have a purpose such as making the participant better able to cope with others. We have chosen to classify them as consummatory because their primary purpose seems to us to revolve around the social-emotional aspect of the group rather than the performance of a specific task or decision-making.

Group evolution follows somewhat different evolutionary phases from those we discussed for dyads, although you will see many similarities. With greater numbers of participants, the nature of the phases changes to a certain extent. Thus we again have several different combinations of structure, function, and evolution in small groups. We will discuss the structure, function, and evolution of groups separately, but instead of having a section that interrelates them at the end of the chapter as we did for dyads, we find it easier with small groups to note the interrelationships as we go along.

SMALL GROUP STRUCTURE

The structure of a small group can be examined from several perspectives. We will focus on the relative status of the group members. Status seems to be the most important structural element other than the number of participants. In the previous chapter on dyads, we discussed the relationship of status to power and role. We identified five different types of power that account for status differentiation. They were reward, coercive, referent, expert, and legitimate power. Status is also related to power in small groups, and these same types of power account for status differences found in small groups. One person can gain status over other members of a group through any one or a combination of these five types of power.

Status carries with it a set of behaviors that applies to that status position. We called these behaviors in a dyad the status role. The only real difference between a status role in a dyad and one in a small group is that there are more possible types of status roles that are enacted in a small group. This increased number of roles leads, of course, to a greater possibility for role and status conflict in small groups.

The effect of status on small group communication is similar to its effect on dyadic interaction. Communication in unequal-status small groups is generally more formal, careful, filtered, distorted, and less honest than communication in equal-status groups. There are more possibilities for crossed and ulterior transactions in unequal-status groups because of the greater number of people enacting their parent, adult, and child ego states. As you can see, we have all of the same structural problems existing in small groups that we had with dyads, but these problems are magnified. We will discuss these small group structural effects under the headings normally used by small group theorists: networks and leadership.

Small Group Networks

The term *network* refers to a set of communication patterns among elements in a system. There is a very simple network involved in the dyad, but with the increased numbers of people in a small group the network is more complex. There are several different types of networks that exist in groups.

Role network In any group, there are various jobs that must be done if the group is to accomplish its function. However, not everyone in the group is willing or able to fill each and every one of those roles. Individuals vary in their ability to fulfill certain roles. In effective groups, people assume the roles for which they are best suited. As each of the roles develops, it begins to interlock with all of the other roles that have developed in the group. This interlocking role development is called a role network. Role networks develop best in small groups in which the group's function can be divided into clear-cut functional divisions, the appropriate role behaviors can be made explicit, and the path to the group's final goal is well planned and shared by all members.

Some of the various roles needed in small groups include contributors, information and opinion seekers, information and opinion givers, elaborators, coordinators, evaluators, energizers, and recorders. These roles are directly related to the group's task. There are also several roles related to the maintenance of the group or to the way the group's members relate to one another. These roles include encourager, harmonizer, compromiser, expediter, standard setter, commentator, and follower. There are also some roles that can be destructive to the group's operation. Some of these are aggressor, blocker, self-confessor, recognition seeker, playboy, dominator, sympathy seeker, and special-interest seeker (Benne and Sheats, 1948). The preceding are just a sample of the types of roles small group members can play. There are many others. As a group determines its function and evolves its role network, some of these roles will be included and others will not. All groups develop some type of role structure, but in some groups the role network is not as explicit as in others. Consummatory groups tend to have a much less explicit role network than instrumental groups.

Status network As the role network develops in groups, there also develops a corresponding status for each of the roles. Group members consider some roles to be more important than others. Some roles carry with them one or more of the types of power discussed earlier. The person with the most status in a small group is often called the "leader." We will devote an entire section to leadership because it is so important to an understanding of small groups. Other roles also develop various statuses, sometimes with appropriate titles and sometimes without any formal designation. There are usually several people who are considered to have more status in the group. There are also some people with rather neutral or undetermined status because they have not yet proved themselves one way or the other. Finally, there is usually at least one person, and sometimes more, who is perceived as having no status or even a negative status. This is usually a person(s) who has developed a destructive role. This person will probably leave the group, but even if not, he or she will be ignored by the other group members. People with low status have a very hard time in making their ideas and feelings known to others. When they do get their ideas recognized, the group usually perceives the idea as coming from someone else with higher status. Our place in the status network of the group determines to a great extent how much influence we have on the group.

There are two ways in which status is attached to roles in a small group. The first is called *ascribed status*. This is status assigned to the individual or the role without any effort on the part of the individual in the role. Ascribed status may come from an individual's position in another group or organization. In a jury, for example, a prominent business person or local public official will often be chosen as foreman because of his or her reputation outside the jury itself. Ascribed status can also be conferred by someone else. A teacher may tell a member of a classroom group to take notes on a meeting and thus ascribes a certain status and role on that person. The second way in which status may be obtained is called *achieved status*. Achieved status refers to attainment of status through performance in the current group. One of the best ways to achieve status in a group is through effective participation.

Once all of the various members of the group have attained their various statuses and developed a status network, this network influences how all of the group's members will behave toward one another. It is important for anyone interested in understanding a particular small group to be aware of both the role and status networks that exist in that group. People with high-status roles behave differently in groups than people with lower-status roles. They tend to talk more and are more often the target for messages from other group members. The nature of the messages that high-status group members output and receive is also different. High-status individuals feel more capable of criticizing and threatening other group members. They are usually less willing to compromise, and they find it easier to neglect or reject the ideas of the other group members. The messages received by high-status group members from lower-status members are often of the approval-seeking nature and are often presented in a deferential manner. The messages of low-status group members are usually easier to understand than the messages sent by a high-status group member. As you can see, these communication effects are very similar to those of status in a dyad.

Communication network A group's communication network is closely aligned with and influenced by the role and status networks within the group. Studies have been conducted on various types of communication networks to determine the effects of such factors as role centrality, access to other members, communication linkages, channel capacity, and access to information. The four most commonly studied communication networks are the wheel, the "Y," the chain, and the all-channel networks. (See Fig. 11.1.)

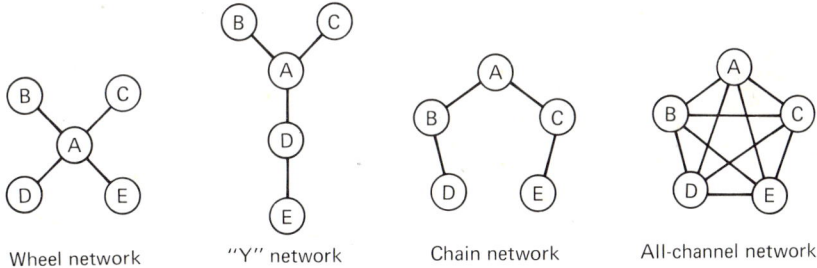

Fig. 11.1 The four most commonly studied communication networks.

First, you may notice in Fig. 11.1 that all four networks have differing degrees of centrality. *Centrality* refers to the access each small group member has to the other members of the group. The wheel network on the left is the most highly centralized, while the all-channel network on the right is the most decentralized. The "Y" network is more centralized than the chain network. In the wheel network, only person A has direct access to all of the other group members. In the all-channel network, each member has direct access to each other member. The communication network that develops in a group is largely dependent on the status and role networks of the group. Usually the more explicit the status network, the more centralized the communication network. The members of the group must "go through channels" in a highly centralized communication network.

The degree of centralization in a group directly affects several other aspects of the group. The person in the most centralized position in the group usually becomes the group's leader, regardless of whether he or she is best qualified for the job. The person in the centralized position usually is also the most satisfied member of the group. Highly centralized groups usually are also the most efficient, although there is some evidence that once a decentralized group establishes a stable work organization, it is as efficient as a centralized group. Decentralized small groups tend to take more time, but the quality of their decisions seems to be higher. Decentralized groups also tend to have more of the members satisfied with their own performance and with the result of the group. The decentralized communication network allows group members an opportunity to participate equally and freely. A centralized network cannot deal as effectively with problems that have more than one possible answer. None of us like to have to communicate through someone else. We like to be right in the thick of the conversation. For this reason, most people prefer a decentralized communication network to one that is highly centralized.

Small Group Leadership

A group's network structure is intimately tied to the type of leadership that exists in the group. Small group leadership has been the topic of many research articles and textbooks and has been examined from several perspectives. One of the first theories of group leadership suggested that some people are born with certain *traits* that make them leaders. This theory has been discarded because a good list of traits could not be found that would consistently distinguish leaders from followers. Other leadership theorists suggested that there are three *styles* of leadership: democratic, autocratic, and laissez-faire. Autocratic leaders want highly centralized communication structures; democratic leaders want more decentralization; and laissez-faire leaders want a group totally decentralized with little or no leadership. This approach can be quite useful theoretically, but it offers few suggestions as to how to recognize or to become a democratic leader, which is often suggested as the best of the three. A third group of leadership theories suggests that a group's leadership must fit the group's *situation*. The group either must have a highly flexible leader who can adapt to the various evolutionary phases or must choose a different leader for each situation it faces. This approach has gained considerable support in recent years and tends to answer many of the questions that have been raised regarding small group leadership. The last approach to defining group leadership. A leader, as we define one, is a person with the formal status role of being in charge of the group. This status role can either be ascribed to or achieved by the leader. The leader does not change throughout the group's evolution. Leadership, on the other hand, refers to the ability get the various group functions accomplished. A person with leadership may or may not be formally tions has not been developed. In this text, we see the situational and functional approaches as highly compatible and we subscribe to both of them.

Thus far, we have discussed leaders and leadership as if they were the same thing. There is, however, a subtle difference between a leader and leadership. A leader, as we define one, is a person with the formal status role of being in charge of the group. This status role can either be ascribed to or achieved by the leader. The leader does not change throughout the group's evolution. Leadership, on the other hand, refers to the ability to get the various group functions accomplished. A person with leadership may or may not be formally designated. Depending on the situation or on the function needed, any member of the group can hold the leadership position at different times. The person who is in the leadership position is the one who is influencing the group at any particular time. This person does not always have to be the group's formal leader. All groups do not need formal leaders, but they do need leadership. Without leadership, a group will eventually disintegrate.

One of the things we do know about persons who are good at providing leadership for groups is that they are sensitive to the needs of the group at any particular time. This sensitivity to the group's needs allows them to provide the direction that is required by the group at a particular point in its development and thus to adapt to the various group phases. This leadership sensitivity often takes one of two forms: a sensitivity to the instrumental needs (those related to the formally recognized goal) of the group and/or a sensitivity to the consummatory needs (those related to interpersonal relationships) of the group. A common finding in small group research is that a kind of *dual leadership* often develops in groups (Bales and Slater, 1955). A group will have one person who is able to supply the group with the direction it needs to complete its purpose or task. This person is frequently referred to as a task leader. Many groups will also have another person who is able to supply the group with the direction it needs to keep its members working well with one another. This person is often called a social-emotional leader. It is difficult to find one person who is capable of performing both types of leadership because they often clash. In order to supply effective task leadership, a person must sometimes be rather "pushy" or the group will never get anything accomplished. This rather hard reality makes it difficult for the same person to be on friendly terms with all of the group members. Dual leadership is very common in small groups, and many role and status networks include such a structure.

SMALL GROUP FUNCTION

A small group's function is also called its goal or purpose. In any case, we are talking about the reason why the group exists. As with the dyad, we have reduced the functions of small groups into what we have called the consummatory function and the instrumental function. The consummatory function refers to the affective or social-emotional aspects of groups, whereas the instrumental function refers to the task side of group operation. There is very little that is different in consummatory small groups and consummatory dyads except, of course, that there are many more social relationships with which to be concerned in a small group. Consummatory small groups have also been used to help people develop an increased awareness of the social aspects of their lives.

In comparing the instrumental small group with the instrumental dyad, it is much harder to separate the informational aspects of small groups from the control aspects. Instrumental small groups are a mixture of controllers, interviewers, controlled, and interviewees. Small groups must develop objectives and methods of reaching those objectives just as instrumental dyads must, but because of the nature of small groups the goals they set for themselves and the capabilities they have for reaching these goals are somewhat different from those we found in dyads.

Consummatory Small Groups

There are basically three types of consummatory small groups that we will mention in this section: the primary group, the therapy group, and the sensitivity group. Our discussion in this section will be concerned with the consummatory aspects of all groups, whether they are totally consummatory or not. We will be focusing most of our attention on that central aspect of groups called *cohesiveness*. Cohesiveness is the social glue that holds groups together. Cohesiveness is the degree to which group members are attracted to one another and to the group.

Primary groups Perhaps the most common type of small group is what sociologists call the primary group. Cooley (1902) defined primary groups as

Small Group Communication

> ... those characterized by intimate face-to-face association and cooperation. They are primary in several senses, but chiefly in that they are fundamental in forming the social nature and ideals of the individual. The result of intimate association, psychologically, is a certain fusion of individualities in a common whole, so that one's very self, for many purposes at least, is common life and purpose of the group.

Examples of such primary groups might include your family, the group of friends with whom you identify, and the people with whom you work. Mead (1934) pointed out that the primary group provides a mirror through which we are able to see ourselves as some "generalized other" might see us. Mead suggested that every significant symbol carries with it some of the social matrix and that therefore the primary group penetrates the individual with every symbol he or she employs or acquires.

Can you identify the instrumental and consummatory small groups and dyads in this picture?
JOHN DUGAN PHOTO

Most of what goes on in primary groups is what we might call consummatory conversation. We meet with our family over dinner. We go out with our colleagues for drinks after work. We talk with our friends at a party. In most cases, the participants in such discussions do not share a common goal other than to talk with one another. The main functions of primary groups are to form the social nature and ideals of the individual and to promote individual growth through the five means discussed earlier: openness, honesty, positiveness, empathy, and supportiveness. Primary groups are a very important type of consummatory group. In some ways, they have more direct impact on our lives than any other type of small group.

Therapy groups A second type of consummatory small group is the therapy group. The therapy group is an alternative to individual psychological counseling. The first real use of this technique came during World War II when the British army had more patients than the psychological staff could handle. One of the first people to use this technique was Bion (1959) at London's Tavistock Clinic. He used a leaderless technique for therapeutic purposes. This means that the psychologist in charge of the group would in no way exercise leadership. The group itself was put in charge of its own fate. He demonstrated that when people are trying to deal with a task, they are also trying to deal with the needs and fears the group arouses in them. He found the leaderless therapy group to be quite effective in helping people understand and deal with their consummatory communication problems.

The advantages that come from such groups are numerous. The atmosphere that is created in such a leaderless group is thought to affect the communicative relationships of all group members. It is felt that the clients must be allowed to help themselves and that a therapist who imposes his or her own interpretations and advice tends to merely aggravate the patient's feelings of helplessness and inadequacy. People must be allowed to find their own answers. When a therapist feels that a more directive atmosphere is needed for a particular problem, individual therapy is the usual pattern rather than the small group. The consummatory purpose of such groups is similar to that in the consummatory dyad. The patients learn to be open and honest with one another through the development of positive, supportive, and empathetic relationships. However, these relationships develop only if the participants are allowed to work on their problems together.

Training or sensitivity groups The third type of consummatory group is the training or sensitivity group. Such groups are a direct outgrowth of the therapy group, but their focus is on "normal" people and they usually occur outside of a medical environment. In recent years, such groups have become something of a fad in the United States. Organizations such as the National Training Laboratories, Esalon, and other human relations workshop groups have grown in size and number. The purpose of the sensitivity or training group is much the same as that of the therapy group. People come together to improve their own interpersonal sensitivity and skills. Such groups normally involve a trained leader who uses the leaderless approach but subtly guides the group's progress toward the desired ends. The chief means of accomplishing this task is open expression of feelings and trust development. Participants are asked to be totally and sometimes brutally honest with one another. Eventually the group members develop a deep level of trust for one another because each knows so much about the other. As pictured in the Johari Window discussed in Chapter 10, it is felt that the smaller the hidden, blind, and unknown selves and the larger the open self, the greater the level of trust that will develop. This process of developing a deeper trust level improves the participants' sensitivity to their own interpersonal relationships outside the training group.

There has been much debate over the values and dangers of such groups. Sensitivity, or training, groups have been attacked for being too open and honest. Critics have said that such an atmosphere is not a true representation of interpersonal relationships outside of the group. They feel that some hidden, blind, and unknown areas must be part of each person's self for that person's own good. When people expose everything about themselves, potential dangers may be created that they may not be able to handle. The critics can even point to many cases in which such groups did more harm than good. Some of this potential danger can be eliminated by a well-qualified leader, but often such groups are not run by persons with the proper qualifications. We do not intend to take a stand either for or against sensitivity or training groups. We merely wish to point out that they are a type of consummatory small group that has as its goals the same qualities of effective interpersonal communication that we advocate in this text. We are not yet convinced, however, that the highly forced means of reaching these ends that are practiced in sensitivity or training groups are the best means available. We tend to think that openness, honesty, positiveness, supportiveness, and empathy are much better and stronger when they arise naturally in the human communication system.

Cohesiveness

As we have said, cohesiveness is the social glue that holds a group together. Cohesiveness is the term used in the small group literature to express the degree of affection, attraction, or liking the group members have for one another and for the group. In purely consummatory groups, cohesiveness may be the only aspect of the group; there may be no instrumental aspect. This is generally the case for the primary, therapy, and sensitivity or training groups described above. Consummatory groups need not have an instrumental function, but instrumental groups do have a cohesiveness dimension.

People join groups for three reasons: because they are attracted to its instrumental purpose, because they are attracted to the other group members, or because they believe the group will increase their prestige (Shaw, 1976). If people join a group because of the group's instrumental purpose, they may or may not be able to develop a strong, cohesive relationship with the other group members. The chances are in their favor, however, because people who have the same taste in group tasks often find one another to their liking. Students, for example, who choose the same major frequently find that they have many other characteristics in common, and they become good friends.

People who choose to join groups because of the other group members normally have little problem in developing cohesiveness, but they may have more difficulty with the group's task. Groups in which all or most of the members have joined because they like the other people have the potential problem of becoming unconcerned with the overall goal of the group. This situation often occurs in fraternities and sororities, in which house leaders can never seem to find anyone when work has to be done around the house but have no trouble in turning up people for social functions.

It is difficult to evaluate the last reason why people join groups (for prestige) in relation to cohesiveness. These people seem to show considerable affection for other group members, but we always get the feeling that they are putting on an act. A person who joins a country club, for example, may make a big deal out of meeting all the members and getting involved in the club's subgroup activities, but we may get the feeling that this person would really rather be someplace else. Such a person may not want to establish good group cohesion and thus in the long run can impede the group.

The degree of cohesiveness that will develop in a group, then, is in part a result of the reasons why the various members joined the group in the first place. People who join a group because they are attracted to its instrumental purpose or because they like the other members have a better chance of developing a higher degree of cohesiveness than people who join the group to increase their own prestige. The reasons why members join a group, however, play only a small part in explaining why some groups become highly cohesive and why others do not. What goes on once the members have joined is of more real importance in explaining cohesiveness development.

The greater the cohesiveness of a group, the more likely it is to achieve success.
PHOTO BY CAROLE DUGAN

Almost everyone who joins a group is interested and enthusiastic at first or they would not have taken the time to attend even one gathering. The several factors that contribute to the eventual outcome of the group for that individual are usually not obvious before joining the group. We have already mentioned some of these factors as being the openness, honesty, supportiveness, positiveness, and empathy that develop or exist in the group. Three other factors of equal importance that have been discussed by Heslin and Dunphy (1964) are what the status structure is in the group and how a person fits into that status structure, how well the group progresses toward its goals, and how much freedom there is to participate in the decisions of the group. As you can see, some of these factors are related to the consummatory function of the group and others are related to the instrumental function.

Cohesiveness and status We have already discussed in general the effects of status in groups. We said that people in the more central communicative roles with higher status are usually the most satisfied with the group. These people are usually the most cohesive. Generally, however, highly centralized groups with strong status roles are usually less cohesive than decentralized groups in which members do not take status roles too seriously. This is very often the case in groups with no formal leader or with no leader at all. In groups that do have a formal leader, better cohesiveness develops if each individual has a relatively stable role and status. This is true of organizations, for example, in which there is a definite chain of command. The people in an organization want to know what their positions are relative to the other roles and positions in the organization.

In groups with formal roles and status, it is quite common to find people of the same status gathered and talking together. They are more cohesive with one another than with people of either higher or lower status. Remember, we said earlier that people are usually more cohesive when status is more or less equal. In such a formal-status group, one might expect the person with the highest status to be the most liked by the other members of the group—especially if this person's status was achieved rather than ascribed. Such is not always the case, however, because the person in the leader role often has to step on the toes of the other group members to get a particular job accomplished. Thus the dual leadership concept discussed earlier becomes important. The social leader often becomes the most liked person in the group because that person does not have task responsibilities and can concentrate on the cohesiveness aspects of the group.

The preceding are only a few of the ways in which status and cohesiveness are interrelated. When we join a group, we are often unsure of our role in the group, our status in relation to the other group members, the nature of the communication network, and our place in that network. All of these factors can create tension and anxiety until they are resolved. Probably the best way to get around this problem is to keep the status, role, and communication differentiation in the group as minimal as possible. The less structural differentiation that exists in the group, the more likely the group is to develop strong cohesiveness among the group members. Cohesiveness is much easier to achieve when a group is smaller. Groups of four, five, or six members usually have less status differentiation than larger groups, and hence cohesiveness in groups of that size is stronger than in larger groups. The triad is not very cohesive because of the unique characteristics that we mentioned. It is possible sometimes to have groups larger than five or six members that operate without much status differentiation and in these cases the cohesiveness is also usually quite high. In groups in which there is a formal leader and strong status differentiation, good cohesiveness can be developed if the differences in status are overlooked as much as possible and a democratic atmosphere is allowed to develop whereby all can participate openly and honestly.

Cohesiveness and participation Status differences in groups can often be overlooked if the group's members are allowed to participate freely and to have a fair hearing. The size of the group also has an effect here. As the size of a group increases, the amount of information any single member of the group is able to contribute is decreased. The nature of the communication that takes place is also different in groups of twelve as compared with groups of five. In the chapter on dyads, we differentiated between a controlling type of communication and an interviewing type of communication. The first involves a sharing of ideas, while the second involves more influence-oriented communication. In larger groups, communication is often more of the control type in which the participants give opinions, while in four- or five-person groups communication is often more of the interviewing type in which the participants ask and answer questions. In groups of larger size, the decrease in the amount of participation by each member and in the control nature of the communication is often accompanied by a corresponding decrease in the level of group cohesiveness.

Most small group members want to be able to participate. If they are not allowed that right, their level of cohesiveness is diminished. This does not mean that every member of the group has to participate for the group to be cohesive. There are often group members who do not want to talk a lot. However, when they do wish to participate, they must feel that they will be given the chance. Nonparticipating group members or less talkative group members can be as important to the group as those who talk a great deal. A person's cohesiveness or worth is not necessarily measured by his or her level of participation. The important thing is that all members feel that they can participate if and when they want to and that their ideas will be given equal consideration with those of other group members. If this is the case, cohesiveness will probably be quite high.

When group members are not allowed to freely participate or if their statements are not given the same consideration as those of other group members, one of the likely outcomes is that the group will split up into coalitions. A *coalition* is a subgroup within the larger group system that forms because of a conflict between its members and the remaining members of the larger group. One of the more common conflicts is that members of the larger group either are not listening to the members of the subgroups or are not giving their opinions equal consideration. Coalitions are a very common occurrence in groups, but when they form they reduce the cohesiveness of the entire group until they dissolve. The cohesiveness among the members of the coalition is quite strong. The only way to dissolve a coalition is to make sure that the ideas of coalition members are given a proper hearing. It is almost impossible to get a coalition to dissolve unless those in it do so voluntarily.

Sometimes, however, a single member of the group rather than a subgroup comes into conflict with the prevailing attitude of the larger group system. When a single member of a group holds a different opinion from that of the rest of the group, the person is called a *deviate*. Again, deviation is common in groups. Whether the deviation involves one group member or a coalition of group members, it should be encouraged in groups. Without competing ideas, communication soon becomes stale. Such deviation should, therefore, be heeded; it should not be discouraged. When such deviation occurs, it does reduce the group's cohesiveness. However, if the deviate is given a fair hearing, the deviation will promote stronger cohesiveness in the long run. Deviation is one way by which group members test the openness, honesty, and supportiveness existing in the group. A truly cohesive group will allow and even encourage deviate participation. All must feel free to express their ideas and feelings openly and honestly and must believe that the group will support the expression of those ideas, whether the members agree with the ideas or not. This is the mark of the truly cohesive group.

Cohesiveness and goal progress Whether the group's goal is consummatory or instrumental, participants must see progress being made toward that goal or cohesiveness will decline. If the goal is extremely difficult to accomplish, group members are willing to accept less progress than if the goal is less difficult to achieve. But even in the former case, they must see *some* form of progress being made. Often groups become highly cohesive because they think they have seen goal progress only to discover that they are headed in entirely the wrong direction. In such a case, the group needs to work extremely hard to get the group moving in the right direction. The easy way out is to give up and to allow the group to dissolve.

The relationship between cohesiveness and a group's goal is nowhere better illustrated than in athletics. When a baseball or basketball team loses game after game, its members begin to bicker with one another and to goof off in practice and even in the games. The cohesiveness declines rapidly. The only way to restore cohesiveness to the group is to find some goal the group can accomplish. Most good coaches realize this fact, and so they may place a game with a rival school at the end of the season schedule. They will then say something like the following to their players: "If we can only win this one game, we will have had a winning season." They make beating the rival more important than the entire season. By using such a strategy, they give the team something to look forward to and a goal that can be obtained. Thus the team's cohesiveness runs high, even through a losing season. Cohesiveness would completely disintegrate if the team had no goal at all. In the same way, members of a winning team often feel defeated if they lose the last game of the season even though they have won every other game. In this case, the coach needs to refer back to all that has been accomplished in the past in order to restore the cohesiveness of the team players. Cohesiveness and goal progress are circular processes, with each building upon the other.

Cohesiveness is a vital element that affects small group communication. Cohesiveness also affects every other aspect of the group. The success of the consummatory function of a small group is expressed in the degree of cohesiveness that exists in the group. If this consummatory function has been successful and cohesiveness is high, the group will probably be perceived as successful. In the following section we will focus on the instrumental function of the small group. Cohesiveness plays an important role in instrumental groups as well.

Instrumental Small Groups

All of us need to make decisions every day of our lives. Some of the decisions we make are not very important, while others have importance for the rest of our lives. Some of the decisions we make are better handled by ourselves alone, while others benefit from the aid of another individual or a group of individuals. We often make the decision about who to involve in our decision making primarily through chance. There are, however, some definite strengths and limitations concerning the various forms of decision making of which you should be aware. The main factors you should take into account in deciding whether or not to use a small group for an instrumental task are (1) the time necessary to complete the task, (2) the nature of the task, and (3) the presence of other people.

Time necessary to complete the task Compared with individuals and dyads, groups are notoriously slow in accomplishing tasks. A large part of this slowness can be attributed to the consummatory function that must be attended to in groups before they can get down to work. As we said earlier, all instrumental groups have cohesiveness needs that must be satisfied before the group can make effective progress toward its instrumental goal. Even when this consummatory function is fulfilled, a group usually takes more time than individuals or dyads because of the increased numbers of ideas and pieces of information that are available in the group. The fact that each of these ideas and pieces of information is examined and discussed by all of the group's members adds time to the task. If time is of utmost concern, you should consider some means of accomplishing the task other than a group.

Nature of the task There are some tasks for which small groups are uniquely suited. There are other tasks for which the possible benefits available through use of a group are not worth the time. The advantages a group brings to any task stem directly from the larger number of people who work on the decision. A small group can divide up the labor and bring more information to bear on the task. These advantages mean that groups are usually more effective for tasks in which much information must be collected, creative thought is necessary, the decision is rather ambiguous, manual skills are needed, and other similar requirements are present. Individuals and dyads do better on uncomplicated and single-answer tasks. On these types of tasks, it is possible to have too much information and to become confused by irrelevant pieces of information. When high expertise is needed to make a decision, highly competent individuals will often make better decisions than a group.

A second aspect of group decision making that has recently been discovered is that groups tend to be more risky than individuals. No one knows for sure why this happens, but, given a task with varying degrees of risk involved, people will choose a less risky alternative when they are working alone than they will when they are part of a group. The most commonly accepted explanation of this phenomenon is that we are capable of transferring part of the responsibility for our decision to the other members of the group, rather than taking all of the responsibility ourselves. If you want a conservative decision, it is better to make the decision individually than in a group.

Presence of other people The presence of other people affects both the time necessary to accomplish a task and the group's productivity. The presence of other people has two other effects that are perhaps even more important to keep in mind. These two effects have most commonly been called groupthink and the assembly effect. The first is considered a drawback to instrumental groups, while the second is considered a bonus to such groups.

Groupthink is the term that has been applied to situations where various group members have been forced to agree with the result instead of being allowed to agree voluntarily. A group can bring considerable pressure to bear on

Small Group Communication

an individual (or people) who disagrees with the majority. In this situation, a really creative decision might be excluded simply because the majority is unwilling to accept it. Such an atmosphere, of course, encourages mediocre decisions. People who apply the term groupthink to small instrumental groups have probably had such an experience. There is no denying that groups can put this kind of pressure on participants, but when dissent is encouraged and given a fair hearing groupthink will not occur.

Open and honest communication by all members of a small group is the key to developing an assembly effect.
PHOTO BY CAROLE DUGAN

When operating effectively, a group can turn the destructive potential of increased numbers of participants into a real bonus. Groups have the potential of developing an *assembly effect*, which refers to a group's ability to go beyond the best efforts of all the group members individually (Collins and Guetzkow, 1964). Think of five people—each working on the same task, but each in a separate room. Now think of these same five people working on a task together. The people working together can produce a better decision because they can experience the assembly effect. The ideas of one member can help produce better ideas from another member, and those combined ideas can produce a still better idea from a third member. The final result is a combination of the ideas of all members and much better than any single member could have created alone. A somewhat trivial example that makes this point clear is the experience you have probably had when telling and listening to jokes in a small group of people. Each joke you hear triggers a joke you heard before but would not have thought of without the proper stimulus. If you had been asked to sit down and write out all of the jokes you could remember, you would have ended up by having far fewer written down than the number you actually told the group. It was the interaction among the group members that brought out the best in all of the members.

It is group communication that produces the assembly effect. The assembly effect is also an illustration of the anti-entropic nature of groups when they are working effectively. There is no assembly effect when individuals are making decisions alone. There is some assembly effect that occurs in instrumental dyads. The assembly effect really begins to show its true potential in the small group. When organizations get too large, many of the advantages of the assembly effect are lost because there is no longer a spontaneous exchange of ideas with unrestricted and immediate feedback. If you have ever been part of a group that is really operating up to its potential, there is a thrill that comes with the final decision that cannot be duplicated in any other context. You end up by feeling you have done better than your best; you have gone beyond self-actualization. You have group-actualized. This is the ultimate assembly effect.

Productivity Not all small groups reach this ultimate outcome, and thus we need some way of measuring the success of a group in accomplishing its instrumental goal. We do this by assessing the group's productivity. Productivity refers to how well the group met the goal it set for itself.

We have already pointed out that social pressure can operate to reduce group productivity. When group members feel they must conform to the expectations of others, they do not feel free to express their own ideas openly and honestly. If such a situation occurs before all opinons have been aired, the productivity of the group will decline. The group's members will have become so dependent on others that they will not make their own ideas known. In order to be productive, small groups must encourage dissent and conflict. It is only in this way that the group can be guaranteed that it is receiving the best participation possible from each and every one of its members. To put pressure on members to conform prematurely or to discourage full and open participation is to negate the potential assembly effect and to reduce productivity.

On the other hand, at some point in the group's progress ideas must be modified and compromises made. Otherwise, the group will never reach its goal. The group must be capable of narrowing down to one solution, and sometimes the only way to accomplish this task is through group pressure. The key here is to be sure that such pressure is not applied too early. Ideally, people change their minds because they see the wisdom of doing things in the way proposed instead of being pressured to change. Social pressure should become important only as a means of bringing people back into the group after they have had their ideas rejected. You must be constantly on the alert, however, for individuals or coalitions who try to use social pressure as a means of subverting open and honest communication and forcing the will of one group on another. When this situation occurs, a loss of productivity is the usual result.

It is also possible to lose productivity because of the group's structure. Highly structured groups with a strict status hierarchy are often the most productive in terms of how much work is actually turned out. But the work tends to suffer in quality. Such groups have real problems in avoiding the effects of premature social pressure. Highly structured role, status, and communication networks tend to restrict the free flow of information and feedback, thus lowering productivity as well. This occurs because group members are often unwilling to commit themselves for fear of being on the opposite side of a powerful group member. It is in this way that leaders create "yes men" without intending to do so. A well-developed status structure is often helpful when the task is more or less routine and mechanical, but it can reduce productivity when the problem is complex and requires creative solutions and unrestricted communication. Even highly structured groups often can get around this difficulty if the high-status members are willing to encourage open and honest communication. This goal is best accomplished by keeping quiet. By remaining silent as much as possible, leaders in therapy and sensitivity training groups avoid the problem of group members becoming dependent on them. This leadership style is also a good idea for high-status persons in groups in which maximum productivity is desired.

The final influence on group productivity is cohesiveness. We said before that cohesiveness and productivity are closely related. As cohesiveness increases, productivity also tends to increase up to a point. That point is reached when the group becomes so involved in the social dimension that they forget about productivity. Don't jump to the conclusion at this point that the cohesiveness causes the productivity. There is just as logical an argument that says productivity causes cohesiveness. We have already indicated that part of a group's cohesiveness comes from the belief that the group is progressing toward its goal. Let's just say that cohesiveness and productivity mutually interrelate with one another and not worry about which causes which.

SMALL GROUP EVOLUTION

The evolutionary phases of small groups that we will discuss were developed by Fisher (1974). They include the orientation, conflict, emergence, and reinforcement phases. The communication activities that take place in each phase are in some ways similar to those found in dyadic evolution. We will review these communication activities plus the unique communication features that result from the increased number of people as we present each evolutionary phase of small groups. We must point out, however, that as with dyads, each phase is distinct from the phases that precede it and those that follow it. Thus the small group in each evolutionary phase should be thought of almost as if it were a new group.

Orientation Phase

Persons entering into a small group relationship, especially with strangers, experience a great deal of tension. Such tension is often labeled *primary tension* and results from the uncertainty each participant has regarding the possible directions the group might take. At this very early stage, people are highly sensitive to the verbal and nonverbal behavior that might indicate something about the other people, the networks, and the interaction itself. Because of this increased sensitivity, the orientation phase is extremely important to the further development of the group. This phase is very similar to the initiating and experimenting stages in the dyad. However, in small groups, this anxiety or primary tension is much stronger because there are more persons toward whom the participants must become oriented. Whereas the role, status, and communication networks into which each participant must fit are relatively simple in the dyad, they are much more complex in the small group. This greater complexity obviously increases the primary tension, and thus the orientation phase often takes much longer in a small group.

The openness, honesty, and supportiveness in the orientation phase in small groups are especially important if the group is to derive the benefits of the assembly effect and to reduce the possible negative effects of group pressure. It is during the orientation phase that group members test the degree of openness, honesty, and supportiveness that will be allowed in the group. They do so by watching not only the effects of their own deviation but also the results of deviation by other members of the group. If they find that social pressure and forced conformity are going to be the group's standard operating procedure, the members with lesser status will tend to become nonparticipating group members. If, on the other hand, they find that all ideas are given an equal hearing and a fair evaluation, they will begin to open up and to express their honest opinions. When this happens, a high level of cohesiveness develops.

Part of the effort in the orientation phase of the group's evolution is devoted to establishing the various role, status, and communication networks that will continue throughout the rest of the group's development. People either attempt to gain a certain role and status or they have a role and status assigned to them by the other members of the group. One of the first roles to be determined is that of instrumental leader. At the same time, the role of social leader may also be developed. Very often in the development of these two very important roles several candidates emerge initially, only to be eliminated later in the group's development. It is quite common for other group roles to be established before the final decision is made regarding the highest roles in the group. If the group formally elects or chooses a leader, the selection process usually occurs during the orientation phase, even though the person chosen may not exert the greatest amount of leadership as the group progresses. Until the role, status, and communication networks in the group are determined, primary tension may continue. Once the various networks are established and each group member feels confident with his or her place in the group, the primary tension begins to dissipate.

In this phase, the members of the group also orient themselves to the goal of the group. They make certain decisions regarding the difficulty of the goal and the means by which they will attempt to accomplish the goal. In many groups, this task is not as easy as it might seem. Very often one or more of the group members have some personal goal that is in conflict with the group's goal. If these individual goals are not identified at this stage, they may interrupt the group's further development. These covert or personal goals are often quite difficult to identify because the group member wants to keep them a secret. Various actions by that participant, however, may disclose the presence of such a hidden goal if the other group members are sensitive enough to recognize its existence. All of the group members should be in agreement with the group's goal prior to entering the next phase of evolution. If it has not reached some kind of consensus before it leaves the orientation phase, the group may have to return to this phase later. Such backtracking is wasteful of both the time and effort of the participants.

Small Group Communication

The interaction that takes place during the orientation phase reflects all of the ideas just presented. It is usually fairly cautious and tentative. Once the interaction starts, it normally consists of mutual exploration. Each person tries to "size up" the others by making very tentative statements and agreeing with almost everything the other members say. During this stage, participants attempt to clarify various matters such as the role and status network, the group goal, and the group's norms. None of the participants want to commit themselves to anything at this stage, so they tend to agree with everything that everyone else says—at least to a certain extent. Opinions and attitudes that are expressed are usually highly ambiguous. Fisher sees these ambiguous statements as signs of the direction that more definite statements will take in future phases. Although we do get a glimpse of things to come, this initial orientation phase is primarily devoted to reducing the primary tension and helping to develop cohesiveness by getting acquainted with one another. As the members become oriented, they begin to take stronger stands on issues and the group moves into the conflict phase.

Conflict Phase

This phase is characterized by disagreement and dispute. The statements by each participant are no longer tentative and ambiguous. Primary tension is no longer present. The participants have adjusted to one another. They begin to argue with one another and to provide reasoning to back up their conclusions. Data, warrants, and backing are all produced to substantiate the claims that are made. At this point, we are most likely to observe reasoning fallacies as well. The participants have chosen sides.

It is during this phase also that the group develops what is called *secondary tension*. Secondary tension results from the conflicts that arise in the group. This form of tension is much more serious than primary tension. This tension results from deviation by individuals or coalitions within the group. The two basic types of conflict (content or realistic conflict and interpersonal or unrealistic conflict) have very different effects on the group. Secondary tensions in the group do not usually become very serious if the conflict is realistic. All good groups need this form of conflict. It is the interpersonal, or unrealistic conflict, that causes the greatest problems for groups and reduces productivity. With the larger number of participants, there is a much greater likelihood that interpersonal conflict will develop between at least two participants. Groups can tolerate only so much unrealistic conflict before the secondary tensions that are created threaten to break up the group. It is even more important here than in dyads that the group learn to manage its conflict. Interpersonal conflict often occurs because the group has not established cohesiveness during the orientation phase. If a group has developed positive and empathic feelings during the orientation phase, most of the group's conflict will be realistic and limited to the group's function.

It is during this conflict phase that serious task suggestions are made by the group members. Because of the greater number of people, the number of proposals is greater and the chance for content conflict is greater than in dyads. At this point, we often find coalitions developing within the group. In each coalition, there is usually a leader who strongly argues that coalition's position against the other proposals in the group. If groupthink is going to occur in the group, this is the point at which we will begin to see it emerge. The various factions attempt to pressure other members into agreeing with them. The group members are no longer tentative about their points of view. They become argumentative and present as much evidence, both logical and illogical, to support their ideas as they can possibly muster. It is during this phase that listening often becomes filtered and selective. Content conflicts occur because none of the participants really understand the point of view of the others. Until the group members begin to listen to one another, the conflict phase will continue. Once they do begin to listen to one another, the group can progress into the emergence phase and achieve the benefits of the assembly effect.

Emergence Phase

It is during the emergence phase that groups begin to show their true value. It is at this point that the ideas of the various conflicting factions can be melded into a truly creative and unique decision that is better than the best effort of any of the members individually. Some of the group members will not give up their position easily and must be convinced that the proposal that is beginning to receive a consensus is the best one. Some form of social pressure can legitimately be applied to those members who refuse to adhere to the emerging decision. The members of the group who are applying the pressure must be sure, however, that all decision proposals have been given a fair and complete hearing. They must believe that all possible evidence and reasoning have been heard and that the rejected proposals are still found lacking.

When dissent begins to slacken off and we see fewer and fewer opposing opinions expressed, the group has entered the emergence phase. The participants will probably not have resolved the underlying conflict, but a tentative outcome has been reached. It is hard to identify exactly when this decision is reached. The participants again revert to ambiguous statements such as those in the orientation phase, but this time the ambiguity occurs because of uncertainty not primary tension. It seems instead to be a means of expressing reluctant acceptance of the outcome. The participants are in the process of modifying their earlier opinions to accept the final outcome. As Fisher states, participants "cannot be expected to change their opinions so abruptly. Thus, dissent changes to assent *via* ambiguity" (p.143). Some participants are probably still opposed to the final outcome, but their opinion is being modified. We begin to hear comments like "Well, this may work out allright," or "This may not be too bad; I'll give it a try." Ambiguous statements are a sign that the group pressure is beginning to work on the deviant members. If the group has been creative and has tried to merge the various proposals into one that is better than any single proposal by any individual member of the group or any coalition of members, it is easier to achieve the agreement necessary in this phase. The reason is that none of the members will feel that they have totally lost and that some other faction has won. If handled properly, all of the group's members can be convinced that they have all won to a certain extent and have all lost to a certain extent.

This is a crucial stage for a small group. A group must reach and progress through this stage for it to be successful. The best that can be hoped for at this point is that the participants achieve some form of agreement and attitude modification. The emergence phase is highly dependent on the earlier success of the orientation and conflict phases. If the group's cohesiveness is of sufficient strength, the participants will be motivated to emerge from the conflict stage and to manage their differences. If not, the group will dissolve prior to or during the emergence stage. It is during this stage that the group may either fall into the groupthink pattern or achieve an assembly effect. It is usually impossible to pinpoint exactly when during this stage the final decision is reached, but that is not vitally important. What is important is how the decision was reached. If it was reached through completely open and honest discussion that utilized evidence and reasoning, not pressure, to arrive at the final decision, the group will have been productive. The decision of the group will probably be the best possible decision, given the information and resources available. Group members cannot ask for anything more than that. All that is left for the group at this point is to reinforce the decision and to reestablish cohesiveness so that the decision will carry the support of the members as they attempt to implement it.

A task completed deserves a toast.
PHOTO BY CAROLE DUGAN

Reinforcement Phase

The reinforcement phase starts out as a continuation of the emergence phase, with continued evidence and support being applied to the group's decision. The group needs this kind of discussion to release the secondary tension that has built up prior to the final decision. It is almost like a teakettle inasmuch as the steam will continue to hiss or to whistle until it has been fully released. Once all of the dissent has vanished and the group's cohesiveness has once again been established, the group becomes almost euphoric. They laugh at and kid one another. They tell each other how good they are and what a good decision they came up with. Each of the participants attempts to reinforce the other. They look for reasons to justify the outcome. They attempt to establish a spirit of unity by reinforcing both their own and others' commitment to the decision.

It is a natural tendency for people to bring their attitudes and behavior into conformity with the group's final decision. This behavior is predictable from consistency theory. If the group members are not given the chance to develop a consistent mental state, they will continue to be anxious over the decision. All of the group members need this reinforcement phase before they will be willing to implement the decision or to defend it to others outside the group. At this point, overt dissent has vanished, although covert dissent and doubt may remain. The more the participants can reinforce one another and provide supporting evidence, the less the covert dissent and the better committed they will be to the outcome. If the outcome is to be given a fair chance after the group is over, the longer the participants remain in this phase the better. At the end of this phase the group will dissolve, having completed its evolution. A great many groups never evolve completely. There are many barriers that must be overcome before a group can complete the four evolutionary stages. If the group has been effective, all of the members will have a real sense of pride in the fact that they have accomplished what they set out to do and that they have achieved a result that was better than any one of them could have accomplished individually. They will once again have discovered the value of the small group as a context for human communication.

SUMMARY

In this chapter, we began by defining the small group and comparing it with the dyad. We suggested that the major difference between these two contexts was the number of participants, but that this size difference had several implications. We looked at the difference between public and private groups and discussed the unique qualities of the triad. Our specific classifications of the structure and function of small groups were basically the same as we developed in the dyadic communication chapter. As you read this chapter, you should have integrated the information about small groups with what you learned about the dyadic context. As we discussed the structure, function, and evolution of small groups, we noted the interrelationships among each of these aspects as we went along.

In the section on group structure, we talked about the three major networks that operate in groups, and we devoted a special section to small group leadership. Small group functions were divided into consummatory and instrumental. We identified cohesiveness with the consummatory function and productivity with the instrumental function. We examined all of the various causes and effects of both cohesiveness and productivity and the relationships between these two aspects of group function. We noted how groups can be used in a destructive groupthink fashion, how they can be used positively, and how they can develop an assembly effect bonus. We discussed the four evolutionary phases of small groups. We mentioned that the orientation and conflict phases are especially affected by the increased number of participants, primarily because of the greater amounts of primary and secondary tension that are created in small groups. Taken together, the two contexts of dyadic and small group communication account for much of the communication that takes place in organizations, which form the focus of the following chapter.

KEY TERMS AND CONCEPTS

- Achieved Status
- Ascribed Status
- Assembly Effect
- Centralized Network
- Coalition
- Cohesiveness
- Cohesiveness and Goal Progress
- Cohesiveness and Participation
- Cohesiveness and Status
- Communication Network
- Conflict Phase
- Consummatory Small Groups
- Decentralized Network
- Decision-Making
- Deviation
- Dual Leadership
- Emergence Phase
- Equal-Status Groups
- Forum
- Functional Leadership Approach
- Group Climate
- Groupthink
- Individual vs. Group Decisions
- Instrumental Small Groups
- Leadership
- Network
- Orientation Phase
- Panel Discussions
- Primary Groups
- Primary Tension
- Productivity
- Public Discussions
- Reinforcement Phase
- Role Network
- Secondary Tension
- Sensitivity Groups
- Situational Leadership Approach
- Small Group
- Social Pressure and Conformity
- Status Network
- Styles of Leadership
- Symposium
- Therapy Groups
- Trait Leadership Approach
- Triad
- Unequal-Status Groups
- Why People Join Groups

SUGGESTED READINGS

Fisher, B. Aubrey, *Small Group Decision Making: Communication and the Group Process*, 2nd ed. New York: McGraw-Hill Book Company, 1979. This text views communication as the organizing element in groups and discusses small group communication from both a structural and process point of view. The student is encouraged to see not only what important elements exist in groups but also how they work in both successful and unsuccessful groups. The book's organizational pattern is easy to follow and flows smoothly. There is a chapter devoted to each of the major aspects of small group communication.

Shaw, Marvin E. *Group Dynamics: The Psychology of Small Group Behavior*, 2nd ed. New York: McGraw-Hill Book Company, 1976. This is one of the most complete and up-to-date reviews of basic research and theory of small groups. This book is written at a somewhat more difficult level than the other two suggested readings. It does, however, provide a series of plausible hypotheses at the end of each chapter that sum up the basic principles discussed in the chapter. This book is especially useful after you have read one of the other two suggested readings.

Suggested Readings

Tubbs, Stewart L., *A Systems Approach to Small Group Interaction*. Reading, Mass.: Addison-Wesley Publishing Company, 1978. This text employs a system's theory approach similar to the one found in our book. A major focus is on how you can be a better group participant and how you can use groups in potential future careers. Each chapter begins with a case study taken from actual situations and includes two relevant readings along with a number of exercises.

12

Organizational Communication

Central to American society is the large organization. We are part of, or transact with, large organizations every day. These can include businesses, educational institutions, government agencies, churches, and social groups. Because they are such a large part of our lives, it is important to understand the role of communication within them. Communication is necessary to the formation of any large organization. An understanding of the channels and systems of communication within any large organization helps us to understand and thus to work more effectively with the organization. Indeed, our career success within an organization, as well as our ability to deal with an organization as an outsider, is dependent on our awareness of organizational communication.

Organizational Communication

With rare exceptions, none of us can live our lives without being significantly affected by or being a part of large organizations. Most of us were born in a hospital and attended schools and churches. Each of these is either a large organization or part of a large organization. In addition to these early contacts with organizations, we also have contacts—as either employees or customers—with large commercial organizations such as department stores, banks, and manufacturing companies. We also deal with government agencies on a fairly regular basis whenever we pay our income tax, build houses, or renew a driver's license. Even when we die, our survivors must cope with various organizations in order to settle our estate, take care of our remains, and seek comfort. It is apparent that large organizations play a major role in our daily existence.

As our population has grown, so has the number of organizations within society. It is not necessary, however, for us to look at contemporary modern society to find large organizations. Even primitive societies include rather large, complex organizations that serve various functions for the individuals and for which the individuals perform various functions. For example, a settlement of natives in Africa or Australia would qualify as an organization. If organizations play such an important role in our lives, what are they and of what importance is communication in organizations? In this chapter, we will attempt to shed some light on these questions by focusing on the organizational context as a type of communication system.

WHAT IS ORGANIZATIONAL COMMUNICATION?

We just discussed the importance of organizations without actually defining them. There have been many attempts to define organizations. Some sample definitions include the following.

> 1. Organizations are viewed as systems which utilize energy (given up by humans and nonhuman devices) in a patterned, directed effort to alter the condition of basic materials in a predetermined manner.
>
> (Perrow, 1965)
>
> 2. An organization may be defined as a structured system of relationships that coordinates the efforts of a group of people toward the achievement of specific objectives.
>
> (Koehler, Anatol, and Applbaum, 1976)
>
> 3. ... the rational coordination of the activities of a number of people for the achievement of some common explicit purpose or goal, through the division of labor and function and through a hierarchy of authority and responsibility.
>
> (Shine, 1965)

As you can see from an examination of these definitions, an organization is a system. We have already discussed in earlier chapters the characteristics of an organization that are included in these definitions. There are some key characteristics that we should always keep in mind, such as the interdependence of activities within the organization, the many different roles and the behaviors associated with those roles, the status hierarchy, the constant change, the inputs and outputs, the existence of communication networks, the collection of subsystems, and the presence of conflict. All of these system characteristics are part of an organization.

The physical layout of a bank reflects its organizational communication system.
SCHAEFER PHOTOGRAPHY

Does this mean, then, that all systems are organizations? In a sense, it does. But from the point of view of common sense, we would consider an organization to be any system composed of more people than the number found in the dyadic and group communication contexts. Such a system might also include public and/or mass communication subsystems. In other words, an organization can include all of the communication contexts we are discussing in this section of the book. It might be useful to think of an organization as a collection of smaller communication systems that are all connected by communication channels and that thus form a larger communication system.

Communication and Organizations

An organization cannot exist without communication. For all of the dyads and small groups and other subsystems within an organization to be coordinated there must be communication. It probably would be more accurate to suggest that any organization is simply a large communication system than to say that communication is a part of the organization. The flow of messages within an organization is what constitutes the operation of the organization. To be sure, were we to look at an organization like Firestone (or any other manufacturing concern), we would see processes occurring that are not communication.

Obviously, the actual physical construction of a tire is not a communication process. However, the planning of the construction of tires and the coordination of the physical processes necessary to construct tires are communication processes. Even something as basic as a manufacturing process is dependent on the ability to communicate within the organization.

Throughout this chapter, we will discuss communication channels, flow of messages, and hierarchies, probably more so than in any other chapter in the book. They are the behaviors we can observe in an organization, and thus they are the behaviors that we most often talk about. As of the writing of this book, the study of organizational communication is still in its early stages. Many scholars in organizational communication recognize that there is much yet to be studied, researched, and learned. In this chapter, we will provide an overview of the area of organizational communication, with the hope that by focusing on the structural, functional, and evolutionary processes in organizations you will better understand the importance of communication in an organization.

ORGANIZATIONAL COMMUNICATION STRUCTURE

In Chapter 9, we indicated that we can define structure not only in terms of elements but also in terms of the elements' interrelationships within a system. In the organizational communication context, it is possible to see who communicates with whom, how often, about what, and with what effect. By observing communication behavior with these points in mind, it is possible to identify both a formal and an informal communication structure within an organization.

Formal Communication Structure

Formal structure in an organization is primarily related to the role and status networks. These formal characteristics have been discussed previously. Status, role, authority, and power also play an important role in organizations. Formal organizational structure grows out of these networks. In organizations, this structure is often represented in a formal organizational chart such as that shown in Fig. 12.1. This is the same chart of a university that was presented in Chapter 9. These factors also create what communication scholars refer to as vertical and horizontal communication patterns.

Vertical communication What we earlier called an unequal-status interaction is called vertical communication in organizations. Vertical communication is communication between and among persons who have different amounts of power and authority in the formal organizational hierarchy. When a student talks to a professor at a university or when a vice-president in a company talks with the president, vertical communication is taking place.

Vertical communication can run both ways. It is possible for messages to be transmitted either upward or downward along the vertical chain of command. Depending on the information needs in the organization and the individual personalities of the people involved, it is possible for messages to go

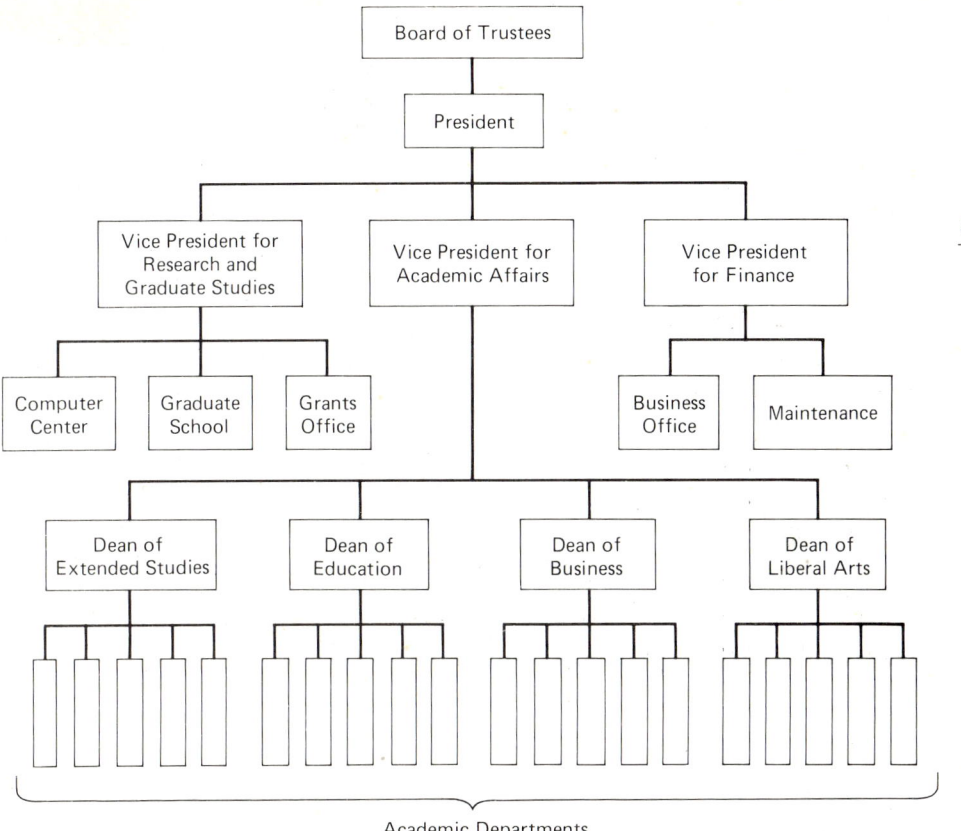

Fig. 12.1 The formal structure of an educational organization.

either from subordinates to superiors (an example of *upward vertical communication*) or from superiors to subordinates (an example of *downward vertical communication*).

Ideally, any organizational communication structure will permit the flow of messages in both directions. When messages are constantly flowing from the top down in downward vertical communication, many problems can result. Those persons in high decision-making positions are frequently forced to make decisions without adequate information. Likewise, problems can develop throughout an organization. If there is no upward vertical communication it is impossible for persons in positions of authority to become aware of problems and cope with them.

Another phenomenon that can frequently result from either upward or downward vertical communication is known as *serial communication*. It is possible to have either upward or downward vertical communication in which the message must go through several persons. This kind of transmittal of messages is referred to as serial communication. Serial communication can occur in both vertical and horizontal communication. One of the unfortunate characteristics of serial communication is that every time a message is received by a person and then transmitted to another person there is a potential loss of information and distortion of the message. These negative effects occur primarily in oral transmission of messages. For example, an employee of a department may discuss a problem with the department head. The department head may then discuss the problem with the division chief, who in turn discusses it with the vice-president, who in turn discusses it with the president. Unfortunately, all the people in that vertical chain interpret the message that they receive, process it in their own minds, and then reformulate it in their own words to pass it on to the next person. As you might guess, this procedure usually results in distortion because of the intrapersonal processing elements as well as the nature of language and nonverbal communication. The factor of memory also plays a part. We must not only receive a message but retain it in our minds until we pass it on to the next person. Of course, we are somewhat selective in terms of what we remember or don't remember, and, therefore, the message is distorted further.

Whenever vertical communication occurs in serial form, the messages that reach the person at the top, or, for that matter, the messages that come down from the top will always be different from the way they started out. Some of you may once have played a game called "gossip," or "rumor," in which you had some message that you passed along through a number of people at a party. It is very funny to see how it comes out at the other end of a line. Unfortunately, in organizations it is not so funny when the essential information or point of the message is lost as a result of serial communication. Policies coming from superiors to subordinates frequently become changed. Likewise, problems that are occurring at lower levels often become modified as they flow up from subordinates to superiors.

Of course, there is sometimes intentional distortion in vertical communication when it occurs in serial form. The phenomenon of *gatekeeping*, or *information absorption*, can prevent messages from reaching a superior or a subordinate. Gatekeeping occurs when a person receives information and decides not to pass it on to the next person. Information is, in effect, "absorbed" by the gatekeeper. Anyone in the organization can be a gatekeeper.

Gatekeeping can occur for a variety of reasons. More often than not, we suspect that persons in a vertical communication chain will stop messages from flowing upward when they believe that the messages will make them look bad or cause them to get into trouble with their superiors. It is not uncommon for someone who is a member of a department in a large organization to bring a problem to the department head, with the result that nothing happens. The reason that nothing happens is that the department head quite often correctly feels that if he or she passes this problem along, someone in a superior position in the vertical chain will begin to wonder how the department head ever let this problem develop in the first place. In order to avoid embarrassment or problems with superiors, the department head simply "forgets" to pass it along.

Such a situation, of course, can also occur in reverse when a superior sends out policies to be transmitted to subordinates, but because some gatekeeper in the vertical chain does not agree with the policy, the policy is never passed along. Excellent examples of this phenomenon occur during the administrations of presidents of the United States. When a person becomes president, that person will wish to put into effect many changes in the ways various units of government will be run. One of the frequent complaints voiced by several past presidents was that they could issue presidential directives and decisions as much as they wanted, but that it was nearly impossible for them to have their directives implemented because they were stopped at various points in the chain of command. Presidents often find that in vertical serial communication there are gatekeepers. These gatekeepers simply stop policies before they reach the people who would have to carry them out. These policies can relate to welfare, environmental protection, foreign policy, and the like. Whatever the area of concern, however, the same phenomenon can occur. Whenever there are vertical communication patterns, there is a real risk that distortion and blockage of messages will occur through gatekeeping and information absorption.

Secretaries are often important gatekeepers in organizations.
PHOTO BY CAROLE DUGAN

There are also some people within organizations who are paid to gatekeep. Secretaries, for example, are often assigned the duty of preventing unnecessary bits of information from reaching their bosses. Thus the gatekeeper wields considerable power within the organization. In many organizations, it is the secretaries who are said to run the place.

Horizontal communication When two department heads in a university talk over a problem, horizontal communication takes place. Horizontal communication in an organization consists of communication between two or more people who occupy positions in the organizational hierarchy that carry similar power, status, and authority. Earlier, we called communication between people of similar power and authority equal-status dyadic and small group interaction. Meetings and interactions in an organization occur primarily in dyads and small groups. Because of the perception of equality in horizontal or equal-status communication, conflict can occur. The people in these communication contexts will be more prone to disagree. One person does not feel subordinate to another and therefore does not feel the need to submerge feelings and disagreements. If the conflict is used properly, however, there is the potential for productivity in horizontal communication.

It is possible for serial communication to occur in horizontal communication channels, just as it can occur in vertical communication channels. When a division head communicates information to another division head, who in turn communicates it to still another division head, serial communication is taking place. The same kinds of problems can occur in horizontal serial communication that can occur in vertical serial communication (i.e., gatekeeping, distortion, and so on).

In "real life" the formal structure of an organization may not reflect the "real" power and status held by people involved in horizontal communication. For instance, although two department heads in an organization may have the same formally designated power and status, it is entirely possible that they may differ considerably because of experiences they have had, friends they have made, and other factors that can contribute to the development of "unofficial power and status." As we talk about informal communication structures it will become apparent that many people develop power and status through contacts, social activities, and the like that have little to do with the formal structure of the organization.

Informal Communication Structure

Essential to the functioning of any system are the consummatory interactions that occur and the cohesiveness that develops. The extent to which people like or dislike each other and can work pleasantly and smoothly with each other has a significant impact on the productivity of an organization. As we discussed earlier, we behave and are motivated because of needs, values, prior attitudes, and the environment we have experienced and are experiencing. As we said, people today are strongly motivated by social and ego needs. Both of these needs can be and frequently are satisfied by interaction with others through the informal structure of any organization. Water coolers, coffee pots, candy machines, and even rest rooms are places where much informal organizational communication often occurs.

This informal structure is sometimes difficult to define precisely in a specific organization, yet it nevertheless affects the formal structure as well.

The extent to which we informally like and interact with someone can affect the way we transmit and receive messages through horizontal and vertical channels as well as the way we interact with people in superior and subordinate positions. The openness, honesty, empathy, supportiveness, and positiveness that develop through informal contacts are often carried over to the formal communication structure. Cohesiveness is as closely related to productivity in organizations as it is in dyads and small groups.

We derive considerable social and ego need satisfaction from our informal interactions with other people in organizations. A pat on the back, a kind word, a smile, an invitation to go out for a cup of coffee—all of these things are the "oil" that the "machinery" of any organization needs to function effectively. However, in addition to having a positive effect on the way an organization functions, the informal structure of an organization can also have an adverse effect on the organization.

The grapevine According to Davis (1972), the term "grapevine" arose during the Civil War. Intelligence telegraph lines were strung loosely from tree to tree in the manner of a grapevine, and the message was often garbled; hence, any rumor was said to be from the grapevine. Certainly the informal communication network is a common occurrence in large organizations. This informal transmission of messages results from the informal organizational communication structure. The grapevine is not always bad for an organization. The grapevine is fast and accurate, and it carries much information.

The grapevine is not necessarily a form of serial communication, a chain in which information passes from one person to another person. Messages in the grapevine usually flow from a small group of people gathered together (for instance, having coffee) who are talking to other small groups or clusters of people. This cluster mode of transmission is what makes the grapevine such a rapid form of communication. In his discussion of the use of the grapevine during the Civil War, Davis cites one message that started in one county on a Monday afternoon, got to over 20 people from several different cities, and the next day reached people attending a meeting in another county some 2500 miles away—all in 36 hours! Within organizations, the grapevine also works very rapidly.

The grapevine is also fairly accurate (Goldhaber, 1979). Estimates are that the grapevine is usually at least 80% accurate, and sometimes higher. However, you may be aware that many people don't trust messages from the grapevine. One of the explanations often given for this fact is that when our grapevine information turns out to be wrong, the situation frequently becomes dramatic because the grapevine transmits information about matters that are usually of great importance or concern to people. Therefore, the mistake is more noticeable. The importance of grapevine information also promotes more care in preserving its accuracy during transmission.

Frequently, rumor is equated with the grapevine. *Rumors* are unsubstantiated pieces of information transmitted informally. In their classic study of rumor, Allport and Postman (1947) suggested that rumors spread faster and further as a result of the importance of the information being transmitted and the ambiguity of the information. Thus, the more important an issue is and the more "fuzzy" the information we have about it, the more it will spread along the grapevine as a rumor. Therefore, if we are working in an organization and if we wish to prevent rumors from occurring, an ideal strategy would be to provide substantiated information to members of the organization. As concrete information is provided and ambiguity is reduced, the likelihood that rumors will spread along the grapevine is reduced. Many management and organizational communication textbooks recommend open administration and management techniques that prevent rumor development.

In our own university, we have seen a new president appointed who decided that when the budget was completed for recommendation to the legislature, all of this information would be disseminated immediately to deans, then to department heads, and finally to members of the faculty. This is an open approach to administration, and it is also a very good way to prevent rumors from occurring about the kinds of requests approved by the central administration. This strategy has cut the amount of rumor about the budget in our university to a minimum.

Informal power and status In the section on formal structure of an organization, we mentioned that the power, status, and authority of an individual in an organization have a significant effect on the way that individual communicates. We would like to point out here that power, status, and authority in an organization often are not derived solely from the formal structure of the organization. All persons in an organization who have power do not necessarily derive it from their formally designated position or role in the organization. Sometimes people derive informal status and power from expertise, relationships with others, and special knowledge of the organization that they have acquired over time. We are sure you know of people in various organizations who wield considerable power that is not based on anything that has been formally ascribed to them by the organization. Some people can acquire formidable power by being part of the right clique, for example, or by being a golfing companion of their superior. Likewise, it is not unusual to find executives and their spouses who seek more power through consummatory relationships with other executives and their spouses. You should never base your estimate of the power an individual has simply on your knowledge of that person's formal role in an organization. Often, a person's informal position in an organization can be of much higher status and can reflect much more power than his or her formal position.

Communication Subsystems

Before concluding our discussion of organizational communication structure, we will consider the relationships between the overall communication structure of an organization and the components within the organization. Although it may not seem immediately obvious, a large organization never really exists as such. Rather, it is a collection of communication subsystems, each possessing its own structural, functional, and evolutionary characteristics. Typically, the communication subsystems are either dyadic or small group.

If you think back to your own experiences in large organizations, it should be clear that you never really communicate with "the organization." Usually, you communicate with one other person in a dyad or with two or three other people in a small group. These dyadic and small group communication subsystems are common in organizations and are the foundation upon which organizations are built. The overall communication patterns we have been discussing thus far are actually a description of the communication links among the various dyadic and small group communication subsystems in organizations. Sometimes these links are formal and sometimes they are informal; however, the communication links among these smaller communication subsystems almost always reflect the power and status of members of these subsystems.

ORGANIZATIONAL COMMUNICATION FUNCTION

As is the case with the other communication contexts, it is possible to view organizational communication in terms of function. We can consider both the function of communication within the organization and the function of communication as it relates the organization to the outside world. As with the other communication contexts, we will view organizational communication in terms of its instrumental and consummatory functions.

Instrumental Organizational Communication

The instrumental function served by organizational communication is the one with which most people seem familiar. When we think of someone as being "all business" in an organization, we are usually responding to that person's instrumental use of communication. Organizational communication, when serving an instrumental function, is used extensively for coordination of activities in the organization. In the spring of 1979, a nuclear incident occurred at a place called Three Mile Island in Pennsylvania. There was great concern that America was going to have its first meltdown in a nuclear reactor. Following the physical handling of the problem, many cries were of course heard for an investigation to discover what had caused this near-catastrophe. The first approach many people took was to examine the equipment in the nuclear reactor and then the qualifications of the persons who were running the reactor. Out of all of the investigations, one overwhelming conclusion began to occur to us as we read the news reports and listened to the newscasts. This fiasco appears to have occurred because a number of procedures that could have prevented the problem were not efficiently transmitted in training programs to the people who would be working with the reactor. Of course, everyone expects communication professors to talk about the importance of communication. However, at the time this book is being written, it is difficult not to believe that a major, if not *the* major cause of this near-catastrophe was the result of inadequate coordination of information and procedures—in other words, poor instrumental organizational communication.

The instrumental function of communication cannot be overemphasized. Although IBM may be in the business of building computers, a large number of activities must be coordinated in order to build those computers. Materials must be procured, parts must be made, the parts must be at different points of an assembly process on time, marketing efforts must be undertaken, and replacement parts must be distributed. In other words, there are hundreds, maybe thousands, of separate activities that must occur for computers to be successfully made and sold. All these coordination activities occur as a result of instrumental organizational communication.

The coordination effort is the job of people commonly termed *managers*. Some people call such a person "the boss." The basic functions of a manager are to coordinate activities in an organization and to provide leadership. We discussed leadership earlier when we were talking about small group communication. It should be apparent that the instrumental function of a leader in an organization is analogous to that of the task leader in a small group. It is the vice-president, the division chief, and the supervisor who must make sure that the activities of the organization—whether they concern manufacturing cars or selling candy bars—mesh together so that the task objective of the company can be realized. Since you are reading this book, you are probably in a university. It should be apparent that the dean of a college has as a primary responsibility the management of many different academic departments so that they can be meshed together and coordinated in such a way that the product, an education, is made available to the consumer, the student. Although we don't often like to talk about education in these terms, the management function, an instrumental one, is quite similar in a university to that in a large business organization.

There are many other activities occurring in any large organization that are instrumental in nature and that require organizational communication. Public relations—persuading the public to accept a company, university, or any other large organization—is quite prevalent today; it too is a part of the instrumental function. People don't engage in public relations programs to have their social needs met in the organization. Rather, they do so because it is good business. If the public is opposed to a company, it is difficult for that company to perform its stated objectives, such as making money, putting out products, and the like. The organization must stay on good terms with its environment.

To effect an organization's interfacing with its environment is an important instrumental function of organizational communication. Lawrence and Lorsch (1969) have discussed the necessity for an organization to interface with its environment. In order to acquire materials to make its products, to glean information about the public's tastes and desires, and to design, market, and sell its products, the organizational system must maintain a successful interaction with its environment and all of the people in it. Whenever an organization neglects this instrumental function of organizational communication, it is doomed to failure. As environments become more unstable, as appears to be the case in these times of scarce energy and fluctuating prices, it is even more important for this interfacing to take place effectively between the organization and the environment.

It may be that one of the reasons why Chrysler Corporation developed such terrible financial conditions in the 1970s was that they neglected to interface effectively with the environment. At a time when gasoline prices were increasing and oil supplies were decreasing, Chrysler Corporation continued to manufacture large automobiles. Chrysler did so at the same time that other auto companies were introducing a line of small, fuel-efficient automobiles. Was their financial crisis the result of their personnel's inability to build automobiles as well as the other companies could? We doubt it. We suspect it is more likely that the instrumental function of organizational communication was neglected at Chrysler and that the interface of that organization with its environment was not what it should have been. Had the people at Chrysler paid more attention to what was going on in the environment, they might have been more likely to design automobiles more consistent with the needs of the public and the times. They have started to do this now.

Of course, we have hindsight now, and it is easy to criticize the management of any corporation that makes a large error. Yet we hope you can see that any organization—be it a manufacturing company, an educational institution, or a government agency—must design departments, hire personnel, and create procedures for instrumental organizational communication which will permit and facilitate effective interfacing with the environment. Public relations, which we mentioned earlier, is certainly a part of this interface. The sales divisions of most companies are also involved in this interface, as are the market research divisions and the marketing divisions. All of these activities in any large organization help fulfill the instrumental function of organizational communication in this necessary interface between the organization and the environment.

Consummatory Organizational Communication

In addition to the task, or instrumental function, organizations also have a social-emotional set of needs, as do small groups. In order for an organization to function effectively, these social-emotional or maintenance needs must be met.

Organizational Communication

These needs are derived from the social or interpersonal needs that we discussed in Chapter 3. They have a significant effect on the way people behave in an organization. As we mentioned earlier, even power and status within the organization can result from the way in which this consummatory function is carried out relative to friendship patterns.

Just as important as the effect of consummatory organizational communication on organizational structure is its effect on morale, turnover, motivation, and the like. We are aware today that in order for an organization to function effectively, the workers in that organization must experience a certain degree of emotional satisfaction, or they must have their social needs satisfied. Many large companies today are paying attention to this fact. Bowling and bridge leagues are formed, and company newletters announcing births and awards are common. Management has begun to realize that attractive eating facilities where people can talk should be made available to workers. Places to take coffee breaks are designed in such a way as to facilitate interaction among people. These efforts on the part of management are the result of research indicating that if people like the people they work with and if they interact with people in a socially satisfying manner, they are more likely to be happy and stay with their jobs. Turnover, of course, is a problem for many organizations, because every time someone is replaced in an organization it costs the organization money to train the replacement. Also, correcting the mistakes a new person inevitably makes costs money. Thus, if you can maintain a positive climate in an organization that will satisfy the social needs of employees, you are more likely to keep them in your organization and have less of a turnover problem.

In addition to preventing turnover, however, effective consummatory organizational commmunication serves the function of motivating people. We don't really want to let down coworkers we like. Thus, a positive social climate can motivate workers to work more effectively with each other. Such a climate doesn't always work, since workers can sometimes enjoy their coworkers so much that they forget what they are there for and perform their work poorly. For instance, in a department store, the sales clerks might develop such an effective social-emotional climate that they would spend all of their time talking with each other rather than waiting on customers. In order to prevent such an occurrence, a manager will have to concentrate more on fulfilling the task leadership function by reminding the clerks of their tasks, reprimanding those who continue to socialize, and rewarding those who attend to the task requirements of their jobs. This is never a pleasant task for an administrator, but it is sometimes necessary.

Today, large organizations are also encouraging people to have social relationships off the job as well as on the job, as long as such socializing doesn't interfere with the work. Repetitive jobs can be made tolerable if a social group can be formed. In Sweden, there are two companies that manufacture automobiles, Volvo and Saab. If you stop to think about the assembly of an automobile, it doesn't sound as if it would be an exciting, stimulating job. In our country, such a job is highly repetitive (i.e., one person puts the same five nuts on the same five bolts of every automobile that comes down an assembly line). Volvo and Saab, on the other hand, have worked out a different arrangement for building an automobile. They have established work groups in their plants. Each work group is a team of workers that builds a car from start to finish. These workers develop both social relationships and job relationships as they plan and execute their task. Thus far, this strategy appears to have resulted in an improvement in quality of workmanship, greater efficiency, lower turnover, lower sickness and absentee rates, and an overall improved level of morale. Greater cohesiveness produces better productivity.

Common interests are the bases for consummatory organizations.
JOHN DUGAN PHOTO

Whether or not this method of automobile construction could be adapted to the very high volume needs of companies like General Motors or Ford is another question. Volvo and Saab together do not manufacture as many automobiles as one division of General Motors, such as Chevrolet. However, the principle is an interesting one to consider, because the two Swedish companies have paid attention to the consummatory function of organizational communication by permitting workers to develop a work group that is also a social group. We would suggest that many companies may need to look at this approach to organizational communication in the future, with an eye toward creating social climates that are more conducive to effective interaction and thus, possibly, to improved output. Never underestimate the power of friendship.

Thus far, we have been discussing consummatory communication functions in task-oriented organizations. However, organizations also exist that have no task function, at least in the sense that we have been discussing. There are organizations that have consummatory outcomes as their primary functions. Fraternities and sororities in colleges and universities are good examples of organizations that serve consummatory functions. The primary reason for their existence is to satisfy the social and ego needs of their members. We could also mention organizations such as bridge clubs, trap-shooting clubs, photography clubs, belly dancing clubs, and dancing clubs, just to name a few. In all of these organizations, the primary objective is to provide social need satisfaction to the members. Satisfactory functioning of the organization is tied to the immediate gratification the members feel from participation in the organization. It is not necessary for the organization to produce a product or to make a profit in order to fulfill its function.

It is, of course, detrimental to the functions of these organizations for members to forget that they are consummatory organizations. Whenever members of a photography club, for example, begin to feel that their primary objective is to win prizes in a contest or to make the club darkroom show a profit, the survival of the club is jeopardized. If some members put pressure on others to achieve these task goals to the exclusion of member satisfaction, the club can no longer fulfill its consummatory function. If this happens, some members may begin to leave. This kind of problem is usually solved by reminding the members of the "reason we are here." A reminder of the consummatory goals will frequently return the activities of the organization to the consummatory function it was formed to serve.

ORGANIZATIONAL COMMUNICATION EVOLUTION

Unfortunately, the research in the organizational communication context regarding evolution has been sparse, to say the least. Certainly, every organization goes through the three generalized phases of initiation, operation, and termination. Every large organization must be formed. Usually, this process involves communication that is intended to set up a structure and develop goals for the organization. In business, for example, the overall goal is usually that of profit, although there can also be secondary goals. In consummatory organizations, the goals are sometimes much harder to identify.

An organization then moves from the initiation stage to that of operation, in which the organization actually produces its product, sells its goods, or, in the case of nonprofit organizations, delivers its services to the appropriate individuals. In the operation phase of any organization we find the existence of dyads, small groups, and other communication systems. These communication contexts have their own separate evolutionary phases that they go through repeatedly. Thus, an organization really is composed of a number of different evolutionary phases through which different units within the organization are progressing in various ways at various times.

Finally, of course, many organizations reach a termination stage, even though one of the goals of many organizations seems to be that of survival. Obviously, organizations provide jobs for people and provide things for people to do. Consequently, there is an interest on the part of most people in an organization in keeping the organization alive. Members of most organizations fight termination vigorously whenever the organization begins to go into this phase. However, as is the case with dyads or small groups, when an organizational communication system ceases to have a function within its environment, it begins to deteriorate and entropy sets in.

A good example of termination would be the manufacturers of buggy whips. At one time, there were many buggy whip manufacturers. When the automobile came into being, there was a resistance to termination by people in many of the buggy whip companies. However, the environment dictated that these organizations no longer had a function to serve. Therefore, these organizations were terminated, or, in some cases, they developed other functions.

There have been other organizations in our society that have terminated. During the 1950s and 1960s, newspapers throughout the country went through termination phases as many ceased publication. This termination phase continued into the 1970s and will probably continue well into the 1980s for many of them. A major reason for the demise of newspapers is that television has begun to take over many of the functions that newspapers once served. Moreover, the public, through their buying behavior and lack of interest in newspapers, caused these large organizations to go into a termination phase.

We hope you can see that every organization goes through the initiation, operation, and termination phases. When and how these phases occur will vary for different organizations, depending on the functions the various organizations serve in their environment. It is also important to keep in mind that within every organization there are many smaller communication contexts that are going through their own evolutionary phases.

In addition to the evolutionary phases that an organization goes through, there has been an evolution of management practices in all organizations in our country. If we look back to the eighteenth century, we did not, of course, have the large organizations of today. Businesses and manufacturing concerns were usually very small shops and even home enterprises. In the nineteenth century, as we entered into the industrial age, large organizations began to come into existence. With the advent of the large organization came an approach to organizational leadership that has been called both *scientific management* and the *classical school of management*. This approach to management was largely concerned with the formal structure of an organization and depended almost solely on instrumental communication. The classical approach to management focused primarily on division of labor and coordination of activities in the manufacturing of a product. There was little, if any, concern for those persons involved in the process. Thus, when the primary concern was the product, as it mainly was in the nineteenth century and early twentieth century, there were sweat shops, horrible abuses of child labor, and working conditions that were unsafe and unhealthy. The concern was not for the individual employees in an organization. The concern was rather with using those employees as one would use a machine, simply fitting people into the right slot to perform a single task and coordinating the many slots.

Probably one of the most dramatic examples in American history of this approach concerned the Swift method of marketing meat in the late nineteenth century. Many of us take for granted the existence of fresh meat in stores and on the table, but at one time, unless you lived on or near a farm, you didn't have fresh meat very often. Swift, on the other hand, developed methods to dissect the animal into its various usable parts on an assembly-line basis. The carcass was hung on a hook and moved down a line of workers who would cut off various parts of the animal. This whole process was a perfect example of the classical approach of management. The men worked in terrible conditions and, no doubt, suffered greatly from their work. But the task was completed, its manufacturing process having been divided into its component parts and put together on an assembly line (or in the case of Swift's meat factories, a disassembly line). This approach continues to be the hallmark of those American manufacturers that use the assembly-line method. The classical school of management represents the first phase of organizational communication thought in the modern post-industrial revolution era.

In sports, as in most organizations, we have seen a move toward the human relations approach to management.
PHOTO BY CAROLE DUGAN

The *human relations approach* came into being in the early to middle part of the twentieth century and was developed partially as a reaction to purely instrumental managers. People began to realize that there were human beings working in the organization and that it might help to pay attention to them and figure out what makes them tick. The approach to organizational communication under the human relations school of thought was to involve workers in decision-making. Call them by name, treat them well, and satisfy some of their needs, with the hope of improving morale. More attention was given in the human relations approach to informal consummatory functions and structures of communication in an organization. This approach to management is still very much with us today. The Harvard Business School was one of the leading proponents of the human relations approach. Today, managers who are what would be considered "enlightened" are using this approach.

In fairly recent years, we have seen the development of the *social systems* approach to management and organizational communication. This is the system that we have been discussing throughout this chapter and, in many respects, throughout the entire book. In this approach to management, there is a greater recognition of the characteristics of systems and the way systems interrelate to one another. There is an awareness that what happens to one person in one division or unit in an organization affects everything and everyone else in the organization. Managers are beginning to realize that they have to comprehend the whole rather than simply to divide things into parts. They have to look at how things interrelate, how one part affects another.

Goldhaber (1979) relates a story about a problem he had on a flight going to the west coast, and we must admit that one of us had a similar problem on an airplane flight going east. In our case, the plane was late in taking off from Denver. When we asked why the flight was late, we were told that the crew had been on another flight that was late and because of regulations from the FAA they were required to get so many hours sleep before they could fly again. As this example shows, to understand a part of an airline you must be acquainted with the entire airline industry and even with government regulations. The airline industry has flights that are late, federal regulations that must be complied with, and a finite number of crew members who get tired. All of these elements must be coordinated into a whole system.

Today, managers schooled in the social system approach attempt to use the principles of systems theory that we have been discussing in this book. By doing so, they are able to maintain a clearer vision of the entire organization with which they are concerned. We feel that although we have evolved through these different management styles over the years, very likely no one style is completely correct. If you will consider for a moment the approach we have been taking in this book, we think you will find elements of each of these management styles in our discussion of communication. Certainly, throughout this chapter, you will find each of these management styles, and we would suggest that as you are considering communication within any organization your best bet probably is to take the best aspects of each of them. We do have to break down activities into component parts and coordinate them. We also must motivate the various people who are members of an organization. Finally, we must think of all of these factors together as they relate to the whole system. There will probably be further evolutions of managerial style by which we will become aware of other factors. Presently, it seems a rather large task just to try to integrate the best features of each of these managerial styles and adapt them to our own personal needs and idiosyncracies. That, however, is the task facing us with organizational communication.

SUMMARY

In this chapter, we have discussed the nature of organizations, recognizing that they are very difficult to define but that they can be defined in terms of structure, function, and evolution. We have discussed the importance of recognizing both formal and informal structure in an organization, as well as the instrumental and consummatory functions of organizational communication. Finally, although it is difficult if not impossible to talk about empirically documented evolutionary phases for an organization, we did discuss the presence of the three general phases of initiation, operation, and termination in every organization. Finally, we concluded with a discussion of the evolution of management and communication styles in all organizations, beginning with the classical approach, proceeding through the human relations approach, and finally concluding with the social systems approach. Many of the concepts discussed in this chapter will be especially applicable as you move on to study the public and mass communication contexts.

KEY TERMS AND CONCEPTS

CLASSICAL SCHOOL OF MANAGEMENT
COMMUNICATION SUBSYSTEMS
CONSUMMATORY ORGANIZATIONAL COMMUNICATION
DOWNWARD VERTICAL COMMUNICATION
FORMAL COMMUNICATION STRUCTURE
GATEKEEPING
GRAPEVINE
HORIZONTAL COMMUNICATION
HUMAN RELATIONS APPROACH
INFORMAL COMMUNICATION STRUCTURE
INFORMAL POWER
INFORMAL STATUS
INFORMATION ABSORPTION
INSTRUMENTAL ORGANIZATIONAL COMMUNICATION
MANAGERS
ORGANIZATIONAL COMMUNICATION EVOLUTION
ORGANIZATIONS
RUMORS
SCIENTIFIC MANAGEMENT
SERIAL COMMUNICATION
SOCIAL SYSTEMS APPROACH
UPWARD VERTICAL COMMUNICATION
VERTICAL COMMUNICATION

SUGGESTED READINGS

GOLDHABER, GERALD M., *Organizational Communication*, 2nd ed. Dubuque, Iowa: Wm. C. Brown Company, Publishers, 1979. This book has been widely accepted as a text in the first course in organizational communication in colleges and universities for good cause. It is easy to read and complete in its coverage. Although the last section of the book on diagnosis and change may not be appropriate for the beginning student, the rest of the book certainly is.

LEWIS, PHILLIP V., AND JOHN WILLIAMS, eds., *Readings in Organizational Communication*. Columbus, Ohio: Grid Publishing, Inc., 1980. This collection of readings provides the reader with a broad perspective concerning organizational communication. Topics covered in this chapter, as well as others, are included for the beginning student interested in this area of study. Although there is a section that focuses on research methods, most of the readings are practically oriented.

SCHODERBECK, PETER P., ASTERIOS G. KEFALAS, AND CHARLES G. SCHODERBECK, *Management Systems: Conceptual Considerations*. Dallas: Business Publications, Inc., 1975. This book was not written from a "communication point of view," and yet it provides an excellent explanation of organizational communication from a systems theory perspective. The first half of the book especially reinforces the material we have presented in this chapter.

13

Public Communication

Public communication has been a vital part of human societies for thousands of years. Even in our modern world of electronic communication, the public context is a frequent form of communication. A major feature of public communication is that it is the only communication context that permits communication to large groups of people with instant feedback and simultaneous adaptation to that feedback. Although it is an old form of communication, it is still important to have an understanding of it.

Public Communication

As you may have noticed, we gradually have been expanding the scope of human communication systems from context to context. First, we considered communication between two people, then communication in small groups, and then communication as it occurs among people within large organizations. Each of these contexts has been an increasingly larger human communication system. In this chapter, we will consider the largest human communication context possible that will still permit immediate feedback. In previously discussed communication contexts, the people participating usually receive immediate face-to-face feedback as part of the system. Regulation of dyadic, small group, and organizational communication systems is ordinarily immediate and direct, except for some special situations. The same is true of public communication systems.

In the public communication context, one person orally presents a preplanned, structured message in a formal situation to a large group of people, who usually sit in front of the speaker. Although it may seem that the person presenting the message has to wait until the message has been presented to get feedback, it is actually possible during the presentation for a speaker to observe nonverbal feedback and to incorporate it into the structuring of the message as it is being presented. Thus, public communication systems include simultaneous regulation and adaptation by communicators during the presentation of the message, as is the case in previously discussed contexts.

THE IMPORTANCE OF PUBLIC COMMUNICATION SYSTEMS

One of the questions frequently raised in a consideration of public communication systems is why we should be interested in them. Many students feel that since they are not planning to be public speakers or to go into public life, the study of public communication systems is a waste of their time. You may feel this way. But, let us suggest that you will participate in public communication systems more often than you think.

Public Communication in Society

It is important to first understand the role of public communication in our society prior to considering its relevance in our own personal lives. We have mentioned throughout the text that communication is a survival mechanism for human beings. In these discussions we have generally considered the survival of individual human beings and small numbers of human beings. However, it is apparent that as societies or cultures grow in size and become more complex, it is necessary that they survive in order to facilitate individual survival. This requires that people within the culture or society be influenced in large numbers. Centuries ago, as cultures began to reach a size that prevented the solution of problems through interpersonal communication, it became more important for people to work out a means of controlling larger groups. The solution to this need was public communication. If we must manipulate large groups, then we frequently do so through this communication context.

The Importance of Public Communication Systems

Public communication has existed as a societal survival mechanism for at least 5,000 years. As we mentioned in Chapter 1, the Egyptians, Greeks, Romans, Europeans, Americans, and others have employed public communication as a means of influencing members of the society in ways speakers felt were conducive to the survival of that society. We would not suggest that all public speaking attempts have necessarily been productive in terms of the survival of a given society. Hitler, for example, presented speeches that eventually led to the fall of the Third Reich. However, the context of public communication has been accepted because it is generally perceived as contributing to the survival of the society.

Public communication by world leaders is necessary, and it demands careful editing because of the possible ramifications of everything they say.
COURTESY OF THE WHITE HOUSE

In addition to politics, the public speech aids in the regulation and governance of our society. Large church organizations make decisions in conferences that employ the public speech. Academic societies evaluate knowledge, discoveries, and research through public presentations. In medical meetings, new advances are presented through the public speech. In our society, the public speech serves an important function, that of influencing members of society in ways we hope are conducive to our culture's survival.

Public Communication and You

The importance of public communication in our society is all well and good, you may say. However, since you don't plan to be a public speaker, you may feel it does not affect you very much. This is not necessarily the case. Because you are reading this book, we assume you are a particular kind of person. You are either a college student or you are educating yourself at the level of a college student. Thus it is safe to assume that with your educational background you will be occupying a role in our society that, interestingly enough, will call upon you to participate in public communication. You will participate sometimes as the speaker and more often as the listener in the audience. In either case, it will be important for you to understand the nature of the process so you can perform better as a speaker and be more responsible as a listener.

Furthermore, we think that an awareness of public communication and the skills developed in public communication are useful to you in another way. If you are under 25 or 30 years of age, your generation is often referred to by older members of our society as "illiterate." Books and articles explain "Why Johnny Can't Read," and although the book has not been written, we suspect the sentiment exists that would provide a ready audience for a book entitled "Why Johnny Can't Think, Talk, or Listen." There has been a deemphasis in many schools on the development of reading, writing, speaking, and listening skills. We have encountered many students who say, "Gee, I know the idea, but I can't say it." Frankly, if you cannot express an idea, you probably don't really have it developed. If you will think back to the discussion of the Sapir-Whorf hypothesis, it should be clear that our ability to express ourselves in spoken language is strongly related to the way we think about things. It is our feeling that an articulate speaker is an articulate thinker. It has been our experience that the people who are the most competent speakers are also usually the most lucid in their conceptualizations. There is no guarantee, obviously, that a person who is a competent speaker will be a good thinker. However, we don't think incompetency as a speaker facilitates competent thinking.

Having considered the importance of public communication, we will now discuss the public communication context. As in the previous chapters on communication contexts, we will consider the nature of public communication from the point of view of the structure, function, and evolution of the public speech communication context.

PUBLIC COMMUNICATION STRUCTURE

We touched on the structure of the public speech communication context when we referred to it as one person talking to a large number of people in a face-to-face setting. Usually, though not always, when a communication system involves around 15 persons or less, it functions more as small group communication. Thus, an important structural characteristic of public communication is that it involves one person speaking to approximately 15 or more people. However, numbers alone do not define the public communication context.

Another structural characteristic that defines the public communication context is the formal setting. The speaker in a public communication context makes a preplanned, formal presentation to people who have tacitly agreed to listen to the presentation. There is an unspoken agreement between speaker and audience that the audience will allow the speaker to make a complete presentation, during which the audience will provide nondisruptive feedback. Although the agreement between speaker and audience is unspoken, it results in a formal structure that determines the manner of interaction that occurs.

The third structural characteristic of public communication systems is the face-to-face setting. There is a great difference between a politician speaking to a group of people in a shopping center face-to-face and a politician speaking to voters over television. In the shopping center, the politician receives immediate nonverbal (and sometimes verbal) feedback and can observe members of the audience who are bored, walking away, or being distracted by other people. In the face-to-face setting, the speaker and the audience must be in the same physical location and aware of the presence of one another.

This is not the case when a politician speaks via television, radio, newspapers, or magazines. Mass communication involves a presentation to an audience that is unseen. Because of the face-to-face nature of the public communication context, the feedback function is more similar to that in dyadic or small group communication systems than that in mass communication systems. Feedback in the public communication context is immediate. This is true even in a large public speaking situation such as the one that occurred in the spring of 1979 in Washington D.C., in which 60,000 to 70,000 people gathered to hear public speeches about the use of nuclear reactors to generate electricity. Even though public address systems were necessary, feedback (in the form of applause, boos, and cheers) in response to what was being said was immediate. The speakers could adapt to this feedback and modify their admittedly preplanned messages while presenting those messages. This opportunity to adapt to an audience during the presentation of the message distinguishes the public communication context from the mass communication context. The structural characteristic of face-to-face interaction is of importance because it means the regulatory function in the public communication context can be immediate and direct. Both speaker and members of the audience can regulate each other's behavior simultaneously throughout the presentation of a message. In order for speakers and listeners to realize the full potential of the public communication context, this immediate regulation must occur. Thus the speaker should make maximum use of the feedback that he or she is receiving and, furthermore, the audience members should provide maximum amounts of nondisruptive feedback to the speaker for the public communication context to function effectively.

We will now consider the structural components of public communication systems so that you will have a better understanding of this context as you participate in it, either as a speaker or a listener. In order to better understand the public communication context, we will consider three of the main components in this context: the speaker, the audience, and the environment. Although the speech can also be considered as part of structure, we feel it is more fruitful to relate it to the evolution of the public communication context and so we will consider it later.

Public Communication

The Public Speaker

A primary element in public communication systems is, of course, the speaker. The way in which a speaker is perceived can have a significant effect on the way in which his or her message is received in any public speaking situation. Two of the primary concerns of all speakers should be the way they are perceived in terms of credibility and the way they are perceived in terms of attractiveness. Because speakers in the public communication context are the people primarily in control of the outcome of the presentation and because they are usually, though not always, the people with the most to gain from the communication interaction, they should take care to insure that the perception of their credibility and attractiveness is as high and as positive as possible. As we said in Chapter 4, credibility consists of three dimensions: competence, trustworthiness, and dynamism. Keep in mind also that perceived credibility may change as the public communication context evolves. We can think in terms of three phases of credibility: initial credibility, derived credibility, and, finally, terminal credibility.

Initial credibility is the credibility that the audience perceives prior to the presentation of the message. This credibility is the result of an audience's knowledge of the speaker's educational background, experience, honesty, and the like. Obviously, our initial credibility is highly dependent on the way in which we are introduced to the audience. When we are about to present a public speech, we have the opportunity to determine the initial perception of our credibility through the use of an introduction. It is never wise to leave the matter of the introduction to chance. The way in which we are introduced to an audience can have a significant effect on the outcome of our presentation. It is probably not a bad idea in any public speaking situation to jot down a few notes, or better yet, to have them typed up and handed to the person who is going to introduce us. Although we can never exercise complete control, we can at least provide some degree of control over the information provided in the introduction. The more we can control our introduction, the more we can control the audience's perception of our initial credibility.

In Chapter 7, we discussed several factors that affect the impressions others form about us. A part of initial credibility results from the clothing a person wears and how neatly groomed the person is. These and other factors of appearance contribute toward the perception of attractiveness and credibility. Obviously, a public speaker should pay close attention to matters of grooming and dress in preparation for any public appearance. Speakers who are dressed inappropriately for a given occasion can do much damage in terms of ultimate acceptance of their message and/or of themselves. Keep in mind, also, that one of the structural characteristics of the public communication context is that it is a formal situation. Because it is formal, appropriate dress in most instances approaches formal dress. This does not mean tuxedos and evening gowns, obviously, but it does usually mean something along the lines of shirt and tie for males and a dress or suit for females. There are, of course, some situations such as a public speech at a county fair in which neither of these forms of dress might be appropriate. On a hot summer afternoon at a county fair, an open collar and casual slacks may be appropriate for a male and a skirt and blouse may be appropriate for a female. The point is, though, to recognize that this is a formal situation calling for attention to dress and that appropriate clothing should be determined according to the situation itself.

Derived credibility is the perception of credibility derived from the presentation of the message. As we present a message, we modify the audience's perception of our credibility. Our expertise or lack of it becomes evident in the kinds of arguments and evidence we use or don't use. The reasoning processes we discussed in Chapter 5 are especially important to our understanding of the public communication context. Keep in mind that the more fair and complete we are in our presentation of supporting materials, the more likely we are to be perceived as both competent and trustworthy. Thus, even if not from an ethical point of view at least from a pragmatic point of view, it is desirable for us to organize our message as intelligently and fairly as possible and to provide as much in the way of supporting materials as we can so that we will be perceived as someone who is thorough in research, expert in knowledge, and fair in the willingness to acknowledge all sides of an issue.

We should also keep in mind that the language used in a public presentation can have a significant effect on the perception of our credibility. If we use highly intense, emotional language, we may be perceived as extreme and less credible in terms of trustworthiness. Likewise, in terms of our nonverbal communication, we would probably do well not to appear too apathetic or lethargic, for fear that on the dynamism dimension of credibility we might be perceived negatively. Of course, nonverbal behavior at the other extreme may cause us to be perceived as too much of a "con artist" and as negative on either the trustworthiness or the dynamism dimension of credibility. As the context evolves, people's perception of us will probably change. And when this happens, the more positive the perception of our credibility, the more likely that what we are presenting will be accepted.

Finally, *terminal credibility* is the positive or negative perception of our credibility after our presentation. It is the sum total of the initial credibility as modified by the presentation in the eyes of the audience. Keep in mind that there are at least two effects of any public presentation. Typically, people think in terms of an acceptance or a rejection of the message. To be sure, this is an important aspect of any public presentation. In addition, however, the communicator should also recognize that another result of any public presentation is the perception of terminal credibility. This factor is important for every speaker, since it will determine not only the acceptance or rejection of the message but also the audience's initial perception of the speaker's credibility at any time in the future.

The Audience

Public communication is the most speaker-oriented form of communication. The linear approach to communication that we discussed earlier has very typically been taken by public speaking teachers. In more recent years, the *receiver-centered approach* has been emphasized. This approach recognizes that the audience, the second major structural component, is as important to the outcome of a public communication as the speaker. We could not agree more. Throughout this book, we have been discussing many factors in the audience that have a significant effect on the outcome of a given presentation.

Although we have already discussed some of these, we will now consider their effect in the public speaking context.

Needs, values, and prior attitudes As we pointed out earlier, the need systems of individuals significantly affect their behavior. Needs play a significant role in determining how audiences will respond to messages in the public communication context. We have already discussed the physical, social, ego, and consistency needs, but we would like to reemphasize consistency needs since they are employed in a public presentation. A speaker should relate the message to all of the needs that he or she thinks an audience has at any given time.

Audiences come in all sizes, and each has different needs, values, and prior attitudes that must be taken into account.
PHOTO BY CAROLE DUGAN

A frequent technique in the public speech is to structure a message in such a way that the position advocated in the message is consistent with the needs or the prior attitudes of the members of the audience. Assume for a moment that you are going to speak to a group of union members about the necessity of wage/price controls. The idea of wage/price controls, at least according to current polls, is not often acceptable to members of unions. Union settlements have typically violated the guidelines set by the federal government. The question then becomes: How do you get this message accepted in spite of the prior attitudes held by union members? An analysis of most union members would suggest that they are usually middle-class people who are having trouble making ends meet. Thus, you might assume that their physiological needs have been threatened because of the increased prices of food and housing. An effective message strategy might be one in which you link federal wage/price controls to the satisfaction of audience needs for food and housing. In this strategy, you would provide evidence that the use of wage/price controls would make food and housing more easily available to them. You would reason adequately and provide good supporting materials for the conclusion that wage/price controls would be consistent with the audience's needs for food and housing. This approach should create considerable inconsistency in the members of the audience. On the one hand, they would desire to have food and housing at lower prices. On the other hand, they might not wish to have wage/price controls because of the possible effect such controls might have on their pay raises. If you provide adequate evidence to support the conclusion that wage/price controls are tied to the satisfaction of their physiological needs, they might resolve this inconsistency by changing their attitude toward wage/price controls. Thus, they would agree with the overall thrust of your presentation. There is no guarantee that this strategy will work. In fact, there is a possibility that by taking too extreme a position you might run the risk of having the audience decide that you are some kind of fanatic, nut, or incompetent, and thus they might become more convinced than ever that they are opposed to wage/price controls. However, if you present a moderate statement with a moderate conclusion and effective reasoning, and if you tie the conclusion you wish them to accept to their own needs, it is quite possible that they might reduce their dissonance by agreeing with the position you are presenting.

This discussion highlights the importance of what is termed *audience analysis*. Until now, we have talked about adapting to audiences and relating the conclusion we are advocating in a message to the needs, values, and prior attitudes of an audience. This approach suggests the importance of spending considerable time in analyzing an audience prior to speaking to it. Before we ever construct a message to present, we should spend much time and effort in determining the needs, values, and prior attitudes of the people to whom we are going to talk. It is not an easy task. Often, we must infer much. When we hypothesized the talk with a group of union members, we had to infer physical needs. We had to take what we knew about their socioeconomic status, probable educational background, and the like, and from these factors we had to infer their need systems, value systems, and prior attitudes. This is a guessing game at best, and we must be careful when we are making our guesses. Nevertheless, we do need to make the guesses. We have to assume certain things about audiences before we talk to them in order to structure a message consistent with their needs, values, and prior attitudes. Without this kind of an analysis, success in public communication is most unlikely.

Environment In addition to the audience and the speaker, there is the environment in which the public presentation occurs. It, too, has an effect on the outcome of an interaction between speaker and audience. The speech of a football coach to a squad of 20 or 30 players is far more effective in a locker room prior to a game than it is the night before the game after a full dinner. The environment in each situation is very different. The environment in the locker room includes people cheering in the stadium, bands playing, and the excitement of the whole day that leads up to the game. All of that helps reinforce and make more important what the coach is saying to the team. On the other hand, after dinner the night before, the same speech would sound a little out of place in a quiet dining room. Because stomachs are full and people are more relaxed, exciting comments and stirring words can fall very flat.

Prior to structuring a message for public presentation, the speaker should do a serious analysis of what environmental influences will exist that could affect the audience's response. What events will be surrounding or accompanying the presentation? Will those events reinforce prior beliefs held by the audience, or will those events reinforce the material presented in the message? Whenever possible, it is desirable for the public speaker to take advantage of and refer to the events occurring in the environment.

The public communication context does not consist simply of a speaker and an audience coming together with their backgrounds. It also includes an environment in which all this is happening. In earlier chapters, we mentioned the importance of environment and the effect of environment on all elements within human communication systems. Nowhere is this more evident than in the public communication context. The audience interacts with their perceived environment, and the speaker interacts with his or her perceived environment. Thus the environment has its own effect on the outcome of any public communication event.

PUBLIC COMMUNICATION FUNCTION

The public speaking context has traditionally been broken down into several functions that fall under the instrumental and consummatory functions discussed earlier. Depending on the particular textbook you happen to read, these have usually included speeches to inform, to persuade, to stimulate, and to entertain. These different speech functions both appeal to our common sense and suggest differing approaches to the preparation of public speeches. However, in keeping with our discussion of human communication systems, we would suggest that as in the case of other communication systems, the basic function of public communication systems is the conscious or unconscious influencing of people in order to meet their various needs. In public communication systems, the function includes both the speaker influencing the audience and the audience influencing the speaker.

In the *informative* speech, the underlying instrumental function of the speaker is to cause a group of people to accept the information presented. Probably one of the best examples of this function is that of the teacher in the classroom. We do not commonly think of such a situation as influence-oriented. However, teachers present material that they want their students to remember. They determine whether or not the students have acquired the information by seeing if the students can perform certain kinds of behaviors on tests which they could not perform prior to hearing the material. Thus, teachers do try to influence students. They attempt to make the students remember information, and they also try to change the students' behavior on tests. This information-retention function is a feature of most informative speeches. Even the home economist who presents information to groups of homemakers about diet and nutrition is, in essence, attempting to influence people to think about the foods that they eat and that they give to their families. The factors that a speaker must keep in mind when presenting an informative speech are very similar to those in any other kind of speech.

Teachers attempt to influence students to learn and to remember information.
PHOTO BY CAROLE DUGAN

The *persuasive* speech, even from the traditional approach to public speaking, is considered to be an instrumental speech designed to change behavior, attitudes, and the like. Thus, the traditional approach to the persuasive speech is entirely consistent with the function that is served by the public informative speech, with the one exception that the receiver must not only retain the information but must also accept it as correct.

In a *stimulative* speech, the speaker traditionally attempts to strengthen beliefs, attitudes, and behaviors that people already have. A speaker at a political convention attempts to make "truer believers" out of people who already believe in the party. If you assume that someone has to change from one belief to a totally different belief in order for there to be influence, then certainly the function of a stimulative speech is not to influence.

It is our feeling, however, that a change from one degree of belief to a stronger degree of belief is a form of influence. Thus, in the example just given, the politician's speech at the political convention is very much an instrumental attempt to influence the members of the audience via the public communication context. Furthermore, in this example we can even identify potential behavior change. A politician presents a stimulative message to the party faithful in order to change their support from apathetic behavior to active behaviors such as recruiting, campaigning, and canvassing. Thus, behavior influence results from what is traditionally called a stimulative speech.

Finally, what traditionally has been called the *entertaining* speech is one that is probably the most difficult for people to identify in terms of influence. At the very least, a speech to entertain, such as a comedy monologue or an after-dinner speech, is designed to influence people to laugh and fulfills a consummatory function. It is also true, however, that one effect of humor may also be a change in people's attitudes and behavior (Freud, 1960). Bergson (1956) suggests that humor is employed to correct faults in other people. Thus, if we have an authoritarian boss at work, we make jokes about authoritarianism in an attempt to modify the boss's behavior toward us. Likewise, the attitude of many governments (and, for that matter, of politicians) toward comedians strongly suggests that entertaining speeches or jokes can influence people. In totalitarian societies, governments do not permit comedians to make jokes about the party in power. There is an instinctive awareness by the people in these governments that jokes about the party in power influence the attitudes of the members of that society. Similarly, many Polish people perceive Polish jokes to be demeaning and harmful toward their position in society. Politicians sometimes perceive jokes about them to have an adverse effect on voters' attitudes and behavior toward them. It is not the laughter itself with which the politician or the person of Polish ancestry is concerned. Rather, it is the possible influence of the laughter that concerns them. It is the possibility that the jokes and laughter will cause people to think incorrectly or less of them. Because of these effects of humor in public speeches, we must conclude that what we call an entertaining "after-dinner speech" may serve an instrumental function and may have a considerable effect on the subsequent information, attitudes, and behaviors of members of the audience. Thus, the entertaining speech also serves the function of ultimately influencing the audience.

PUBLIC COMMUNICATION EVOLUTION

We find evolutionary phases in the public communication context just as in other communication contexts. Every public communication system proceeds through at least three evolutionary phases. These phases have been traditionally discussed in terms of the organization of the speech itself. However, it is also apparent that speakers and members of audiences go through phases also. We will discuss the general phases of initiation, operation, and termination as they apply to the public communication context.

Initiation

There are several components of the initiation phase. One, obviously, is the introduction of the speaker. As we said earlier, it is important that speakers control the way in which they are introduced so that they are presented in a favorable manner. An effective introduction of a speaker can create a perception of positive initial credibility. The more positively the audience perceives the speaker's credibility, the more likely the acceptance of the message.

Many public speaking teachers traditionally stress the importance of what they call the attention step in public speaking. In this step, the speaker attempts to gain the attention of the members of the audience so that they will listen to the speech. Frankly, we feel it is easy to gain the attention of an audience. When a person stands up to speak in a formal situation and the members of the audience are seated in front of this individual, it is unlikely that they won't pay attention to the person. This part of the initiation phase is part of the agreement between the speaker and the audience and is necessary for effective public speaking. The initiation phase in the speech is usually referred to as the introduction. The introduction, or beginning part of a speech, is intended to heighten attention and to introduce the material that is about to be presented.

Preceding introductions and attention steps is one other important step in public communication. This step is preparation. Every public speaker must research his or her topic, prepare an outline, develop the wording of some or all of the message, and practice delivery, with attention given to nonverbal communication. Some people think that a public speech can be given with little or no preparation, but this is not the case. An effective public presentation requires much time and effort spent in preparation. If the presentation is short, it will require even more time and effort to prepare than a longer presentation. It actually does take more time to prepare an effective short presentation than it does to prepare a long speech. The reason is that there is less time and effort that the speaker can afford to waste in the preparation of the shorter message. We once heard a story about President Woodrow Wilson who, when asked if he would be willing to make an after-dinner speech, replied that if the speech was to be a ten-or fifteen-minute speech he would need several months to prepare, but if he had no time limit he was already prepared. This anecdote should suggest to you that the typical public speech requires much preparation.

Operation

Traditionally, the operation phase in any public communication context is referred to as the body of the speech. You may be familiar with this term if you have taken either a public speaking course or an English course in which you studied essay writing. The operating phase in public speaking is simply the presentation of the bulk of material that the speaker wishes the audience to hear. We will consider the organization of the material when we consider the speech itself later.

Termination

Most often called the conclusion of a speech, the termination phase of any public communication includes summaries, restatement, and the like. At this point in the speech, the speaker tries to make certain that the audience has grasped the essentials of what was presented during the speech. The speaker also attempts to leave the members of the audience with some kind of a strong statement that will, in the speaker's eyes, move the audience closer to the main objective in the message.

All public communication contexts involve these three evolutionary phases. There is always an evolutionary cycle in any public speaking situation in which the speaker and the audience together move through an initiation of the formal presentation, the main process of presentation, and termination. In our following discussion of the speech you will see that these three phases are manifested in speech organization patterns. These three phases form the primary focus of our discussion.

The Speech

Central to every public communication presentation is the speech. It is the speech that links the speaker with the audience. This connection is accomplished through the use of organization, language, supporting materials, and so on. Since this section is concerned with evolutionary phases, we will focus primarily on the organization of the speech rather than go into detail about the other elements of a speech previously covered.

Let us briefly suggest that in terms of language, the key to an effective public presentation is the use of language that is appropriate to the audience. It is important to use language that is familiar and not outside the bounds of acceptability of the people to whom you are speaking. Moderation in language is desirable. Don't make extreme statements, and don't use highly intense language. As we discussed in Chapter 6, the extremely intense presentation can very easily lead to a boomerang effect that can turn an audience against the speaker.

In terms of supporting materials, always keep in mind the four basic types of evidence discussed in Chapter 5: observation, examples, statistics, and testimony. We use one or more of these types of evidence to draw reasoned conclusions. Review the characteristics of each type of evidence and reasoning and the problems and advantages of using each. Remember that the effective use of reasoning and evidence can go a long way toward creating a positive perception of your credibility as a speaker. Always try to avoid reasoning fallacies, and never try to misuse evidence. The ultimate acceptance of the conclusions of the speech often depends on the way supporting materials have been employed and arranged in a speech.

Prior to choosing language and supporting materials, it is necessary to organize the message we are preparing. The way we organize a speech determines the evolution of the public communication context. One thing to keep in mind is that there is no such thing as a "correct" organizational sequence. Rather, there are many different organizational patterns, all of which can work, depending on the topic and the occasion. The important decision to be made is which organizational pattern is most appropriate to the topic and the occasion. When we let the organizational pattern grow out of the topic and the message function, we are most likely to achieve an effective organizational pattern. There are many different types of patterns of arrangement. The ones that seem most common include the chronological, spatial, causal, priority, need-satisfaction, topical, and difficulty patterns.

Chronological pattern When we are delivering a public speech concerned with an event(s), an effective form of arrangement—especially for informative speeches—is the chronological pattern. This organizational pattern focuses on the time sequence in which events occurred. Were we to give a speech about the Watergate incident and the demise of Richard M. Nixon's presidency, we might begin with the break-in of the Watergate apartments. We might next discuss the reaction to the discovery of the break-in by Nixon and his subordinates. This might be followed by a discussion of Nixon's first statement to the public. Our speech then could proceed chronologically to consider the various statements in court by different witnesses, Mr. Nixon's public statements, the events leading up to his resignation, and finally the resignation itself. In other words, a chronological sequence would be an extremely effective way of discussing the Watergate affair. By following a time sequence, it would be possible to discuss each element and individual involved in the Watergate incident that led up to Mr. Nixon's resignation. The time sequence would tie everything together and produce greater understanding.

Spatial arrangement A frequent form of organization is the spatial arrangement—an arrangement according to geographical location. For instance, in discussing oil shortages we might begin with the United States, go north to Canada, east to Europe, and further east to the Middle East. We would thus be discussing oil supply and demand in terms of geography. Notice that although we would be talking about oil, we would be organizing our speech according to geographic locations in the world.

Causal pattern We often reason from cause to effect. A speech that is organized according to causes and effects is following the causal pattern. A speech on automobile safety regulations might focus on the accidents that occurred with the Chevrolet Corvair and the Ford Pinto. These accidents would be seen as the major factors that subsequently caused the creation of a federal agency to supervise the safety of automobiles and that led to new safety regulations. It would be possible to organize the entire speech around the Corvair, with the problems related to the Corvair as the causes and the regulations we have today as the effects. Such an organizational pattern would make much of what we have today in the way of automotive regulations more understandable to a group of people listening to our speech.

Priority pattern Sometimes it is possible to break a topic down into priorities. One of the best examples we ever saw of this pattern was a magazine article entitled "Upgrading Your Stereo System." We could easily envision this article as a speech. Although it might not seem obvious to all readers at first, the point of the article was that if you are going to upgrade or improve your stereo system you should begin by replacing those components that have been changed the most in recent years. Thus the article suggested that if you had a turntable and cartridge that were more than five years old, they should be the first components in your current system to replace. Those particular pieces of equipment would have the greatest priority because the greatest changes had occurred in them. The article was then structured so that each piece of equipment discussed was arranged in order of relative importance, or priority. By setting up a system of priorities based on when the most recent technological improvements had occurred, the author of this article used the priority pattern to organize the entire presentation. Not all topics lend themselves to a priority approach. However, it is an effective pattern of arrangement in certain instances.

Need-satisfaction pattern Whenever we can break a topic down, relate it to needs people have, and show how what we are advocating relates to the satisfaction of those needs, a very effective pattern of arrangement has emerged. An excellent example of the need-satisfaction arrangement might be one in which we begin by talking about people who are overweight and the necessity of losing weight. Once we have discussed a need(s), we could present material about a particular diet such as a high-fiber, a low-carbohydrate, or a high-protein diet. Any of these would be well suited to the need-satisfaction pattern. In the first part of the speech, we would develop the need, discussing the dangers and cosmetic effects of being overweight. In the rest of the speech, we would present the diet so that it would naturally grow out of our organizational

Public Communication

pattern. One of the most complete approaches to the need-satisfaction sequence was one that we discussed earlier in the text. Monroe's primary contribution was the motivated sequence, in which he broke the need-satisfaction sequence into five steps through which a speaker can proceed and lead the audience step-by-step through the need-satisfaction pattern (Ehninger, Monroe, and Gronbeck, 1978).

Step 1: Attention. As we have already mentioned, the first phase in the public communication context is that of initiation. We said earlier that this phase is frequently referred to as an attention step. In a public speech, this step is most often accomplished by making a statement that relates to audience needs, values, interests, prior attitudes, and the like. For instance, if we were presenting a speech on the desirability of dieting, we might begin the speech with a statement to the effect that it is very possible to cut five to ten years off one's life simply by following a poor diet. This revelation should get the attention and interest of many people, since it would relate to their physical needs.

Step 2: Need. The function of this second step of the motivated sequence is to begin what we earlier called the body of the speech. It is necessary to take an audience whose interest you have and show them how they have a need to listen to what you are about to present to them. If you can show an audience that what you are about to present is important to them and that they need to know what you are about to say, they will do most of the work for you.

In our example of the diet, a statement relating to the need step might focus on the fact that clothes may be ill-fitting for some members of the audience and that the extra weight carried around the neck, chin, stomach, and thighs may make them less attractive to members of the opposite sex. A statement like this is designed to amplify the initial attention step and, at the same time, to relate the speech to the social needs of the audience. It would even be possible to go further and make statements about the lack of pride people would probably experience if they should allow themselves to remain overweight. This statement would appeal to the ego needs of the audience.

Step 3: Satisfaction. In this step, which is another component of the body of the speech, the speaker attempts to satisfy the need aroused in step 2. In our example of a speech concerning diet, the speaker can say to the audience, "You may be 10% overweight, but by simply making an overall slight reduction in the amount of food eaten at all meals, eliminating second helpings, and skipping between-meal snacks, it will be possible to lose that excess weight at approximately the rate of one pound per week." In other words, in this particular step the speaker presents a solution to the problem developed during steps 1 and 2.

Step 4: Visualization. This step can occur both in the body of the speech and at the conclusion of the speech. In many speeches, it will overlap these two evolutionary phases. In this step, an attempt is made to make the solution presented in step 3 more graphic. It is not enough to simply say that we need to cut down on eating. In this step, we try to visualize the benefits of accepting the recommended course of action and the ease with which members of the audience can accomplish this diet. For instance, we could talk about a more attractive figure to be gained from the diet, or the increased athletic prowess and endurance that could result. In the visualization step, we try to graphically portray the benefits of adopting the recommended solution presented in the satisfaction step.

Step 5: Action. This last part of the motivated sequence usually occurs at the conclusion of most speeches. This step involves a call to action. Up to this point in our example, the speaker has been talking about the need for dieting, how to go about it, and its benefits. In this step, the speaker tells the audience to do it. This is a quite stimulative part of the speech in which the speaker is trying to "jack the audience up" and get them to go out and do what has been recommended.

Monroe's motivated sequence is based on sound psychological principles, and the overall pattern he follows is that of presenting a need followed by satisfaction of that need. As a pattern for organizing a speech, we think Monroe's motivated sequence holds up well. This conclusion on our part is confirmed by the still substantial acceptance of Monroe's book in its current edition. This approach to organizing messages is taught in public speaking courses throughout the nation.

Topical pattern This pattern of arrangement is one that absolutely must grow out of the subject matter itself. Whenever a subject can be broken down into familiar topics or subtopics, you can arrange the speech around those topics. For instance, if a person were giving a speech about the energy crisis in America, it would be possible to break it down into topics such as waste, conservation, insulation, exploration, drilling, transportation, refining, sales, and profit. We don't pretend that these topics are necessarily exhaustive of the overall topic, and yet at the same time we hope you can see that it would be possible to talk about the energy crisis in terms of these different topics, with each topic serving as the heading of a section in the speech.

Difficulty pattern This last approach to the organization of a message is based on the complexity of the topic. This organizational pattern also grows out of the topic. Although all of the organizational patterns should be suited to the topic, this organizational pattern, like the previous one, is especially adapted to subject matter. In this organizational pattern, we break down the topic into its components and assess the degree of difficulty of each. The objective in organizing the speech is to begin with the topics that are easiest for the audience to understand and then to build gradually on these topics to the more difficult topics. If you stop to think about it, the classroom is a good example of this organizational sequence. If you take a course in statistics, the professor will begin the course by presenting the concepts that are the simplest and with which the students are most familiar. Gradually, the professor will proceed to the more difficult topics. If we were to present a speech on the benefits of solar power, it would be especially advantageous to use this organizational pattern, since this topic is somewhat complex. Using examples, we could begin with the basic principles of solar heating, and we could then work up to more complicated heating systems such as those used in apartment buildings and office complexes.

As you can see, the public communication context permits a wide variety of organizational patterns in a message and thus also permits varied evolutionary phases. Although a speech will follow the overall general pattern of initiation, operation, and termination, it can vary somewhat, depending on the specific organizational pattern selected for the message. This pattern, in turn, grows out of the topic and the occasion.

As you can see, the public communication context shares much in common with other human communication systems. The particular context alters to some extent the evolutionary phases, and there are differences in structure from context to context. But you may note that the goal of a public communication context is essentially the same as that of any other human communication context. We are still concerned with social influence based upon needs. Because the presentation of the speech brings to life all that we have discussed thus far, we will move now to a consideration of delivery. Keep in mind that delivery interacts with all of the characteristics of the public communication context: structure, function, and evolution.

PRESENTING THE SPEECH

Obviously, a message is not a speech until it is presented, much as a script is not a play until the actors trod the boards and present it to the audience. Since this is the case, delivery and presentation of a speech should not be ignored or considered unimportant. Delivery and presentation can be just as important as organization, reasoning, supporting materials, and the like. Both our nonverbal and verbal behavior in any communication system are of considerable importance in determining the outcome of the interaction. This is certainly true within the public communication context. The way in which credibility and attractiveness are perceived is affected by the way people dress, articulate and pronounce words, and use eye contact, in addition to the words they choose. We don't wish to overemphasize delivery so that it appears as if a glib, attractive person can be successful without attention to the content of a message. However, we have seen many speakers who have been able to make much more out of a message than the content would suggest. Likewise, we have seen speakers who have had very significant, well thought-out content, and who were unable to achieve success because of their method of presentation.

A major question regarding delivery concerns how formal or informal a speaker should be. A second question is: Should a speaker memorize, write out a speech, or speak from outlined notes? These two questions are related. A very formal presentation tends to result from a memorized speech or one that is written down word for word and read. A more informal presentation tends to result from a speech that is outlined with supporting materials on note cards and in which the speaker extemporaneously "speaks around" the notes.

In earlier days, it was the pattern to write out speeches which were either memorized or read verbatim. This pattern has changed in recent years. People want more spontaneity, informality, and naturalness in a presentation, as opposed to a rehearsed, practiced presentation. People prefer public speakers who will speak *with* them rather than perform *for* them. This is not to say that the formal, practiced, memorized speech is totally a thing of the past. Such speeches do occur occasionally, but the more commonly accepted form of public speaking today is the extemporaneous one.

When we use the word "extemporaneous," we should point out that we do not mean "impromptu." There is sometimes confusion between these two terms. An *impromptu* public speech is one in which speakers have had no forewarning that they will be making a presentation, and they are forced to speak to an audience without any prior preparation. An *extemporaneous* speech, on the other hand, is one that has been planned, researched, and structured but is not written out word for word. This kind of speech is usually outlined, and the only material that is written out word for word is the supporting material or evidence. The speaker speaks around the outline. This kind of speech may be rehearsed in advance so that the speaker can practice wording and yet, at the same time, the wording can be different, depending on the audience and the situation at any given moment.

One advantage of the extemporaneous speech over the manuscript (written) or memorized speech is the informality and spontaneity that usually result from this approach. In addition, because the speaker is not locked into specific, preplanned wording, he or she is more likely to adapt to the feedback provided by the audience while presenting the speech. This adaptation to feedback can result in a very intimate relationship between speaker and audience in which the two interact with each other throughout the experience.

We should not overemphasize the relationship of delivery and credibility, but it is an important one that should not be forgotten. First, as we mentioned earlier, this is a formal situation. The way a person dresses should be somewhat formal. The other question regarding delivery that is interesting to us concerns fluency. How fluent should a speaker be? Research indicates that the more conversational we can be in our delivery, the more our message will be accepted.

The more fluent and slick our delivery, the less effective we will be in gaining acceptance of our message (Dietrich, 1946). We suspect that this difference in response to styles of delivery relates to the dimension of credibility discussed earlier, trustworthiness. Very likely, as people perceive an overly enthusiastic, fluent speaker they tend to think of someone who is practiced in putting on an act, much like the used-car salesperson who has the pitch down pat. One of the best examples of this negative response to style is that of Richard Nixon. Nixon was a very highly skilled college debater and subsequently became a very fluent political speaker. Many people do not trust him or feel warmth for him, and we suspect it may have much to do with his very methodical, practiced approach to public speaking. Whenever possible in public speaking, the speaker should probably strive for a conversational delivery that even includes some nonfluencies (although not too many).

Practice

Just as in many sporting activities such as golf or tennis, the more we practice, the more we can perfect skills. Similarly, the more we practice faults, the more ingrained they can become. Practice doesn't always make perfect; sometimes it just makes faulty behavior permanent. The public speaker who does not become aware of how he or she appears to others will have a problem. If possible, every public speaker should practice before a mirror, audio recorder, or a videotape recorder. Find out what nonverbal behaviors you use while speaking so that it will be possible for you to eliminate the objectionable ones instead of practicing them until they become permanent liabilities. If you don't have access to recording equipment, it is an excellent idea to have a very close, very honest friend listen to and watch you while you are practicing a speech. This friend can provide you with honest feedback so that you can work to eliminate problems and to develop your assets. This technique is based on the imitation-reinforcement model we talked about in earlier chapters.

Feedback

As we said, when compared with mass communication, one of the distinguishing characteristics of public communication is that the direct, face-to-face situation permits use of feedback to modify the message while it is being presented. This characteristic suggests that speakers should never allow themselves to ignore the responses of the audience. The primary advantage of presenting a speech live in a public, face-to-face situation is that the speaker has the opportunity to adapt to the audience as the audience is receiving the message. Thus we should pay attention to the way people are sitting, the number of coughs, whether or not people are talking to each other, or whether any are going to sleep. We should take advantage of these observations and modify our message in an attempt to overcome negative responses and to take advantage of positive responses.

In addition to paying attention to feedback from the audience, we should also pay attention to the environment. If the seats are uncomfortable or if the room is hot or cold, we should attempt to make the message shorter or more interesting. Or it may even be desirable to move around to maintain attention. Recognize that environmental factors as well as message content factors can

Once you learn the proper way to present a speech, you must practice to improve your skills.

PHOTO BY CAROLE DUGAN

have an adverse effect on the way the message is received. The point of this discussion is that feedback is one characteristic of a public message that distinguishes public communication from mass communication. If we do not take advantage of the feedback provided by an audience, then we might as well write the message out in advance, hand out mimeographed copies of it, and treat it as a mass communication system.

SUMMARY

We hope you can see that the public communication context is not a simple process. We hope also that you have been able to see that public communication plays a major role in our society. It is through public communication that decisions are made and leaders are chosen. We also hope you realize that because of your role as a college student and professional in the future, you may be in public speaking situations quite often. In public communication, many of the concepts discussed earlier in this book come together in a very complex yet satisfying human communication system. The public context makes communication more difficult, but not impossible.

The basic structure of a public communication system includes the speaker, the message, and the audience. We considered the importance of the development of positively perceived credibility for the speaker. We also considered the characteristics of an audience that should be analyzed prior to the presentation of a message.

We have indicated that the basic function of public speeches is that of influencing the members of the audience. We discussed the instrumental types of audience influence that are associated with speeches to inform, speeches to persuade, speeches to stimulate, and the consummatory speeches to entertain. All of these involve influence attempts, although of different types.

We also considered the evolutionary phases through which a public communication system progresses. These basic phases were those of initiation, operation, and termination. In addition, we indicated that there exist several organizational patterns we can use in a speech to move through the evolutionary phases, including the chronological, spatial, causal, priority, need-satisfaction, topical, and difficulty patterns of arrangement.

Finally, we discussed the presentation of the speech, with a consideration of the differences among extemporaneous, impromptu, manuscript, and memorized speeches. The advantages and disadvantages of each were considered, with the suggestion that for most of us, the extemporaneous speech is the most effective in most situations.

We hope this chapter has helped you to better understand the public communication system. With this understanding, along with formal training, you should be able to improve your own effectiveness as a public speaker and audience member.

KEY TERMS AND CONCEPTS

AUDIENCE ANALYSIS
CAUSAL PATTERN
CHRONOLOGICAL PATTERN
DERIVED CREDIBILITY
DIFFICULTY PATTERN
ENTERTAINING SPEECH
ENVIRONMENT
EXTEMPORANEOUS PUBLIC SPEECH
IMPORTANCE OF PUBLIC COMMUNICATION
IMPROMPTU PUBLIC SPEECH
INFORMATIVE SPEECH
INITIAL CREDIBILITY

MEMORIZED PUBLIC SPEECH
MONROE, ALAN
MOTIVATED SEQUENCE
NEED-SATISFACTION PATTERN
PERSUASIVE SPEECH
PRIORITY PATTERN
PUBLIC COMMUNICATION STRUCTURE
RECEIVER-CENTERED APPROACH
SPATIAL ARRANGEMENT
STIMULATIVE SPEECH
TERMINAL CREDIBILITY
TOPICAL PATTERN

SUGGESTED READINGS

Barker, Larry L., *Communication.* Englewood Cliffs, New Jersey: Prentice-Hall, Inc.: 1978. Although this book was not written as a public communication text, it provides an excellent perspective on this communication context. Barker relates the various communication contexts to each other and in so doing, provides greater insight into the public communication context.

Ehninger, Douglas, Alan H. Monroe, and Bruce E. Gronbeck, *Principles and Types of Speech Communication*, 8th ed. Glenview, Illinois: Scott Foresman and Co., 1978. The first edition of this book appeared in 1935. Since then, it has been a dominant force in public communication. The motivated sequence is a major feature of the book. The book is extremely readable and complete.

Ross, Raymond S., *Speech Communication*, 4th ed. Englewood Cliffs, New Jersey: Prentice-Hall, 1977. First appearing in 1965, this book had a major influence in moving the study of public communication toward the research in the behavioral sciences. The book has been widely accepted because of this behavioral orientation, and it continues to be much used. Ross explains the application of empirical research findings to the public communication context in a very clear and understandable manner.

14

Mass Communication

In this chapter, we will be examining the structure, function, and evolution of the mass communication context. The two main categories of mass communication are the print and electronic media. We will examine the media elements and the relationships between those elements. We identify six basic mass communication functions: economic, entertainment, educational, socializing, tranquilizing, and persuasive. Finally, you will be introduced to the way in which newspapers, books, magazines, still and moving pictures, radio, and television evolved historically. This is the last of the major communication contexts and one of the most important in our modern society.

Mass Communication

At first glance, you might assume that what we have called public communication in the last chapter and what we call mass communication in this chapter are very similar. What is the real difference between communicating to the "public" and communicating to the "masses?" Obviously, part of the problem lies in the terms that have traditionally been chosen to refer to these two contexts. The real difference beween public and mass communication lies not in the audience but in the means by which the audience receives the message, which results in delayed feedback. Public communication usually involves a face-to-face message, whereas mass communication requires the use of other channels or media to reach a large audience. We can, therefore, define mass communication as the use of media other than the face-to-face channel to communicate with large numbers of people. This definition excludes media like the telephone, telegraph, personal letter, and memo, which are not face-to-face but are used to influence one or two people rather than mass audiences. We will examine in later sections the similarities and differences among the structure, function, and evolution of mass communication. First, however, we will operationally define mass communication by listing each of the mass media individually.

The two main categories of mass communication are print media and electronic media. Both are characterized by the channel through which the audience receives the message. Print media are produced by mechanical means. They include books, newspapers, magazines, photography, comic books, billboards, handbills, placards, posters, direct mass mailing, consumer packaging, mass produced T-shirts, buttons, and bumper stickers. Electronic media are produced by and received by electronic means. Radio, television, satellite, and cable are often referred to as telecommunication because they travel a distance before reaching the audience. They transmit their signals through the air—a commodity belonging to the public. Other media in this category are phonograph records, videotapes, and audiotapes.

MASS COMMUNICATION STRUCTURE

In this section, we will compare and contrast the structural elements and relationships of mass communication to those that exist in the other communication contexts. The basic structural elements of sender, message, channel, and receiver exist in the mass communication context as they do in the other contexts we have previously discussed. In this context, however, many of the elements differ somewhat from those we have already examined. There are also some important differences in the relationships that exist among the various elements in mass communication. In this section, we will present several mass communication models and theories that attempt to picture and to explain the ramifications of the structural differences found in the mass communication context.

Structural Elements

Sender We begin by examining the mass communication sender. In mass communication, the person (or group) who wishes to send a message and the person (or group) who actually does the sending are often different. These two potential senders are commonly referred to as the source and the encoder. The *source* of a mass communication message is often a business or a concerned group that needs to communicate to a mass audience. Many times these sources do not have the expertise to actually encode and transmit the desired message. They therefore hire trained, professional *encoders*, such as advertising agencies, journalists, public relations or marketing experts, and broadcasters. In the mass media, it is not as easy to separate the source and the encoder as these definitions might imply. What actually occurs is a kind of nesting of sources and encoders. A reporter who gets a story from a source could be called the encoder of that story, but the editor and copywriter and even the newspaper publisher could also be called encoders. The editor may have given the reporter the story assignment and would therefore be a source. A newspaper columnist who creates and writes a story is both the source and encoder. The source and encoder may be two people or just one person, or there can be several sources and several encoders. It can get rather confusing, but for our purposes it is sufficient to remember that in the mass communication context, the source and encoder do not have to be the same person. This division of the sending element into the two parts of source and encoder is rather unique in human communication. In most of the previous contexts, these processes were combined in one person or group.

Message Like the messages in most of the other contexts we have discussed, messages from the mass media are transient and usually designed for one time consumption. There is, however, considerable message repetition over the mass media. You will often get the same message over several different media channels. You may see a newscast on television or hear it on the radio, get it again the next day in your newspaper, and finally be exposed to it once more in a magazine or book. Even on the same medium there is much repetition. A commercial, for example, will be replayed over and over again. Sometimes you see or hear the same message so often you get sick of it. This repetition is one strategy of mass communication sources. They want you to see and hear the same message so often that you memorize it and, they hope, react positively to it. We're sure all of you have had the experience of finding yourself repeating, singing, or humming a commercial you heard on radio or television.

One of the advantages of mass communication messages for a source is that the cost per receiver is relatively low when compared to other message output forms. It would take much more time and effort to reach as many people as quickly through any of the previous contexts we have mentioned, including public communication. The distances covered by the mass media are also an important factor. Mass communication reaches almost every corner of the globe. Many authors have remarked that the media's worldwide distribution is making the world smaller psychologically. People all over the globe are becoming more and more informed about and involved with one another. This "global reach" can have both good and bad consequences.

Channel The channel is a unique characteristic of mass communication. McLuhan (1967), a mass communication theorist, suggests that the "medium is the message." By this statement he means that the channel used to transmit a message has a profound influence on how the message is perceived by the audience. If you see or hear the "same" message presented face-to-face, on the

Mass Communication

radio, over television, via a newspaper, or by any other medium, you will actually perceive the message differently in each case.

Using a continuum, McLuhan differentiates among the various message channels. On one end of the continuum are what he calls the *hot* media and on the other end are what he calls the *cool* media. Various mass communication media are placed along this continuum, depending on the amount of receiver participation and involvement. A hot medium requires much receiver involvement, whereas a cool medium does not. He classifies the print media as generally on the hot end of the continuum and electronic media on the cool end. According to McLuhan, people receive information from the print channels in a linear or one-word-at-a-time sequence, but they receive "all-at-once" messages from the electronic channels. With a hot medium, the receiver must supply many of the details to fill in the gaps, but with a cool medium, all of the receiver's senses are involved all of the time and the receiver needs to supply little information. McLuhan suggests that children who have grown up in the electronic media age have been reshaped and therefore make different demands on their mass communication channels than adults who grew up primarily with the print medium. Electronic-age children demand channels that supply information all-at-once and not one-word-at-a-time. Whether you agree with McLuhan's hot and cool continuum, or not (and there is much debate as to its premises and conclusions), there are few who question his basic belief in the importance of the channel as a vital element in communication structure.

What basic structural elements of mass communication do you notice in this scene?
PHOTO BY CAROLE DUGAN

Receiver The receivers, or audience, for mass communication are potentially in the billions. One single television program or commercial can reach over 75 million households at one time. The average household family watches television an estimated 6 1/2 hours per day. Because of this large audience size, the receivers are a fairly undifferentiated, heterogeneous group. They are of all ages, races, religions, educational levels, and socioeconomic classes—particularly television and newspaper audiences. Some of the other media such as certain magazines and radio stations attempt to appeal to a more select or homogeneous audience. A country and western radio station or *Playboy* magazine would be examples of a medium's attempt to appeal to a more select audience. Even so-called select audiences are still rather diverse. Therefore, in these cases, the sender must adapt the language and reasoning level to reach a majority of the audience. The language and reasoning level turn out to be rather low. The average television language level, for example, is appropriate for an 11-year-old child.

Receivers of mass communication have the potential to filter and select what they will hear and see over the mass media. As a matter of fact, it is easier for the mass communication receiver to be selective than it is for someone in a face-to-face interaction context. The receiver of mass communication simply has to change the dial or decide not to purchase some printed material. In the public communication context, we often are hesitant to leave the room in which a speech is being delivered, but in the mass communication context, we do not hesitate to turn off our TV set. This selection potential gives the receiver considerable power. It forces senders to develop messages that they think the audience wants to receive. William Paley, longtime chairman of CBS, insists that "in this business, at least, one always has to remember that he is not scheduling a network to please himself; he has to do it in order to please his audience" (1979). Professionals in the print media like to think they are better than the electronic media in this regard. Columnist Russell Baker suggests that "the difference is that people in the newspaper industry tend to blame themselves for the low-quality stuff while TV executives tend to shift the blame to their audiences" (Paley, 1979). This statement is not completely true. We often see sensationalized headlines and stories in the newspapers and magazines designed to attract an audience at any cost. What we get throughout mass communication sources is what we, the audience, are willing to buy. We can blame ourselves as much as anyone else for the quality of the messages we receive via mass communication.

Gatekeeper There are two structural elements that are somewhat unique to mass communication. The first of these is the gatekeeper. A gatekeeper is any person (or group) who has the power to filter or distort the mass communication message that finally reaches the receiver. The gatekeeper serves a function in mass communication similar to that discussed in the chapter on organizational communication. All mass communication messages go through several "gates" where they can be altered or stopped. Two potential determiners of what we see and hear are the source and encoder of the message. Either of these senders can filter or manipulate the message. A gatekeeper, however, is somewhat different. A gatekeeper alters or stops the message after the source has requested its creation and after the encoder has created it. If either of these people came back into the process at that stage, that person could also be called a gatekeeper. For example, if the encoder shows the message to the source before it is transmitted, the source could act as a gatekeeper. The more common types of gatekeepers in the mass media are editors, proofreaders, station owners, programmers, reviewers, magazine distributors, government agencies, and newscasters such as Dan Rather and Jessica Savitch. These are the people who decide not only what you will receive over the media but how and when you will receive it. In most cases, the gatekeeper is neither a source nor an encoder. Rather, the gatekeeper comes between the sender and the receiver in the mass communication chain. The gatekeeper is a very important element in the mass communication process.

Opinion leader The last but not least important element in the mass communication context is the opinion leader. An opinion leader is a person who has the ability to influence what the receiver thinks relative to what he or she receives through mass communication. The opinion leader is known by the receiver, whereas many gatekeepers are not known. The opinion leader does not usually control what, when, and how the receiver will obtain the mass communication message but does help control what the effect of the message will be on the receiver. Opinion leaders are similar to high-status persons in small groups and organizations with whom others check before they make a decision or take an action. Research on the characteristics of opinion leaders reveals that they have greater exposure to the mass media, have greater social participation, have higher social status, are more innovative, and are generally more modern than their counterparts—opinion followers (Rogers, 1971).

Before any mass communication message can have a significant effect on opinion followers, it must be endorsed by an opinion leader. The followers will withhold their opinions and decisions until they can check their potential behavior with someone whose opinion and decisions they respect. This fact suggests that the mass media's persuasive effect is in part controlled by opinion leaders. We will return to a discussion of this hypothesis later.

Relationships Among the Elements

Now that we have examined the basic nature of the mass communication elements, we will discuss how these elements are related to one another. We have already implied some of these relationships. We said that a source feels a need to communicate through the mass media. The source either encodes the message personally or recruits a professional media encoder to prepare the message. At this point, the source and/or encoder select a mass media channel. Gatekeepers can enter the process as the message is being transmitted or after it has been transmitted, but, in either case, before it reaches the receiver. Once the message has been sent, it can be rejected or filtered by the receiver, acted upon directly, or discussed with an opinion leader prior to accepting, rejecting, or filtering it. The one basic relationship we have not yet mentioned is that between the receiver and the sender—the relationship we have previously referred to as feedback. We will discuss this relationship immediately and then present several models that have been developed to picture and explain in more detail some of the mass communication relationships.

Feedback The nature of the feedback that occurs in mass communication is very different from the nature of the feedback that occurs in the other contexts we have examined. In a face-to-face communication situation, the sender can immediately and directly evaluate the receiver's response to the message. Senders can even alter a message as it is being presented in order to better adapt it to the receiver(s). The information that is fed back to a mass media source is much less immediate and direct. In fact, mass communication sources have considerable trouble in getting honest, factual feedback from their audience. Hiebert, Ungurait, and Bohn (1974) suggest six characteristics of mass communication feedback that make it different from feedback in the face-to-face contexts. They suggest that mass communication feedback is (1) representative, (2) indirect, (3) delayed, (4) cumulative, (5) institutionalized, and (6) quantitative.

By *representative*, they mean that the feedback received by mass communication senders reflects the direct opinions of a representative sample of all the receivers. Very often, mass media senders hire agencies like the A.C. Nielsen Company to sample the total audience. Other media use unsolicited telephone calls and letters from viewers as a form of feedback, assuming that, in general, they may be representative of all receivers. All of these forms of feedback are *indirect*; that is, the feedback does not go directly from the receiver to the source but goes through an agency, editor, secretary, or some similar third party.

Because of the nature and form of mass communication feedback, it is almost always *delayed*. It takes time for people to write letters or for agencies to conduct polls and surveys. Mass communication feedback is almost always too late to affect the transmission of a single message, although it can often change future messages on the same topic. The *cumulative* nature of the feedback reflects this aspect of delay. Mass media senders usually use the feedback that has resulted from several similar messages rather than the feedback from any one single message in order to make their long-range decisions.

The feedback is *institutionalized* insofar as it is collected by formal institutions such as the A.C. Nielsen, Pulse, American Research Bureau, Trendex, Hooper, Gallup, Roper, and Harris companies. The feedback often lacks the emotional and spontaneous flavor of face-to-face feedback. Finally, the feedback is *quantitative* and not necessarily qualitative. All that most sources and encoders and, for that matter, even gatekeepers usually see is a set of figures representing how various percentages of the receivers felt about the message.

In summary, then, we can say that the feedback relationship for mass communication is rather poor as compared with the other contexts. Even though the receivers of the media have considerable power, it takes much time for the feedback to get to the people who can do what the audience wants them to do.

Relationship Models

There have been many models developed to picture and present various aspects of the relationships existing between the mass communication elements. We will focus on only a few of the more important ones in this section. They include one-step flow models, the Shannon-Weaver Model, the DeFleur Model, the two-step flow model, the Westley-MacLean Model, and multi-step flow models. Finally, we will discuss a model we have developed that we think combines the best features of all of the other models. We present all of these models because we think each has something to add to our understanding of communication in the mass context.

One-step flow models The one-step flow models represent some of the very first attempts to understand the relationships among the structural elements in the mass communication context. Perhaps the earliest of these attempts is the *hypodermic needle model* (Fig. 14.1). This model suggests that the various mass communication media affect the receivers in a very direct, immediate, and powerful manner. Early theorists felt that mass communication is similar to dyadic communication but perhaps has even a greater effect since the receivers have little or no chance to question or refute the sender. The model pictures the mass media as similar to a large hypodermic needle that plunges all forms of messages directly into a passive, nonresistant audience. The media are seen as having an all-powerful or omnipotent influence on human behavior. In some respects, this model may be correct. There are probably some people in the mass audience who do accept without question most or all of the messages that come to them through the mass media. For the most part, however, we believe this model is greatly exaggerated.

Fig. 14.1 Hypodermic needle model.

A modified form of the hypodermic needle model is based on data regarding the effects of mass communication on receivers. It is simply called the *one-step flow model*. It differs from the hypodermic needle model only in that the audience is credited with a much more active role in the mass communication process. This model still does not recognize the existence of gatekeepers or opinion leaders, and it does not provide for feedback. But it does recognize that the media are not all-powerful. It gives the audience credit for having some choice in what they will accept or reject. It states that different receivers will be affected differently by what is transmitted through the media. Although it is not explicitly stated, this model begins to imply that such factors as the amount of media exposure, the nature of the channel and of the message, and many others can act to modify the effect of the media.

The one-step flow models seem to explain the effects of the mass media as "awareness-creating" or "knowledge-getting" channels. We do seem to get much of our information or knowledge about objects and events in our environment from mass communication. The media are often our first source of such information. This information is, in fact, an immediate and direct effect of the mass media. However, this effect does not imply that we believe or accept these messages or use them as the basis for forming our opinions or determining our behavior. As we will see in later models, there seem to be other factors that enter in before we act on the information we receive from mass communication.

The Shannon-Weaver model The Shannon-Weaver (1963) model was originally designed for the Bell Telephone Company to help them explain and understand the mechanical and electronic transmission of messages. It has come to be used, however, to help understand all forms of mediated communication, or communication in which the channel is not face-to-face. As you can see in Fig. 14.2, much of the same type of thinking that went into the one-step flow models also appears in the Shannon-Weaver model. This model closely resembles the linear models discussed in Chapter 2. The transmission of the message from the sender to the receiver is pictured as a one-way or linear process, with little or no feedback. It does, however, split up the sender into two separate elements: an information source and a transmitter. More recently, the term encoder has come to be used instead of transmitter and implies more than simply the transmission function. This model also suggests the idea of including a destination as well as a receiver. Along with the transmitter element, the model further suggests the idea of gatekeepers and opinion leaders as part of the mediated communication process. However, Shannon and Weaver do not develop these concepts in their model. The final and perhaps most important aspect of this model is the noise source. Noise refers to any form of interference that can affect the message. Shannon and Weaver discuss noise as static and as irrelevant sounds that can affect message transmission. It would not be totally incorrect, however, to think of noise as also referring to the effects of the medium itself, as was suggested by McLuhan. The authors of the model do not think of it in that way, but that does not mean it does not apply. This model was the main source for the DeFleur model.

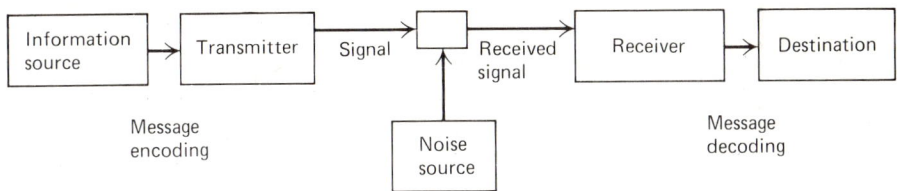

Fig. 14.2 Shannon-Weaver model.
From Claude E. Shannon and Warren Weaver, *The Mathematical Theory of Communication* (Urbana, Ill.: University of Illinois Press, © 1949, 1977). Reprinted by permission.

The DeFleur model One of the most profound theorists of mass communication is DeFleur (1970). In his classic text, *Theories of Mass Communication*, DeFleur presents the model illustrated in Fig. 14.3. The model comes directly from the one developed by Shannon and Weaver, but several features are added that make it important. First, the model introduces a feedback link between the sender and the receiver. Not only is feedback added, but it has built within it the recognition that some device is needed for feedback in mass communication. This recognition of the need for a feedback device springs from an

Mass Communication

awareness of the indirect nature of feedback to the mass media sender. The feedback device can take the form of ratings, letters, telephone calls, responses from professional critics, and the like, but in almost all cases the feedback is mediated in some way. Further, the model recognizes the existence of gates in the feedback mechanism as well as in the transmission mechanism.

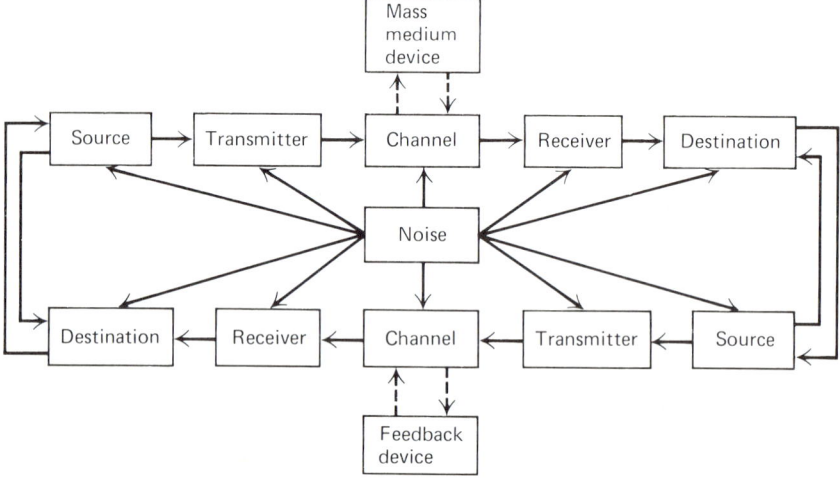

Fig. 14.3 DeFleur model.

From *Theories of Mass Communication*, 3rd ed. by Melvin L. DeFleur and Sandra Ball-Rokeach. Copyright © 1966, 1970, and 1975 by Longman Inc. Reprinted by permission of Longman Inc., New York.

The second major addition to our understanding of mass communication provided by the DeFleur model is the concept that noise can enter into the mass communication context, as it can into any other context, not only through the channel but also through all of the other elements of the mass communication structure. Finally, this model puts some direct emphasis on the medium itself. This emphasis suggests the importance of the medium chosen for message transmission. The DeFleur model leaves out much for our complete understanding of mass communication, but as you will see later, it also includes much that later models leave out.

Two-step flow model The two-step flow model developed out of a classic study of the 1940 presidential election by Lazarsfeld (1944). He and his colleagues found, to their surprise, that few voting choices were directly influenced by the mass media. They found that messages often flowed from the mass communication source to opinion leaders and then from the opinion leaders to the rest of the mass audience. The term "two-step flow" comes from this message movement from the source to the opinion leader (step one) and from the opinion leader to the followers (step two). It was later found that this model explained receiver behavior in many situations, especially when messages included a persuasive element. Step two seemed to be the important step in regard to receiver influence. This model was the first to indicate that there is a direct relationship between mass and face-to-face channels of communication.

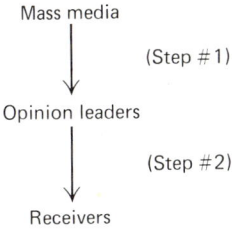

Fig. 14.4 The two-step flow model.

As important as the two-step flow model is, it has some severe limitations. Rogers (1971) lists five of the most important limitations. First, the model suggests that only opinion leaders are active information seekers, while the rest of the mass audience is passive. As we said in discussing the one-step flow models, the audience does not seem to be that passive, whether or not they are opinion leaders. Both groups have the capability of being either active or passive receivers. Sometimes receivers seek out opinion leaders, and sometimes the reverse occurs. Second, the model suggests that the whole process involves two—and only two—steps. As we have demonstrated earlier, in some situations the process involves only one step and in other situations it may involve more than two steps. Third, the two-step flow model implies that opinion leaders get most or all of their information and form their opinions from the mass media alone. The truth of the matter seems to be that opinion leaders as well as receivers of all kinds get messages from many channels as well as from their own perceptions of the environment. Fourth, the model makes no differentiation as to channel operation based on the evolutionary phase of the mass communication process. The evidence suggests that different channels play different roles at different times. This differing channel usage occurs for both opinion leaders and the mass audience of followers. Finally, the two-step flow model implies that all members of the mass communication audience can be divided into opinion leaders and opinion followers and further, that all opinion followers depend on an opinion leader. Actually, the process does not appear to be that simple. Some people are opinion leaders for a very narrow range of topics and not for others. Also, some nonleaders are not followers; they make up their own minds directly but are not opinion leaders for others and do not follow the opinions of others.

In spite of its limitations, the two-step flow model is very important. It just does not go far enough. It does, however, make explicit the role of opinion leaders. Moreover, it paved the way for the more detailed models that follow, such as the Westley-MacLean and multi-step flow models.

The Westley-MacLean model The Westley-MacLean (1957) model, pictured in Fig. 14.5, is probably the most widely known of all mass communication models. It grows directly out of the two-step flow model. There are three persons or groups represented in this model: A represents the sender (both the source and encoder), B represents the receiver or final destination for the mass message, and C represents either a gatekeeper or opinion leader who comes between the sender and the receiver. The Xs on the far left signify objects or events in the environment that are capable of being perceived by the various elements in the model. X′ is a message that A transmits to C about events as A perceives them in the environment. X″ is a message that C transmits to B about events as C personally perceives them in the environment—perceptions that C receives from A about the events and objects in the environment. The dotted lines going from right to left represent feedback from B to A (f_{BA}), from B to C (f_{BC}), or from C to A (f_{CA}).

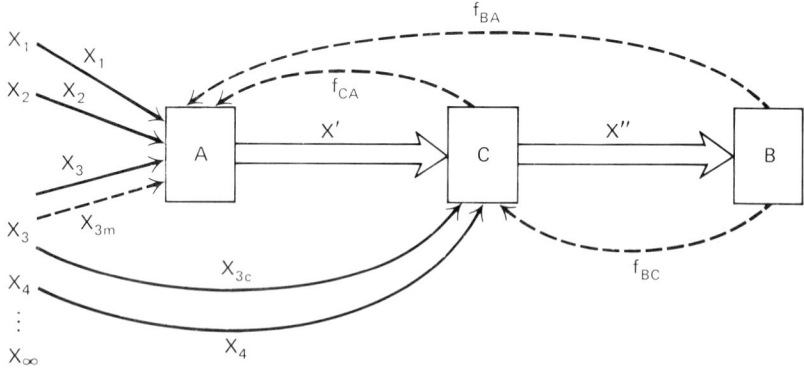

Fig. 14.5 The Westley-MacLean model.

From Bruce Westley and Malcolm S. MacLean, Jr. "A Conceptual Model for Communication Research," *Journalism Quarterly* 34 (1957): 31-38. Reprinted by permission.

This model incorporates many of the ideas presented thus far, such as the opinion leader and gatekeeper roles, the various aspects of feedback that can occur in mass communication, and the direct perception of the environment by both A and C. The major drawback of the Westley-MacLean model is that it places the receiver in entirely too passive a role. The receiver (B) may also directly perceive the objects and events in the environment. As we saw in the one-step flow model, it is also possible for the mass media (A) to send a message directly to the receiver (B) without the use of a middle element (C).

The models we have reviewed thus far have been on either one extreme or the other in that they have made the receiver almost entirely passive or they have made the receiver almost omnipotent. The evidence suggests that the receiver can be either or neither of these and that receivers change depending on the message type, the channel used, the nature of the source, the presence or absence of opinion leaders and gatekeepers, and other factors. This model is important, however, because of its historical influence on our understanding of the structure of mass communication and because of the added dimensions it brings to the structural relationships of mass communication elements. In this model, we begin to visualize for the first time how complex the mass communication context really is when both the mediated and face-to-face aspects of the process are included. The following multi-step flow models and the model we develop to explain mass communication structure are elaborations of the Westley-MacLean Model.

Multi-step flow models The original notion of a multi-step flow model came from Rogers. He did not diagram such a model, but he described it in the following statement:

> The multi-step model is based on a sequential relaying function that seems to occur in most communication situations. It does not call for any particular number of steps nor does it specify that the message must emanate from a source by mass media channels. This model suggests that there are a variable number of relays in the communication flow from a source to a large audience. Some members will obtain the message directly through channels from the source, while others may be several times removed from the message origin. The exact number of steps in this process depends on the intent of the source, the availability of mass media and the extent of audience exposure, the nature of the message, and salience of the message to the receiving audience.
>
> (Rogers, 1971, p. 209)

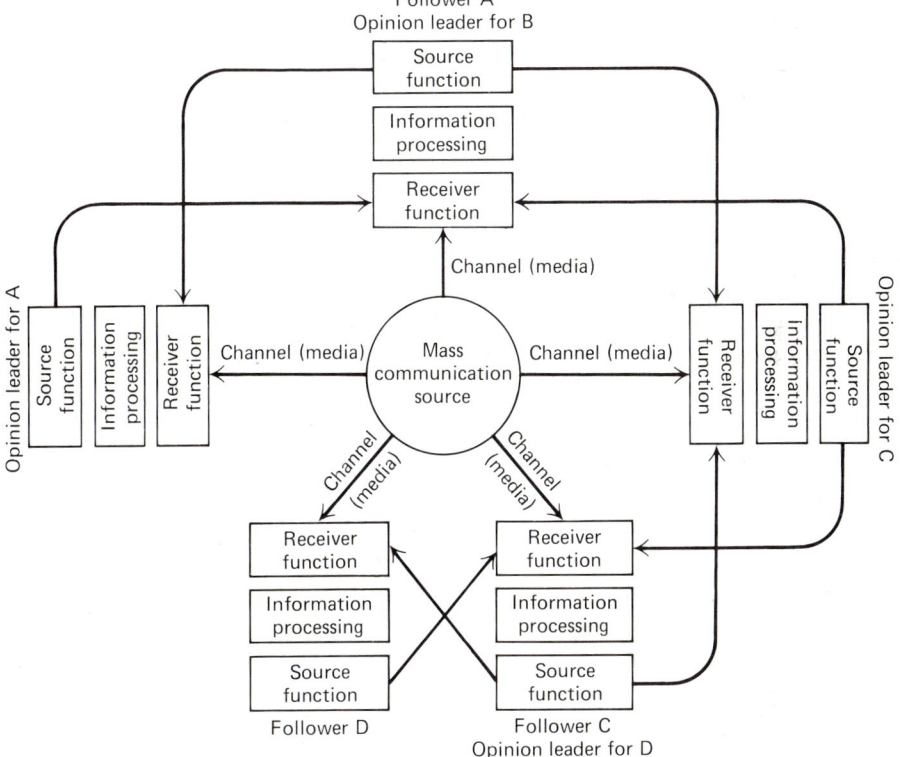

Fig. 14.6 Multi-cycle, multi-step flow model.

From James C. McCroskey and Lawrence R. Wheeless, *Introduction to Human Communication*. Copyright © 1976 by Allyn and Bacon, Inc., Boston. Reprinted with permission.

Mass Communication

McCroskey and Wheeless (1976) present a pictorial representation of the Rogers concept, with certain modifications of their own. They call their model (see Fig. 14.6) a *multi-cycle, multi-step flow model*. As you can see, it locates the mass communication source at the very hub of the model. Messages go out from the mass communication source to opinion leaders and followers alike. The model pictures the interaction beween opinion leaders and followers as two-way, with messages and feedback going in both directions. The greatest contribution of this model is that it shows how a single person can be a follower and/or an opinion leader, depending on the various factors mentioned above by Rogers. These roles are constantly changing for most of us all of the time. What this model leaves out is any feedback between the opinion leaders or followers and the mass communication source. The McCroskey-Wheeless multi-cycle, multi-step flow model is, however, one of the more sophisticated representations of mass communication structure yet developed. In the following section, we will enlarge on this model by adding some of the details noted in other models in order to make it as complete as possible, given our current understanding of the mass communication context.

A synthesis model We call the model that you see illustrated in Fig. 14.7 a synthesis model because we have tried to incorporate what we believe to be the most significant aspects of all the models we have presented. This synthesis model may at first look somewhat complicated, but that feature is unavoidable when explaining a complicated set of structural interrelationships.

As you can see, the basic form of the model follows the McCroskey-Wheeless model, with the substitution of our own triangular representation of the people involved. We have also added a gatekeeper element to the representation of the mass communication source. This element comes from the encoder/transmitter concept found in the Shannon-Weaver and DeFleur models. It is important for you to realize that mass communication sources have gatekeepers as well as receivers. This gatekeeper element is also meant to imply the feedback devices or mediated feedback that exist for mass communication sources. You will notice that follower D and follower C are indicated as both receiving information from and feeding back information to the mass communication source through the gatekeeper. The other persons involved in the process are not pictured as providing such feedback because in the mass communication context only a few receivers either attempt to or are given the opportunity to feedback messages to the mass communication source. For many of the receivers, the message flow is only one-way. We have also added the concept of noise to our model, in keeping with the ideas presented by Shannon, Weaver, and DeFleur. Finally, we added several Xs to our model to represent objects and events in the environment, in the same fashion as they are used in the Westley-MacLean model. However, we have represented the followers, as well as the opinion leaders and senders, as capable of perceiving the objects and events in the environment. This aspect of the model does not mean that followers will always have those perceptions, but that they have the capacity to do so.

We do not suggest that this model is complete; however, it represents an attempt to pictorially represent the elements and the relationships between the elements in the mass communication context as we currently understand them. We feel this model incorporates the best of the ideas presented by the other models we have discussed. It should also provide you with an overall perspective with which to understand the function and evolution of mass communication.

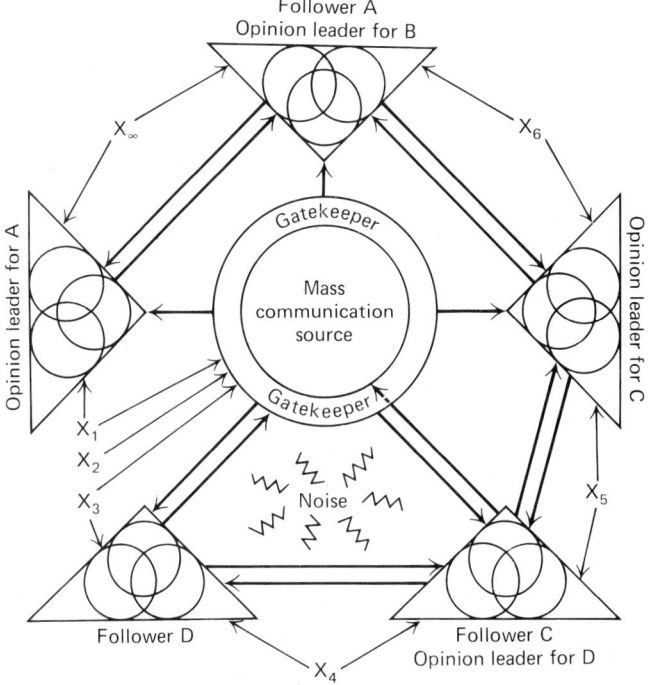

Fig. 14.7 A synthesis model of mass communication.

MASS COMMUNICATION FUNCTIONS

In this section, we will consider the functions, or purposes, of mass communication. As we examine each of the functions of mass communication, there are several things you must keep in mind. First, few of the media attempt to serve only one function. Each tries to serve several functions, and sometimes the various functions overlap. For example, an advertisement that is designed to persuade an audience to buy a product may also provide humor that is designed to entertain the audience. Obviously, the advertiser thinks that humor will increase the effectiveness of the persuasive message. Nevertheless, two of the basic functions of the media are being served at the same time. It is hard to analyze any single media message and say that it is serving one function alone, even though the functions we will present in this chapter represent broad categories of purpose.

The second thing to remember while you read this section is that all of these functions are not necessarily of equal importance. As you will see much more clearly in our section on the evolution of mass communication, the main functions of the mass media have changed over time. Even now, there is confusion and debate over what should be the main function or functions of mass communication.

Finally, as you read this section you should remember that the receivers of mass communication give it their attention for a variety of reasons. The same receiver may watch television at one time to be informed, at another time to be entertained, and at still another time to be persuaded. When you multiply these changing needs by the over 200 million people in the United States alone, you can see how many functions are demanded of the media by the mass audience. As you will see from our list of mass communication functions, the audience is often not even aware of some of the effects the media are having on them. The audience also may not be consciously aware of some of their own needs that the media are satisfying. If you keep these three factors in mind as you read this section, you will understand the functions of mass communication much better. Our list of mass communication functions includes the following: an economic function, an entertainment function, an educational function, a socializing function, a tranquilizing function, and a persuasive function. In the following paragraphs, we will discuss and interrelate each of these various functions of mass communication.

The Economic Function

It might seem strange to you to discuss the economic function of mass communication first. The fact is, however, that none of the other media functions are as important to senders as the economic function. Critics of the media may attack it for not paying enough attention to some of its other functions, but they are just kidding themselves if they believe that any other function will mean as much to mass media producers as money. We must remember that first and foremost, mass communication is a business, and as in any other business, the people in it attempt to maximize financial rewards and to minimize the costs. The only media that are relatively free of this basic function are those media that are subsidized in some way, usually by the federal government. Examples of such media are public broadcast television and radio stations in this country. In many other countries, most notably England, more of the media are subsidized and controlled by the government. In this country, we have steered away from such governmental control, both financial and otherwise, in the belief that the media must be free to print and broadcast the news as they see fit. Hence, we have left control of the media in the hands of private individuals and groups who must in turn finance their operation on their own. Thus the economic function becomes of primary concern. The media cannot perform any of their other functions if they are out of business.

The economic function goes far beyond keeping the media running and making a profit. The media play an important role in the economic health of our nation and of its local communities as well. The materials essential to produce mass communication messages, such as paper, machines (both mechanical and electronic), chemicals, dyes, wires, tubes, and so on, as well as the people necessary to provide these materials and use them represent a significant aspect of our economy. Mass communication is as important to our economy as the automobile industry or any other major industry.

Finally, mass communication serves the economic function of offering a showcase for the goods and services produced. It allows buyers and sellers to get together. This function is achieved primarily through advertising. Advertising is the most efficient way of finding out what goods are available, where they can be found, and the prices at which they are available. The advertisers pay enough to allow the mass media to provide other types of information to you, such as notices for meetings, news reports, and much additional information for which there is no charge. We are not suggesting that you should not get a little upset when you see a half dozen commercials in a row or when you read of the large profits and salaries available to those in the media, but do not ever assume that the economic function is necessarily bad or unneeded. It is one of the most crucial, if not the most crucial, of mass communication functions.

The Entertainment Function

In great part because of the importance of the economic function of the mass media, probably the second most important function is entertainment. As Pember (1974, p. 36) puts it, "Entertainment is the shill that brings the crowds to the media pitchmen." Most of us think of the electronic media when we think of entertainment, but this function continues to have real importance for the print media as well. How much actual "news" do you find in your local newspaper? There are large sections devoted to comics, sports, movies, restaurants, cooking, and so on, all of which could be considered entertainment. Many magazines are totally devoted to entertainment activities such as sports, decorating, movie and TV gossip, and crossword puzzles. Even with all of these entertainment functions in the print media, however, the electronic media have become our greatest source of mass communication entertainment, as you will see in the section on mass communication evolution.

The Educational Function

The success of mass communication in fulfilling its educational function depends on how we define the word "education." If we think of education as simply the formal process we normally find in a classroom, we can say that the mass media have done very poorly in fulfilling their educational function. This is particularly true of the electronic media. Television especially has the potential to make all of our homes into classrooms, but very little of this potential has been achieved. The success that has been realized has primarily occurred over public television. People in commercial television have not attempted to fulfill this function, in fear that such attempts will cause them to lose a large part of their audience and therefore a large part of their profits. There are indications that this situation may change somewhat with the rapid growth of cable television, which is attempting to attract more select audiences for its programming. We will have to wait to see if formal educational programming draws enough of an audience to make it a regular part of cable television.

On the other hand, if we define education as the informal process of acquiring and imparting general knowledge, we arrive at a totally different conclusion as to how the media are performing this function. The media are constantly imparting knowledge of all sorts to their audiences. They impart product knowledge, news knowledge, scientific knowledge, stock market knowledge,

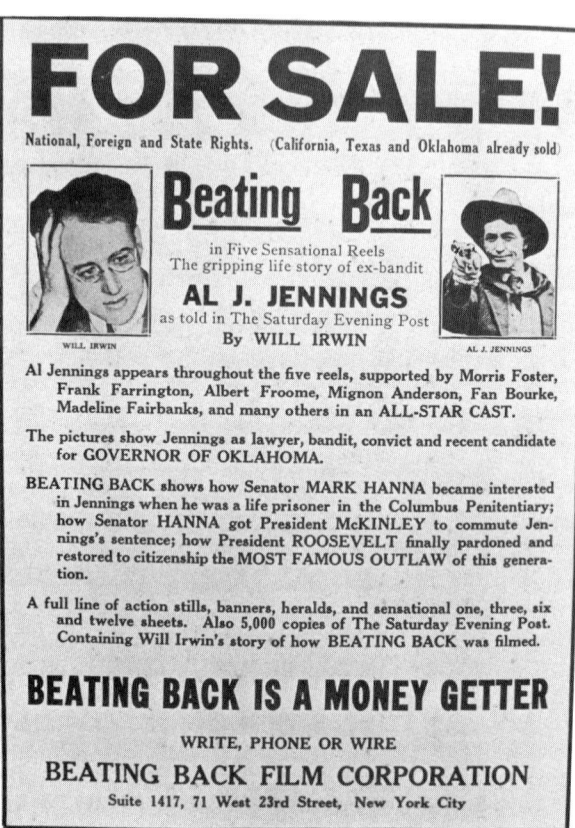

There has always been a strong link between the economic and entertainment functions of mass media.

weather knowledge, and so on. The media have a great ability to focus the attention of the audience on the important problems, persons, and issues in the world around them. As we said in the last section, one of the things that the media do best is to provide information for their audiences. The United Press International (U.P.I.) and Associated Press (A.P.) wire services provide timely and accurate information to both the print and electronic media about people and about events that are happening all over the world. Combine this information with the information gathered by staffs of the local mass media companies, and you have the greatest pool of knowledge available to the public ever created. In terms of informal education, the mass media are performing this function very well. Most people who are out of school, and many who are still in school, for that matter, get much of their education from mass communication. We might also suggest that the public is better informed now than ever before, in great part because of the efforts of the mass media to fulfill their educational function.

The Socializing Function

The socializing function of mass communication implies that the media help to establish and maintain the social norms of our society. We have previously discussed the idea that people learn to live with one another and survive through the process of communication. We said that we learn the norms of our society through imitation and reinforcement by our parents and others around us. Mass communication theorists feel that much of our socializing also comes from the mass media. They believe that the media provide us with the values, opinions, and rules that society has prescribed for its members. This process is usually unspoken; people imitate the people they see, hear, or read about through mass communication and are rewarded for their behavior by society.

The major question regarding the socializing function is whether mass communication has the power to change our cultural norms or whether it can merely reinforce the norms set by society. The current theory suggests that the socialization function is predominately one of reinforcement rather than change.

> **The media can *reinforce* cultural norms, as they do every day, and thus indirectly play a part in shaping conduct along established lines. They can undoubtedly *activate* a considerable amount of behavior, providing it is consistent with the needs of the individual and socially approved within the existing structure of cultural norms. (The classic case here is the Kate Smith marathon radio broadcasts which sold 15 million dollars' worth of war bonds in a single day.) The media can even *create* new norms in areas of behavior which are not currently controlled by strong socio-cultural constraints. It remains much in doubt, however, that the media alone have any effective power to *convert* populations from one form of conduct to another by changing definitions of the situation among the relevant actors. It seems clear, in other words, that the media do not *change* deeply institutionalized norms and thereby significantly alter conduct.**

(DeFleur, 1970, p. 134)

The Tranquilizing Function

We have inserted the notion of tranquilizing function for the mass media because of their ability to make people think that they are directly involved, when in reality they are not. Lazarsfeld and Merton (1971) call this ability *vicarious performance*. People confuse the knowledge they receive about current events with some type of decision or action on their part. This vicarious performance tends to tranquilize receivers and make them apathetic. Sports is another good example of this tranquilizing effect. Many of us sit and watch football, gymnastics, or golf on television rather than participate directly in a sport ourselves. Somehow we are tranquilized into believing that viewing a sport is related to partaking in that sport. Millions of viewers vicariously play football every weekend in the fall. We have become a nation of bystanders, in part because of the effects of mass communication.

There may, however, be some benefits of the tranquilizing function. Many experts believe that one of the values of violent programs on television is that these programs allow viewers to release their frustrations vicariously rather than overtly. These experts suggest that we are tranquilized by watching someone else get punched in the mouth, and we no longer yearn to do the punching ourselves. In this same manner, television tranquilizes us by giving us a way to get our minds off our own problems. When we come home, we can sit in front of the television and relax. We can get our minds off our own problems by watching situation comedies. By providing a fantasy world for us to get lost in, many of the mass media allow us to relax and "turn off our minds." There is little doubt that many of us use the entertainment supplied by mass communication for this very purpose. And for this purpose, much of what is presented on television, at least, is ideally suited. You certainly don't have to think in order to watch many of the programs presented over commercial television.

The Persuasive Function

As several of the models we presented earlier suggest, the intervening variable or element in the persuasive function for the mass media seems to be the opinion leader, although there are some situations in which the media do have a direct and immediate persuasive effect on the audience. The mass media may directly persuade us to choose a particular brand of cheese or a particular deodorant, but they seldom persuade us to vote for a candidate or to make a major financial investment. In these cases, the media provide us with appropriate information, but our opinion leaders supply the real influence or persuasion.

There is one group of communication scholars interested in the way the mass communication media combine with face-to-face communication to create persuasive effects on the mass audience. They refer to their area of specialization as the *diffusion of innovations*, which they describe as a "special" type of communication. The main concern of scholars of innovation diffusion is "to explore how social systems are changed through the diffusion of new ideas" (Rogers, 1971, p. 1).

By examining many successful innovation diffusion efforts, these scholars have determined that there are four basic stages or phases that need to occur before an innovation will be adopted. These four phases are the knowledge, persuasion, decision, and confirmation phases.

The *knowledge phase* includes the initial exposure to the innovation and the gaining of some understanding of how the innovation operates. It is at this stage that mass communication plays its most important role. This phase is closely aligned to the educational function discussed earlier.

The *persuasion phase* occurs when the potential adopter forms either a favorable or unfavorable attitude toward the innovation. Part of this persuasion may come from the mass media, as we pointed out in the one-step model, but it is more likely that much of the persuasion will occur because of the efforts of opinion leaders and change agents. The only difference between an opinion leader and a change agent is that the latter is a professional persuader while the former is not necessarily paid to produce changes in the audience.

The *decision phase* occurs when one (or more) receiver(s) initiates behaviors that lead to adoption or rejection of the innovation. In the persuasion phase attitudes are changed, but in the decision phase actual behaviors must occur. The receiver buys the microwave oven, tries the new method of farming, practices birth control, teaches his or her students in the new manner, tells the contractor that a new house must face south, or initiates any number of other possible innovative behaviors.

The *confirmation phase* occurs when the adopter seeks reinforcement for the innovation that he or she has adopted. If you have just purchased a new trash compactor, you seek out people to confirm that you have made a wise decision. If you do not find such confirmation, you may return the product and thus reject the innovation. In the same way, if you have considered solar hot water heating but have decided not to install such a system, you may seek out others who will suggest that the costs are still too high. These people will thus confirm your decision to reject the innovation at this time. Like the persuasion and decision phases, the confirmation phase relies heavily on interpersonal persuasion.

In summarizing the persuasive values of mass media channels versus interpersonal channels, Rogers (1971) suggests the following as the main advantages of mass media:

1. They can reach a large audience rapidly.
2. They can create knowledge and spread information.
3. They can lead to changes in weakly held attitudes.

Rogers also suggests the following advantages of interpersonal channels, which best accomplish the formation and change of strongly held attitudes:

1. They can allow a two-way exchange of ideas. The receiver may secure clarification or additional information about the innovation from the source individual. This characteristic of interpersonal channels sometimes allows them to overcome the social and psychological barriers of selective exposure, perception, and retention.
2. They can persuade receiving individuals to form or change strongly held attitudes. (Rogers, 1971, pp. 252-253)

This, then, concludes our discussion of the six basic functions of mass communication. To summarize, the mass media perform economic, entertainment, educational, socializing, tranquilizing, and persuasive functions. Some of these functions are done better than others, but in one way or another they are all performed by mass communication, as you will see in the following section.

MASS COMMUNICATION EVOLUTION

Because of the diverse nature of the various mass communication media and their many different characteristics, we have chosen to approach mass communication evolution somewhat differently from the way in which we presented the evolution of other communication contexts. There are no real stages or phases of evolution that characterize communication in the mass context, as there are in the other contexts. We feel, instead, that the aspect of mass communication evolution that will be of the most practical interest is a short chronology of how some of the major forms of print and electronic media have developed and evolved (few have terminated). This approach allows us to suggest some of the important forces that have shaped both the structure and function of mass communication into what it is today.

The Print Media

We begin by focusing on the print media primarily because they came into being much earlier than the electronic media. In our history of communication presented in Chapter 1, we discussed the development of writing and the invention of printing. Therefore, we will begin this discussion of the print media at the point at which we left off in Chapter 1. In this section, we will cover the evolution of newspapers, books and magazines, and still and cinema photography.

Newspapers In the initiation stage, newspaper-like publications began with broadsheets (one event, one sheet), diurnals (official news when there was some available), and the coranto (pamphlet) for foreign news dissemination. These were the main mass communication sources for Europeans after Gutenberg invented movable type. They served an educational function. They were not published on a regular basis, primarily because they reported official news and rulers often practiced censorship, not wanting news or comment on public affairs to reach the common people. The first established newspaper, the "Strasborg Relation," appeared in 1609. In 1665, the first full-sized newspaper, the Oxford "Gazette," was founded. It moved to London and primarily reported official notices of the royal court. The "London Gazette" is still performing much the same educational function and is the longest-lived English language newspaper.

In the United States, the pattern was similar. Formal restrictions were placed on the use of the press. The first newspaper published in the colonies, "Publick Occurences Both Forreign and Domestick," was printed in Boston in 1690. One of the greatest inspirational victories for the press against censorship occurred in the 1730s. John Peter Zenger published an antigovernmental newspaper, for which he was arrested and charged with publishing "scandalous, virulent, and seditious reflections upon the government." His lawyer, Andrew Hamilton, appealed directly to the jury and not to the bench, which was made up of hand-picked government officials. He pleaded the right of free men to publish and to speak the truth. This defense, which had failed to succeed in the past, did succeed for the first time in the Zenger case. Even today, the only defense against libel and defamation for all mass media is proof that the published or broadcast message is truthful.

Repression and censorship, prevalent in the early history of newspapers, accounted in great part for the many safeguards regarding the press that were built into the Constitution. The First Amendment prohibits Congress from abridging the freedoms of press and speech. These rights are as jealously guarded today by people in communication as they were when the Constitution was first written. People in the media cannot hope to truly accomplish the media's functions without these guarantees.

Until the 1880s, many newspapers were sold for 6¢, a price out of reach for the average person. In 1833, Benjamin H. Day founded the "New York Sun," a 1¢ paper. He established advertising in the paper and, by using sensationalism, he cornered an audience. At this point, we see the beginning of economic and entertainment functions in newspapers. The rise of the *penny press* brought a whole new concept to newspapers. It gave more attention to news (rather than politics); it was smaller in size; and it had the personal, editorial style of its publisher. Transportation advances like the railroad, pony express, and steamships to Europe decreased the time factor in dissemination of information. Competition for the news market became high and to solve some of the problems, New York's 17 newspapers formed a cooperative to gather and share information. It was and still is called the Associated Press. AP was the first American wire service developed to help accomplish the media's functions. Later, other wire services were added for the same purpose.

Newspapers are put together in what is known as the composing room.
PHOTO BY CAROLE DUGAN

The post-Civil War years brought newspapers out of the initiation stage and into the operation stage. From then until the 1900s, there was a new social climate brought on by large-scale immigration. Technological advancements produced growth in the press and other media—faster presses, telegraph cables, and longer-reaching railroads; the invention of electricity and of telephones; and substantial manufacturing, economic, and educational growth. Newspapers followed the railroads to the West. This climate produced a social conscience and a renewed socializing function in the press. Several publishers represented a "new" journalism with ethics and objectivity.

At the same time, publishers were again wedding the economic and entertainment functions—using entertainment as the shill to bring the crowds to the media pitchman. It was during this time that the term *yellow journalism* came to be used. This term referred to press sensationalism. In the early 1900s, another term cropped up—*jazz journalism*. This was supersensationalism with illustrations and photographs as well as stories. The leader of this field was the "New York Daily News," until it printed a picture of a woman being electrocuted and the public protested. At that point, many of the tabloids switched from sensationalism and turned into very respectable, responsible newspapers.

After World War II, newspaper publication leveled off because of competition, monopolies, standardization, and the use of wire services. At the same time, the *activist press* emerged and attempted to serve a persuasive function. These papers all "had an idea" or an ax to grind that was ignored by the established press. When the idea either died or became popular, the newspaper also died or broadened its scope. The "Boston Guardian," founded in the late 1940s, was the first real activist paper. It was political (leftist) in nature. The "Village Voice" (1955) dealt with social causes. It eventually expanded its views and turned establishment, losing its original readers. "Mohammad Speaks" (1957) was an activist paper in Chicago dealing with minority views. In the late 1950s and early 1960s, there was an explosion of these single-idea, persuasive papers. The premise of all of them was that reporters should have viewpoints and should express them and that the establishment should recognize its dirty linen and air it publicly.

Since World War II, there has been a decline in the metropolitan daily newspapers. The main causes are economics and the population shift from large cities. The biggest potential danger in this decline is a monopolization of the viewpoint that the reader receives. Congress has since passed the Newspaper Preservation Act, enabling papers to compete more economically. They are now exempt from antitrust laws, and two papers can share the same equipment and facilities. The papers may not, however, use joint editorial staffs or personnel. These provisions keep the cost of publication down and the competition up on the finished product. Today, newspapers primarily serve economic and educational functions with persuasion, entertainment, and socialization as secondary functions.

Books and magazines Books were the first print medium. During their developmental stage, they suffered from the same problems as newspapers. They were censored by the Catholic church and by Henry VIII in England, and they were subjugated to stamp acts and licensing. They were the first printed material in the American colonies.

Magazines developed later. Ben Franklin had the first idea for a magazine called *General Magazine and Historical Chronicle*, but Andrew Bradford beat him to the newsstands by three days with *The American Magazine*. Both were local political opinion magazines. Magazines and books were not economically successful at first for two main reasons: People didn't have the leisure to sit and read, and they didn't have a cultural curiosity because they were mostly involved in survival.

In the thirty years preceding the Civil War, print media were growing, and great magazines like *Harper's Monthly* were founded. The post-war social changes affected books and magazines as they did newspapers. Both the educational and socializing functions came to the forefront. Many major history books were published that reflected the emergence of national pride. An increase in the number of literary, scientific, and sociological books indicated the intellectual growth of the times.

In the late 1880s and early 1890s, increased social concern in large cities produced a boom of books and magazines and signaled the operation stage for both. The push for social reforms was strong. Books and magazines were used to socialize and to persuade the public. The term *muckrakers* was first used by Theodore Roosevelt when criticizing what he called untruthful, sensationalized writers. *The Octopus* (1891) was a significant book, as were Jack London's *Iron Hill* and Upton Sinclair's *The Jungle*, a book about the Chicago meat-packing industry. Magazines that fell in the same category were *Colliers* and *Cosmopolitan*. Muckraking was criticized as an activity that offered no solutions, but it was still condoned by the public because it brought problems to the attention of Congress. In the early 1900s, legislation was passed that focused on some of the problems the muckrakers had pointed out: the Pure Food and Drug Act; the Newspaper Publicity Act that dealt with truth in advertising; and much antitrust legislation. With immediate goals accomplished, muckraking and the functions it served pretty well died out until the 1960s.

In the late 1920s, comic books were published to serve an entertainment function. Because it was a postliterate era and because comic books were easy to understand, comic books came to be considered as part of an antiliterary revolution. There was a large variety of comic books, and many of the more popular ones reflected the feelings of the times. For example, Superman is thought to have provided an escape for men who felt psychologically impotent during a time of national economic depression. It is interesting to note that in the late 1970s with the growth of equal opportunities for women in the nation's labor force and with the increasing necessity for both adults in a family to work outside of the home because of spiraling inflation, there has been a resurgence of the superhero (and emergence of the superheroine) in all media.

Despite the antiliterary revolution, magazines and books continued to flourish because they fulfilled educational needs that the newspaper could not. Books are considered storehouses of knowledge. They are historically the longest-lived, most detailed, and most enduring of the mass media. Books like Dr. Spock's *Baby and Child Care* were purchased by the millions. Magazines also had national circulation that produced a democraticizing and socializing influence. You could live in Maine and read about western cattle ranches, learn southern cooking, and follow the lives of Hollywood film stars. The depth of coverage for various events or ideas could not be done in newspapers, but it could be accomplished in magazines and books.

The trend in magazines is specialization. Magazines on fishing, hot rods, interior design, mechanics, travel, and many other topics are published for specialized audiences. In recent years, the cost of publishing magazines has become prohibitive, especially the cost of postage, which has spiraled circulation expenses. In an effort to fight rising costs, many publishers have reduced the size of their magazines, changed the paper weight, increased ads, and specialized the focus. Many have folded, but there are now still more than 20,000 magazines catering to special interests in the United States. Some general interest magazines like *Life*, which folded in the early 1970s, were revived late in the decade because of public demand.

A big event in the book world was the advent of paperbacks after World War II. The lower cost of the paperbound volume to both the reader and publisher significantly boosted the circulation of a single work. With the proliferation of books and magazines in this country, it is easy to see why publishing is one of the largest industries in the United States and why the United States is the largest producer of books in the world.

Because of their long-lasting effects and diversity, books and magazines serve the widest range of functions of all the mass media. It is difficult to single out any primary function for these media.

Pictures: still and moving The use of pictures both still and moving as a means of mass communication could legitimately be classified as part of either the print or electronic media. Still pictures and photojournalism are an important part of all print media. Moving pictures, on the other hand, are nothing more than a series of still photographs viewed in rapid succession—a procedure that gives us the illusion of motion because of a phenomenon called "persistence of vision." When motion pictures, in the form of film, are projected onto a screen, the final product is very similar to television, both in its means of projection and in its overall effect. We have chosen to treat these mass communication media at this point in the discussion because of their proximity to both the print and electronic media.

Practical photography was first presented to the public by Louis Daguerre at the Paris Exposition in 1839. The daguerrotype was a positive image on a copper plate and could not be reproduced. It was not until the end of the nineteenth century, however, when Frederick Ives had developed the halftone process, that the practical mass production of photographs in the print media was made possible. Film had progressed from tin to glass plates to paper with a celluloid base that could be put on a spool. Prior to 1900, Thomas Edison had developed an incandescent bulb capable of projecting pictures onto a wall. William Dickson, an assistant to Edison, had developed a camera and projecting device that utilized the new bulb. The first moving picture recorded a man sneezing, and it lasted 15 seconds. Most early developmental "movies" lasted only five to seven minutes and cost a nickel. They were shown in theaters called "nickelodeons." The content was usually pretty dull, like a rising sun or random scenes in a city. Nevertheless, people flocked to see this new entertainment medium.

Dr. Erich Salomon is considered to be the "father of modern photojournalism." He specialized in using available light and in taking candid shots of politically important people as they attended meetings. He became so successful and so internationally accepted that a "famous diplomat was once heard to remark, 'Where is Salomon? If we begin without him people will think this conference is not important'" (Davis, 1976, p. 30). The 1930s, however, were significant years for photojournalism. In an effort to socialize the country and to document the depression, Franklin Roosevelt established the Photographic Unit of the Farm Security Administration. The FSA Unit photographed and produced an amazing documentary of the period. Their work took them from one end of the country to the other from 1935 until 1941, when Pearl Harbor ended the project. "It was an inspired project which told the story of the depression more powerfully and directly than words could possibly have done" (Davis, 1976, p. 32). The potential for still pictures to serve functions other than entertainment was established. This signaled the beginning of the operation stage of still photos.

The motion picture industry also experienced rapid growth during the era from the beginning of the century until World War II. In their earliest days, films had been shown between vaudeville shows to encourage people to leave the theater. However, the first "real" movie, *The Great Train Robbery*, was released in 1905, and it was a tremendous financial success. From that point on, films were on their way to becoming a mass medium in their own right. In 1915, D.W. Griffith's *Birth of a Nation* started the operation stage by proving that motion pictures could serve not only an economic function but socializing and persuasive functions as well. It is considered "the most influential silent film ever made" (Whetmore, 1979, p. 201).

Early "talkies" actually used only music, but by 1930 almost all films contained sound of all sorts. In 1928, color came to movies, but no one seemed to care until 1964 when television executives told the movie industry that they would buy only color films. The 1930s was the decade of the gangster movie. Producers were severely criticized for showing criminals as the good guys, thereby misleading the young. During this whole period, however, and perhaps even today, the primary functions of films were entertainment and tranquilization. Movies have always provided us with an escape from reality. Even *Citizen Kane*, released in 1941 and considered to be perhaps the most important American film ever made, was originally produced for purely entertainment purposes. The only sustained period during which the movie industry tried to fulfill educational, persuasive, or socialization functions was during World War II, when it produced newsreels and main features that attempted to inspire American patriotism.

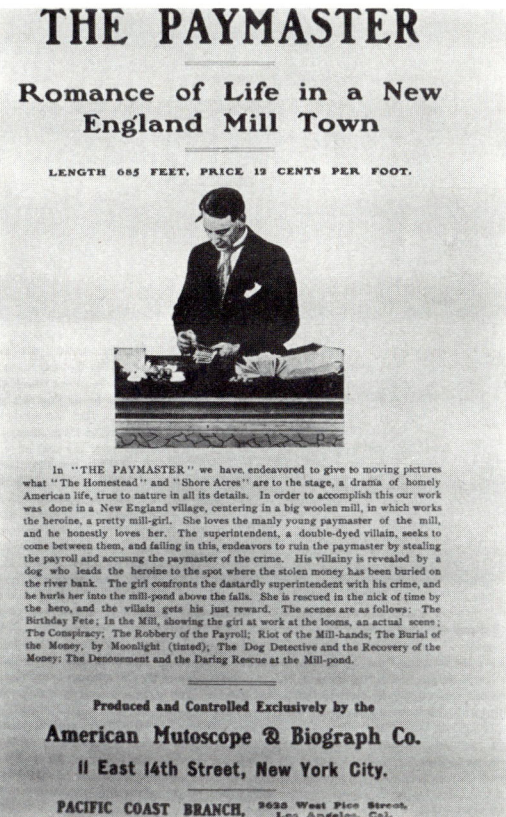

During the war, it was actually the still photographers and radio that brought the front "home." Photojournalists were the ones who attempted to socialize and to persuade the mass audience about the war rather than to simply record it. Still photographers have continued that emphasis until the present. Much of the photojournalism we see today has a definite "editorial" style. Although photography began to decline in the magazine format during the 1950s and 1960s (primarily because of the popularity of television), photojournalism has become more widespread in newspapers and in television news. Through the use of a standardized procedure developed in the 1960s for taking, developing, and printing photographs for fast, uniform results, it is possible for evening news programs on TV to have up-to-the-minute quality photos in time for their broadcasts. The media intimacy and immediacy during the Vietnam conflict had a profound influence on public opinion. Social comment, with few or no words, is the photojournalist's primary function today.

The changes that took place in motion pictures after the war related more to the audience than to the functions motion pictures served. The young became film's main audience after television won the adults away from the movie theater. Movies became a form of escape for the young rather than a retreat from reality for everyone. Films also attempted to deliver forms of entertainment that could not be found on television. Motorcycle movies, monster movies, science fiction movies, disaster movies, horror movies, pornographic movies, and popular-music movies were all successful because they either were considered unsuitable television fare or they appealed to a more specialized audience. Moving pictures are still serving the same basic functions they served in their very beginning: entertainment, tranquilization, and economics.

The Electronic Media

The electronic media did not develop as quickly as the print media because it took longer to perfect the necessary technology. Once it developed, however, it had significant and wide-ranging effects on the mass communication context. McLuhan (1971) says that the advent of the electronic media marked a shrinking of the world back to a tribal or village size, to what he calls a "global village." According to McLuhan, whereas the print media encouraged city, town, and national factions to develop because they failed to perceive the whole, the electronic media tend to break down these social and ethnic barriers by making all people familiar with one another. The electronic media make communication instantaneous and whole. Not everyone agrees with Professor McLuhan, but none can deny that the electronic media have had some profound effects on all of us. Radio (AM and FM) and television are the electronic media that will be the focus of this section, but we will also look at some of the newly emerging electronic media.

Radio (AM—amplitude modulation) Marconi developed a device that without the use of wires would transmit sparks to a destination one mile away. The Italian authorities weren't interested, so he took the device to England. The British navy wanted it for communication between ships, and the business community wanted it for communication between branch offices throughout the world. British and American Marconi Corporations were established, and a world-wide monopoly was anticipated. However, the Americans would not allow a monopoly. Just prior to the war, David Sarnoff, an employee of American Marconi, had the idea to build receivers and transmit music, but his idea was turned down. When World War I came along, there was a compelling reason for the development of a good radio. The radio would be used as a military device. Because it had to be made into a compact size, the realization came that radio might be usuable for mass communication purposes.

In November of 1920, KDKA of Pittsburg, Pennsylvania aired the returns of the Harding-Cox election. This was the first real radio station. Two months later, there were 30 more licenses, and shortly afterwards, 200 more. Radio was not yet financially profitable, so nonprofit groups like religious and educational organizations became involved. Radio was undergoing an identity crisis. People just didn't know what to do with it or how to cope with costs. In 1922, the American Telephone and Telegraph Company built station WEAF (now WNBC) in New York and introduced commercial broadcasting. It was a powerful station and whoever wanted to broadcast had to pay a toll. Radio began to fulfill its economic function. Early broadcasts were primarily of an entertainment nature. The money from advertisers paid for talent, which built up an audience and produced a loyalty between the listener, product, and program. This loyal audience gave the advertiser considerable control.

For most of its first decade, radio broadcasting had few laws affecting it. There were many stations and receivers, and the only law was the Radio Act of 1912 that required a license to operate a radio station. To get a license, you just wrote to Washington and asked. As a result, by the mid-1920s chaos reigned on the airwaves. Congress, after a direct appeal from the president, finally established the Radio Act of 1927. This act provided for a temporary five-member Federal Radio Commission. The Radio Act also decreed that the airwaves were the property of the public and that "licensed broadcasters are obliged to operate in the interest, for the convenience, and at the necessity of the public." In 1934, President Roosevelt proposed that a new agency known as the Federal Communications Commission be given authority over the services "which rely on wires, cables, or radio as a medium of transmission." Congress passed the Communications Act of 1934. This act provided for the FCC and incorporated, with amendments and refinements, most of the Radio Act of 1927. Although frequently amended, the Communications Act of 1934 is still the governing law for interstate and international communications by wire, radio, TV, and satellite transmission today.

In 1949, the FCC developed what is called the "fairness doctrine." This doctrine states that broadcasters are to be encouraged to present editorials, that they have a duty to present controversy, and that coverage is to be fair and balanced. This decision brought the persuasive function to broadcasting. The commission went even further and stated that it is an "affirmative responsibility" of broadcasters to "provide a reasonable amount of time for the presentation over their facilities of programs devoted to the discussion and consideration of public issues..." (13FCC1246). Similar regulations do not exist for the other mass commmunication media. Congress has been studying and recommending a complete overhaul of the Communication Act of 1934, but as of this writing, no major steps have been taken in accepting the revised proposals.

During the depression, radio competition sprang up in earnest, and 5¢ movies also began to serve an entertainment function. Radio was free, though, and it provided "escape" and helped serve a tranquilizing function for the multitudes who needed it during these hard times. Programs improved, and money came in from advertisers, thereby solving both the economic and content problems of radio. AM radio became fully operational.

Colleges and universities provide "hands on" training for persons interested in a mass communication career.
PHOTO BY CAROLE DUGAN

By 1934, radio had begun to serve educational (news) and economic functions. Thus, a rivalry developed between the newspapers and radio. By the second World War, the public considered radio the prime source of news. During World War II, radio probably had its "finest hour." The government did not take over the broadcasting industry as it had taken over the wireless stations in World War I. Instead, the government enlisted the help of the industry for the war effort. Radio continued to serve the economic, entertainment, tranquilizing, and educational functions described earlier, but it added the functions of persuasion and socialization. It expanded programming to include documentaries, news commentary, on-the-spot news reports, and speeches by world leaders. Information and propaganda from the government concerning the war as well as public service spots on victory gardens and buy-a-bond campaigns were all aimed to keep the public informed and to raise morale during the war effort.

Following the war, the fortunes of AM radio began to decline. By the end of the 1940s, the nation was having economic problems and television was making itself felt as a mass medium. Radio was losing advertisers and audience to the "upstart," and as the 1950s progressed, the future of network radio looked glum. The result was a switch from live program formats to local station control and a return to primary emphasis on the entertainment function. It was the birth of the deejay! Today, some educational programming is still provided by the networks in the form of news, sports, and special events, but for the most part, the formats are locally oriented. Radio today is in pretty good shape. It survived the lean years and has done well in the past decade.

Radio (FM—frequency modulation) There are many advantages to FM radio. The higher frequency range produces a better fidelity of sound and thus eliminates much of the static and distortion found on AM radio. "Line of sight" transmission limits the coverage and allows multiple use of the same frequency by stations within a relatively short geographical range.

In the 1930s, Edwin Armstrong developed an FM radio and transmitter. The FCC authorized the commercial use of FM radio, but when America entered the war in 1941, expansion came to a standstill. After the war, it grew quickly. In two years, there were approximately 1,000 FM stations operating, but there were problems. A converter was necessary to hear FM on AM receivers, and FM sets did not carry AM. Inexpensive receivers lacked fine tuners and overall quality. Programming on FM was geared toward small audiences and special interests. As a result, advertisers were hard to find. They could reach many more people on AM or on TV.

With improvements in technology and the increased availability of quality receivers, FM has become solidly entrenched and operational as a mass medium. Today, its main function is also primarily that of entertainment. In the late 1950s, it diversified by multiplexing—that is, by sending a second signal on the same frequency that is received on sets with multiplex capabilities. Multiplexing enables FM stations to feed selected background music to businesses, usually for a tranquilizing effect. It also enables transmission in stereophonic (two-channel) sound—a step approved by the FCC in 1961. These added abilities of FM have meant an increased economic base as well as an efficient use of broadcast frequencies.

Television Although inventions relating to television started in the 1880s, it wasn't until 1939 that TV went public in America. RCA demonstrated the device at the New York World's Fair with an NBC telecast of President Roosevelt's remarks during the opening ceremony. It was seen by few people, but it began a new era in mass communication.

The 1950s were the "golden age" of television. The number of stations boomed. To encourage people to buy TV sets, the emphasis was placed on entertainment programming. Programs were live, and the offerings were varied. Comedy, drama, documentaries, and variety shows saturated the airwaves. The number of homes with television sets grew, and today over 98% of all American homes have at least one television set. Almost all programs today are in color, and with larger screens the impact of color makes programs seem more "real."

Like the other mass media we have discussed, television has tended to focus on different functions at different times. One of the best ways to follow these changes is to examine electronic media management group(s). In the early days, the main television functions were tranquilization and entertainment. Thus management was, to a great extent, show biz. Producers and entertainment entrepreneurs were the main force in mass media at that time. In the

1950s, competition between radio and TV and beween networks meant competition for revenue. The management force then was made up of people with backgrounds in sales and economics. In the 1960s and 1970s, the FCC rules and regulations (i.e., bureaucracy) became important, and people oriented in law led the field in management. In the past fifteen or so years, as in the print media, there has been a shift away from almost total emphasis on the economic and entertainment functions toward a growing awareness of social responsibility to the viewing public. The current trend in management, therefore, is to turn toward people grounded in social science who are attempting to expand television's socializing function.

There is no doubt that television producers and managers are still out to make the big buck. However, with their own growing social awareness reinforced by groups of concerned citizens and government agencies, these producers and managers are changing the picture, so to speak, if only slightly. We still see too many shows aimed at a 12-year-old level and shows that tend to glorify antisocial behavior. Recently, however, there has been a glimpse on occasion of more "quality" programs reminiscent of the 1950s. There is less violence on prime-time TV, and advertisements during children's programming on Saturday morning have been sterilized to a great extent. However, we must always remember that what we watch is what we get. With few exceptions, the top-rated shows in this country are still those aimed at the 12-year-old level.

New Developments We have just begun to see the potential for television as a means of mass communication. In recent years, we have seen the development and expansion of cable and satellite transmission for television. The predictions are that by 1985 most of us will be able to talk back to our television. Tests are currently being conducted on such a system, which would solve the feedback problems we discussed earlier. Television will become more like the interpersonal contexts we have examined.

In the very near future, we will be receiving direct satellite television transmission to our homes.

Cable, CATV (community antenna TV), had its beginnings in 1948. The original idea was to bring TV into remote areas by means of improved reception. By hoisting an antenna atop a mountain and feeding the relay to homes via cable, the inventors of cable TV made the poor reception in these areas a thing of the past. CATV has unlimited possibilities. Because a coaxial cable is used to transmit, every channel can be put to use. By means of microwave stations and satellites for relaying, programs can be brought to and from the most remote areas of the country or world. CATV has capabilities beyond entertainment. It can virtually affect our everyday life style. Banking, shopping, weather watching, and much more can all be done with cable facilities. Even fire and burglar alarms can be set up on cable TV. These functions have been in the works for years and are just now beginning to hit the public market on a large scale. Cable offers entertainment, news, and sports features not available by regular transmission, but it hasn't as yet become the mass center of communication that it has the potential to be.

In the past several years, audiovisual transmission via satellite has become a normal procedure. It has been most extensively used in news, special events, and sports programming. Signals that are almost instantaneously relayed from anywhere in the world are now seen throughout this country. Satellite transmission enables people in most of the world to see the same program simultaneously. The technological advances in satellites have established them as a world-wide telephone and television communication system. The next step is direct relay to homes rather than relay through networks into home sets. The potential uses of satellites in communication are mind-boggling. Above all else, the use of satellites has completely eliminated time and space problems in mass media and truly made us a global village.

The very popular television commercial with "Mean" Joe Greene and his little friend has been highly successful because it incorporates most of the elements of good human communication.
COURTESY OF THE COCA-COLA COMPANY

SUMMARY

The mass communication context is becoming more and more an important aspect of human communication. The electronic media particularly are assuming a great deal of importance. There are some very definite differences between the structure, function, and evolution of mass media and the structure, function, and evolution of interpersonal channels. The basic structural elements of sender, message, and receiver are very similar. The differences occur in the elements of channel, gatekeeper, and opinion leader. In this chapter, we discussed several relationship models to demonstrate how the various mass communication elements interrelate. We concluded with our own model—a model that, in our opinion, incorporates the best aspects of the other models.

We specified six basic functions for mass communication: economic, entertainment, educational, socialization, tranquilizing, and persuasive. All of the media are primarily concerned with the economic function and serve that function best of all. In fact, the media label their main geographical area of coverage not by the city name but by the "market area." In the section on evolution, we pointed out that the educational function is being served very well by newspapers, magazines, and photography. Television, radio, and moving pictures are providing more entertainment and tranquilization. All of the media make some attempts to socialize and to persuade, but they have only qualified success because of the role played by opinion leaders in the accomplishment of these two functions.

In 1960, Leo Rosten cited what he believed to be the ten main complaints about the mass media.

1. The mass media lack originality.
2. The mass media do not use the best brains or the freshest talents.
3. The mass media do not print or broadcast the best material that is submitted to them.
4. The mass media cannot afford to step on anyone's toes.
5. The mass media do not give the public enough of adequate information about the serious problems of our time.
6. The aesthetic level of the mass media is appalling; truth is sacrificed to the happy ending, escapism is exalted, romance, violence, melodrama prevail.
7. The mass media corrupt and debase public taste. They create the kind of audience that enjoys cheap and trivial entertainment.
8. The mass media are what they are because they are operated solely as money-making enterprises.
9. The mass media are dominated—too much influenced—by advertisers.
10. The mass media do not provide an adequate forum for minority views—the dissident and unorthodox.

(Cassata and Asante, 1979, p. 183)

These complaints bring up perhaps the most important fact of all about the mass communication context. As in all human communication contexts, it is the receiver who perhaps plays the most important role. Communication occurs only when the receiver chooses to heed the message. In the mass communication context, the receiver has even more potential to select and filter the media's messages. We cannot blame the mass media entirely for the complaints cited above. We must take much of the blame ourselves.

KEY TERMS AND CONCEPTS

AM RADIO EVOLUTION
BOOK EVOLUTION
CABLE TELEVISION EVOLUTION
CONFIRMATION PHASE
COOL MEDIUM
CUMULATIVE FEEDBACK
DECISION PHASE
DEFLEUR MODEL
DELAYED FEEDBACK
DIFFUSION OF INNOVATIONS
ECONOMIC FUNCTION
EDUCATIONAL FUNCTION
ELECTRONIC MEDIA EVOLUTION
ENTERTAINMENT FUNCTION
FEEDBACK CHARACTERISTICS
FM RADIO EVOLUTION
GATEKEEPER
HOT MEDIUM
HYPODERMIC NEEDLE MODEL
INDIRECT FEEDBACK
INSTITUTIONALIZED FEEDBACK
KNOWLEDGE PHASE
MAGAZINE EVOLUTION
MASS COMMUNICATION
MASS COMMUNICATION CHANNEL
MASS COMMUNICATION ENCODER
MASS COMMUNICATION MESSAGE
MASS COMMUNICATION RECEIVER
MASS COMMUNICATION SENDER
MASS COMMUNICATION SOURCE
MOTION PICTURE EVOLUTION
MULTI-CYCLE, MULTI-STEP FLOW MODEL
MULTI-STEP FLOW MODELS
NEWSPAPER EVOLUTION
NOISE
ONE-STEP FLOW MODEL
OPINION LEADER
PERSUASION PHASE
PERSUASIVE FUNCTION
PRINT MEDIA EVOLUTION
QUANTITATIVE FEEDBACK
REPRESENTATIVE FEEDBACK
SATELLITE EVOLUTION
SHANNON-WEAVER MODEL
SOCIALIZING FUNCTION
STILL PICTURE EVOLUTION
SYNTHESIS MODEL
TELEVISION EVOLUTION
TRANQUILIZING FUNCTION
TWO-STEP FLOW MODEL
VICARIOUS PERFORMANCE
WESTLEY-MACLEAN MODEL

SUGGESTED READINGS

DEFLEUR, MELVIN L., AND SANDRA BALL-ROKEACH, *Theories of Mass Communication*, 3rd ed. New York: Longman, Inc., 1975. Since its first edition in 1966, this text has been the classic reference in mass communication theory. This third edition includes much new information that guarantees that it will continue to be the primary source in the area. The focus of this book is the role that mass communication plays in contemporary society. The dependency theory of audience-media-society relations, which DeFleur and Ball-Rokeach present in the final chapter of the book, represents some of the most advanced thinking in this area to date. The book also examines the influence of motion pictures, the press, and the broadcast media on society, as well as emerging media systems, media violence, and the persuasive potential of mass communication.

GUMPERT, GARY, AND ROBERT CATHCART, eds., *Inter/Media: Interpersonal Communication in a Media World*. New York: Oxford University Press, 1979. As the title of this book suggests, the editors have tried to examine the interrelationship of interpersonal and mass communication. "We believe that it is misleading to study interpersonal communication and pretend that media do not influence the nature of the phenomenon. It is equally misleading to represent the media world as one disconnected from our interpersonal relations" (p. v). The book examines the effects of mass communication on interpersonal intimacy, perception, and roles. The authors of the readings presented in this text represent the most advanced thinking in both the fields of mass communication and interpersonal communication. The editors themselves each represent one of these hitherto artificially separated disciplines.

WHETMORE, EDWARD JAY, *Mediamerica: Form, Content, and Consequence of Mass Communication*. Belmont, Calif.: Wadsworth Publishing Company, 1979. This is a delightfully written contemporary examination of the history and role of mass communication in America. Whetmore looks at both the print and electronic media in an honest and often humorous way. He suggests the major issues confronting each of the media and tries to supply possible answers to each issue. Perhaps the strong point of the book, however, comes in the last three chapters in which he looks at the effects and future of mass communication.

BIBLIOGRAPHY

Bibliography

Adler, M.J., "The Confusion of the Animalists," in *The Great Ideas Today* (New York: Praeger, 1975):72-89.

Aiken, L.R., "The Relationship of Dress to Selected Measures of Personality in Undergraduate Women," *Journal of Social Psychology* 59 (1963):119-128.

Aldefer, C.P., *Existence, Relatedness, and Growth: Human Needs and Organizational Settings* (New York: Free Press, 1972).

Allport, G., and L. Postman, *The Psychology of Rumor* (New York: Henry Holt, 1947).

Ardrey, R., *Social Contract* (New York: Atheneum, 1970).

Argyle, M., *Social Interaction* (Chicago: Aldine-Atherton, 1969).

Argyle, M., *Psychology of Interpersonal Behavior* (Baltimore: Penguin, 1971).

Arnold, W., and R. Hirsch, *Communication Behavior* (Lexington, Mass.: Xerox College Publishing, 1977).

Asch, S.E., "Forming Impressions of Personality," *Journal of Abnormal and Social Psychology* 41 (1946):258-290.

Bales, R.F., and P.E. Slater, "Role Differentiation in Small Decision-Making Groups," in *The Family, Socialization, and Interaction Process*, eds. T. Parsons, *et al.* (Glencoe, Ill.: Free Press, 1955):259-306.

Barker, Larry L., *Communication* (Englewood Cliffs, N.J.: Prentice-Hall, 1978).

Beer, M., *Leadership, Employee Needs and Motivation* (Columbus: Bureau of Business Research, Ohio State University, 1966).

Benne, K.D., and P. Sheats, "Functional Roles of Group Members," *Journal of Social Issues* 4 (1948):41-49.

Bergson, H., "Laughter," in *Comedy*, ed. W. Sypher (Garden City, N.Y.: Doubleday Anchor Books, 1956).

Berlo, D.K., *The Process of Communication* (New York: Holt, Rinehart and Winston, 1960).

Berlo, D., J. Lemert, and R. Mertz, "Dimensions for Evaluating the Acceptability of Message Sources," *Public Opinion Quarterly* 33 (1969):563-576.

Berne, E., *Games People Play* (New York: Grove Press, 1969).

Berne, E., *What Do You Say After You Say Hello?* (New York: Grove Press, 1972).

Bernstein, B., "A Sociolinguistic Approach to Socialization: With Some References to Educability," in *Directions in Sociolinguistics*, eds. J. Gumperz and D. Hymes (New York: Holt, Rinehart and Winston, 1972).

Bion, W.R., *Experiences in Groups* (New York: Basic Books, 1959).

Brooks, W.D., *Speech Communication*, 2nd ed. (Dubuque, Ia.: Wm. C. Brown, 1974).

Brooks, W.D., and P. Emmert, *Interpersonal Communication*, 2nd ed. (Dubuque, Ia.: Wm. C. Brown, 1980).

Carroll, L., *Alice's Adventures in Wonderland, Through the Looking Glass, and The Hunting of the Snark* (New York: Modern Library 1925).

Cassata, M.B., and M.K. Asante, *Mass Communication: Principles and Practices* (New York: Macmillan, 1979).

Collins, B.E., and H. Guetzkow, *A Social Psychology of Group Processes for Decision Making* (New York: John Wiley, 1964).

Cooley, C.H., *Human Nature and the Social Order* (Glencoe, Ill.: Free Press, 1956).

Coser, L., *The Functions of Social Conflict* (Glencoe, Ill.: Free Press, 1956).

Dance, F.E.X., "Speech Communication: The Sign of Mankind," in *The Great Ideas Today* (New York: Praeger, 1975):40-57.

Davis, K., *Human Behavior at Work* (New York: McGraw-Hill, 1972).

Davis, P., *Photography*, 2nd ed. (Dubuque, Ia.: Wm. C. Brown, 1976).

DeFleur, M.L., *Theories of Mass Communication*, 2nd ed. (New York: David McKay, 1970).

DeFleur, M.L., and S. Ball-Rokeach, *Theories of Mass Communication*, 3rd ed. (New York: Longman, 1975).

Denes, P.B., and E.N. Pinson, *The Speech Chain: The Physics and Biology of Spoken Language* (Bell Telephone Laboratories, 1963).

DeVito, J.A., *The Psychology of Speech and Language* (New York: Random House, 1970).

DeVito, J.A., *The Interpersonal Communication Book* (New York: Harper and Row, 1976).

DeVito, J.A., *Communicology: An Introduction to the Study of Communication* (New York: Harper and Row, 1978).

Dietrich, J.E., "The Relative Effectiveness of Two Modes of Radio Delivery and Influencing Attitudes," *Speech Monographs* 13 (1946):58-65.

Ehninger, D., A.H. Monroe, and B.E. Gronbeck, *Principles and Types of Speech Communication*, 8th ed. (Glenview, Ill.: Scott Foresman, 1978).

Ekman, P., and W.V. Friesen, "The Repertoire of Nonverbal Behavior: Categories, Origins, Usage and Coding," *Semiotica* 1 (1969):49-98.

Ekman, P., and W.V. Friesen, *Unmasking the Face* (Englewood Cliffs, N.J.: Prentice-Hall, 1975).

Festinger, L., *A Theory of Cognitive Dissonance* (Evanston, Ill.: Rowe Peterson, 1957).

Fisher, B.A., *Small Group Decision Making: Communication and the Group Process* (New York: McGraw-Hill, 1974).

Fisher, B.A., "Communication Study in System Perspective," in *General Systems Theory and Human Communication*, eds. B.D. Ruben and J.Y. Kim (Rochelle Park, N.J.: Hayden, 1975):191-206.

Fotheringham, W.C., *Perspectives on Persuasion* (Boston: Allyn and Bacon, 1966).

Bibliography

French, J.R.P., Jr., and B. Raven, "The Bases of Social Power," in *Studies in Social Power*, ed. D. Cartwright (Ann Arbor, Mich.: Institute for Social Research, 1959):150-167.

Freud, S., *Jokes and Their Relation to the Unconscious*, trans. and ed. J. Strachey (New York: W.W. Norton, 1960).

Gerard, R.W., "Units and Concepts of Biology," in *Modern Systems Research for the Behavioral Scientist*, ed. W. Buckley (Chicago: Aldine, 1968):51-58.

Gibb, J.R., "Defensive Communication," *Journal of Communication* 11 (1961):141-148.

Goffman, E., *Presentation of Self in Everyday Life* (Garden City, N.Y.: Doubleday, 1959).

Goldhaber, G.M., *Organizational Communication*, 2nd ed. (Dubuque, Ia.: Wm. C. Brown, 1979).

Hall, A.D., and R.E. Fagen, "Definition of a System," *General Systems Year Book* 1 (1956):18-28.

Hall, E.T., *The Silent Language* (New York: Doubleday, 1959).

Harris, T., *I'm O.K., You're O.K.* (New York: Harper and Row, 1967).

Harrison, R.P., *Beyond Words: An Introduction to Nonverbal Communication* (Englewood Cliffs, N.J.: Prentice-Hall, 1974).

Hastorf, A.H., D.J. Schneider, and J. Polefka, *Person Perception* (Reading, Mass.: Addison-Wesley, 1970, 1979).

Hayakawa, S.I., *Language and Thought in Action*, 2nd ed. (New York: Harcourt, Brace and World, 1964).

Heider, F., "Attitudes and Cognitive Organization," *Journal of Psychology* 21 (1946):107-112.

Heider, F., *The Psychology of Interpersonal Relations* (New York: John Wiley, 1958).

Heslin, R., and D. Dunphy, "Three Dimensions of Member Satisfaction in Small Groups," *Human Relations* 17 (1964):99-112.

Hiebert, R.E., D.F. Ungurait, and T.W. Bohn, *Mass Media* (New York: David McKay, 1974).

Janis, I.L., *Victims of Groupthink* (Boston: Houghton Mifflin, 1972).

Kahane, H., *Logic and Contemporary Rhetoric*, 2nd ed. (Belmont, Calif.: Wadsworth, 1976).

Kahn, F.J., Jr., ed., *Documents of American Broadcasting*, rev. ed. (New York: Appleton-Century-Crofts, 1972).

Kendon, A., "Some Functions of Gaze-Direction in Social Interaction," *Acta Psychologica* 26 (1967):22-63.

Knapp, M., *Nonverbal Communication in Human Interaction*, 2nd ed. (New York: Holt, Rinehart and Winston, 1978a).

Knapp, M.L., *Social Intercourse: From Greeting to Goodbye* (Boston: Allyn and Bacon, 1978b).

Koehler, J.W., K. Anatol, and R.L. Applbaum, *Organizational Communication: Behavioral Perspectives* (New York: Holt, Rinehart and Winston, 1976).

Kuhn, A., *The Study of Society: A Unified Approach* (Homewood, Ill.: Richard D. Irwin, and Dorsey Press, 1963).

Lasswell, H.D., "The Structure and Function of Communication in Society," in *The Communication of New Ideas*, ed. L. Bryson (New York: Harper, 1948):37-51.

Lawrence, P.R., and J.W. Lorsch, *Developing Organizations: Diagnosis in Action* (Reading, Mass.: Addison-Wesley, 1969).

Lazarsfeld, P.F., et al., *The People's Choice* (New York: Duell, Sloan and Pearce, 1944).

Lazarsfeld, P.F., and R.K. Merton, "Mass Communication, Popular Taste, and Organized Social Action," in *The Process and Effects of Mass Communication*, rev. ed. (Urbana, Ill.: University of Illinois Press, 1971):554-578.

Litterer, J.A., *Organizations: Systems Control and Adaptation*, vol. 2, 2nd ed. (New York: John Wiley, 1969).

Luft, J., *Of Human Interaction* (Palo Alto, Calif.: National Press, 1969).

Maslow, A.H., "Dynamics in Personality Organization," *Psychological Review* 50 (1943):514-539.

Maslow, A.H., *Motivation and Personality* (New York: Harper and Row, 1954).

McClelland, D., "Business Drive and National Achievement," *Harvard Business Review* 40 (1962):99-112.

McCroskey, J.C., and T.A. McCain, "The Measurement of Interpersonal Attraction," *Speech Monographs* 41 (1974):261-266.

McCroskey, J.C., V.P. Richmond, and J.A. Daly, "The Measurement of Perceived Homophily in Interpersonal Communication," *Human Communication Research* 1 (1975):323-332.

McCroskey, J.C., and L.R. Wheeless, *Introduction to Human Communication* (Boston: Allyn and Bacon, 1976).

McGuire, W.J., "Attitudes and Opinions," *Annual Review of Psychology* 17 (1966):475-514.

McLuhan, H.M., and Q. Fiore, *The Medium is the Message* (New York: Random House, 1967).

McLuhan, H.M., *War and Peace in the Global Village* (New York: Bantam Books, 1971).

Mead, G.H., *Mind, Self and Society* (Chicago: University of Chicago Press, 1934).

Mehrabian, A., *Nonverbal Communication* (Chicago: Aldine-Atherton, 1972).

Miller, G.A., *The Psychology of Communication: Seven Essays* (Baltimore, Md.: Penguin Books, 1967).

Bibliography

Murray, H., ed., *Explorations in Personality: A Clinical, Experimental Study of Fifty Men of College Age* (Cambridge: Oxford University Press, 1938).

Newcomb, T.M., "An Approach to the Study of Communicative Acts," *Psychological Review* 60 (1953):393-404.

Nummenmaa, T., "The Language of the Face," *Jyvaskyla Studies in Education, Psychology and Social Research* 9 (1964) Jyvaskyla, Finland: Jyvaskylan Yliopistoyhdistys.

Ogawa, D., "Small Group Communication Stereotypes of Black Americans," *Journal of Black Studies* 1 (1971):273-281.

Ogden, C.K., and I.A. Richards, *The Meaning of Meaning* (New York: Harcourt, Brace and Company, 1946).

Osgood, C.E., G.J. Suci, and P.H. Tannenbaum, *The Measurement of Meaning* (Urbana: University of Illinois Press, 1957).

Osgood, C.E., and P.H. Tannenbaum, "The Principle of Congruity in the Prediction of Attitude Change," *Psychological Review* 62 (1955):42-55.

Paley, W., "The Powerless Powerful," *Time* (April 16, 1979):118.

Pember, D.R., *Mass Media in America* (Chicago: Science Research Associates, 1974).

Perrow, C., "Hospitals: Technology, Structure, and Goals," in *Handbook of Organizations*, ed. J. March (Chicago: Rand McNally, 1965):913.

Piaget, J., *The Language and Thought of the Child*, trans. M. Gabain (New York: Meridian Books, 1955).

Porter, L., *Organizational Patterns of Managerial Job Attitudes* (New York: American Foundation for Management Research, 1964).

Porter, R.E., "An Overview of Intercultural Communication," in *Intercultural Communication: A Reader*, ed. L.A. Samovar and R.E. Porter (Belmont, Calif.: Wadsworth, 1972):3-18.

Pribran, K.H., *Languages of the Brain* (Englewood Cliffs, N.J.: Prentice-Hall, 1971).

Riccillo, S.C., and M.C. Liebig, "Language, Speech and Communication: A Functional Relationship," from First V.P.'s program on *Speech as the Focus of Our Discipline* (Speech Communication Association Annual Convention, Washington, D.C., 1977).

Rogers, C.R., *On Becoming a Person* (Boston: Houghton Mifflin, 1961).

Rogers, E.M., with F. Shoemaker, *Communication of Innovations*, 2nd ed. (New York: Free Press, 1971).

Rokeach, M., *The Nature of Values* (New York: Free Press, 1973).

Rosenthal, R., J. Hall, D. Archer, R. Matteo, and P. Rogers, *Sensitivity to Non-Verbal Communication* (Baltimore: Johns Hopkins University Press, 1979).

Ruben, B.D., "General Systems Theory: An Approach to Human Communication," in *Approaches to Human Communication*, eds. R.W. Budd and B.D. Ruben (Rochelle Park, N.J.: Hayden, 1972):120-144.

Scheflen, A.E., and A. Scheflen, *Body Language and Social Order: Communication as Behavioral Control* (Englewood Cliffs, N.J.: Prentice-Hall, 1972).

Scheidel, T.M., *Persuasive Speaking* (Palo Alto, Calif.: Scott Foresman, 1967).

Scheidel, T.M., *Speech Communication and Human Interaction*, 2nd ed. (Glenview, Ill.: Scott Foresman, 1976).

Schoderbek, P.P., A.G. Kefalas, and C.G. Schoderbek, *Management Systems: Conceptual Considerations* (Dallas: Business Publications, 1975).

Schutz, W.C., *The Interpersonal Underworld* (Palo Alto, Calif.: Science and Behavior Books, 1958, 1966).

Shannon, C., and W. Weaver, *The Mathematical Theory of Communication* (Urbana, Ill.: University of Illinois Press, 1949, 1977).

Shaw, M.E., *Group Dynamics: The Psychology of Small Group Behavior* (New York: McGraw-Hill, 1976).

Sherif, C.W., M. Sherif, and R.E. Nebergall, *Attitude and Attitude Change* (Philadelphia: W.B. Saunders, 1965).

Sherif, M., and C.I. Hovland, *Social Judgment* (New Haven: Yale University Press, 1961).

Shine, E.H., *Organizational Psychology* (Englewood Cliffs, N.J.: Prentice-Hall, 1965).

Stewart, C.J., and W.B. Cash, Jr., *Interviewing: Principles and Practices* (Dubuque, Ia.: Wm. C. Brown, 1978).

Thayer, L., *Administration Communication* (Homewood, Ill.: Richard D. Irwin, and Dorsey Press, 1961).

Toulmin, S., *The Uses of Argument* (Cambridge: Cambridge University Press, 1958).

Wahaba, M.A., and L.G. Bridwell, "Maslow Reconsidered: A Review of Research on the Need Hierarchy Theory," *Proceedings of the Academy of Management* (1973):514-520.

Weir, R., *Language in the Crib* (The Hague: Mouton, 1962).

Westley, B., and M. MacLean, Jr., "A Conceptual Model for Communication Research," *Journalism Quarterly* 34 (1957):31-38.

Whetmore, E.J., *Mediamerica: Form, Content, and Consequence of Mass Communication* (Belmont, Calif.: Wadsworth, 1979).

Whorf, D.L., *Language, Thought, and Reality*, ed. J.B. Carroll (Cambridge, Mass.: The M.I.T. Press, 1956).

Wilden, A., "Analogue and Digital Communication: On the Relationship Between Negation, Signification, and the Emergence of the Discrete Element," *Semiotica* 6 (1972):64.

Wilmot, W., *Dyadic Communication*, 2nd ed. (Reading, Mass.: Addison-Wesley, 1979).

Wood, B.S., *Children and Communication: Verbal and Nonverbal Language Development* (Englewood Cliffs, N.J.: Prentice-Hall, 1976).

INDEX

Index

Abdicrat, 64, 65
Abstraction, 135, 136, 137
Academic departments, development of, 18, 19, 20
Activity component, 146, 147, 148, 149
Adaptors, 173
Adler, M., 137
Affect displays, 173
Aiken, L., 190, 382
Aldefer, C., 58, 382
Allport, G., 90, 91, 309, 382
AM radio, 372, 373, 374, 375
American Marconi Corp., 372
American Research Bureau, 351
American Telephone & Telegraph Co., 373
Analogic code, 166
Anatol, K., 302, 385
Anchor point, 99
Applbaum, R., 302, 385
Archer, D., 386
Ardrey, R., 7, 382
Argyle, M., 88
Aristotle, 14, 15, 16, 30
Armstrong, E., 375
Asante, M., 373, 378, 383
Asch, S., 87
Assimilation effect, 101, 102
Associated Press, 362, 367
Attributes, 225
Audience analysis, 327, 328, 329, 330
  environment, 329, 330
  needs, values, and prior attitudes, 328, 329
Autocrat, 65

Baby and Child Care, 369
Bacon, F., 17
Baker, R., 349
Balance theory, 108
Bales, R., 281, 382
Barker, L., 212, 343, 382
Basic emotions, 185
Benne, K., 277, 382
Bergson, H., 331, 382
Berlo, D., 20, 25, 110, 382
Berne E., 245, 246, 382
Bernstein, B., 208, 209, 382
Bible, 16
Bion, W., 283, 382
Birth of a Nation, 371
Body orientation, 173, 174, 181, 182
Body posture, 173, 174, 181, 182, 188
Bohn, T. W., 351, 384

Books, 368, 369, 370
"Boston Guardian," 368
Bradford, A., 368
British Marconi Corp., 372
Brockreide, W., 130
Bronson, C., 19
Brooks, W., 58, 62, 88, 382
Burgoon, J., 193

Cable television, 376, 377
Caesar, Julius, 15
Carroll, L., 153, 382
Carter, J., 121
Cartwright, D., 384
Cash, W. B., Jr., 387
Cassata, J., 278, 373, 383
Categorization, 82, 83, 136
Christ, 12
Cicero, 15, 16
Citizen Kane, 371
Classical school of management, 317, 318
Closed questions, 254
Closed systems, 35, 106
Coalition, 287
Cognitive competence, 138, 139
Cohesiveness, 281, 284, 285, 286, 287, 288
  and goal progress, 288
  and participation, 286, 287, 288
  and status, 286
Colliers, 369
Columbus, Christopher, 17
Communication
  contexts, 20, 22, 23, 24, 221-380
  definitions based upon intent, 44, 45, 46, 47
  definitions based upon perceived meaning, 44, 46, 47
  development of, 203, 204, 205, 206, 207, 208, 209, 210
  dyadic, 23, 239-271
  elements, 20, 21, 22, 51-130
  Emmert-Donaghy model, 40
  importance of, 4, 5, 6, 7
  inputs, 22, 131-219
  mass, 23, 24, 345-380
  models, 29, 30, 31, 32, 33
  nonverbal, 22, 165-194
  organizational, 23, 301-320
  outputs, 22, 131-219
  prehistoric evidence of, 9, 10, 11, 12, 13
  processing elements, 21, 22, 51-130
  public, 23, 321-343

391

Index

sending and receiving mechanisms, 195-219
sensitivity, 210-217
small group, 23, 273-299
survival value of, 7, 8, 9
verbal, 22, 133-163
Communication systems, 40, 41, 42, 43
  characteristics of, 33, 34, 35, 36, 37, 38, 39
  communication functions, 231, 232, 233
  definitions of, 43, 44, 45, 46, 47
  Emmert-Donaghy model, 40
  regulatory function, 42
  subsystems, 311
  types, 47, 48, 49
Communications Act of 1934, 373
Communicative competence, 138
Communicator, 40, 41
  communicator intent, 85, 86
  communicator role, 229
Conclusion, 114, 115, 116
Conflict, 262-266
  content, 263
  dyadic, 262, 263, 264, 265, 266
  intensity, 263
  interpersonal, 263
  management, 264, 265, 266
  phase, small group, 294, 295
  status, 244, 245
  types, 263
  values of, 263, 264
Congruity theory, 109
Consistency, 106, 107, 108, 109
  definition of, 106
  needs, 55, 60, 61
  theories, 106, 107, 108, 109
Consummatory function, 232, 233
Context, 224
Contextual meaning, 144, 145
Contrast effect, 101, 102
Control dyad, 255, 256, 257
Cool medium, 348
Copernicus, Nicholas, 17
Corax, 13
Cosmopolitan, 369
Credibility, 92, 93, 94
  competence component, 92, 93
  derived credibility, 327
  dynamism component, 93
  initial credibility, 325, 326
  terminal credibility, 327
  trustworthiness component, 93

Daguerre, L., 370
Dale, P., 218
Daly, J., 96, 385
Dance, F., 137, 138, 383
Davis, K., 309, 383
Day, B., 366
Decision-making, 276, 288, 289, 290, 291, 292
  individual vs. group, 288, 289, 290, 291
Decoding, 83, 84
Deduction, 114, 115, 116
Delayed feedback, 226, 351
Democrat, 65
Deviation, 287, 288
DeVito, J., 137, 383
Dickson, W., 370
Differentiation, 39
Diffusion of innovation phases, 364, 365
  confirmation phase, 365
  decision phase, 364
  knowledge phase, 364
  persuasion phase, 364
Digitial code, 166
Displacement activities, 187, 188
Display rules, 210
Dissonance theory, 106, 107, 108
Donaghy, W., 197, 198
Drive-reduction needs, 55, 56, 57, 58, 59, 60
Dunphy, D., 285, 384
Dyadic communication, 239-271
  consummatory, 241, 248-252
  control, 255, 256, 257
  definition of, 240
  equal-status, 240, 242, 243, 244, 245, 246, 247
  evolution, 241, 242, 257, 258, 259, 260, 261, 262
  function, 240, 241, 247-257
  instrumental, 241, 252-257
  integrating components, 266, 267, 268
  interview, 252, 253, 254, 255
  structure, 240, 242, 243, 244, 245, 246, 247
  unequal-status, 240, 242, 243, 244, 245, 246, 247

Edison, T., 370
Ehninger, D., 31, 130, 336, 383
Ekman, P., 172, 173, 383
Elaborated code, 208, 209
Electronic media, 372, 373, 374, 375, 376, 377

Ellsworth, P., 104
Elocutionary movement, 18
Emblems, 173
Emmert, P., 58, 62, 88, 197, 198, 382
Emotion cues, 179, 185-189
   eye behavior, 186
   facial expression, 186
   hand movement, 187, 188
   head movement, 187, 188
   personal artifacts, 188, 189
   posture, 188
   vocalics, 188
Emotional words, 154
Empathy, 250, 251
Enthymeme, 114, 118
Entropy, 36
Environment, 42, 43
Environmental inputs, 207, 208, 209
Environmentalist position, 205
Equal-status, 240, 242-281
Equifinality, 39
Equipment, child's, 204, 205, 206, 207
Evaluation component, 146, 147, 148, 149
Evans, D., 270, 271
Evidence, 110, 111, 112, 113
   classification of, 110
   types of, 110, 111, 112, 113
Evolution, 233, 234, 235
Evolution, mass communication, 365-379
   AM radio, 372, 373, 374, 375
   book, 368, 369, 370
   cable television, 376, 377
   electronic media, 372, 373, 374, 375, 376, 377
   FM radio, 375
   magazine, 368, 369, 370
   motion picture, 370, 371, 372
   newspaper, 366, 367, 368
   print media, 366, 367, 368, 369, 370, 371, 372
   satellite, 376, 377
   still picture, 370, 371, 372
   television, 375, 376
Evolution phases, small group, 292-297
   conflict phase, 294, 295
   emergence phase, 295, 296
   orientation phase, 292, 293, 294
   reinforcement phase, 296, 297
Evolution stages, dyadic, 241, 257, 258, 259, 260, 261, 262
   avoiding stage, 242, 261
   bonding stage, 241, 259, 260
   circumscribing stage, 242, 260, 261
   coming apart, 242, 260, 261, 262
   coming together, 241, 257, 258, 259, 260
   differentiating stage, 241, 260
   experimenting stage, 241, 257
   initiating stage, 241, 257
   integrating stage, 241, 258, 259
   intensifying stage, 241, 258
   stagnating stage, 242, 261
   terminating stage, 242, 261, 262
Examples, 111
Extemporaneous public speech, 339
Eye behavior, 171, 172, 180, 181, 186
   functions of, 172

Facial control, 180, 186
Facial expression, 170, 171, 180, 186
Facts, 110, 111
Fagen R., 225, 384
Fallacies. *See* Reasoning fallacies
Farm Securities Administration, 370
Federal Communications Commission, 373
Feedback, 37, 38, 42, 226
   delayed, 226
   immediacy of, 226
Feedback, mass communication, 350, 351
   characteristics, 350, 351
   cumulative, 351
   delayed, 226, 351
   indirect, 351
   institutionalized, 351
   quantitative, 351
   representative, 351
Festinger, L., 106, 107, 108, 383
Fiore, Q., 347, 348, 385
Fisher, B., 224, 292, 293, 294, 295, 296, 298, 383
FM radio, 375
Fonda, J., 122
Formal communication structure, 304-308
   horizontal communication, 308
   vertical communication, 304, 305, 306, 307, 308
Fotheringham, W., 232, 383
Franklin, B., 18, 368
French, J. P., Jr., 224, 384
Freud, S., 331, 384
Friesen, W., 172, 173, 383
Function, 230, 231, 232, 233
   individual functions, 230, 231
   system functions, 231, 233
Functions, mass communication,

Index

359-365
  economic, 360, 361
  educational, 361, 362
  entertainment, 361
  persuasive, 364, 365
  socializing, 363
  tranquilizing, 363, 364

Galilei, Galileo, 17
Gallup, 351
Gatekeeping, 306, 349, 350
General Magazine and Historical Chronicle, 368
General systems perspective, 33
Generalization, 114
Gerard, R., 224, 384
Gestalt approach, 79, 80, 81, 87
Gibb, J., 251, 384
Gilbert, M., 130
Goal seeking, 34
Goldhaber, G., 309, 384
Good form, 80, 81
Grammar, 139, 149, 150, 151, 152
  sentence structure, 149, 150
  word appropriateness, 150, 151, 152
Grapevine, 309, 310
Great Train Robbery, The, 370, 371
Greene, D., 73
Greene, "Mean" Joe, 377
Griffith, D., 371
Gronbeck, B., 31, 336, 383
Group climate, 284, 285, 286, 287, 288
Groupthink, 289, 290
Gumpers, J., 382
Gutenberg, Johann, 16, 366

Hall, A., 225, 384
Hall, E., 174, 384
Hall, J., 386
Hamilton, A., 366
Hand movements, 172, 173, 187, 188
Harper, N., 25
Harper's Monthly, 368
Harris, L., 351
Harris, T., 245, 384
Harrison, R., 168, 384
Hastorf, A., 83, 104, 384
Hayakawa, S., 233, 384
Head movements, 172, 173, 187, 188
Hearn, M., 270, 271
Heider, F., 108, 109, 384
Henry VIII, 368
Heslin, R., 285, 384

Heterophily, 96
Hiebert, R., 351, 384
Hierarchy, 38, 39
Holism, 34
Homer, 12
Homophily, 96
Honesty, 249, 250
Hooper, 351
Horizontal communication, 308
Hot medium, 348
Human relations approach, 318
Hymes, D., 382

Illustrators, 173
Imitation-reinforcement model, 205, 211
Implicit personality theory, 87, 88
Impression formation, 87, 88, 89, 90, 91, 92, 93, 94, 95, 96
Impromptu public speech, 339
Indexing, 154
Individual functions, 230, 231
Induction, 116, 117
Inference, 113
Inferential reasoning, 117, 118, 119
  backing, 118, 119
  claim, 118, 119
  data, 118, 119
  qualifier, 118, 119
  rebuttal, 118, 119
  warrant, 118, 119
Informal communication structure, 308, 309, 310, 311
Information absorption, 306
Initiation, 233, 234, 235
Inputs, 35, 40
Instrumental dyad, 241, 252, 253, 254, 255, 256, 257
Instrumental function, 232, 233
Instrumental small group, 281, 288, 289, 290, 291, 292
Interaction cues, 169-179
  body orientation, 173, 174
  body posture, 173, 174
  eye behavior, 171, 172
  facial expression, 170, 171
  hand movement, 172, 173
  head movement, 172, 173
  proxemics, 174, 175
  vocalics, 170
Interaction distances, 174, 175
Interdependence, 33, 34
Interfacing, 41
Interference, 40, 43

Interpersonal attitude cues, 179-185
  body orientation, 181, 182
  body posture, 181, 182
  eye behavior, 180, 181
  facial expression, 180
  personal artifacts, 184
  proxemics, 184, 185
  touch, 182, 183
Interpersonal attitude dimensions, 179-184
  immediacy, 180
  power, 180
  responsiveness, 180
Interpersonal communication systems, 48
Interpersonal needs, 55, 61, 62, 63, 64, 65, 66, 67
  affection needs, 62, 65, 66, 67, 179, 180
  control needs, 62, 64, 65, 179, 180
  deficient responses to interpersonal needs, 63, 64, 65
  excessive responses to interpersonal needs, 64, 65, 66
  inclusion needs, 62, 63, 64, 179, 180
Interview dyad, 252, 253, 254, 255
  techniques, 253, 254, 255
  types, 252
Intrafacing, 41
Involvement, 103
Iron Hill, 369
Isocrates, 13
Ives, F., 370
Ivey, A., 270, 271

Janik, A., 130
Janis, I., 384
Johari window, 249
Jones, R., 104

Kahane, H., 119-127, 384
Kahn, F., 384
KDKA, 373
Kefalas, A., 320, 387
Kendon, A., 172, 384
Kennedy, J., 122
Kim, J., 383
Knapp, M., 194, 210, 211, 241, 242, 257-262, 271, 384
Koehler, J., 302, 385

LaFrance, M., 194
Language, 137, 138, 139
  cultural differences, 158, 159, 160
  developing sensitivity, 211, 212, 213, 214
  improving effectiveness, 160, 161, 162
  intensity, 155
  problems, 153-160
  spoken, 137
  and thought, 152, 153
Lasswell, H., 30, 385
Latitudes, 101
  of acceptance, 101
  of noncommitment, 101
  of rejection, 101
Lazarsfeld, P., 354, 363, 385
Leadership, small group, 9, 280, 281
  dual, 281, 286
  functional approach, 280
  situational approach, 280
  styles of, 280
  trait approach, 280
Leakage cues, 187
Lepper, M., 73
Lewis, P., 320
Liebig, M., 138, 386
Life positions, 251
Linear models, 30
Linguistic competence, 138
Listening, 212, 213, 214
  attention, 212
  hearing, 199, 212
  misconceptions, 212, 213, 214
  remembering, 212
  understanding, 212
Litterer, A., 33, 385
London "Gazette," 366
London, J., 369
Luft, J., 249, 385

MacLean, M., Jr., 355, 356, 387
Macromeaning, 83, 84, 143
Magazines, 368, 369, 370
Major premise, 114
Marconi, G., 372
Maslow, A., 56, 57, 58, 59, 74, 385
Mass communication, 23, 24, 345-380
  channel, 347, 348
  definition of, 346
  encoder, 347
  evolution, 365-377
  function, 359-365
  message, 347
  receiver, 348, 349
  sender, 346, 347
  source, 347
  structure, 346-359

Index

systems, 48
Mateo, R., 386
Mayo, C., 194
McCain, T., 95, 385
McCroskey, J., 95, 96, 357, 358, 385
McLuhan, H., 347, 348, 372, 385
Mead, G., 282, 385
Meaning, 139-149
   arbitrary meaning, 141
   associated meaning, 140, 141, 147
   change in, 155, 156
   components of meaning, 145-149
   connotative meaning, 141
   contextual meaning, 144, 145
   cultural differences, 158, 159, 160
   denotative meaning, 141
   dimensions of meaning, 145-149
   macromeaning, 143
   micromeaning, 143
   multiple meanings, 153, 154
   structural meaning, 143, 144
   triangle of meaning, 141, 142, 143
Mehrabian, A., 179, 385
Memory, 202, 203
Merton, R., 363, 385
Message perception, 96-103
Micromeaning, 84, 143
Micromomentary expressions, 171
Miller, G., 206, 385
Milton, J., 17
Minor premise, 114
Miscue, 168, 169
Missed cue, 168
Models, mass communication, 351-359
   DeFleur, 353, 354
   hypodermic needle, 352
   multi-cycle, multi-step flow, 357, 358
   multi-step flow, 357, 358
   one-step flow, 352, 353
   Shannon-Weaver, 353
   synthesis, 358, 359
   two-step flow, 354, 355
   Westley-McLean, 355, 356
"Mohammad Speaks," 368
Monroe, A., 31, 336, 383
Motion pictures, 370, 371, 372
Motivated sequence, 31, 336, 337
Motivation, 40
   defined, 54, 55
   and environmental effects, 71, 72, 73
Motivational perspective, 29, 32

Nativist position, 204, 205

Nebergall, R., 104, 387
Needs, 7, 8, 9, 56, 57, 58
   esteem needs, 7, 8, 9, 57, 58
   long-term maintenance needs, 56, 57
   physiological needs, 7, 8, 9, 56
   safety needs, 56, 57
   self-actualization needs, 58
   short-term maintenance needs, 56
   social needs, 7, 8, 9, 57
Nervous system, 196, 197, 198
   brain, 9, 202, 203
   effector organs, 196, 197, 198, 199
   neurons, 196, 197, 198
   receptor organs, 196, 197, 198, 199, 200, 201
Nesting, 38, 39
Network, small group, 277, 278, 279
   centralized, 279
   communication, 279
   decentralized, 279
   role, 277
   status, 278
"New York Daily News," 367
"New York Sun," 366
Newcomb, T., 109, 386
Newspapers, 366, 367, 368
Newton, Isaac, 17
Nielsen, A. C., 351
Nixon, R., 120, 122
Noise, 353, 354
Nonverbal communication, 165-194
   believability of, 167
   characteristics of, 167-169
   conscious vs. unconscious, 168
   cues, 169-192
   definition of, 166
   holistic nature of, 167
   sensitivity, developing, 214, 215, 216, 217
   universality of, 166, 167
   vs. verbal channels, 166, 167
   and verbal interaction, 175, 176, 177, 178, 179
Nummenmaa, T., 186, 386

Observations, 110, 111
Octopus, The, 369
Ogawa, D., 90, 386
Ogden, C. K., 141, 142, 386
One-way models, 30
Open questions, 254
Open systems, 35, 106
Openness, 248, 249

Operation, 233, 234, 235
Opinion leader, 350
Order, 81, 82
Organizational communication, 23, 301-320
   consummatory, 313, 314, 315, 316
   evolution, 316, 317, 318, 319
   instrumental, 311, 312, 313
   systems, 48
Organizations, 302, 303
   and communication, 303, 304
Osgood, C., 145, 146, 386
Outputs, 35, 40
Outputs, child's, 209, 210
Overpersonal person, 66, 67
Oversocial person, 64
Oxford "Gazette," 366

Paley, W., 349, 386
Parsons, T., 382
Pember, D., 361, 386
Perceived attractiveness, 94, 95, 96
   physical appearance component, 95
   social-liking component, 95
   task-respect component, 95
Perception, 40, 78-85
Perrow, C., 302, 386
Person perception, 85-96
   cultural effects, 90, 92
Personal artifacts, 184, 188, 189, 190
Personal individual, 67
Personal space, 184
Personality cues, 189, 190, 191, 192
   personal artifacts, 190
   physical appearance, 189, 190
   public artifacts, 190
   vocalics, 191, 192
Physical appearance, 189, 190
Physical structure, 225, 226, 227
Piaget, J., 209, 210, 386
Plato, 14, 15, 16
Playboy, 349
Polefka, J., 83, 384
Positiveness, 251, 252
Postman, L., 90, 91, 309, 382
Potency component, 146, 147, 148, 149
Power, 244
   informal, 310, 311
   types of, 244
Prejudice, 158
Pribram, K., 203, 386
Primary group, 281, 282
Primary tension, 292, 293

Print media, 366, 367, 368, 369, 370, 371, 372
Printing, development of, 16
Probability, 116, 117
Process world, 233
Processing elements, 21, 22, 40, 51-130
   motivation, 21, 53-74
   perception, 21, 75-104
   reasoning, 21, 22, 105-130
Productivity, small group, 291, 292
Prosodic features, 170
Protagoras, 13
Proxemics, 174, 175, 184, 185
Proximity, 79, 80
Public artifacts, 190
Public communication, 23, 48, 321-343
   importance of, 322, 323, 324
   memorized public speech, 339
   receiver-centered approach, 327, 328
Public communication evolution, 332-338
   causal pattern, 335
   chronological pattern, 334
   difficulty pattern, 338
   initiation, 332
   need-satisfaction pattern, 335, 336
   operation, 333
   priority pattern, 335
   spatial arrangement, 335
   the speech, 333
   termination, 333
   topical pattern, 337, 338
Public communication function, 330, 331, 332
   entertaining speech, 331, 332
   informative speech, 330
   persuasive speech, 331
   stimulative speech, 331
Public communication structure, 324-330
   the audience, 327, 328, 329, 330
   the public speaker, 326, 327
Public discussions, 374, 375
   forum, 374
   panel discussion, 374
   symposium, 374
Public speaker, 326, 327
   presenting the speech, 338, 339, 340, 341
"Publick Occurences Both Forreign and Domestick," 366
Pulse, 351
Pupil dilation, 180
Pure Food and Drug Act, 369

Quintilian, 16

Index

Radio Act of 1927, 373
Raven, B., 244, 384
Reagan, R., 122
Reasoning, 40, 105-130
   barriers to, 127, 128
   definition of, 105, 106, 107
   fallacies of, 119-127
   forms of, 113-119
   how people reason, 109-113
   why people reason, 106, 107, 108, 109
Reasoning fallacies, 119-127
   ad hominem, 122
   ambiguity, 121
   appeal to authority, 120
   begging the question, 126
   defined, 119
   false charge of, 127
   false dilemma, 125, 126
   hasty conclusion, 123
   inconsistency, 126, 127
   invalid reasoning, 120, 121, 122, 123, 124
   irrelevant reason, 120, 121
   provincialism, 120
   questionable analogy, 124
   questionable cause, 123, 124
   questionable classification, 123
   questionable evaluation, 125
   questionable premise, 124, 125, 126, 127
   slippery slope, 121, 122
   straw man, 125
   suppressed evidence, 124
   tokenism, 123
   two wrongs make a right, 122, 123
   unknown facts, 124, 125
   valid reasoning, 124, 125, 126, 127
Redford, R., 122
Reference process, 142
Referent, 142
Regulations, 37, 38
Regulators, 173
Relationship structure, 227, 228, 229, 230
Relationships, 42
Response matching, 181
Restricted code, 209
Rhetoric, 13, 14, 15, 16, 17, 18
   colonial, 17, 18
   five canons of, 14
   Greek, 12, 13, 14, 15, 16
   medieval, 16
   Renaissance, 16, 17
   Roman, 15, 16
Riccillo, S., 138, 386

Richards, I., 141, 142, 386
Richmond, V., 96, 385
Rieke, R., 130
Rogers, C., 213, 386
Rogers, E., 350, 355, 357, 364, 365, 386
Rogers, P., 386
Rokeach, M., 67, 68, 71, 74, 386
Role, 244
Roosevelt, F. D., 370, 373, 375
Roosevelt, T., 369
Roper, 351
Rosenthal, R., 386
Ross, R., 343
Rosten, L., 378
Ruben, B., 383
Rumors, 309, 310

Saine, T., 193
Salomon, E., 370
Sapir, E., 152
Sapir-Whorf hypothesis, 152, 153
Sarnoff, D., 373
Satellite, 376, 377
Scheflen, A., 181, 387
Scheidel, T., 240, 241, 268, 387
Schneider, D., 83, 104, 384
Schoderbeck, C., 320, 387
Schoderbeck, P., 320, 387
Schutz, W., 61, 63
Scientific management, 317, 318
Secondary tension, 294
Selective perception, 97, 98
Selective reception, 96, 97
Selective retention, 98
Self-fulfilling prophecy, 88, 89
Self-image, 189
Self-reflexiveness, 137
Sensitivity, communication, 210-217
   listening, 212, 213, 214
   nonverbal, 214, 215, 216, 217
   verbal, 211, 212
Sensitivity group, 283, 284
Serial communication, 305, 306
Shannon, C., 353, 387
Shaw, M., 284, 298, 299, 387
Sheats, P., 177, 382
Sherif, C., 104, 387
Sherif, M., 98, 104, 387
Shine, E., 302, 387
Shoemaker, F., 350, 355, 357, 364, 365, 386
Sign, 139
Skelton, R., 106
Slater, P., 281, 382

Small group communication, 273-299
  consummatory, 281-288
  defined, 274
  equal-status, 276-281
  evolution, 292, 293, 294, 295, 296, 297
  function, 281-292
  instrumental, 281, 288, 289, 290, 291, 292
  structure, 276-281
  unequal-status, 276-281
  why people join, 284, 285
Smell, 201
Social individual, 64
Social judgment involvement, 98-103
Social pressure and conformity, 289, 290, 291, 292
Social systems approach, 318, 319
Societal norms, 169
Socrates, 114, 115
Sophists, 13, 14
Speech
  chain, 199
  vs. "communication," 20
  egocentric, 209, 210
  vs. "English," 18
  production mechanism, 199
  vs. "public speaking," 18, 19
  reception mechanism, 199, 200
  sensitivity, 211, 212
  socialized, 210
Speech analysis, levels of, 198, 199, 200, 201, 202, 203
  acoustic, 198
  linguistic, 198
  physiological, 198, 199, 200, 201, 202, 203
Spock, B., 369
Stabilization, 83
Statistics, 112, 113
Status, 242, 243, 244, 245, 246, 247
  achieved, 278
  ascribed, 278
  and cohesiveness, 286
  conflict, 244, 245
  dyad, 242, 243, 244, 245, 246, 247
  network, small goup, 278
  and power, 244
  and role, 244
Stereotype, 90, 156, 157, 158
Stewart, C. J., 387
Still pictures, 370, 371, 372
Stimulus-response perspective, 29, 30, 31
"Strasborg Relation," 366
Structural meaning, 143, 144

Structuralist approach, 78
Structure, 225-230
  physical structure, 225, 226, 227
  relationship structure, 227, 228, 229, 230
Subcultures, 159
Suci, G. J., 145, 146, 386
Supportiveness, 251
Syllogism, 114, 115, 116, 118
  categorical, 115
  disjunctive, 115, 116
  hypothetical, 116
Symbol, 137, 142
Symbolization, 139, 142

Tannenbaum, P., 145, 146, 386
Taste, 201
Television, 375, 376
Termination, 233, 234, 235
Testimony, 113
Therapy group, 283
Time binding, 134, 135
Touch, 182, 183, 201
Toulmin, S., 113, 117, 118, 119, 130, 387
Trait approach, 87
Transactional analysis, 245, 246, 247
  complementary transactions, 246
  crossed transactions, 246, 247
  ego states, 245, 246, 247
  ulterior transactions, 247
Transactional perspective, 32
Transformation, 36
Trendex, 351
Triad, 275, 276
Triangle of meaning, 141, 142, 143
Truth vs. validity, 114, 115
Tubbs, S. L., 299

Uhlemann, M. R., 270, 271
Underpersonal individual, 65, 66
Undersocial person, 63, 64
Unequal-status, 240, 242, 243, 244, 245, 246, 247, 276-281
Ungurait, D. F., 351, 384

Value judgment, 125
Value systems, 67, 68, 69, 70, 71
  function of value component, 69, 70, 71
Values, 55, 67, 68
Verbal models, 30
Vertical communication, 304, 305, 306, 307, 308
  downward vertical communication, 305
  upward vertical communication, 305

Index

Vicarious performance, 363
"Village Voice," 368
Visual reception mechanism, 200, 201
Vocabulary, 139-149
Vocalics, 170, 188, 191, 192

Wallace, K., 25
Weaver, W., 353, 387
Weir, R., 206, 387
Westley, B., 355, 356, 387
Wheeless, L., 357, 358, 385

Whetmore, E., 371, 387
Whorf, B., 152, 387
Williams, F., 218, 219
Williams, J., 320
Wilmot, W., 262, 271, 387
Witherspoon, J., 18
Wood, B., 204-210, 219, 387
Writing, development of, 9, 10, 11, 12

Zenger, J., 366